THE CAMBRIDGE COMPANION TO GLOBAL LITERATURE AND SLAVERY

The Cambridge Companion to Global Literature and Slavery reveals the way recent scholarship in the field of slavery studies has taken a more expansive turn, in terms of both the geographical and the temporal. These new studies perform area studies–driven analyses of the representation of slavery from national or regional literary traditions that are not always considered by scholars of slavery and explore the diverse range of unfreedoms depicted therein. Literary scholars of China, Central Asia, the Middle East, and Africa provide original scholarly arguments about some of the most trenchant themes that arise in the literatures of slavery – authentication and legitimation; ethnic formation and globalization; displacement, exile, and alienation; representation and metaphorization; and resistance and liberation. This *Cambridge Companion to Global Literature and Slavery* is designed to highlight the shifting terrain in literary studies of slavery and collectively challenge the reductive notion of what constitutes slavery and its representation.

LAURA T. MURPHY is the author of *Freedomville: The Story of a 21st Century Slave Revolt; The New Slave Narrative: The Battle over Representations of Contemporary Slavery;* and *Metaphor and the Slave Trade in West African Literature.* She is a recipient of the National Endowment for the Humanities Public Scholar Award and has been a fellow of the National Humanities Center and the British Academy.

T0382275

THE CAMBRIDGE COMPANION TO GLOBAL LITERATURE AND SLAVERY

EDITED BY

LAURA T. MURPHY

Sheffield Hallam University

CAMBRIDGE
UNIVERSITY PRESS

Shaftesbury Road, Cambridge CB2 8EA, United Kingdom

One Liberty Plaza, 20th Floor, New York, NY 10006, USA

477 Williamstown Road, Port Melbourne, VIC 3207, Australia

314–321, 3rd Floor, Plot 3, Splendor Forum, Jasola District Centre, New Delhi – 110025, India

103 Penang Road, #05–06/07, Visioncrest Commercial, Singapore 238467

Cambridge University Press is part of Cambridge University Press & Assessment,
a department of the University of Cambridge.

We share the University's mission to contribute to society through the pursuit of
education, learning and research at the highest international levels of excellence.

www.cambridge.org
Information on this title: www.cambridge.org/9781316512647

DOI: 10.1017/9781009070928

First published 2023

A catalogue record for this publication is available from the British Library.

ISBN 978-1-316-51264-7 Hardback
ISBN 978-1-009-06891-8 Paperback

Contents

Contributors

SAM H. BASS is Visiting Assistant Professor in the Department of Central Eurasian Studies at Indiana University. He teaches and researches about Mongolian history and culture from the thirteenth century to the present day.

NIENKE BOER is Assistant Professor of Humanities (Literature) at Yale-NUS College, Singapore. Her articles have been published in *MLN*, *Research in African Literatures*, *Journal of Commonwealth Literature*, and *Comparative Literature Studies*, and on the online platform Global South Studies: A Collective Publication with the Global South.

DAVID BROPHY is a senior lecturer in modern Chinese history at the University of Sydney. He is the author of *Uyghur Nation: Reform and Revolution on the Russia–China Frontier* (Harvard University Press, 2016) and the translator of *In Remembrance of the Saints: The Rise and Fall of an Inner Asian Sufi Dynasty* (Columbia University Press, 2021).

JASON FRYDMAN is an associate professor of English and comparative literature at Brooklyn College, the City University of New York, where he has also directed the Caribbean Studies interdisciplinary program. He is the author of *Sounding the Break: African American and Caribbean Routes of World Literature* (University of Virginia Press, 2014). His essays, on topics including Muslim slave writing in the Americas, reggae and dancehall culture in the Cold War, and comparative memory of Caribbean slavery and the Holocaust, have appeared in such journals as *Small Axe*, *Interventions*, and *Critical Arts*, as well as in the edited volumes *The Global South Atlantic* and *The Routledge Companion to World Literature*.

WENDY S. HESFORD is Professor of English and Ohio Eminent Scholar of Rhetoric, Composition, and Literacy at the Ohio State University. She is the author of seven books, including, most recently, *Violent*

Exceptions: Children's Human Rights and Humanitarian Rhetorics (Ohio State Press, 2021), which focuses on strategic deployments of the humanitarian figure of the child-in-peril in late twentieth- and early twenty-first-century American political discourse.

MARTINO LOVATO is a visiting lecturer in Classics and Italian at Mount Holyoke College. He specializes in the Mediterranean as site of inter-disciplinary inquiry across the Arabic, French, and Italian literatures and cinema, with a focus on literary history, migration, and human rights. He has published essays on the Renaissance traveler Leo Africanus/Al-Wazzan and on the Algerian and Italian film directors Merzak Allouache and Francesco Rosi.

EWA MACURA-NNAMDI is an assistant professor at the Institute of Literary Studies of the University of Silesia in Poland. Her main research interests include postcolonial Anglophone literatures of Africa, refugees, and migration in cinema and literature. She is currently working on a book project provisionally titled *Fictions of Water: Refugees and the Sea*.

ALEXANDRA S. MOORE is Director of the Human Rights Institute and Professor of Human Rights and the Humanities, Department of English, Binghamton University, USA. She has published two mono-graphs, *Vulnerability and Security in Human Rights Literature and Visual Culture* (Routledge, 2015) and *Regenerative Fictions: Postcolonialism, Psychoanalysis, and the Nation as Family* (Palgrave Macmillan, 2004), and numerous edited collections and essays on human rights and literature, film, and photography. Her current research focuses on representations of human rights abuses in the War on Terror.

LAURA T. MURPHY is Professor of Human Rights and Contemporary Slavery at the Helena Kennedy Centre for International Justice in Sheffield Hallam University, UK. She is the author of *Freedomville: The Story of a 21st Century Slave Revolt* (Columbia Global Reports, 2021), *The New Slave Narrative: The Battle over Representations of Contemporary Slavery* (Columbia University Press, 2019), *Survivors of Slavery: Modern-Day Slave Narratives* (Columbia University Press, 2014), and *Metaphor and the Slave Trade in West African Literature* (University of Ohio Press, 2012). She is currently researching forced labor in the Uyghur region of China.

SUPRIYA M. NAIR is a professor in the Department of English Language and Literature at the University of Michigan–Ann Arbor. She is the author of *Caliban's Curse: George Lamming and the Revisioning of History* and *Pathologies of Paradise: Caribbean Detours*. She is the coeditor of *Postcolonialisms: An Anthology of Cultural Theory and Criticism* and the editor of *Teaching Anglophone Caribbean Literature*. Her research and teaching interests include postcolonial, feminist, diaspora, African, Caribbean, South Asian, and cultural studies.

MATTHEW OMELSKY is an assistant professor of English at the University of Rochester. His work on topics ranging from time-consciousness and theories of black fugitivity to African speculative fiction and climate change aesthetics has appeared in the *Black Scholar*, *Cultural Critique*, *South Atlantic Quarterly*, and *Research in African Literatures*, among other venues.

KWABENA OPOKU-AGYEMANG is a senior lecturer at the University of Ghana's Department of English. He is also Academic Director of the School for International Training's study-abroad program in Ghana. His research interests revolve around African digital literature.

JOHANNA S. RANSMEIER is a historian of China and the author of *Sold People: Traffickers and Family Life in North China* (Harvard University Press, 2017). She is currently Associate Professor of History and the College at the University of Chicago and a visiting research scholar at the Institute of Modern History, Academia Sinica.

KIRK B. SIDES is an assistant professor in the Department of English at the University of Wisconsin Madison. He has published articles in the *Cambridge Journal of Postcolonial Literary Inquiry*, *Safundi: Journal of South African and American Studies*, and others. A specialist in African environmental literatures and humanities, his current book manuscript, *African Anthropocene: The Ecological Imaginary in African Literatures*, explores the relationship between environmental and decolonial thinking in African literary and cultural production across the twentieth century. In 2021, he was a fellow at the Rachel Carson Center for Environment and Society and a visiting research scholar in the Humanities Institute at the Pennsylvania State University.

PARISA VAZIRI is Assistant Professor of Comparative Literature and Near-Eastern Studies at Cornell University. Her forthcoming book, *Racial Blackness and Indian Ocean Slavery: Iran's Media Archive*, explores Iranian cinema as a site of historical transmission for legacies of African slavery.

SUBHA XAVIER is Associate Professor of French at Emory University and a scholar of migration and the Global South. She is the author of *The Migrant Text: Making and Marketing a Global French Literature* (McGill-Queen's University Press, 2016) and the forthcoming book *Transcultural Fantasies: China, France and the History of Sino-French Literary Exchange*. She is currently at work on a new monograph on transnational boat migration.

Acknowledgments

My humblest gratitude goes to all of the contributors to this volume, many of whom took this project as an opportunity to explore new avenues in their research or to pick up lost threads, and all of whom did so with enormous grace and generosity in a year that stole so much from us. I am also grateful to all of the people who have told their stories of enslavement and exploitation whose work we hope to amplify in these pages. Thanks to Ray Ryan for insisting on this volume and to Edgar Mendez and Phil Dines for making the process simple. Thanks go as well to Olive Malone for stitching all of the pieces together. This project was supported by Sital Dhillon and the Helena Kennedy Centre for International Justice at Sheffield Hallam University.

Chronology

It almost certainly goes without saying that writing a chronology of critical events in the history of global slavery is a daunting task. Slavery has existed since antiquity and has operated both through institutions that keep records and on the margins where little record has been kept. Perhaps, the most important moments in slavery's trajectory and the ones that many of the writers of literature are most interested in – those in which oppressed people fought back, won their freedom, or resisted in their daily lives – are more often silenced by the record instead of being touted in a chronology such as this one. As contributor Parisa Vaziri wrote in response to a request for items for this timeline,

> The traditional historiographic method fails to give us a lucid understanding of this past; neither does it help us to orient our present in relation to this past ... It is worth remembering that slavery is itself the very obliteration of orientation. Timelines do not do justice, and at worst, potentially conceal, the absolute disorientation of sense that slavery is ... As Saidiya Hartman and other Black Studies scholars have so powerfully instructed, it is facile to correlate the end of a historical institution like slavery with a date, with a legal decree, or other putatively significant moment in history. Slavery is not an event and does not fit comfortably with the order of eventuality crafted by timelines.

With this caution in mind, the contributors to this volume collectively submit this compilation of dates that would be better understood as a timeline of institutional investments in and geopolitical responses to slavery that are most relevant to the essays collected in this volume.

500	Trade route developed through the Straits of Malacca, linking the Indian Ocean to the South China Sea
642–1220	Slavery expands and fuels growth of the Islamic Empire under the Ummayads, Abbasids, and

	Persian dynasties. From the beginning, slavery in the Near East was domestic, sexual, and military, but also in certain cases agricultural, and contributed to the economic and political growth of the region
711	Arab conquest of the Iberian Peninsula and Sind
780	Islamic mosque constructed in Shanga, on the east coast of Africa
869–893	Zendj rebellion
1050	Muslim dynasty established at Kilwa, on the East African coast
1206–1294	Conquest and consolidation of the unified Mongol Empire across Eurasia; continent-spanning forced displacement of people, including enslavement of subjugated people
1488	Portuguese explorer Bartolomeu Dias rounds the southern tip of Africa, opening the way for a sea route from Europe to Asia
1502–1736	Enslaved people from East Africa and the Caucasus employed at various levels of society under the Safavid and, eventually, the Qajar dynasties
1508–1582	The height of power of the Tümed Mongols under Altan Khan; significant Chinese migration to Mongolian regions, including enslavement of Chinese by Mongols
1602	Founding of the Dutch East India Company (Vereenigde Oost-Indische Compagnie, VOC)
1636–1691	Incorporation of Inner and Outer Mongolia into the Qing Empire; Qing colonial legal regime adapts to and redefines the terms of slavery in Mongolia
1652	Dutch East India outpost established at the Cape of Good Hope
1680	Junghar Mongol conquest of the Tarim Basin; beginning of deportation of Muslim peasantry to Ili Valley
1685	Code Noir instituted in order to codify punishments for marronnage that was taking place in the Caribbean colonies; evidence of marronage apparent as early as 1655 in Martinique, 1657 in Guadeloupe, and 1700 in Guyana

1760	Qing Dynasty completes its conquest of Xinjiang and begins transportation of Muslim peasants to "Muslim farms" in the Ili region
November 1781	The *Zong* massacre (142 enslaved people are thrown overboard by Captain Luke Collingwood so that he can claim insurance on the value of the drowned)
August 29, 1793	Haitian revolutionaries force France to abolish slavery in the colony of Saint Domingue
February 4, 1794	France abolishes slavery throughout its colonies
1795	British forces take the Cape of Good Hope, Cochin, and Malacca from the VOC
July 8, 1801	Toussaint L'Ouverture publishes Haiti's 1801 colonial constitution that abolished slavery
1802	Napoleon Bonaparte reinstitutes slavery and the slave trade in colonies
May 20, 1805	Article 2 of Haitian Constitution abolishes slavery and puts an end to the slave trade
1806	Transatlantic slave trade abolished in the United Kingdom
1807	Transatlantic slave trade abolished in the United States
February 8, 1815	Declaration of the Powers on the Abolition of the Slave Trade, Congress of Vienna Act XV, often cited as the first international instrument to call for an abolition of the slave trade
1817	Establishment of mixed maritime commissions (whose courts operated from 1819 to the 1860s)
1828	Suppression of Jahangir Khoja's uprising (in present-day Central Asia); enslavement of some 1,600 relatives of participants in Ili
1828	Through the Treaty of Turkmenchay, Russia gains control of the Caucasus and ends the slave trade from the Caucasus to Iran, intensifying demand for slave labor from the African continent
1834	First indentured laborers arrive in Mauritius

1835	Emperor Daoguang (China) orders release of captives enslaved in the wake of Jahangir Khoja's uprising
1848	Nasser al-Din Shah Qajar formally forbids importation of enslaved people to Iran; in practice, slavery continues through the early twentieth century
1851	Iran signs a treaty with Great Britain to allow British patrollers to search slave ships
1870s	Jim Crow era begins in the United States
February 26, 1885	Article VI, General Act of the Conference of Berlin, divides Africa into European colonies and abolishes slavery in those colonies
July 2, 1890	Brussels Antislavery Conference
1913	The Natives Land Act (South Africa) passed
1921–1923	Abolition of personal servants (*qamjilġ-a*) by decree of the Provisional State Khural of Mongolia and constitutional guarantee of equality of all Mongol citizens
1926	Slavery Convention of the League of Nations
1929	The anti-slavery bill ratified by the Iranian National Parliament
1930	General Conference of the International Labour Organization, Forced Labour Convention (No. 29)
1956	Supplementary Convention on the Abolition of Slavery, the Slave Trade, and Institutions and Practices Similar to Slavery
1957	International Labour Organization, Abolition of Forced Labour Convention (No. 105), United Nations
1976	Bonded Labor System Abolition Act India
December 12, 2000	United Nations Protocol to Prevent, Suppress, and Punish Trafficking in Persons, Especially Women and Children, supplementing the United Nations Convention against Transnational Organized Crime

January 18, 2002   United Nations Convention on the Rights of the Child: Optional Protocol on the Sale of Children, Child Prostitution, and Child Pornography

February 12, 2002   United Nations Convention on the Rights of the Child: Optional Protocol on the Involvement of Children in Armed Conflict

Introduction

Laura T. Murphy

Despite its utterly inhumane contours, slavery is a wholly human endeavor, an exploitative relationship between an extractor of labor and a producer of labor. At the same time, as an institution endemic to capitalism's expansion, it suffuses global systems of exchange, consumption, and desire that are so often and so ironically touted as inherently liberatory. As an expression of power and control, in the sphere of both the market and the intimate, slavery appears to have existed for all of human history and may very well continue to exist as long as humans continue to commodify labor. Indeed, despite it being considered morally reprehensible and legally illegitimate in practically every society today, slavery still infects our global supply chains, our battlefields, and our domestic spaces.

This very human injustice is thus unsurprisingly an underlying current in global literatures from the Caribbean to the Middle East, from Africa to Asia. Local in its iterations but global in its trajectories, slavery produces its own grammar of violence that is in turn shaped by its interpersonal scenes of subjection. Writers throughout literary history have grappled with slavery's footprint on both the intimate spaces and the planetary circuits, depicting both our capacity to subject one another to the most hideous tortures and our indomitable capacity to rise up against the worst forms of oppression.

The literary treatment of slavery in North America – from Wheatley to Whitehead – has been celebrated and analyzed for decades. From the early 1970s, rediscovery of the vast body of thousands of first-person testimonies of the formerly enslaved to the exposure of slavery's afterlives in the language of twenty-first-century African American satire and neo-slave narratives, the field of slavery studies has engaged in active conversation about the literary representation of slavery for nearly a hundred years.[1] *The Cambridge Companion to Slavery in American Literature* highlights some of the most significant analytical approaches to the literature of slavery in the United States.[2] Unfortunately, American scholarship on antebellum

transatlantic slavery dominates scholarly conversations and often obscures
or ignores the intersecting and intertextual global literary currents in
respect to slavery. Even Paul Gilroy's provocative call to a more globalized
approach to slavery in *The Black Atlantic* nearly exclusively ponders
American depictions of the transatlantic trade.[3] Furthermore, theoretical
and critical approaches to slavery have often focused on the era and
destination geographies of the transatlantic slave trade and hardly reached
any further, rarely even to trace the origination locations, effects, and
afterlives in the literature of slavery in Africa.[4]

The essays collected in this volume, *The Cambridge Companion to
Global Literature and Slavery*, pursue new itineraries for scholarship in
the field of slavery studies, suggesting a more inclusive turn, in both the
geographical and the temporal. These studies of global literature depicting
slavery have taken an area studies approach, performing deep-dive analyses
on national or regional literary traditions typically overlooked in the study
of literature and slavery, and they reflect on the diverse range of unfreedoms depicted therein. Literary scholars of China, Central Asia, and the
Middle East recognize, analyze, and represent slavery and its legacies in
regions of the world where slavery does not always take on the form of
racialized chattel slavery of people of African descent that is so familiar to
Western scholars. Even when the authors take on genres or geographies
familiar to those who study transatlantic slavery, such as slave narratives,
for instance, the authors reconfigure our worldview, subordinating the
transatlantic or undermining the European and American dominance over
the discourse, even as they often reveal the way black African bodies and
experiences have come to stand in for a wide variety of forms of labor
exploitation in the global imaginary. Other scholars are rejecting the
Eurocentric mythology that slavery was effectively abolished in the nineteenth century to analyze the slave narrative and other representations of
slavery as they have been developed to account for twenty-first-century
forms of unfreedom and forced labor.

The Cambridge Companion to Global Literature and Slavery is designed
to highlight the shifting terrain in literary studies of slavery and collectively
challenge the reductive notion of what constitutes slavery and its representation. The essays contained herein provide original scholarly arguments about some of the most trenchant themes that arise in the
literatures of slavery – themes that seem to transcend time and suggest
that slavery encodes its own language, structures, and grammars in our
representations of it. While discussing vastly different archives, literatures,
and cultures, these articles return time and again to themes of

authentication and legitimation; ethnic formation and globalization; displacement, exile, and alienation; representation and metaphorization; and resistance and liberation. Contributors to this volume repeatedly reflect on the failures of law to provide protections of rights, such that even after emancipation – by law or by escape – formerly enslaved people tend to experience a sense of not-yet-freedom, physically freed but not quite fully recognized by law or even interpellated within society as entirely human. Their contributions suggest the myriad ways literature has approached the daunting historical reality – and seeming inevitability – of forced labor in the era of the rise and flourishing of global capitalism. Collected together, they are as much a contemplation of our human endeavor for freedom as they are of the human capacity to enslave.

It would be impossible to have sufficient coverage of slavery's many avatars or its locations across all of human history. Instead, these essays are shaped by scholars who present ideas that are global in perspective even when local in their articulations. The essays address forms of slavery that have developed contemporaneously with the transatlantic slave trade as well as those that long postdate it. Contemporary forms of forced labor, human trafficking, and other bonded labor are contemplated both as and in relationship to slavery, depending on the location and reflecting literary writers' own approaches to these forms of unfreedom. Thus, representations of slavery as diverse as those that have emerged in South, West, North, and East Africa; China, Mongolia, and Central Asia; India; the Middle East; and the Indian Ocean and Mediterranean worlds are all represented here. These varied geographies, many of which have been defined at least in part by the routes of commerce and thus slavery that cross them, are considered not only in terms of how writers contend with the existence of slavery but also in terms of the way the legacy of slavery continues to dominate corporate and personal relationships long into the twenty-first century. In some cases, those legacies are represented through metaphors for contemporary exploitation; in others, slavery is evoked as a literal and practical description of the very real circumstances of the present. Those representations are both engaged for their explanatory power and critiqued for their potentially problematic and global political implications.

Read together, these essays pursue some of the thornier questions confronting slavery studies at this moment. The authors contend with the definition of slavery as it has changed over time and migrated across continents. They interrogate the way the literary representation of slavery has reemerged as both a trope and a weapon in our current globalized discourse. They identify the way American forms of racialized chattel slavery and its legacies have informed racialized practices as far away as Iran or South Africa. They pursue the effects of the representation of slavery, including the ways it sometimes allows both the oppressive practices inherent in slavery and the opportunities of resistance to it to resonate across borders. To understand the contours of this vast field of discourse, we have opened the doors to an interdisciplinary group of scholars interested in questions of slavery's representation and communication and who work not only in literary studies but also in history, philology, anthropology, and linguistics.

The collection opens with two pieces that establish some of the contested terrain upon which the rest of the essays travel. In Chapter 1, Alexandra Moore argues that contemporary global literatures of slavery contend with and critique exclusionary, Eurocentric narratives of human rights discourse that emerged in response to nineteenth-century slavery and that continue to obscure the reality of rights violations today. Through a reading of Mahasweta Devi's short story "Douloti the Bountiful" and Chris Abani's *Becoming Abigail,* Moore situates the seemingly familiar genre of the slave narrative within the context of international human rights and anti-slavery legislation to show the way contemporary global fictions of slavery decolonize the genre and thereby defamiliarize the reductive and colonial logic of slavery and freedom that are inscribed in two centuries of supposedly liberatory anti-slavery legislation. Largely ignorant of such critiques, a renewed "abolitionist" movement has sprung up in the last twenty years as awareness of contemporary forms of global slavery has risen. In Chapter 2, Wendy Hesford moves the conversation to the contemporary fictions of slavery promulgated by conservative groups in the United States that coopt the gravity of rights discourse and humanitarian tropes to amplify their conspiratorial agendas that are xenophobic, sexist, and racist. She performs a literary-critical exegesis of the discourse of contemporary anti-slavery to suggest that the "field of contemporary slavery studies scholarship needs to become more attuned to the powerful grip of humanitarian politics in order to more effectively counteract its parasitic logics and violence perpetrated in its name."

With those cautions in mind, the contributors in Part I engage with the genres and tropes of slavery, in contexts more and less familiar to slavery studies. In Chapters 3 and 4, Matthew Omelsky and Kwabena Opoku-Agyemang present contemporary genre fiction as the literary space in which West African authors have chosen to extend African experiences of enslavement beyond the narrow frame of the transatlantic to contend with the radical dispossession of contemporary life. Omelsky's chapter on slavery in African speculative fiction is a tribute to the long history of the struggle for freedom in worlds, minds, and bodies dominated by slavery's shape-shifting forms. His chapter moves inward, to the continent's interior and into the interior spaces of the mind and body subjected to slavery, where there is room for both dissent and liberation, dissociation and revolution. Opoku-Agyemang's chapter turns outward to the streets, where disconnected youth in Ghanaian microfiction are attempting to dodge the exploitative labor systems that prey on their poverty. West African writers employ the accessibility of flash fiction and digital journals to explore marginalization and servitude through an interplay of isolation and conflict in order to communicate to broad audiences about new forms of slavery that emerge from the radical inequality experienced in the region. These chapters together reveal the way the narrative of slavery moves away not only from the transatlantic but also from the first-person narrative and into the genres most widely consumed by readers, creating a popular counter-discourse to the exploitative structures that are depicted in their pages – whether they're describing Oxford Road in Accra today or a distant planet in the twenty-second century.

In a counterpoint to the reimagining of slavery's familiar tropes in new genres, Chapters 5–7, about literary representations of slavery in Asia from the medieval period to the nineteenth century, serve to broaden the scope of the archive of slavery studies, introducing tropes and discursive strategies at once familiar and differently imagined. In Chapter 5, David Brophy turns to two genres – hagiography and folk tale – to understand the experiences of slavery and resistance in seventeenth- to nineteenth-century Central Asia, in what is now known as East Turkestan or Xinjiang. He zooms in on the famous legend of Nazugum, a young woman who successfully fled slavery and captivity, and describes how this and other acts of resistance have echoed through the ages to shape contemporary Uyghur imaginations of the struggle against colonial oppression. In Chapter 6, Johanna Ransmeier focuses her analysis primarily on one of the world's most famous novels, *The Dream of the Red Chamber*, to discover the tropes by which slavery is encoded in Chinese cultural representations and traditions, even as it remains hidden in the subtext. Her excavation of the figures of enslavement in the text reveals characters who are at once the lynchpins upon whom all action depends and the invisible mirror counterpoints to those who are ostensibly in power. Her analysis reveals a dynamic of slavery that is potentially universal – the reliance of slaveholders upon those they enslave, both for their practical needs and for the definition of their own subjectivity. In Chapter 7, Samuel Bass takes a linguistic approach, tracing the shifting language of slavery back to the oral traditions of the medieval period in Mongolia and into epic literatures to reckon with the way the language both reflects and refracts cultural practices. Metaphorized at times, representations of slavery existed as both recognition of practices of captivity, bondage, and forced labor and, at the same time, a means of imbuing power in or critiquing social relations. As Bass points out, mobilizations of the language of slavery change over time and context and can be interpreted in some contexts as indicating appropriate behaviors for subordinate classes and at other times be deployed to describe the injustice of contemporary leadership.

Slavery influences our cultures, practices, interpersonal relationships, and institutions, even long after it has been abolished. Recent scholarship and political advocacy campaigns have identified the legacies of American chattel slavery in the unequal distribution of resources, in the project of mass incarceration of black lives, in health disparities between the races, and in many other forms of systemic racism that plague the United States. The same can often be said in other countries where slavery was institutionalized and remains salient in institutions generations after it has been abolished. In Part III, on afterlives and legacies, contributors look to the literatures of Iran, northern Africa, the Indian Ocean, and Nigeria to examine how the literary evocation of the history of slavery can illuminate the crises of the contemporary period. In Chapter 8, Parisa Vaziri reveals the literal blackness and the literary blackface of a well-known mythological figure in Iranian culture to argue that the character both reveals and obscures the fact of slavery in Iranian history. Her chapter undermines the notion of the "happy slave" in that context and at the same time critiques scholarship that congratulates itself for hearing the voice of the enslaved, even when that voice is entirely silenced or silent. Her consideration of the archive as a perversion that undermines the historiographical claim to truth provides an important context for the chapters that follow. In Chapter 9, for instance, Martino Lovato traces the contemporary representations of the ninth-century Zendj revolt that has been celebrated as a triumph for egalitarianism in the Arab-Islamic world. Lovato analyzes Jamel Eddine Benchecikh's 1998 novel *Rose noire sans parfum* and Tareq Teguia's 2013 film *Révolution Zenj* that appropriate the history of Zendj rebellion and the figure of its leader to contemplate the radical inequality in contemporary Algeria. The powerful mythology of the originary revolutionary figure can obscure present-day realities, but the authors evoke these rebels as models of discontent, a usable past that can be mobilized to critique contemporary inequalities. The allegories of the films pinpoint not a shared history of regional egalitarianism but instead "a historical presence" that reveals "a shared history of slavery, racism, and oppression." In Chapter 10, Nienke Boer focuses on what is spoken and what is silenced in eighteenth- and nineteenth-century Indian Ocean literature by placing it in contrast to the Black Atlantic archive. She writes, "If the anglophone Black Atlantic, then, is a sphere of autobiographical speech and legal silence, the Indian Ocean world of enslavement can be seen as one of autobiographical silence, but legal speech." The enslaved voices of Indian Ocean slavery and the counter-narratives they produced survive only in court testimonies and thus shape how contemporary Indian Ocean writers, such as Yvette Christianse, Amitav Ghosh, and so many others, render "slavery" and "indenture" – sometimes risking collapsing the two related but not quite equal systems of exploitative labor – in a kind of fictional erasure of contractual differences that exclude the enslaved entirely but provide mobility for the indentured. Boer's chapter unpacks the way the archive destabilizes truth in both the historiography of the period and in contemporary debates regarding forms of unfreedom. In Chapter 11, Supriya Nair reflects on author Uwem Akpam's short story about twenty-first-century human trafficking in Nigeria to reveal the way in which the emphasis of the archive of transatlantic slavery has so dominated discourses of slavery that it obscures other geographies and other experiences, including those in West Africa. Akpam's work asks us to shift attention away from the Afropolitan, Nair argues, and toward more local contexts where the experiences of the most marginalized – in this case, impoverished and exploited children – point to a continuum of precarity between past and present that is largely silenced by the archival obsession with the transatlantic.

In Part IV, contributors ponder the role of literary and intellectual migrations in the shaping of our understanding of slavery across borders. These chapters together provide a re-visioning of the tropes of transatlantic slavery from a Global South perspective to quite different ends. In Chapter 12, Jason Frydman centers the "cosmopolitan grandeur of African history" in nineteenth-century African writer Edward Wilmot Blyden's work. Frydman reveals how Blyden's traversal of the Muslim world allowed him to collect slave narratives written in Arabic by Muslim victims of the transatlantic trade, whose works "emerge as bids to reclaim a sacred, cosmopolitan subjectivity, a pious breath of freedom, across the rupture of the Middle Passage." Blyden's amplification of the experience of enslaved Muslims, while far from condoning slavery, nonetheless maps out an alternative vision of blackness and even slavery for his English readers, upending the power of racial categories and undoing the binary of enslaved vs. free. Documenting a more nefarious trajectory for intellectual migrations, in Chapter 13, Kirk Sides provides a close literary-critical reading of the sociological and ethnographic/academic literature from South African architects of the then-emerging Apartheid system to reveal the ways American slavery and Jim Crow segregation helped them define (in relief and in contrast) a set of racialized policies and also desires that formed the ideological bedrock of Apartheid. Sides argues that the South African social experiment of Apartheid reveals the power of American chattel slavery in the imagination of slavery and blackness. The United States serves "as a testcase; a laboratory for the testing and development, and subsequent dissemination to the larger colonial world of racial/ist technologies designed and implemented around the enslavement of 'Black peoples.'" Chapters 14 and 15, which almost feel like a generative conversation between Subha Xavier and Ewa Macura-Nnamdi, situate the recent migration of African people across the Mediterranean within the ambivalence of agency in border crossings that so often result in exploitation and even death. Both chapters remind us that, as Xavier puts it, "migration, especially in today's climate crisis, is above all else a human impulse that challenges the logic of inequality that slavery and colonialism have cast upon black lives, offering up movement as the dynamic imperative of life today." And yet, as Macura-Nnamdi points out, journalistic and scholarly representations so often emphasize black bodies' proximity to death rather than life. She points out the way mythologies of saving and rescuing black bodies are legacies of the historic slave trade and have migrated into the discourse of migration itself. In Chapter 15, Macura-Nnamdi cautions us that those narratives of refugee rescue go no further than the boundaries of the sea, revealing a callous disregard for the systemic injustice that mobilizes migrants in the first place and that meets them on the other side if they survive the journey. Nonetheless, Xavier suggests that we reject the notions of migration as vulnerability and suffering that are legacies of the transatlantic trade and instead embrace migration as a defiant logic grounded in not only agency but also a dynamic human impulse to move.

Together, this diverse collection of scholarly essays is meant not only to provide readers a grounding in the field as it stands today but also to be a force in shaping the field of global literary studies of slavery. It puts in conversation those scholars who have worked within the established traditions and geographies of slavery studies with those who are forging a path for the study of slavery in other regions of the world right up to the present moment. Readers who come to the volume expecting to find discussions of the transatlantic trade in literature will find innovative turns in that subfield, but the collection seeks to expand the imagination of the wider temporal and geographic scope of literary representations of slavery. In this way, we hope the companion can serve both as a reflection of the field and a beacon of light for potential future itineraries.

Notes

1 For studies of slave narrative as literature, see, for instance, William Andrews, *To Tell a Free Story: The First Century of African-American Autobiography* (Urbana, IL: University of Illinois Press, 1986); John W. Blassingame, *Slave Testimony: Two Centuries of Letters, Speeches, Interviews, and Autobiographies* (Baton Rouge: LSU Press, 1977); Vincent Carretta, *Unchained Voices: An Anthology of Black Authors in the English-Speaking World of the Eighteenth Century* (Lexington: University Press of Kentucky, 2013); Frances Smith Foster, *Witnessing Slavery: The Development of Ante-Bellum Slave Narratives* (Madison: University of Wisconsin Press, 1979); Henry Louis Gates Jr., *Introduction to the Slave's Narrative*, ed. Charles T. Davis and Henry Louis Gates, Jr. (New York: Oxford University Press, 1985); Gates Dwight McBride Jr., *Impossible Witnesses: Truth, Abolitionism, and Slave Testimony* (New York: NYU Press, 2001); James Olney, "'I Was Born': Slave Narratives, Their Status as Autobiography and as Literature," *Callaloo*, no. 20 (1984): 46–73; Sidonie Smith, *Where I'm Bound: Patterns of Slavery and Freedom in Black American Autobiography* (Westport, CT: Greenwood Publishing, 1974). For studies of a variety of forms of neo-slave narrative, see, for instance, Bernard Bell, *The Afro-American Novel and Its Tradition: Fabulation, Legend, and Neo-Slave Narrative* (Amherst, MA: University of Massachusetts Press, 1987); Ashraf Rushdy, *Neo-Slave Narratives: Studies in the Social Logic of a Literary Form* (New York: Oxford University Press, 1999); George Handley, *Post-Slavery Literatures in the Americas: Family Portraits in Black and White* (Charlottesville, VA: University Press of Virginia, 2000); Timothy Cox, *Postmodern Tales of Slavery in the Americas from Alejo Carpentier to Charles Johnson* (New York: Garland Publishing, 2001); Joy James, *The New Abolitionists: (Neo) Slave Narratives and Contemporary Prison Writings* (Albany, NY: State University of New York Press, 2005). For studies of the afterlives of slavery, see, for instance, Christina Sharpe, *In the Wake: On Blackness and Being* (Durham, NC, and London: Duke University Press, 2016); Yogita Goyal, *Runaway Genres: The Global Afterlives of Slavery* (New York: New York University Press, 2019); Taiwo Adetunji Osinubi, "Chinua Achebe and the Uptakes of African Slaveries," *Research in African Literatures* 40, no. 4 (Winter 2009): 25–46.
2 Ezra Tawil, *Cambridge Companion to Slavery in American Literature* (New York: Cambridge University Press, 2016).

3 Paul Gilroy, *The Black Atlantic: Modernity and Double Consciousness* (London: Verso, 1993).

4 See, for instance, Saidiya V. Hartman, *Scenes of Subjection: Terror, Slavery, and Self-Making in Nineteenth-Century America* (New York: Oxford University Press, 1997); Sharpe, In the Wake; Stephen M. Best, *The Fugitive's Properties: Law and the Poetics of Possession* (Chicago: University of Chicago Press, 2004), Achille Mbembe, *On the Postcolony* (Berkeley, CA: University of California Press, 2001).

PART I

Contexts and Contestation

CHAPTER I

Genres of Slavery and Human Rights
Alexandra S. Moore

In *The Slave Trade and the Origins of International Human Rights Law*, Jenny S. Martinez intervenes in histories that take the Nuremburg military tribunals as their point of departure, to argue that the nineteenth-century "slave trade courts were the first international human rights courts," and "the abolition of the transatlantic slave trade ... the most successful episode ever in the history of international human rights law."[1] Martinez's analysis of the maritime slave trade courts, which were established through bilateral treaties between Britain and Spain, Portugal, and the Netherlands, focuses on their success in adjudicating over 600 cases and freeing approximately "80,000 slaves found aboard illegal slave trading vessels" sailing under the flags of the courts' signatories.[2] This legal history highlights the combined strength of Britain's naval power and its abolition movement to drive the mixed (multinational) commission courts, even as it underscores that the courts operated in the *absence* of a comprehensive international prohibition against the slave trade and without the cooperation of major slaveholding powers such as France and the United States. Given that context, her argument invites a critical examination of the links between empire, law, and the literary genres through which slavery and emancipation become legible. Whereas Martinez's scholarship draws well-deserved attention to the work of the mixed commissions, this essay takes her argument about their success as a point of departure to consider what contemporary literature might illuminate about slavery in the context of human rights. Building on the work of Third World approaches to international law (TWAIL) scholars, I look at the limitations of international law and the human rights legal framework more specifically in addressing slavery, and the ways in which contemporary global fiction puts pressure on normative legal and literary conceptions of slavery and freedom.

This essay proceeds in two parts to examine briefly the following questions: how slavery and the slave narrative take shape in the context

13

of international law that is rooted in colonial encounters and predicated on
the differential recognition of humanity; how normative twentieth-century
human rights law delimits the concepts of slavery and freedom; and how
several contemporary global fictions challenge the familiar, generic logic of
the slave narrative and, with it, human rights imaginaries of freedom.

1.1 Slavery in Nineteenth-Century and Twentieth-Century Declarations and Legal Instruments

An overview of the legal prohibition against slavery and the slave trade as
well as the legal right to protection against enslavement provides a window
onto the emergence of international human rights within the larger context
of international law. Antony Anghie (2004), among others, traces the roots
of international law to European colonial encounters. His analysis emphasizes the development (as opposed to the application) of key concepts
including sovereignty, cultural and racial difference, and property ownership in law that asserts itself as a universal, civilizing force even as it
facilitates European colonization. Focusing on international law as a means
of hierarchical differentiation that adapts to and takes shape within shifting
historical, legal and political, and rhetorical registers (natural law, positive
law, the exercise of sovereign and biopolitical power in the modern state,
and national development agendas), he describes law's development in
terms of "the endless process of creating a gap between two cultures,
demarcating one as 'universal' and civilized and the other as 'particular'
and uncivilized, and seeking to bridge the gap by developing techniques to
normalize the aberrant society."[3] The process of normalization further
cements the dominance of erstwhile colonial nations and institutions that
undergird international law.

Anghie's overview of the uneven evolution of international law illuminates its role in securing European colonial, postcolonial, and neocolonial
power, through mechanisms that facilitate geographic control along with
resource and labor extraction, as well as through the yoking of freedom,
among other rights, to legal personhood. His analysis provides a compelling reminder that, as Stoyanova writes succinctly, "[h]istorically, international law served to authorize and justify slavery"[4] as well as colonization,
in addition to maintaining different legal and moral norms within versus
beyond Europe.[5] Returning to the nineteenth century, even a brief examination of key declarations and instruments during this period – the
Haitian Constitution (1805), Declaration of the Powers on the Abolition
of the Slave Trade at the Congress of Vienna (1815), the mixed maritime

commissions (inaugurated in 1817 and whose courts operated from 1819 to the 1860s), and General Act of the Conference at Berlin (1885) – reveals the knotty relationship between colonial interests and the push for emancipation in the development of international law.

Although the Congress of Vienna (1815) concluded with a declaration often cited as the first international instrument to call for the abolition of the slave trade, it is helpful to begin with the more radical recognition of shared humanity as the basis for freedom articulated a decade earlier in the Haitian Constitution. A national document with international implications, the Constitution recognized the equality of "all mankind" (Preamble) as the foundation of articles that both abolished slavery (Article 2) and understood citizens of the sovereign nation to be "brothers at home," whose "equality in the eyes of the law is incontestably acknowledged, and there cannot exist any titles, advantages, or privileges, other than those necessarily resulting from the consideration and reward of services rendered to liberty and independence" (Article 3).[6] Positing the human being as the bearer of rights before the citizen or the individual (the focuses of the U.S. and French Constitutions, respectively), the Haitian Constitution grounded equal standing and protection to formerly enslaved persons in shared humanity as opposed to legal recognition and liberal personhood.[7] Based on this framework, the Haitian Constitution, according to Siba Grovogui, provides a crucial example of the "multiple genealogies" of human rights, including those arising from the Global South and "existing outside of Western norms, without negating the possibility of universalism or universality."[8] At the same time, the limitations of a national, as opposed to international or universal, approach to emancipation became evident when refugees from Haiti in that era, despite having been declared free persons, were vulnerable to re-enslavement in other jurisdictions on the basis of pre-emancipatory property claims.[9]

Describing the slave trade as "repugnant to the principles of humanity and universal morality," the Congress of Vienna claimed a broader geographic purview. The Declaration of the Powers on the Abolition of the Slave Trade proclaimed its European signatories' "wish of putting an end to a scourge."[10] Participants could readily assent to the declaration's moral condemnation because the agreement was legally nonbinding and included no enforcement mechanism or definitive time frame; it noted instead that "this Declaration cannot prejudge the period that each particular Power might consider as most advisable."[11] The language of moral condemnation also gained acceptance by coding European sovereigns as the safeguards of civilized conduct. As Vasuki Nesiah points out, the document's conception of "humanity and universal morality" explicitly referenced "those of 'civilized countries,'" which it quickly parsed as 'several European governments' and finally ... as 'all the Powers possessing colonies in different parts of the world.'"[12] In Martinez's more generous terms, the declaration could "be classified as soft law at best, and cheap talk at worst,"[13] and she argues that the maritime commissions arose in the institutional and legal vacuum it helped to define.

Hearing cases in Sierra Leone, Cuba, Brazil, and Suriname, the mixed maritime commissions drew particular strength from the British government's commitment to them as well as from the power of its navy to stop, search, and seize slave ships. The British navy took the lead in seizing suspected slave ships, actions that at once reflected and enhanced its power: whereas individual officers received prize money for each ship captured and at times bounties on its enslaved persons, and the proceeds from forfeiture of the ship funded the courts and their signatory governments, the enslaved received certificates of freedom.[14] These radically uneven outcomes – the inherent freedom of the navy officers versus the bestowal of freedom by all-white courts adjudicating their empires; the freedom of movement and full citizenship of the mixed court jurists versus the certificate of freedom that transforms the enslaved into colonial subjects; the bounties and prize money awarded to naval officers versus the lack of reparations or repatriation for those freed – demonstrate the imbrications of the maritime commissions' successes in racialized, colonial empires.

Two decades after the mixed commissions ended, the Berlin Conference (1884–5) provided another stark example of the ways in which abolition rhetoric, Eurocentrism, and colonization continued to coexist. Taking place after nearly a century of international law prohibiting first the slave trade and then enslavement, the Berlin Conference employed the argument that by defining the terms of European control over Africa, colonization would make possible the efficient suppression of the slave trade. Racist paternalism again informs the language of the General Act of the Conference. Article 6, for example, stipulated that the colonizing powers will: "bind themselves to watch over the preservation of the native tribes, and to care for the improvement of the conditions of their moral and material well-being, and to help in suppressing slavery, and especially the Slave Trade."[15]

This volume underscores that slavery has been a global and transhistorical phenomenon which takes different forms depending upon context. Within the modern era, the central role of colonialism in slavery manifests in two additional examples with different racial logics. First, at the beginning of the 1800s, British, Dutch, and U.S. naval power and "gunboat diplomacy" ended the practice by Algiers, Tunis, and Tripoli of enslaving captured foreign sailors and holding them for ransom. Second, British naval power and the Brussels Conference of 1890 curtailed the slave trade of an estimated 7 million sub-Saharan Africans who were transported for domestic labor and concubinage to North Africa and the Middle East.[16] Here, too, colonial interests resound in the language and process of abolishing the slave trade, as Article 1 called for the "organization of the administrative, judicial, religious, and military services in the African territories placed under the sovereignty or Protectorate of civilized nations."[17] Again and again, the abolition movement, bolstered by British naval power, helped to infuse international law with the racially-coded, "civilized" power of colonial empires to provide a rationale for the expansion of their institutions as well as racial capitalism.

This history produces what Nesiah terms a "jurisprudence of failure" when it comes to freedom.[18] Contrary to the characterization of the maritime commissions' freed persons as "silent bystanders" and "beneficiaries of the system,"[19] Nesiah writes extensively about the paucity of "liberty authorized by 'the law.'"[20] Freedom through the mixed commissions placed no responsibilities on either slavers or the courts toward formerly enslaved persons: "in the majority of cases, the 'freed' found themselves hundreds or thousands of miles from home, in an environment where they did not speak the local language and did not have the resources or geographic knowledge to return to their families."[21] The law thus produced another form of radical precarity, including vulnerability to other forms of exploitative or forced labor, extreme poverty, and severance from familiar social contexts that typically form pathways for survival and human flourishing. More broadly, as this sketch of key nineteenth-century instruments against slavery and slave trade indicates, legal emancipation of enslaved persons was predicated on differential rule and the production of "juridical humanity," conditioned by and through law, rather than either a moral, legal, or political conception of what might be termed universal human rights.[22]

In addition to shaping the law, the central role played by the nineteenth-century British abolition movement catalyzed the formation of the Atlantic slave memoir as a distinct and influential genre. As Joseph Slaughter demonstrates, "law favors and enables some narrative plots and literary genres over others," and "genres [themselves] emerge and become conventional (both publicly common and formally regular) to the extent

that they make collectively legible – if sometimes distorted – both actual
and possible (desirable and undesirable) social formations and relations."[23]
Extensive Anglophone scholarship on the slave memoir emphasizes its
generic conventions, which include a verifiable and sentimental escape
story addressed to white audiences.[24] Typically conditioned by either
paratextual frames or amanuensis by a white editor or co-author, slave
narratives functioned in parallel to international law in the appeal toward
readers with full legal personhood to demonstrate their own "civilized,"
often Christian morality by bestowing recognition on another. Meanwhile,
the author's freedom, no matter how precarious or constrained, manifested
in the literacy that made the narrative possible and therefore placed little
responsibility on readers other than sympathy. The importance of British
and Anglophone power in the nineteenth-century abolition movement
points at once to the role of empire in shaping international law and to the
need for a volume such as this one to account for other, alternative
narratives of slavery and forced labor. This need is compounded by the
fraught definition of slavery in law.

    The development of international law prohibiting slavery and the slave
trade throughout the nineteenth century (and earlier) took place without
clearly defining its objects. The 1926 Slavery Convention of the League of
Nations offered the first legal definition, one that limited slavery to "the
status or condition of a person over whom any or all of the powers
attaching to the right of ownership are exercised."[25] The definition has
become more capacious in subsequent legislation, although tension
between competing interpretations of slavery continues to affect how
contemporary cases are adjudicated.[26] Recognizing "that freedom is the
birthright of every human being" (a phrase that significantly ties freedom
to humanity rather than legal personhood), the Supplementary
Convention (1956) also identifies serfdom, debt bondage, familial trafficking, and traffic in children as conditions "similar to slavery" (Article 1).
Clearer articulations of the central role of forced labor in slavery and
related conditions, as opposed to the initial focus on ownership, appear
in conventions in 1930 and 1957 that prohibit compulsory labor, whether
conducted under threat (1930, Article 2) or, in the later convention, as a
means of punishment, political coercion, economic exploitation, or discrimination (1957, Article 1).[27] Finally, the Palermo Protocol (2000)
establishes a link between trafficking and exploitation through forced
labor, slavery, and servitude.[28] This most recent instrument echoes the
paternalism of nineteenth century conventions with discourse weighted
toward humanitarian rescue of victims by powerful states rather than the

rights of trafficked persons: its provisions pay particular attention to women and children, define prostitution as inherently exploitative (against the arguments of sex workers) (Article 3), empower police and border control agents, and, with respect to trafficked persons, pledge "[a]ssistance to enable their views and concerns to be presented and considered at appropriate stages of criminal proceedings against offender" (Article 6.b).

Even this cursory and selective overview of antislavery twentieth-century legislation raises crucial questions, taken up in this volume, about how freedom from slavery might be imagined beyond the normative rhetoric of victims who need sympathy or rescue by the institutions and persons tied historically to their exploitation, of the formerly enslaved whose humanity has been granted in the form of certificates of freedom, or, as Saidiya Hartman has shown in the U.S. context, of recognition as "individual subjects whose capacities could be quantified, measured, exchanged, and alienated."[29] Rather than employ the nineteenth-century slave narrative as a model for reading contemporary literature across geographic and historical contexts, I turn briefly to two novellas that take place within the "jurisprudence of failure" to undermine generic assumptions and open expectations for the remainder of this volume.

1.2 Contemporary Imaginaries of Enslavement and Emancipation at the Edge of Law

Legal scholars, literary authors and critics, and poets invite us to read normative laws and literary genres contrapuntally for the structures upon which they depend, the failures they mark, as well as for alternative narrative frameworks they might offer. Anghie, for instance, asks, would "international law be different if authored by these 'outsiders' [the enslaved and their ancestors] whose oppression was justified precisely by all these systems?"[30] What narrative and legal possibilities emerge when the enslaved human being's perspective prevails over the structures that would contain it? Or even when a narrative marks specific epistemological or enunciatory failures that prohibit that expression? "Douloti the Bountiful" by Mahasweta Devi and *Becoming Abigail* by Chris Abani open up these questions. Situated in the context of legal failure, they illuminate the workings of structural oppression within the postcolonial state and insist on the interiority of characters which the law fails to consider. The short form of both texts signals the impossibility of fulfilling the generic expectations of the emergence of full personhood that accompany the *Bildungsroman* or the slave narrative, even as the authors' careful crafting of language and voice bring forth other, often submerged histories and perspectives.

Mahasweta Devi's "Douloti the Bountiful" (translated by Gayatri Chakravorty Spivak and published in *Imaginary Maps*, 1995) takes place during the first decades of India's independence, from 1947 to the beginning of the Emergency in 1975, although it traces the effects of the dispropriation of adivasis (indigenous tribal populations) from communal lands in favor of land privatization and redistribution, and, thus, tribals' entry into bondslavery, during the British colonial era. While the story ends just prior to the passage of the 1976 Bonded Labor System Abolition Act, Mahasweta's larger oeuvre underscores violence and discrimination occasioned by the law and continuing in its aftermath in order to emphasize bondslavery as a problem law alone cannot solve.[31] She writes consistently about the gap between law and the material conditions of survival, between legal recognition and political power, and between incommensurable civilizational worldviews. As she notes in the introduction to *Imaginary Maps*, "[d]ecolonization has not reached the poor," and "Douloti" addresses the inner workings of the bondslavery or kamiya system and the particular commoditization of women and girls for rape under these conditions.[32]

Central to the thematics of "Douloti" (from the Bengali "doulot," meaning "wealth") are the layered meanings of "reckoning," which appears in both noun and verb forms in Spivak's translation of the story.[33] When used by the brothel owner, madam, and proprietary rapist, reckoning refers to the careful computation of Douloti's valuation as well as of the compound interest that keeps her – bonded for 300 Rs at age fourteen to release her incapacitated father from debt – enslaved for the remainder of her life, despite having generated over 40,000 Rs for others. At the beginning of the story, her father Ganori Nagesia "can't reckon what is and is not his job," nor how his condition might be otherwise: "Crook Nagesia is Munabar Singh Chandelar's kamiya. Who reckons how long the Crook Nagesias have been their servant-kamiya-seokia? It's a matter of hundreds of years."[34] Mahasweta details the interconnected disposability, substitutability, and intergenerational devaluation of adivasis through the transfer of the father's debt to the daughter. When Ganori Nagesia is crippled (and thus becomes useless to his master) by being forced to pull a plow like an ox as punishment, a brothel owner settles the debt ostensibly to marry Douloti. Like her father, she remains unable to calculate fully her own exploitation: after "the boss has made [Douloti and the other "kamiya-whores"] into land" to be repeatedly exploited, "[s]he understood now that this is natural. Now she has no fear, no sorrow, no desire."[35] The narrator's matter-of-fact tone does not confirm the "naturalness" of bondslavery, but rather draws attention to the alienation of kamiyas from the structures of the postcolonial (and corrupt) state which promise to emancipate them.

The incommensurability of worldviews persists throughout the text in the reference to the machinations of the modern state which seek to count but not empower adivasis (e.g., the arrival of the ominously described "body count or census") as well as to national events which seem to have no meaning:

> Hey, you are all independent India's free people, do you understand? No, Sadhuji.[36]

Even when the local schoolteacher, white missionary, and representatives of humanitarian and political organizations meet with Douloti to compute the profits she has generated, their calculations result in little more than a data point in a report to the government rather than her release from slavery. "The first job is to abolish this system by law," states Father Bomfuller as they depart the where she remains.[37]

Gender also emerges as an inflection point through the moral and political senses of reckoning as an accounting to God or of holding someone to account. Here the text emphasizes the way caste and religious tradition – shown through the repeated slide between master and god, when Douloti and her emasculated father address those in power – collude to encourage them to understand their condition as "fate's decree."[38] However, Mahasweta also imagines alternative reckonings in violent resistance and political organizing through various male characters (although for the "fierce bonded prostitutes ... there is no opportunity for collective resistance").[39] Both Douloti and her Uncle Bono are ruptured through violence, Douloti through her initial rape and Bono in murdering a liquor store owner who sought to exploit the community and stealing his money for Bono's self-emancipation from bondslavery – murder he understands as committed by "[n]ot me. Just my hands."[40] Whereas for Bono, the actions of his hands catalyze other forms of labor and organizing (although he still searches for someone else to "light the fire") at the expense of introspection, Douloti's hands offer the narrative's only extended access to her interiority when, brought together with her uncle toward the end of the story, she massages his feet: "Douloti's fingers said, Why grieve, Uncle Bono?" as she physically conveys affective reminiscences of their family and village life.[41] Mahasweta insists on the problem of representation – narratological, political, legal – of adivasi bondslavery rather than its triumphant resolution in fiction through competing discursive registers (more various than those briefly mentioned here) whose reckonings (in the sense of the characters' considerations, ability to give an accounting, and moral, political, and economic calculations) never cohere.

In contrast to Mahasweta's strategic focus on structural oppression as opposed to interiority, in *Becoming Abigail* (2006), Chris Abani builds the full humanity of his protagonist in the blind spots of the law. In his story of Abigail, a Nigerian teenager who is trafficked by family members to London, where she is repeatedly raped and assaulted by her cousin Peter and misrecognized, dismissed, and denied by the law, Abani offers one of what he calls his "[s]tories of transformation, that lean into transcendence, but that are never sentimental, that never look away from the darkest things about us."[42] For Abigail, that darkness includes her mother's death in childbirth and father's suicide, childhood sexual abuse that presages the future, as well as a series of misrecognitions and blindnesses that first conflate her with her mother and then foreclose the flourishing of her worldliness, agency, desire, and self-authorship. The novella includes horrific scenes of dehumanizing entrapment and attempted forced prostitution, particularly when Peter chains her in the backyard like a dog and rapes her twice daily; however, even those most brutal textual moments in which she "felt caught in the sheath of men's plans" include elements of other temporalities to map the complex layering of experience and identity.[43] Escape from the backyard brings her under state control, where she is only barely legible. Eschewing, first, the sentimentality and linearity of the slave narrative's trajectory and, second, the dichotomy between enslavement and freedom in the law, Abani employs the lyric mode to address the entanglements of desire and abuse across the temporalities of "Then" and "Now" through which the novella is structured.

In the various time-spaces or chronotopes of the novella, the state apparatus in Nigeria and England (the traffic between them facilitated by imperial history) fails Abigail as a person before the law: the fact of her being trafficked for sex and the fake passport under which she is smuggled go unnoticed, rendering her a "ghost" in the system. Once her abuse in London demands state intervention, her designation as a minor in need of saving turns out to contain its own violence, although readers may disagree about the form that violence takes.[44] Nesiah's "jurisprudence of failure" occurs when the law paternalistically frames Abigail solely as a victim to be saved and, in doing so, negates her own agency and desire. As an alternative to misrecognition and foreclosure, Abani renders Abigail's attempts at self-inscription in images of branding through which she maps her desire: "These dots. Me. Abigail."[45] That self-telling on the skin resonates throughout the novella in the overlapping contexts of self-harm, the branding of live property, and a childhood ritual, thereby refusing readings of writing as liberation.

Underscoring the work of imagining Abigail's interiority, Abani's lyrical third person narration moves across temporalities and thematic contexts, mostly focalizing through Abigail perspective, yet also at points marking its distance from her: "Of course Abigail didn't think like that. Not in those words."[46] Through such shifts, Abani destabilizes generic expectations, particularly regarding the reader's positionality. As opposed to the sympathetic reader of the nineteenth-century slave narrative or contemporary sentimental human rights bestseller, Abani's readers are often positioned uncomfortably. In the scene of Abigail's self-branding, for example, readers learn what each dot means alongside Derek, the married, white social worker with whom she has just willingly had intercourse while his wife sleeps upstairs. In the end, Derek is fired for his sex with a minor and client, and his punishment (which denies her desire) – in the name of protecting Abigail – becomes her final, unsurvivable betrayal. Perhaps in keeping with Abani's comment that "there is no such thing as freedom, only power," Abigail's final act asserts her right to control (the end to) her own life as she follows the stub of her cigarette into the river.[47]

In *Zong!*, her poetic reimagining of the slaveship whose captain ordered the purposeful drowning of human cargo for its insurance value in 1781, M. NourbeSe Philip begins with the deconstruction of the law which could only see the drowned as property:

suppose the law
is
not
does
not
would
not
be
not[48]

For Phillip, the initial bid to "suppose" otherwise makes possible the radical emergence of voices, languages, stories, and forms that exist outside the law's purview and lexicon. That possibility also comes with a challenge to readers to think critically about the ways in which literary forms, genres, and languages delimit our imaginations. Although "Douloti the Bountiful" and *Becoming Abigail* conclude with the deaths of their young, central female characters, much as Philip reimagines the cries of the enslaved as they drown, the failure or refusal of legal personhood necessary for normative human rights claims in these texts takes place alongside the imagination of other subject positions, histories, and forms of both testimony and rights.

Notes

1 Jenny S. Martinez, *The Slave Trade and the Origins of International Human Rights Law* (Oxford: Oxford University Press, 2012), p. 11 and p. 17.
2 Martinez, *The Slave Trade*, p. 11.
3 Antony Anghie, *Imperialism, Sovereignty, and the Making of International Law* (Cambridge: Cambridge University Press, 2004), p. 4.
4 Vladislava Stoyanova, "United Nations Against Slavery: Unravelling Concepts, Institutions and Obligations," *Michigan Journal of International Law* 38, no. 3 (2017): 365.
5 Jean Allain, *The Law and Slavery: Preventing Human Exploitation* (Leiden: Koninklijke Brill, 2015), p. 5.
6 Constitution of Hayti, 1805, from The L'Ouverture Project. https://thelouvertureproject.org/index.php?title=Haitian_Constitution_of_1805
7 Siba N. Grovogui, "To the Orphaned, Dispossessed and Illegitimate Children: Human Right Beyond Republican and Liberal Traditions," *Indiana Journal of Global Legal Studies* 18, no. 1 (2011): 48.
8 Grovogui, "To the Orphaned, Dispossessed and Illegitimate Children," 62.
9 Rebecca J. Scott, "Under Color of Law: *Siliadin v. France* and the Dynamics of Enslavement in Historical Perspective," in *The Legal Understanding of Slavery: From the Historical to the Contemporary*, ed. Jean Allain (Oxford: Oxford University Press, 2012), pp. 156–161.
10 Declaration of the Powers on the Abolition of the Slave Trade, Congress of Vienna Act XV (February 8, 1815).
11 Declaration of the Powers on the Abolition of the Slave Trade.
12 Vasuki Nesiah, "Freedom at Sea," *London Review of International Law* 7, no. 2 (2019): 165.
13 Martinez, *The Slave Trade and the Origins of International Human Rights Law*, p. 26.
14 Martinez, *The Slave Trade*, pp. 9, 64, 69–70.
15 Article VI, General Act of the Conference of Berlin (Feb. 26, 1885), 23 Stat. 332, reprinted in Barbara Harlow and Mia Carter (eds.), *Archives of Empire Volume II: The Scramble for Africa* (Durham, NC: Duke University Press, 2003), p. 31.
16 Jean Allain, *The Law and Slavery: Preventing Human Exploitation*, pp. 39–40.

17 General Act of the Brussels Conference relative to the African slave trade, Brussels, July 2, 1890 (London: Printed for H. M. Stationery Office by Harrison and Sons, 1892), p. 37.

18 Vasuki Nesiah, "Freedom at Sea," *London Review of International Law* 7, no. 2 (2019):, 150.

19 Martinez, *The Slave Trade*, p. 87.

20 Nesiah, "Freedom at Sea," 150.

21 Vasuki Nesiah, "The Law of Humanity Has a Canon: Translating Racialized World Order into 'Colorblind' Law," *PoLAR* (November 15, 2020).

22 See Samera Esmeir, "On Making Dehumanization Possible," *PMLA* 121, no. 5 (October 2006): 1544–1551.

23 Joseph R. Slaughter, *Human Rights, Inc.: The World Novel, Narrative Form, and International Law* (New York: Fordham University Press, 2007), pp. 10, 11.

24 See, e.g., Yogita Goyal, *Runaway Genres: The Global Afterlives of Slavery* (New York: New York University Press, 2019), p. 3 and James Olney, "'I Was Born': Slave Narratives, Their Status as Autobiography and as Literature," *Callaloo* 20 (Winter 1984): 50–51.

25 1926 Slavery Convention.

26 See, for instance, Rebecca J. Scott, "Under Color of Law: *Siliadin v. France* and the Dynamics of Enslavement in Historical Perspective," in *The Legal Understanding of Slavery*, pp. 152–164.

27 1956 Supplementary Convention on the Abolition of Slavery, the Slave Trade, and Institutions and Practices Similar to Slavery, General Conference of the International Labour Organization, Forced Labour Convention, 1930 (No. 29) and International Labor Organization, Abolition of Forced Labour Convention, 1957 (No. 105), United Nations.

28 Protocol to Prevent, Suppress, and Punish Trafficking in Persons, Especially Women and Children, supplementing the United Nations Convention against Transnational Organized Crime, 2000.

29 Saidiya V. Hartman, *Scenes of Subjection: Terror, Slavery, and Self-Making in Nineteenth-Century America* (Oxford University Press, 1997), p. 117.

30 Anghie, "Slavery and International Law: The Jurisprudence of Henry Richardson," *Temple International and Comparative Law Journal* 31, no. 1 (2017): 14.

31 E.g., see the fine readings of Mahasweta Devi's stories "Salt" and "Dhowli" in Jennifer Wenzel, *The Disposition of Nature: Environmental Crisis and World Literature* (New York: Fordham University Press, 2020), chapter three.

32 Mahasweta Devi, *Imaginary Maps: Three Stories by Mahasweta Devi, Translated by Gayatri Chakravorty Spivak* (New York: Routledge, 1995), p. xx.

33 Gayatri Chakravorty Spivak, "Woman in Difference: Mahasweta Devi's 'Douloti the Bountiful,'" *Cultural Critique* 14 (Winter 1989–90): 128.

34 Mahasweta Devi, "Douloti the Bountiful," *Imaginary Maps*, pp. 20, 20–21.

35 Mahasweta, "Douloti," pp. 60, 61.

36 Mahasweta, "Douloti," pp. 31, 41.

37 Mahasweta, "Douloti," p. 86.
38 Mahasweta, "Douloti," p. 22.
39 Spivak, "Woman in Difference," p. 125.
40 Mahasweta, "Douloti," p. 26.
41 Mahasweta, "Douloti," pp. 88, 87.
42 Chris Abani, "On Humanity," TED2008. www.ted.com/talks/chris_abani_on_humanity
43 Chris Abani, *Becoming Abigail* (New York: Akashic Books, 2006), p. 75.
44 Abani, *Becoming Abigail*, p. 110.
45 Abani, *Becoming Abigail*, p. 53.
46 Abani, *Becoming Abigail*, p. 79.
47 Personal conversation with the author, College Park, MD, October 11, 2019.
48 M. NourbeSe Phillip, *Zong!* (Middletown, CT: Wesleyan University Press, 2011), p. 20.

CHAPTER 2

Humanitarian Attachments: Contemporary Anti-slavery and Anti-trafficking Discourses

Wendy S. Hesford

SAVING OUR CHILDREN IS FAR MORE IMPORTANT THAN A FAKE PANDEMIC. THE REAL PANDEMIC IS CHILD TRAFFICKING. THE REAL PANDEMIC IS PEDOPHILIA – WE DO NOT BELIEVE IN THE ELECTION INFECTION #SAVE THE CHILDREN!

These declarations appeared on the signs of QAnon followers at anti-trafficking and Trump rallies leading up to the 2020 U.S. presidential election. Host to anti-vaxxers and anti-maskers, and with strong links to evangelical religious organizations, QAnon followers claim that the global coronavirus pandemic is a liberal hoax designed to undermine the Trump presidency. QAnon conspiracy theorists assert that satanic-worshipping pedophiles, congressional Democrats and Hollywood elites among them, are running a global child sex trafficking ring. Amidst the rise in coronavirus cases and pandemic lockdowns in the spring of 2020, QAnon followers hijacked #SavetheChildren and infiltrated anti-trafficking rallies across the United States and United Kingdom. Ignoring evidence that families, employers and acquaintances are the chief perpetuators of child trafficking, QAnon circulates stranger danger narratives about predators snatching children off the streets and using COVID-19 mask regulations as cover.[1] In August 2020, Save the Children, a nongovernmental international humanitarian relief organization, released a public statement on QAnon's appropriation of its name in an attempt to counter the spread of trafficking myths and misinformation.

Not only has QAnon exploited the global pandemic to advance its conspiracy theories, but it has also hijacked the humanitarianism themes of the contemporary anti-slavery movement and its emphasis on child trafficking as the most egregious form of modern-day slavery. QAnon feeds on public fears about domestic child trafficking to advance its conspiratorial agenda. White women influencers drawn to child redemption narratives populate QAnon's "mommy blogosphere" with human trafficking myths.[2] Indeed, white women's presence in QAnon is vital to its human-itarian appeals. As sociologist Julia O'Connell Davidson observes, "This interlacing of the terms 'trafficking' and 'modern slavery' produces an extremely broad appeal to humanitarian feeling."[3] Anti-trafficking cam-paigns and conspiracy theories humanitarian attachments lie in the con-vergence of moral panics and public anxieties pertaining to childhood innocence, gendered vulnerability, trafficking in the sex industry, racial diversity, globalization, and immigration.

This chapter examines the humanitarian imperatives of contemporary anti-slavery and anti-trafficking campaigns and their calculated appropria-tions and parasitic logics. Central to this chapter is the following question: In what contexts, under what conditions of visibility and legibility, and in support of what political investments are humanitarian tropes deployed? To better understand the contemporary anti-slavery movement's perpetu-ation and parasitic appropriation of humanitarian tropes, this chapter turns our attention to the rhetorical mediation of human trafficking subjects and their stories. Understanding these mediations is important because how trafficking subjects and their stories are framed sets the parameters for public recognition and political action.

The contemporary anti-slavery movement, specifically anti-trafficking campaigns, hosts competing and often conspiring parasitic logics and publics. Rhetorical studies scholars Kyle R. Larson and George F. McHendry Jr. argue that a parasitic public "articulates with and feeds off of the power structure's oppressive norms through demagogic rhetoric intended to limit discursive space for others and strengthen its own circulatory, material power."[4] The parasitic logics of anti-trafficking cam-paigns are tied to humanitarianism's emergency imaginary and threshold politics, that is, attention and action are sparked by the determination that a moral line has been crossed.

Contemporary slavery studies scholarship needs to become more attuned to the powerful grip of humanitarian politics in order to more effectively counteract its parasitic logics and violence perpetrated in its name. These humanitarian attachments harm efforts to systemically com-bat the intertwined problems of human trafficking, gender violence, racial oppression, economic dispossession, and labor exploitation. Within some sectors of U.S. political discourse on human trafficking, these attachments feed on white resentment, the repressive sexual politics of rescue, anti-migration agendas and postracial fantasies, and consequentially deepen the ethical void at the core of humanitarian politics, which must rely on the willingness of those in power to relinquish resources.

Below, I elaborate on how contemporary right-wing conspiracy theorists appropriate humanitarian tropes to justify vigilante violence in the name of averting the trafficking of children and protecting the vulnerable nation-state. These appropriations, part of the rhetorical machinery of white supremacy, perpetuate the parasitic logic of humanitarian recognition and its conferment, and give immunity to white privilege in discounting structural violence and racial inequities.

2.1   Vigilante Humanitarianism and White *Ressentiment*

Donald J. Trump's rhetoric epitomizes the moral and political economies of white *ressentiment* and affective charge of whiteness as embattled.[5] Rhetorical studies scholar Casey Ryan Kelly aptly defines the concept *ressentiment* (re-sentiment) as a "generative force" that accounts for "the unique interaction where powerful sentiments and self-serving morality are coupled with feelings of powerlessness and ruminations on past injuries."[6] White fears about the decentering of white privilege, particularly white masculinity, serve as warrants for doubling down on traditional gender roles and a conspiratorial stream of nativist narratives about white victimization.[7] Trump specifically capitalized on white male *ressentiment* and directed that resentment toward political opponents, the press, communities of color, liberal immigration and racial diversity policies, the #MeToo movement, and globalism understood as a worldwide conspiracy aspiring to limit the sovereignty of nation-states.[8]

Through the embattled rhetoric of righteous victimization, Trump's appeal to white rage relies on an "emotional-moral framework in which victimization, resentment, and revenge are civic virtues."[9] In contrast to white perceptions of Black rage as threatening, white rage is construed as virtuous. Trump feeds on white *ressentiment* fueled by the loss of the traditional hallmarks of white privilege and neoliberalism's economic injuries to save a nation perceived as under siege by predatory outsiders. The enemy may be conspiratorial and elusive, but this elusiveness drives vigilantes' revenge fantasies and violent actions. Trump's discrediting of the 2020 presidential election emboldened right-wing conspiracy theorists and white supremacists toward acts of vigilante violence framed as civic virtue. In this regard, President Trump might be best described as the "vigilante-in-chief." MAGA hats and QAnon signs sported by those who stormed the United States Capital building on January 6, 2021, demonstrated that white *ressentiment* is not simply a psychological disposition on which conspiracy feeds, but a political tool of white nationalist violence.

On October 28, 2017, an anonymous user Q declared on the 4chan website that they would use their alleged government security clearance to inform the public about President Trump's battle against the "deep state." Many reporters suggest that QAnon emerged from the conspiracy fiction that came to be known as Pizzagate, which falsely implicated government officials, including then presidential candidate Hillary Rodham Clinton, in a global child sex trafficking ring. QAnon followers claimed that references to "pizza" in the hacked emails of Democrat party officials, including John Podesta, Clinton's campaign manager, were references to child trafficking. The conspiracy led Edgar Maddison Welch, a 28-year-old man from North Carolina, to travel to the Comet Ping Pong pizzeria in Washington D.C. to investigate the alleged global child sex trafficking ring. Upon arrival, he fired a rifle to break open the lock of a storage room door behind which he believed children were held captive. Welch was subsequently charged with assault and possession of a firearm during the commission of a crime.

In 2019, the FBI designated QAnon as a domestic terror threat. On October 2, 2020, the United States House of Representatives passed Resolution 1154, which characterized QAnon as "an ideology that has demonstrated its capacity to radicalize to violence individuals at an alarming speed," and denounced QAnon adherents for "harming legitimate efforts to combat child exploitation and sex trafficking, including by overwhelming antitrafficking hotlines with false reports."

By contrast, QAnon followers implicit coding of violence perpetuated in the name of protecting vulnerable children and the nation suggest that white nationalist violence be viewed as acts of *vigilante* humanitarianism. Vigilante humanitarianism may not be beholden to the state, but it is a "state effect" and in that respect parasitic. My invocation of the concept of "state effect" is derived from French philosopher Michael Foucault's theory of the state not as an *object* but as a *process* that permeates the body, behaviors, actions, and time of individuals.[10] As a state effect, vigilante humanitarianism might be understood as part of the continuum of carceral humanitarianism, the latter of which refers to the state's "control and manage[ment of] populations and their movements."[11] Vigilantes are beholden to remedy problems that the state has created but is perceived as incapable of correcting. Despite the violent and anti-democratic acts of QAnon supporters, several high-ranking members of the Republican Party express alliance with QAnon, and President Trump had retweeted accounts aligned with QAnon and other conspiracy theorists on at least 145 occasions.[12] When confronted by reporter Savannah

Guthrie about his knowledge of QAnon at a town hall meeting in the lead up to the 2020 presidential election, Trump first denied knowledge of the group and then managed to endorse them in a series of disambiguating claims. Guthrie said, "Let me ask you about QAnon – it is this theory that Democrats are a satanic pedophilia ring and that you are the savior of that. Now can you just once and for all state that that is completely not true and disavow QAnon in its entirety?" Trump responded, "I know nothing about QAnon. I know very little . . . I do know they are very much against pedophilia."[13]

Trump's series of disambiguating claims destabilize the presumption of veracity and the burden of proof in an attempt to diffuse opposition and foreclose deliberative debate. Through appeals to popular belief and incredulity, Trump entitles QAnon's position as beyond reproach. The rhetorical fallacy is something like: "How bad can QAnon be if they are against pedophilia," or "You can't argue with QAnon because they are against pedophilia." Trump's use of "phantom sources" seemingly allows him to make claims without accepting any responsibility.[14] As rhetoric and communications scholar Ryan Neville-Shepard observes, for Trump, the impact that a claim serves in advancing his position is more important than the source of the information.[15]

Whereas QAnon and Trump seize humanitarian rhetoric to advance conspiratorial theories about white victimization and government corruption, neo-abolitionists along the political spectrum coincide in their turn to humanitarian appeals in their fight to abolish prostitution globally. These alliances are facilitated by anti-trafficking legislation and humanitarian attachments to gendered vulnerability and the neoliberal privatization of gender violence. This fusion appears in cultural representations of sex trafficking as well as in domestic U.S. and international human trafficking policies, specifically through *sexual humanitarian* discourse. Below I highlight how sexual humanitarianism mediates contemporary anti-trafficking campaigns and call for a more critical engagement attuned to these mediations and their consequences.

2.2 Sexual Humanitarianism and Trafficking Narratives

Sexual humanitarianism is one of the prevailing discursive frameworks for contemporary literary representations of human trafficking, particularly sex trafficking – a framework that is impoverished in its obsession with sexual constraint, coercion, and choice instead of power. *Sexual humanitarianism*, a phrase coined by queer migration studies scholar Nicola Mai, "operates by containing through social interventions the mobility of migrant groups that are strategically essentialized and othered as 'pure' victims of sexual oppression and exploitations."[16] Sexual humanitarianism thrives on a lexicon of moral sentiments and graphically sexualized dichotomies between victimization and agency and between freedom and slavery, and melodramatic heteronormative narratives of sexual danger and rescue.[17] The concept of sexual humanitarianism points to the hypervisibility of female violation, eroticization of violence and gendered vulnerability, the politics of rescue, and heteronormative cultural and political agendas.

Despite the achievements of transnational feminists and critical trafficking studies scholars and lawyers (Bernstein,[18] Beutin,[19] Brysk,[20] Chuang,[21] Cojocaru,[22] Davidson,[23] Fukushima,[24] Hesford, Hua,[25] Madhavi,[26] Russo,[27] Shih,[28] Suchland,[29] Vance,[30] Warren,[31] among others) in framing sex work and sex trafficking as part of the gendered global economy, the trafficking of white savior narratives proliferates. Literary and cultural representations of sex trafficking that are targeted at Western audiences often depict victims of sex trafficking as foreign and non-autonomous, as innocent young women and girls betrayed by cultural traditions. As cultural anthropologist Lila Abu-Lughold has noted, mass-marketed literature on trafficking is dominated by themes of force and bondage (such as Alyaan Hirsi Ali's *The Caged Virgin*, Azar Nafisi's *Reading Lolita in Tehran*, Zana Muhsen's *Sold: A Story of Modern Slavery*, and Patricia McCormick's young adult novel *Sold*). Moreover, Abu-Lughold argues, there are "surprising similarities between slave plantation pornography," that is, images of abused Black bodies in U.S. abolitionist literature, and writing on gender oppression and sexual slavery in the Muslim world that target Western readers.[32] Similar to the George W. Bush administration's strategic use of the discourse of women's human rights to justify the U.S. bombing of Afghanistan post-9/11, recent mass media coverage of sex slavery within the context of Islamic terrorism has been strategically deployed to support U.S. humanitarian military interventions and occupations. Sexual humanitarianism discursively binds U.S. counterterrorism and U.S. anti-trafficking campaigns.[33]

Nicholas Kristof's *New York Times* editorials and book *Half the Sky: Turning Oppression into Opportunity for Women Worldwide*, co-authored with Sheryl WuDunn, exemplify a form of sexual humanitarianism enabled by the terms of the global sex trade – the purchase of human beings. In *Half the Sky*, Kristof writes about his travels with *New York Times* videographer Naka Nathaniel to Cambodia, and his efforts to rescue girls and young women working in brothels. He writes, "We became slave owners in the twenty-first century, the old-fashioned way: We paid cash in exchange for two slave girls and a couple of receipts. The girls were then ours to do with as we liked. Rescuing girls from brothels is the easy part, however. The challenge is keeping them from returning."[34] Kristof acknowledges that these girls and young women's agency is reduced by their limited choices, but in the end, he sees himself as both the consumer and the change agent. His purchase of these young women's freedom turns them into valuable commodities, which not only sets into motion a rescue narrative but also creates "a new market in abduction and redemption."[35] Kristof's raid and rescue narrative allows him to emerge as a virtuous reporter, as a humanitarian hero.

Literary scholars working at the intersection of feminist studies and life narrative, including new slave narratives (Gilmore,[36] Johnson,[37] Murphy,[38] and Whitlock[39]) spotlight the colonial cosmopolitan gaze that drives much contemporary humanitarian storytelling. With regard to new slave narratives, white, Western narrators often serve as intermediaries for formerly enslaved non-Western sex trafficking victims, or those miscon-strued as such. In some cases, the women represented have consented to sex work but not to its exploitative structures. This narrative seizure "perform[s] a gendered and colonialist ventriloquism" that more often than not "attaches credibility to a white, Western, and male narrator as spokesperson" and "proxy witness."[40] These proximate relations and attachments to whiteness reinforce the neo-abolitionist movement's para-sitic relationship to rescue and redemption. In *Half the Sky*, Kristof emerges not only as a humanitarian hero but also as a "vigilante abolitionist."[41] Sociologist Elena Shih describes "vigilante abolitionism" as a "carceral extension of neoliberal U.S. state power" that privileges criminal justice rather than social justice approaches to human trafficking.[42] Vigilante abolitionism and its close cousin vigilante humanitarianism, as I discuss below, also contour feminist abolitionist anti-trafficking campaigns.

2.3 Feminist Abolitionist Anti-trafficking Campaigns

Contemporary feminist abolitionist anti-trafficking campaigns and organi-zations such as the Coalition against Trafficking in Women likewise deploy sexual humanitarian rhetoric in criminalizing prostitution and recasting justice in carceral terms – an emphasis that fails to address the structural inequities and the economic determinants of human traffick-ing.[43] Contemporary feminist abolitionists tend not to distinguish between consensual sex work and sex trafficking, and thus conflate prostitution and human trafficking. Indeed, in neo-abolitionist campaigns, feminist and otherwise, prostitution is framed as slavery. Neo-abolitionist campaigns employ humanitarian rhetoric in their appeals to regulate female sexuality under the pretext of protecting vulnerable women, and in this regard echo the late-nineteenth- and early-twentieth-century "white slavery" campaigns and early anti-prostitution laws.

The Mann Act of 1910, initially named the White Slave Traffic Act, outlawed the transport of individuals across state lines for prostitution. The Mann Act was based on provincial fears about young white girls from rural areas becoming sexual victims to foreign city dwellers. The modern-day slavery analogy for sex trafficking draws on these earlier twentieth-century characterizations of the social evils of prostitution. Dominated by repressive moralists, anti-white-slavery campaigns forged alliances with religious and social purity organizations and feminist organizations that sought to abolish prostitution.[44] Opportunistic alliances between neo-abolitionist feminists and Christian right-wing groups continue to flourish, united in their commitment to the carceral paradigms of gender justice.[45]

Carceral feminist abolitionist understandings of human trafficking contrast with transnational feminist views of human trafficking as a "sociopolitical process codified by local, national, and institutional law shaped by perceptions of labor and migration and embedded in indentured mobility."[46] The Global Alliance against Traffic in Women (GAATW), for example, has long argued for the application of human rights principles to address trafficking as a complex problem that involves context-specific issues of migration and labor exploitation. GAATW aims to combat the restrictive trends of crime-control campaigns and neo-abolitionist agendas, which the organization argues infringe on the rights and protection of trafficked persons. GAATW's position is that trafficking as a concept is insufficient because it does not account for the link between trafficking and migration. Sensational representations of stranger abductions and depictions of trafficked women as passive and naive victims lured or tricked into sex work nevertheless remain pervasive tropes in global anti-trafficking campaigns as well as in U.S. domestic legislation designed to address trafficking, including the Trafficking Victims Protection Act of 2000 (TVPA).[47]

Moral panics about the "Other" have long consumed American politics and generated paternalistic policies destined to protect those deemed deserving victims. Yet these policies have also subjugated and criminalized these very same victims. The long-standing law-and-order emphasis of international and domestic U.S. trafficking policies has served as a precursor to recent legislation directed at the prohibition of the use of the internet to promote prostitution, which includes the 2012 criminal case against Backpage.com brought before the court by the former Attorney General of California, Kamala Harris, and more recent trafficking legislation signed into law by the Trump administration in 2018 to hold "web sites liable for any content posted by their users that 'facilitates' prostitution."[48] A year after signing the "Stop Enabling Sex Traffickers Act" and "Allow States and Victims to Fight Online Sex Trafficking Act," Ivanka Trump invited neo-abolitionists, faith-based groups chief among them, to the White House to renew alliances. Conservative political operatives and congressional representatives, evangelical brothel raiders, and a longtime feminist anti-porn activist were among the attendees.[49] Neo-abolitionist alliances' prioritization of the criminalization of prostitution not only further stigmatizes sex workers but distracts attention from the economic harms, gender discrimination, and reproductive healthcare needs of those working in the sex industry (see Russo, "Online Sex Trafficking Hysteria").

2.4 Carceral Humanitarianism: Trafficking Security

Scholars have persuasively argued that anti-immigration sentiment undermines the humanitarian imperatives of anti-trafficking legislation in the United States.[50] Indeed, the Trump administration's anti-immigration rhetoric and policies were fervent hosts to parasitic human trafficking myths. While humanitarian configurations of the United States obscure the nation's complicity in global economic structures that lead to conditions that propel mass migrations and human trafficking, anti-immigration's parasitic racial logics entail white nationalists' reclamation and domestication of humanitarian recognition. Consider the Trump administration's mobilization of human trafficking as a presumably morally unimpeachable cause to amass support for stricter immigration policies. Trump zealously seized human trafficking tropes with his Executive Order on Border Security just days after his inauguration in an attempt to heighten public fear and to engender support for building the wall along the Southern border. The introduction to the EO states:

> Border security is critically important . . . . Transnational criminal organizations operate sophisticated drug-and human trafficking networks and smuggling operations on both sides of the southern border, contributing to a significant increase in violent crime . . . . Among those who illegally enter are those who seek to harm Americans through acts of terror or criminal conduct.

Claiming that the nation was vulnerable to "foreign others," Trump produced the ultimate stranger danger narrative. Here anti-trafficking is used as a warrant for anti-immigration platforms that reserve humanitarian recognition for those deemed victimized by foreign others, which, as sociologist Nandita Sharma puts it, "gives a humanitarian gloss to national anti-immigration controls."[51] Notwithstanding evidence by experts that building a wall would exacerbate trafficking,[52] throughout his presidency Trump continued to mobilize trafficking myths and nativist fear-based rhetoric.

In his televised "Address to the Nation on the Crisis at the Border" on January 8, 2019, the third week of a partial shutdown of the U.S. federal government, President Trump framed the situation at the U.S.–Mexico border as "a humanitarian crisis – a crisis of the heart and a crisis of the soul." Trump claimed, "Last month, 20,000 migrant children were illegally brought into the United States, a dramatic increase. These children are used as human pawns by vicious coyotes and ruthless gangs." Not only did Trump manipulate the 20,000 statistic, which refers to the total number of children, parents, and legal guardians caught together at the border (*Washington Post*), but his exclusive focus on coyotes and gangs shifted the humanitarian gaze from migrant children to U.S. citizens as the "true" victims deserving of humanitarian recognition. The President's nativist rhetoric reinforced the notion that all Americans are "hurt by uncontrolled, illegal migration." "Among those hardest hit," he argued, "are African Americans and Hispanic Americans." He continued, "I've held the hands of the weeping mothers and embraced the grief-stricken fathers." "America's heart broke," he said, "when a young police officer in California was savagely murdered in cold blood by an illegal alien, who just came across the border." The President then delivered a litany of gruesome murders: an "Air Force veteran was raped, murdered, and beaten to death with a hammer by an illegal alien with a long criminal history," and "an illegal alien was recently charged with murder for killing, beheading, and dismembering his neighbor." He asked, "How much more American blood must we shed?"

President Trump claimed the power of the white humanitarian benefactor to gift those whom he construed as deserving of humanitarian recognition, such as "weeping [US citizen] mothers," and he withdrew recognition from those fleeing violence and those exposed to the inhumanity of the administration's policies. The apocalyptic spectacle of violence that the President's litany of crimes created erased the humanity of those presently detained and discounted the lives of the children who have died in U.S. custody at the border, or soon after they were released. Not only was his characterization of illegal crossings as an "invasion" misleading, since the numbers of illegal crossings remain below higher levels of earlier years, but the President also pitted differentially oppressed groups against each other – a strategy deployed to uphold white authority. Additionally, far more Americans have been injured or killed by white supremacist citizen terrorists and domestic violence than have been victims of violence by undocumented immigrants.[53] Yet the Trump administration did not afford these victims the same level of humanitarian concern.

Deflecting attention from his own administration's complicity in perpetuating human trafficking, including the detention of children at the border, Trump argued "traffickers" were "to blame for the crises of children in cages." The separation and detention of children crossing the U.S.–Mexico border might be viewed as an exemplar of *carceral humanitarianism* – the "two sides of state sovereignty." "These two pillars, humanitarian aid and humanitarian war," as Kelly Oliver argues, "operate according to an autoimmune logic by which the greatest threat to survival is also what sustains them, bloody wars, terror attacks, and human suffering."[54] The violence of humanitarian governance – the dual role of confinement in the protection and violation of children's human rights – became devastatingly clear when news spread of the conditions of some of the detention centers and the death of several children in U.S. border custody.

Moreover, as Haynes notes, Trump selectively conferred humanitarian recognition on "foreign" women and girls whose trafficking experience fit the "rare, but much more frequently depicted (often rather luridly) tragedy of women and girls abducted for sex slavery."[55] In an attempt to exploit the government shutdown to secure funds for the wall, Trump repeatedly circulated the same sensationalist abduction narratives and set of exaggerated claims that contour sexual humanitarian discourse to reinforce its anti-immigration agenda. Those crossing the U.S.–Mexico border, he claimed, "come in and they have women tied up. They have tape over their mouths ... And they have three, four, five of them in vans, or three of them in back seats of cars ... And if we had a barrier of any kind ... they wouldn't be able to make that turn. They wouldn't even bother trying." These images of female bondage – women shackled in chains and bound by rope – build on the cultural eroticization of female victimization.

The hypocrisy of the administration's depiction of the U.S.–Mexico border as a humanitarian crisis lies not only in its selective conferment of humanitarian recognition, but also in its criminalization of humanitarian aid. Under the Trump administration, U.S. border patrol agents harassed humanitarian groups and charged members with felonies for assisting migrants crossing the desert. "Trumpian humanitarianism requires not just a wall between Mexico and the United States," as political anthropologist Elizabeth Cullen Dunn perceptively notes, "but one between the present and some imagined dystopian future, one in which invaders wreak death and destruction on American citizens."[56] Humanitarian attachments served as a cover for the Trump administration's perpetuation of human rights violations at the border. Democrats' extension of humanitarian appeals may have highlighted their outrage against the administration's policies, specifically the forced separation and detention of children, but these appeals likewise failed to fully address no less resolve the paradoxes of humanitarianism, including violence exercised in its name.

Above, I considered how contemporary anti-trafficking campaigns serve as hosts to conspiratorial publics, white nationalist and nativist platforms, and the repressive sexual politics of rescue. Below, I consider how contemporary anti-trafficking campaigns' uncritical embrace of the transatlantic slavery analogy reproduces temporal postracial fantasies with little to no regard for the legacy of slavery and its aftermath.

2.5   Postraciality: Trafficking the Slavery Analogy

Numerous contemporary anti-trafficking organizations frame human trafficking as a form of modern-day slavery, including Free the Slaves, Anti-Slavery International, and the Polaris Project. The Polaris Project describes fighting "trafficking and slavery in the spirit of a modern-day Underground Railroad."[57] The Polaris Project web site describes the original of the organization as follows, "Founded in 2002, Polaris is named for the North Star, which people held in slavery in the United States used as a guide to navigate their way to freedom. Today we are filling in the roadmap for that journey and lighting the path ahead" (polarisproject.org). U.S. political leaders have seized upon the transatlantic slavery analogy and description of contemporary human trafficking as modern-day slavery because "it allows them to present their efforts to control borders as part of a moral struggle for human rights and against slavery."[58]

In her analysis of the U.K.-based initiative Antislavery's Usable Past and its use of images of racial chattel slavery to advance awareness about contemporary human trafficking, communication studies scholar Lyndsey Beutin points to the risk that such juxtapositions run in reproducing "the racialising and capitalist logics that underpinned racial chattel slavery in the first place."[59] These juxtapositions also risk perpetuating the ontological project of anti-blackness through humanitarian negation. Apropos to the content of this chapter is Beutin's analysis of the project's juxtaposition of a nineteenth-century drawing of an African American woman on an auction block and a photograph of a young South Asian woman in a Plexiglas box with a placard that reads "Child Prostitute, Bangladesh, c. 2009." The photograph, derived from the 2009 Save the Children Australia campaign, reproduces racist colonial stereotypes of an uncivilized global South in need of rescue by a civilized global North. The juxtaposition problematically lacks differentiation between past and present systems of oppression.[60] "[T]he points that do converge," Beutin argues, "the effects of capitalism's accumulation through dispossession via colonialism or enslavement – are not discussed."[61] This political investment in postraciality and the notion that race is no longer a structuring principle in inequity relocates the violence of racial capitalism to the precarious refuge that is humanitarianism.

Equally troubling are deployments of the transatlantic slavery analogy that erase the history of racial oppression in the United States and position slavery as part of a contemporary narrative and "national mythology of progress toward pluralism, equality, and liberty."[62] In such instances, the slavery analogy props up myths about racial progress, erases struggles against ongoing racialized state violence, and sidelines prison abolitionist campaigns against the mass incarceration of Black bodies. Neo-abolitionist Kevin Bales' *Disposable People: New Slavery in the Global Economy* exemplifies the contemporary anti-slavery movement's investment in postracial fantasies. In this work, Bales, former president of Free the Slaves, asserts that in the "new slavery" "race means very little." "The criteria of enslavement today do not concern color, tribe, or religion; they focus on weakness, gullibility, and deprivation."[63]

In addition to the investment of certain sectors of the contemporary anti-trafficking movement in postraciality, the movement recasts the contradictory use of humanitarian appeals of earlier periods. While early abolitionists turned to humanizing tactics to counter the cruelties of slavery, including the humanization of enslaved children, proslavery advocates and apologists deployed infantilizing discourses to justify slavery. Proslavery advocates construed enslaved people as childlike and as requiring the oversight of paternalistic whites. Slavery apologists also mobilized the figure of the enslaved child to bolster benevolent slaveholders' humanitarian narratives, namely that they were providing orphaned children protection.[64] Similar rhetorical patterns characterized reconstruction, wherein northern abolitionists used stories of slavery's cruelty to push for the rights of southern Blacks; whereas former slaveholders turned to proslavery humanitarian rhetoric to support the argument that emancipation would contribute to Black poverty, starvation, and misery.[65]

Although contemporary anti-trafficking campaigns evoke the humanitarian themes of earlier abolitionist campaigns, they are distinguished in their exchange of "black suffering [with] non-black, non-racial political demands."[66] The modern-day slavery analogy "parasitically feeds" on the "specter of slavery."[67] When deployed in ways that transcend systems of gender and racial hierarchy, the modern-day slavery analogy casts the United States as morally supreme and masks violence perpetuated in the name of humanitarianism, including its deep entanglement with settler colonialism and the genocidal logics of elimination.[68]

Contemporary anti-trafficking campaigns uncritical embrace of the modern-day slavery analogy brings contemporary abolitionism face-to-face with humanitarianism's enduring contradictions. In addition to advancing the myth of the United States as an "exemplary racial democracy,"[69] anti-trafficking and anti-immigration policies collude in limiting protections for migrants. In this regard, contemporary anti-trafficking policies function as the "moral reform arm of contemporary anti-immigrant politics."[70] Additionally, neo-abolitionist campaigns that uphold corporations and consumers as exemplary modern-day abolitionists naturalize neoliberalism's economic dispossession of communities of color. Among these campaigns are the The Body Shop's campaign against child sex trafficking and Ivanka Trump's promotion of anti-slavery campaigns while having her clothes sourced from factories with exploitative labor conditions. In sum, if we are to counteract myopic understandings of freedom perpetuated by neo-abolitionists and conspiracy theorists alike, we need a more robust critique of the parasitic logics of humanitarianism and violence of humanitarian negations.

2.6   Conspiratorial Humanitarian Politics

I conclude by returning to QAnon's hijacking of #SAVETHECHILDREN and earlier discussion of vigilante humanitarianism as a state effect. The racial logics undergirding vigilante humanitarianism's parasitic relation to the state and the state as host to human trafficking myths became vividly clear to me while looking at a photograph that accompanied a local news story about a rally held in Mansfield, Ohio in August 2020, just an hour north of Columbus, Ohio where I live. Inspired by national protests, the group of five protesters featured in the photograph held up signs that read: KIDS JUST DON'T DISAPPEAR #SAVEOURCHILDREN. ABOLISH ICE. I WANT EVERY PERSON IN POWER WHO WAS INVOLVED IN EPSTEIN'S PEDO-RING TO BE PUT BEHIND BARS FOR LIFE. PROTECT HEAL SAVE #PIZZAGATE.

Abolish ICE has been deployed by progressives in their critiques of the Trump administration's zero tolerance policy that led to the separation and detention of hundreds of migrant children. Although deportation rates peaked under the Obama administration, and Trump's policies amplified the Obama administration's policies, it was not until the emergence of news reports of young "tender age" children held in cages at the U.S.–Mexico border that calls to Abolish ICE gained traction in mainstream U.S. media and politics. The Black Lives Matter movement reignited calls to Abolish ICE in the wake of the murder of George Floyd. In these contexts, Abolish ICE bespeaks a structural critique of the carceral state that includes addressing the limits of police reform platforms. Legislators across the political spectrum – from progressives to libertarians – have adopted these critiques to advance their own agendas.

When juxtaposed with #PIZZAGATE, Abolish ICE takes on conspiratorial meaning and reverberations, which include QAnon supporters' attribution of civic virtue to vigilantes fighting against the "deep state" and its alleged involvement in running a global child sex trafficking ring. Thus, these protest signs present different examples of actual, potential, and fabricated child abuse as equivalent, and problematically so. Conspiracy fictions about child trafficking are treated on par with the material realities of child separation and dispossession that immigrants and other communities of color continue to face in the United States. In juxtaposition with #SAVEOURCHILDREN, the Abolish ICE sign might be read as an endorsement of postraciality in that the rights category of child trafficking is without racial valence to the protesters. In rendering all particularity illegible and categories of social difference fungible – substitutable and exchangeable – these protest signs epitomize the epistemic and ontological violence of conspiratorial humanitarian politics. These signs and their differing critiques of the state collude in their attachment to the humanitarian figure of the trafficked child. The conspiratorial dimension allows for the glaring conflict between calls for Abolish ICE and #SAVEOURCHILDREN. The Mansfield, Ohio protestors may not have been aware of these contrasting ideological allegiances. But taken together, these child trafficking narratives shine a spotlight on the parasitic logics that undergird humanitarian attachments.

Notes

1 Elle Hardy, "Inside the Save The Children conspiracy theory that's targeting suburban mums in the US". *ABC News.* September 19, 2020. www.abc.net .au/news/2020-09-20/how-growing-conspiracy-movement-critical-to-us-election/12661592. Accessed 5 Jan 2021.
2 Hardy, "Inside the Save The Children conspiracy theory that's targeting suburban mums in the US."
3 Julia O'Connell Davidson, "New Slavery, Old Binaries: Human Trafficking and the Borders of Freedom," *Global Networks* 10, no. 2 (2010): 244–261.
4 Kyle R. Larsen, and George F. (Guy) McHendry Jr., "Parasitic Publics." *Rhetoric Society Quarterly* 49, no. 5, 2019: 517–541, p. 519
5 Casey Ryan Kelly, "Donald J. Trump and the Rhetoric of Ressentiment," *Quarterly Journal of Speech* 106, no. 1, 2020: 2–24.
6 Kelly, "Donald J. Trump and the Rhetoric of Ressentiment."
7 Kelly, "Donald J. Trump and the Rhetoric of Ressentiment."
8 Kelly, "Donald J. Trump and the Rhetoric of Ressentiment.".
9 Kelly, "Donald J. Trump and the Rhetoric of Ressentiment."
10 Stephen W. Sawyer, "Foucault and the State," *The Tocqueville Review* 36, no. 1 (2015): 135–164, p. 136.
11 Katie Oliviero, *Vulnerability Politics: The Uses and Abuses of Precarity in Political Debate* (New York University Press, 2018).
12 Adrienne LaFrance, *The Atlantic*, June 2020, pp. 26–38, p. 30.
13 "Guthrie to Trump: You're the President, you're not some crazy uncle!" *CNN Business.* www.cnn.com/videos/media/2020/10/16/trump-town-hall-nbc-guth rie-coronavirus-qanon-masks-orig.cnn-business. Accessed January 5, 2021.
14 Ryan Neville-Shepard, "Post-presumption Argumentation and the Post-truth World: On the Conspiracy Rhetoric of Donald Trump," *Argumentation and Advocacy* 55, no. 3 (2019): 175–193, 184.
15 Neville-Shepard, "Post-presumption Argumentation and the Post-truth World."
16 Nicola Mai, "Between Embodied Cosmopolitism and Sexual Humanitarianism: The Fractal Mobilities and Subjectivities of Migrants Working in the Sex Industry." In *Borders, Mobilities and Migrations, Perspectives from the Mediterranean in the 21st Century*, ed. V. Baby-Collins and L. Anteby (Peter Lang, 2014), 175–192.
17 Carole S. Vance, "Thinking Trafficking, Thinking Sex," *GLQ*, 17, no. 1 (2010): 135–143.
18 Elizabeth Bernstein, *Brokered Subjects: Sex Trafficking and the Politics of Freedom* (University of Chicago Press, 2019).
19 Lyndsey P. Beutin, "Black Suffering for/from Anti-trafficking Advocacy," *Anti-trafficking Review*, no. 9 (2017): 14–30.
20 Alison Brysk, "Rethinking Trafficking: Human Rights and Private Wrongs." In *From Human Trafficking to Human Rights: Reframing Contemporary*

Slavery, ed. Alison Brysk and Austin Choi-Fitzpatrick (University of Pennsylvania Press, 2013), 73–85.

21 Janie Chuang, "United States as Global Sheriff: Using Unilateral Sanctions to Combat Human Trafficking," *Michigan Journal of International Law* 27, no. 437 (2006): 430–494.

22 Claudia Cojocaru, "Sex Trafficking, Captivity, and Narrative: Constructing Victimhood with the Goal of Salvation," *Dialect Anthropology* 39 (2015): 183–94.

23 O'Connell Davidson, "New Slavery, Old Binaries", pp. 244–261.

24 Annie Isabel Fukushima, *Migrant Crossings: Witnessing Human Trafficking in the U.S.* (Stanford University Press, 2019).

25 Julietta Hua, *Trafficking Women's Human Rights* (University of Minnesota Press, 2011).

26 Pardis Mahdavi, *From Trafficking to Terror: Constructing a Global Social Problem* (New York: Routledge, 2013).

27 Regina A. Russo, "Online Sex Trafficking Hysteria: Flawed Policies, Ignored Human Rights, and Censorship," *Cleveland State Law Review* 68 (2020): 314–345.

28 Elena Shih, "Not in My "Backyard Abolitionism": Vigilante Rescue against American Sex Trafficking," *Sociological Perspectives* 59, no. 1 (2016): 66–90.

29 Jennifer Suchland, *Economies of Violence: Transnational Feminism, Postsocialism, and the Politics of Sex Trafficking* (Duke University Press, 2015).

30 Carole S. Vance, "Thinking Trafficking, Thinking Sex," *GLQ* 17, no. 1 (2010): 135–143.

31 Kay Warren, "Troubling the Victim/Trafficker Dichotomy in Efforts to Combat Human Trafficking: The Unintended Consequences of Moralizing Labor Migration," *Indiana Journal of Global Legal Studies* 19, no. 1 (2012): 105–120.

32 Lila Abu-Lughod, *Do Muslim Women Need Saving?* (Harvard University Press, 2013), p. 82.

33 Wendy S. Hesford, and Amy Shuman. "Precarious Narratives: Media Accounts of Islamic State Sexual Violence." In *Precarious Rhetorics*, ed. Wendy S. Hesford et al. (The Ohio State University Press, 2018), 41–61.

34 Nicholas Kristof, and Sheryl WuDunn. *Half the Sky: Turning Oppression into Opportunity for Women Worldwide* (New York: Knopf, 2009), 35.

35 Leti Volpp, "Disappearing Acts. On Gendered Violence, Pathological Cultures, and Civil Society," *PMLA* 121, no. 5 (2006): 1631.

36 Leigh Gilmore, *Tainted Witness: Why We Doubt What Women Say about Their Lives* (New York: Columbus University Press, 2017), pp. 122–123.

37 Kelli Lyon Johnson, "The New Slave Narrative: Advocacy and Human Rights in Stories of Contemporary Slavery," *Journal of Human Rights* 12, no. 2 (2013): 242–258.

38 Laura Murphy, *The New Slave Narrative: The Battle Over Representation of Contemporary Slavery* (New York: Columbia University Press, 2019).

39 Gilliam Whitlock, *Soft Weapons: Autobiography in Transit* (Chicago: University of Chicago Press, 2010).

40 Leigh Gilmore, *Tainted Witness: Why We Doubt What Women Say about Their Lives* (New York: Columbus University Press, 2017), 122–123.

41 Elena Shih, "Not in My "Backyard Abolitionism": Vigilante Rescue against American Sex Trafficking," *Sociological Perspectives* 59, no. 1 (2016): 66–90.

42 Shih, "Not in My "Backyard Abolitionism."

43 Elizabeth Bernstein, *Brokered Subjects: Sex Trafficking and the Politics of Freedom* (University of Chicago Press, 2019).

44 Jo Doezema, "Loose Women or Lost Women? The Re-Emergence of the Myth of White Slavery in Contemporary Discourses of Trafficking in Women," *Gender Issues* 18, no. 1 (2000): 28.

45 Elizabeth Bernstein, *Brokered Subjects: Sex Trafficking and the Politics of Freedom* (University of Chicago Press, 2019).

46 Fukushima, *Migrant Crossings*, p. 160.

47 For incisive analyses of the spectacle of female victimization and coupling of femininity and death in contemporary anti-trafficking campaigns, see Rutvica Andrijasevic, "Beautiful Dead Bodies: Gender, Migration, and Representation in Anti-Trafficking Campaigns," *Feminist Review* 86 (2007): 24–44; Fukushima, *Migrant Crossings*; Wendy S. Hesford, *Spectacular Rhetorics: Human Rights Visions, Recognitions, Feminisms* (Durham, NC: Duke University Press, 2011); and Hua, *Trafficking Women's Human Rights*.

48 Melissa Gira Grant, "White Mom's Burden," *The New Republic* (July–August 2019): 10–11.

49 Grant, "White Mom's Burden."

50 Christina Doonan, "A House Divided: Humanitarianism and Anti-immigration Within US Anti-trafficking Legislation," *Feminist Legal Studies* 24 (2016): 273–293, p. 276.

51 Nandita Sharma, "Anti-Trafficking Rhetoric and the Making of a Global Apartheid," *NWSA Journal* 17, no. 3 (2005): 88–111.

52 Dina Francesca Haynes, "Sacrificing Women and Immigrants on the Alter of Regressive Politics," *Human Rights Quarterly* 41 (2019): 777–822.

53 Daniel Sipes, "Right-Wing Radicals a Higher Threat to US than Undocumented Immigrants Ever Were," *The Global Post*, November 9, 2018. https://theglobepost.com/2018/11/09/right-wing-radicals-immigrants/ . Accessed May 26, 2022.

54 Kelly Oliver, *Carceral Humanitarianism: Logics of Refugee Detention* (University of Minnesota Press, 2017), 37.

55 Haynes, "Sacrificing Women and Immigrants on the Alter of Regressive Politics," 777–822.

56 Elizabeth Cullen Dunn, "Humanitarianism, Trump Style," *Public Anthropologist. Journal Blog*, 14 Jan. 2019, https://publicanthropologist.cmi.no/2019/01/14/humanitarianism-trump-style/. Accessed January 5, 2021.

57 Hua, *Trafficking Women's Human Rights*, p. 97.

58 O'Connell Davidson, "New Slavery, Old Binaries", pp. 244–261.

59 Lyndsey P. Beutin, "Black Suffering for/from Anti-trafficking Advocacy," *Anti-trafficking Review* 9 (2017): 14–30, p. 15.
60 Beutin, "Black Suffering for/from Anti-trafficking Advocacy," p. 21.
61 Beutin, "Black Suffering for/from Anti-trafficking Advocacy," pp. 14–30, 21.
62 Hua, *Trafficking Women's Human Rights*, p. 101.
63 Kevin Bales, *Disposable People: New Slavery in the Global Economy* (University of California Press, 2012), 11.
64 Anna Mae Duane, *Suffering Childhood in Early America* (University of Georgia Press, 2010), 15.
65 Margaret Abruzzo, *Polemical Pain: Slavery, Cruelty, and the Rise of Humanitarianism* (Johns Hopkins University Press, 2011), 236.
66 Tryon Woods, "Surrogate Selves: Notes on Anti-trafficking and Anti-blackness," *Social Identities* 19, no. 1 (2013): 120–134, p. 130.
67 Woods, "Surrogate Selves," p. 120.
68 Krista Maxwell, "Settler-Humanitarianism: Healing the Indigenous Child-Victim," *Comparative Studies in Society and History* 59, no. 4 (2017): 974–1007.
69 Neda Atanasoski, *Humanitarian Violence: The U.S. Deployment of Diversity* (University of Minnesota Press, 2013), 4.
70 Sharma, "Anti-Trafficking Rhetoric and the Making of a Global Apartheid," pp. 88–111.

PART II

Forms and Figures

CHAPTER 3

Speculative African Slaveries
Matthew Omelsky

African speculative fiction is indisputably here, and always was. If, from Thomas Mofolo to Ngugi wa Thiong'o to Ben Okri, African fiction has long borne traces of the mystical and the fantastic, we've come to a moment in the last fifteen years when the speculative demands its own space in African literature. Writers from across the continent have won some of the world's most prestigious literary prizes working in this fluid field that encompasses any genre – such as science fiction, fantasy, and horror – that somehow contorts our understanding of the world as we know it. Among the genre's dominant themes of (post)apocalypse, war, climate change, and artificial intelligence, is slavery. Not just any kind of bondage, certainly, but slavery radically reimagined, sutured into water worlds, ghost stories, invented mythologies, and alien encounters. The twenty-first-century texts I want to focus on in this chapter posit alternative futures and revised histories. They're all undergirded, in their own distinct ways, by the dialectic of subjection and desired freedom that animates the iconic eighteenth- and nineteenth-century slave narratives of Olaudah Equiano, Ottobah Cugoano, Harriet Jacobs, and others. Except these African visions of slavery are shot through an – often literal – otherworldly lens.

Like all African speculative fiction (sf), these speculative slaveries are in some way, as Nnedi Okorafor might put it, "organic" to the continent, "bloom[ing] directly the soil of the real."[1] Indeed this is how many of its creators envision African sf more broadly, even if the terms are contested. Some, like Sofia Samatar and Wanuri Kahiu, maintain that African specificity can be cultivated within the larger rubric of Afrofuturism, a term coined in 1994 by critic Mark Dery to describe a black American aesthetic that broadly incorporates "images of technology and a prosthetically enhanced future."[2]

Kahiu, for one, sees Afrofuturism in the creation myths of the Dogon peoples of Mali and the Kikuyu of Kenya, and in the way the spirit realm

49

permeates African fiction.[3] Okorafor and Mohale Mashigo, on the other hand, need new names, something that distinguishes African radical (re) imaginings from those shaped in the diaspora by the descendants of those stolen from the continent. For Mashigo, the insistent placeholder, "_____," holds out for the precision that might discern the specificity of "Africa's future 'post-colonialism'" and the continent's diverse modes of "reimagining a fantasy present."[4] Okorafor likewise sees the historical, political, and aesthetic convergences of African and diasporic experiences, but insists on the particularity of what she calls "Africanfuturism" and "Africanjujism" – the former being a subgenre of science fiction that's "directly rooted in African culture, history, mythology and point of view," while the latter, much like Kahiu's point of focus, "acknowledges the seamless blend of true existing African spiritualities and cosmologies with the imaginative."[5] My point here, however, is less about the terms themselves than the common ground among these voices. For these artists, sf is shaped by the continent's diverse histories, cultures, and cosmologies, and this is certainly the case in the field's disparate representations of slavery. To read these forms of subjection is to witness how, from African soils, power, freedom, and the world might be imagined otherwise.

Because these speculative slaveries span a range of representations, from shapeshifting cyborgs to zombie robots, teleportation to time travel, and because not all of the works discussed here explicitly name "slaves" or "slavery," some provisional terms are necessary. Speaking specifically to the continent, though broadly enough to encompass African sf's disparate expressions, Achille Mbembe asks the fundamental question, "who is a slave, if not the person who, everywhere and always, possesses life, property, and body as if they were alien things?" "Slave is the forename," he maintains, of the "man or woman whose body can be degraded, whose life can be mutilated, and whose work and resources can be squandered – with impunity." The slave, in other words, is relegated to the world of things, of objects to be manipulated, controlled, and devastated for another's gain. Another name that organizes these characteristics, Mbembe contends, is the native, historically constituted through colonialism's "grammar of animality," excluded from the "field of the human," belonging instead to the "family of eminently mechanical, almost physical things."[6] All the works I discuss here of "unrestrained imagination," as Mashigo describes African sf, contain some aspect of the dispossession, alienation, and/or proximity to violence of which Mbembe speaks.[7] The figures in these works, in one way or another, have been stripped of their being and reduced to the brute force of creatures and things.

To be sure, writing that speaks to the trans-Atlantic slave trade is prominent among African sf representations of slavery. Works like Biram Mboob's space odyssey "Luminal Frontier" (2018) and Nuzo Onoh's ghost story "Our Bones Shall Rise Again" (2015), for instance, reimagine histories of slaves being thrown, or willfully fleeing, overboard into the Atlantic. Along with Efe Okogu's "An Indigo Song for Paradise" (2016), Ekari Mbvundula's "Montague's Last" (2015), and other stories, citations of Atlantic slavery have an important place in contemporary African sf, and ought to be read alongside the wealth of diasporic speculative fictions by writers like Octavia Butler, Rivers Solomon, and Nalo Hopkinson that do related work. In this chapter, though, I want to attend to the more sizable body of African sf that imagines slaveries removed from the middle passage and chattel slavery in the Americas, including works with no clear historical analogue. If, for novelist Walter Mosley, science fiction plays a critical imaginative role for black Americans who have been "cut off from their African ancestry by the scythe of slavery," then what (re)imaginative function, we might ask, do African sf slaveries with no trace of that "scythe" enact?[8] What does it mean to imagine slaveries not ostensibly burdened by the "natal alienation" of being severed from kin and transformed into a fungible object in the "New World"?[9] Or, for that matter, slaveries unconnected to, or only obliquely allegorical of, other historical trades, such as the Indian Ocean trade that preceded the trade across the Atlantic? In what follows, I want to excavate the continent's radical (re) imaginings of subjection and desired freedom by isolating two especially prominent genres of slavery in contemporary African speculative fiction removed from the Atlantic.

3.1 Cosmologies of Subjection

In the first of these categories, slavery is structured around an invented metaphysics, a singular way of understanding time, space, society, and ontology. These often overtly religious systems of belief function much like Stuart Hall's description of the operations of ideology: "The mental framework – the languages, the concepts, the categories, imagery of thought, and the systems of representation – which different classes and social groups deploy in order to make sense of, define, figure out and render intelligible the way society works."[10] The metaphysics – or cosmologies, we might call them – in these speculative works similarly organize the social and epistemological order, functioning as a mechanism to maintain the collective understanding that one group is meant to be

slaves, and another masters. Sacred texts provide the strictures, representations, and narratives that undergird the given order; clerics are the
enforcers, prophesying, divining, and judging to keep all in their place.
In most cases, these cosmologies regulate subjection. But in some of these
novels and stories we find the rise of new, insurgent "mental frameworks,"
counter-cosmologies and retooled cosmologies that open up the pathways
of revolution. In all of these systems of thought, though, what's sure is that
they bear the surreal, magical, reconfigurative hallmarks of the speculative.

Nnedi Okorafor's 2010 World Fantasy Award winning *Who Fears
Death* is the most prominent among these. A coming-of-age story set in
a sprawling postapocalyptic desert, the novel traces the young life of
Onyesonwu as she seeks to avenge her sorcerer father for raping her
Okeke mother, and in turn, break apart the caste structure that justifies
the extermination of the fictional Okeke ethnic group by the Nuru people.
Though very much removed from our twenty-first-century world, the idea
for the novel's larger structure of subjection emerged, Okorafor says, from
the actual slaughter of African farming communities by government-
backed militias in the Darfur region of Sudan in the 2000s, where the
Janjaweed used epithets like "black slave" as they systematically raped
women and destroyed villages.[11] *Who Fears Death* supercharges this historical ethnic violence with magic and reconfigured cosmologies. The
Great Book, an authoritative and revered religious text, reinforces dominance and submission, reasoning that Ani, the Igbo goddess of the earth,
has enslaved the Okeke as punishment for disrupting the earth's climatic
and biological systems: "The Nuru to this day point at the Okeke and say,
slave and the Okeke must bow their heads in agreement."[12] But the
narrative is driven by a prophecy that says that the Great Book will be
rewritten, and change will come. Another metaphysical system, the Okeke
Great Mystic Points, which Onye learns to harness, makes possible that
force of change. Throughout, she uses these Points to escape danger and
change the world around her, shapeshifting into a vulture that soars
through the sky, slipping in and out of the otherworldly "wilderness"
"where there is no time or flesh" (232). She even manipulates the wind
during an attempted rape: "I gathered the wind, gray and black in my
hands, and pressed it together, elongating it into a funnel," pressing the
men to the ground (205). For critic Lisa Dowdall, the novel's Mystic
Points are not just a revolutionary toolkit, but as "a way of understanding
the world," a "meditation on otherness, a disavowal of totalizing ideologies
that foreclose the future."[13] Ultimately, the larger arc of the novel can be
read through these contending systems of belief: the one serving to

"degrade" the body, to "mutilate" life "with impunity," as Mbembe might put it; the other signaling a new, freer world.

Other instances of this confluence of slavery and cosmology appear in short fiction by Dilman Dila and Sofia Samatar, two of the leading voices in the field. Published in his 2014 collection *A Killing in the Sun*, Dila's "The Healer" has a lot in common with *Who Fears Death*: one fictional ethnic group, the Cuku, has for centuries enslaved another, the Twa, transforming them into zombie robot forced laborers, using Oksism, its sacred text, and its priests to reinforce this otherworldly subjection. The story is also set in a world deep into the Anthropocene: "Forests were vanishing, animals were becoming extinct, the climate was changing at an alarming rate, all because Oksism made people believe this world was not their home," that their paradise lay "beyond the stars."[14] The Twa, not just the Cuku, have become followers of this religion invented thousands of years ago by a king "wary of the power of magicians." The narrative revolves around Benge, a juju-practicing healer, and his quest to "decolonize the minds" of the enslaved Twa – Dila extending Ngugi wa Thiong'o's iconic expression to futurist, anticolonial struggles not dissimilar to those of the twentieth century.[15] Benge does this by convincing the Twa and "liberal" Cukus that his myriad powers, including teleportation and instantaneous healing, make him and other healers "the true servants of Oks." So he "plays on their beliefs" when he's been sentenced to death by fire and makes the flames vanish, reasoning to the gathered crowd: "I should be roasted alive by now, but Oks protected me. He asks me to deliver to you a simple message. You've been deceived for too long. The book has been misinterpreted" (28). Here religion is stripped down to unveiled ideology. Instead of contending with another system of thought, Benge sutures his own into that dominant system, doubly retooling that mental framework as both an insurgent, emancipatory politics and a radical recuperation of a devastated earth.

Samatar's "An Account of the Land of Witches," included in her 2017 collection *Tender*, is remarkably different from these other works. Instead of legitimizing slavery, the story's metaphysics clears an otherworldly escape route. Told in five parts, the story revolves around the first, an enslaved person's first-person account of the Land of Witches – a mystical place where time is "shaped" and "eroded," where "onerous tasks pass swiftly, while a pleasure may last for weeks or, indeed, forever."[16] The story's other parts directly address this narrative, including a "refutation" of the slave's account by her former master, who, we're told, "purchased this Arta for no small sum in the country of the blacks," and a twenty-first-century researcher's attempt to decipher both the account and the refutation (152). In her account, the un(self)named slave describes traveling to the Land of Witches, where she learned to harness Dream Science: a literally transporting meditative practice that "obliterates distance as well as time," where the thought of a single word will deliver the mind, and perhaps the body, to a nebulous elsewhere (149). To dream of pomegranates, for instance, is to inhabit, or be consumed by, "black bile," "a cloister," "the rattling of dry leaves," and, inexplicably, to find oneself in the Place of Mourning. By the end of her account, after the enslaved person has described using Dream Science "to reduce the time beneath my master to almost nothing," we're left to assume she uses this cognitive vanishing to escape from bondage. The modern-day researcher's diary entry eventually brings a layer of disorienting realism, suggesting that the enslaved woman was likely Somali, and that her account, written on papyrus, was found in a ninth-century BCE grave in twenty-first-century Sudan. But this scholar seems just as baffled as us: *"Is it simply an unusual autobiographical record? Or is it (as Kircher surmised – "autobiography being unknown in the Kingdom of Kush") some sort of occult text, written in a coded language known only to the priesthood?"* (156, original emphasis). Dream Science, it seems, refuses empiricism. Its mysticism evades rational thought, and indeed, narration, just like Arta evades the grasp of her master, fugitively vanishing, we presume, to some kind of freedom where she might once again feel human.

In all three of these texts, I want to suggest, religion is inseparable from ideology, cosmology can't be severed from power. Systems of belief establish and maintain submission, but in each they also open up new worlds, leading the enslaved – potentially, proleptically even – toward the field of the human. Or perhaps toward another order of being altogether, one that transcends what Sylvia Wynter calls the colonial "ethnoclass mode of being human, Man," and its overrepresentation as that of "the human species as a whole."[17] Perhaps these works signal the excessive, unmappable ontology that Fanon alludes to at the end of *Black Skin, White Masks* (1952), where he insists, "I am a part of Being to the extent that I go beyond it."[18] That "beyond," for him, is not a concrete space, threshold, or structure of being. It marks an openness to contingency, to possibility, to the prospect of another form of life, another genre of being-in-the-world. An ontology that hasn't merely been decolonized, but instead, has been remade and recreated in excess of colonialism's field of legibility. This is the work the speculative does for these writers. Arta's vanishing signals an open set, a lunging beyond the known toward a remade self. Benge and Onyesonwu perhaps also evince a kindred desire for that fugitively elusive state of being, leaning toward the horizon of an unknown freedom that's been evacuated of this world.

Significantly, in all of these works, slavery is named. Subjection is given a recognizable label, one that we, as readers, can connect to the constellation of associations we have with the terms "slave" and "slavery." Samatar and Okorafor's uses of these terms, combined with their geographical settings, evoke specific histories of enslavement, whether of the Janjaweed's discursive use of the term, some ancient iteration of the trans-Saharan slave trade, or more precisely in the Kingdom of Kush in ancient Nubia. Even Dila's explicit use of the term – despite the story's indeterminate spatial and temporal setting – evokes an array of religiously sanctioned historical slaveries. In this next category, though, slavery isn't given that name. Instead we have to assemble the pieces of subjection, sift through hyper-technological worlds to gather the contours and the attributes that might correspond to that name.

3.2   Cyberpunked Slavery

These unnamed slaveries appear in distinctly African versions of cyberpunk, the dystopian subgenre of science fiction that came to prominence in the 1980s with writers like William Gibson and Bruce Sterling, featuring some combination of gritty city streets, a repressive corporatized state, sprawling virtual infrastructures, and insurgents revolting against the existing order. Perhaps most characteristic, though, is technology that's "inside, not outside, the personal body and mind itself," which is where the question of enslavement arises, even if it's rarely named as such in the texts themselves.[19] The presence, I argue, of African bodies, African geographies, and African histories in cyberpunk from the continent demands that we examine the bodily infiltrations and radical social exclusions in these works as a form of slavery. A futurist genre of slavery that very much evokes, in certain instances even literalizes, Mbembe's flexible notion of the native qua slave as "eminently mechanical," as one who "possesses life, property, and body as if they were alien things." Nnedi Okorafor's 2015 *The Book of Phoenix* – the biotech-saturated prequel to *Who Fears Death* – is a prominent example of slavery in African cyberpunk, featuring an "accelerated biological organism" bred to be a flying nuclear weapon who leads a revolution to destroy LifeGen Technologies and liberate the world's genetically engineered "speciMen."[20] To expand this

discussion on speculative slaveries, though, what follows focuses on influential works beyond the world of the Great Book.

The first of these is *Moxyland*, the 2008 debut novel by Arthur
C. Clarke award winner Lauren Beukes. Saturated with virtual landscapes,
a hyper-corporatized state, and futurist vestiges of South Africa's apartheid
system, the Cape Town-set novel provides at least two kinds of
technology-infused slavery. Lured by superhuman immunity and beautiful
skin, one character consents to have the Ghost Corporation inject her with
a "nano-enhanced hormone" that makes her increasingly addicted to
Ghost Drink and gives her a luminous tattoo of the company's logo,
effectively transforming her into a living advertisement. When she
demands her freedom from a company that has transformed her body
into something alien to her, she's euthanized by Ghost – the technology is
permanent, and she's deemed to be no longer of use. The other form of
slavery, though perhaps less evident, comes through the state's manipula-
tion of mobile phones: the state builds "social controls and access passes
and electroshock pacifiers into the very technology we need to function
day to day," another character observes, "so you've got no choice but to
accept the defuser in your phone or being barred from certain parts of the
city because you don't have clearance."[21] A clear intensification of
apartheid-era surveillance infrastructures, the cell phone is attended by
the constant anxiety of becoming a "disconnect": denied access to official
cellular networks that facilitate the navigation of everyday life, thus
becoming "relegated to homeless, out of society," leading, as Sheryl
Stobie aptly puts it, to the "obliteration of the individual."[22] If, following
Orlando Patterson, Frank Wilderson suggests that forced labor in itself is
not constitutive of slavery, then *Moxyland*'s state of "disconnection" may
very well be a kind of slavery, an ontological position in which "the slave is
not a laborer but an anti-Human, a position against which Humanity
establishes, maintains, and renews its coherence."[23] In Beukes's novel, the
disconnects are the refuse that confirm the privilege, even the personhood,
of the connected. And just as, for Patterson, the slave's "social death" only
forecloses the "recognition of legitimacy" of slave sociality – not their
actual "informal social relations" – the discarded in *Moxyland*, led by the
insurgent and voluntary-disconnect, Tandeka, collaborate covertly to disrupt the world, organizing protests and bombings, hacking government
systems, and exposing the state's weaponized use of the Marburg virus.[24]

Another of these cyberpunk works is Tade Thompson's epic Nommo
and Arthur C. Clarke Award winning *Wormwood* trilogy (2016–2019). Set
largely in the 2050s and 2060s, the three novels chart the emergence of

Wormwood, a massive bubble-like living organism that sprang from the soil in rural Nigeria, serving as the home base for an alien takeover of the planet. The trilogy is global in scope – the dome first emerged in 2012 in London, and the United States has "gone dark," completely insulating itself from the rest of the world – but it's meticulously stitched into Nigerian culture and history, including the country's history of British colonialism: "When Wormwood surges into awareness, we are unimpressed, even in our knowledge that it is the most significant event in Earth's history. We've seen colonisers before, and they are similar, whether intercontinental or interplanetary."[25] At its core, the trilogy presents a *Moxyland*-like cyberpunk conceit – cyborg drones, communication systems implanted in the body, ubiquitous state surveillance, post-internet virtual spaces – overlaid by a radically imaginative biopunk conceit. The latter centers on xenoforms, "strands of alien fungi-like filaments and neurotransmitters" invisible to the naked eye, which, distributed everywhere on earth over thousands of years, "have an affinity for nerve endings and quickly access the central nervous system."[26] These filaments can heal the human body, "reanimate" the recently deceased, and, significantly, enable select human "sensitives," like Kaaro, to access the "psycho-field" called the "xenosphere," where he can see (and interact with) all human and alien thought – past, present, future, and "alternative versions" – as an overwhelmingly sprawling and volatile virtual landscape.

Slavery in the trilogy centers on these xenoforms. In search of a new planet, the alien endgame is to transfer the data existences of billions of Homians, as they're called, into the bodies and minds of all individual humans through a slow cellular takeover, gradually increasing the xenoforms in each body until mankind has become fully alien. In a way it's a speculative reconfiguration of Rob Nixon's influential notion of "slow violence," as Hugh O'Connell perceptively notes, a kind of scifi hyperintensification of the attritional ecological violence distributed across time and space characteristic of the Anthropocene.[27] At the end of the trilogy's first installment, *Rosewater*, we learn that a homeless Londoner was the first human to be taken over entirely by Wormwood, and alien-controlled duplicates of this man have been distributed throughout the world to mine for information on human biology, behavior, and environments. In a way, all of this is reminiscent of Kendra's subjection to Ghost in *Moxyland*: people initially only see the healing benefits of Wormwood, but this healing is really the xenoforms progressively taking over bodies and forcing them to work and gather data, all without a known reversal mechanism, until colonization is complete and slavery gives way to, essentially, genocide. But by the third novel, *Redemption*, it seems that a clean takeover may not be possible, that this enslavement to aliens could be ceaseless. It's discovered that the reanimated dead, taken over by alien life, may retain traces of their original human consciousness – suggesting a kind of endless dystopian bondage where one can't help but be at least partially aware of being used, controlled, and manipulated like a puppet. This indeed brings entirely new meaning to Mbembe's formulation that the slave "possesses life, property, and body as if they were alien things." But this is cyberpunk, a subgenre that typically involves some kind of counter insurgency, a gesture to another world. *Wormwood* is no exception, ending with Kaaro hacking into the mind of a soon-to-be-alien-occupied reanimate with a virus that seeps into the Homian interstellar servers, deleting the billions of alien data-beings waiting to be uploaded into human bodies.

In Thompson's novels, as in *Moxyland*, slavery emerges from technology's proximity to the body, that infiltration and "alienness" inhabited by the flesh. There may be related forms of enslavement in Gibson's *Neuromancer* (1984), Ridley Scott's *Blade Runner* (1982), and other works, but there's something distinct, politically trenchant even, in the Africanness of these cyber worlds. The way cultures, modes of thought, and histories of subjection and liberation from across the continent saturate them. Like so much African sf, these are mutant formations, mutant slaveries. Of the continent but also of the world. Just as influenced by Achebe, Okri, and Laing as by William Gibson, Octavia Butler, and Paolo Bacigalupi.

3.3   Critical Speculation

That political entrenchment of the speculative, what Hortense Spillers might call its "critical edge," is fundamental.[28] Speculative fiction's function is not to predict the future or provide a mindless escape, but to "defamiliarize and restructure our experience of our present," to enact a certain "perceptual renewal" so that, when we step away from the text, we might see something new in what we've always known, or awaken to the unthought, the unanticipated.[29] The traces of recognizable histories, cultures, environments, and forms of life in speculative fiction are the threads that tether our world to the seemingly distant and otherworldly, the fragments that trigger that renewed perception, that insist the devastated earths, the racisms, the misogynies, and the coercive ideologies generated by the speculative might not be that far removed from our own. These threads transform speculative fiction into radical politics, into a laboratory for conjuring new worlds, new ethics, new ways of breathing and being.

This certainly holds for the freedom dreams and the structures of subjection in African sf. It's a stunning moment in Dilman Dila's 2014 short story "A Wife and a Slave" when we realize that an unnamed autocratic African state has enslaved former white colonialists as a form of postcolonial retribution, sequestering them in camps.[30] It turns both history and future upside down, it entangles the familiar and the unfamiliar, it challenges how we conceive of the past, present, and future of power on the continent. Dila's story, and works like *Who Fears Death* and the *Wormwood* trilogy, may be cautionary, heedful of possible futures, but they're also excavations of the imagination, insistent questionings of what it means to be human, what it means to construct and perpetuate difference, what it means to wield and experience power, what it means to bring new worlds into existence. And a story as baffling as Samatar's "Land of Witches" isn't just a curious escape for the reader, but a burst of queries into the limits of human experience and historical knowledge, asking whether some chapters of history will always be unrecoverable, and what precisely constitutes the relationship between thought and freedom.

The slaveries of African speculative fiction demand that we check our assumptions of what we know the diversity of life on the continent to be. This is at least one of the (re)imaginative functions of African sf that hasn't been "scythed," as Walter Mosley puts it, by the middle passage. For Mosley, that scythe generates alienation, a remove from an originary sense of belonging. Perhaps these African speculative slaveries bear the invisible marks of that severing, occupying the traces of those lost to the hold like a phantom limb. But is it the same alienation? These representations may be allied with that diasporic alienation, but the sense of inhabiting a body that can be animalized and degraded with impunity that we find in these un-Atlantic-ed speculative fictions reflects a fundamentally different structure of loss, one that emerges from continental histories, cosmologies, and anxieties. Slavery, in the latter reconfiguration, is in the traces of (African) consciousness that remain in alien controlled human bodies in Thompson's *Redemption*, a speculative phenomenon strongly suggestive of twentieth-century colonialism; freedom, potentially, is in the virus that Kaaro puts into the interstellar servers that forestalls the full erasure of indigenous life on the continent. No matter how debilitating the anxiety, these African speculative fictions still inhabit a historicity, an ancestrality, a cosmological intimacy uncut by the scythe. One that generates not just its own reimaginings of subjection, but its own constellation of freedom dreams. Its own visions of transformation and possibility. Its own ways of being, and becoming, (more than) human.

Notes

1 Nnedi Okorafor, "Organic Fantasy," *African Identities* 7, no. 2 (2009): 278.
2 Mark Dery, "Black to the Future: Interviews with Samuel R. Delany, Greg Tate, and Tricia Rose," *Flame Wars: The Discourse of Cyberculture*, ed. Mark Dery (Durham: Duke University Press, 1994), 180.
3 "Afrofuturism in popular culture: Wanuri Kahiu at TEDxNairobi." www .youtube.com/watch?v=PvxOLVaV2YY. See also Sofia Samatar, "Toward a Planetary History of Afrofuturism," *Research in African Literatures* 48, no. 4 (2017): 175–191.
4 Mohale Mashigo, *Intruders* (Johannesburg: Picador Africa, 2018), x–xi.
5 Nnedi Okorafor, "Africanfuturism Defined." http://nnedi.blogspot.com/ 2019/10/africanfuturism-defined.html. For another take on this desire to devise news terms beyond Afrofuturism, see Pamela Phatsimo Sunstrum, "Afro-mythology and African Futurism: The Politics of Imagining and Methodologies for Contemporary Creative Research Practices," *Paradoxa* 25 (2013): 113–129.
6 Achille Mbembe, *On the Postcolony* (Berkeley: University of California Press, 2001), 235–236.
7 Mashigo, *Intruders*, xv.
8 Walter Mosley, "Black to the Future," *New York Times Magazine*, November 1, 1998, 32.
9 Orlando Patterson, *Slavery and Social Death* (Cambridge, MA: Harvard University Press, 1982), 5.
10 Stuart Hall, "*The Problem of Ideology: Marxism and Cultural Studies*," eds. David Morley and Kuan-Hsing Chen (London: Routledge, 1996), 25, 26.
11 In the acknowledgements to *Who Fears Death* Okorafor cites Emily Wax's 2004 Associated Press article "We want to make a light baby" about "weaponized rape in the Sudan" as inspiration for the novel.
12 Nnedi Okorafor, *Who Fears Death* (New York: DAW Books, 2010), 92–93. Original emphasis. Further citations in parentheses. It's worth noting that Okorafor creates fictional African ethnic identities and cosmologies in her novel (the Okeke, the Nuru, and sacred text of the Great Book, for instance), but also draws on actually existing African ethnicities and cosmologies (the most notable being the figure of Ani, the Igbo goddess of the earth).
13 Lisa Dowdall, "The Utopian Fantastic in Nnedi Okorafor's Who Fears Death," *Paradoxa* 25 (2013): 10.

14 Dilman Dila, "The Healer," *A Killing in the Sun* (Johannesburg: Black Letter Media, 2014), 35. Further citations in parentheses.
15 See Ngugi wa Thiong'o, *Decolonising the Mind: The Politics of Language in African Literature* (Oxford: James Curry, 2005): 16, 87.
16 Sofia Samatar, "An Account of the Land of Witches," *Tender* (Easthampton, MA: Small Beer Press, 2017), 147. Further citations in parentheses.
17 Sylvia Wynter. "Unsettling the Coloniality of Being/Power/Truth/Freedom: Towards the Human, After Man, Its Overrepresentation – An Argument." *CR: The New Centennial Review* 3, no. 3 (2003): 313.
18 In the French, this passage reads, "Je suis solidaire de l'Etre dans la mesure où je le dépasse." Frantz Fanon, *Peau noire, masques blancs* (Paris: Éditions du Seuil, 1952), 186.
19 Darko Suvin, *"On Gibson and Cyberpunk SF," Storming the Reality Studio: A Casebook of Cyberpunk & Postmodern Science Fiction*, ed. Larry McCaffery (Durham: Duke University Press, 1992), 325.
20 Nnedi Okorafor, *The Book of Phoenix* (New York: DAW Books, 2015).
21 Lauren Beukes, *Moxyland* (Nottingham: Angry Robot, 2008), 155.
22 Beukes, *Moxyland*, 113; Cheryl Stobie, "Dystopian Dreams from South Africa: Lauren Beukes's *Moxyland* and *Zoo City*," *African Identities* 10, no. 4 (2012): 372.
23 Frank Wilderson, *Red, White & Black: Cinema and the Structure of U.S. Antagonisms* (Durham: Duke University Press, 2010), 10–11.
24 Patterson, *Slavery and Social Death*, 6.
25 Tade Thompson, *Rosewater* (New York: Orbit, 2016), 225.
26 Thompson, *Rosewater*, p. 76.
27 Hugh O'Connell, "'Everything is changed by virtue of being lost': African Futurism between Globalization and the Anthropocene in Tade Thompson's *Rosewater*," *Extrapolation* 61, no. 1–2 (2020): 122.
28 Hortense Spillers, "The Idea of Black Culture," *CR: The New Centennial Review* 6, no. 3 (2006): 26.
29 Fredric Jameson, *Archaeologies of the Future: The Desire Call Utopia and Other Science Fictions* (New York: Verso, 2007), 286–287.
30 Dilman Dila, *"A Wife and a Slave," A Killing in the Sun* (Johannesburg: Black Letter Media, 2014).

CHAPTER 4

Contemporary and Historical Slavery in West African Digital Literature

Kwabena Opoku-Agyemang

This chapter examines how the general topic of slavery is treated in African literary digital short stories. While one story explores exploitative conditions of children in contemporary times in urban Ghana, the other narrative is crafted as historical fiction and through parody, imagines child trafficking in a pre-independent Nigerian setting. Having child labour and child trafficking as major themes in both stories links directly with slavery, as explained by organizations such as the United Nations' Children's Fund (UNICEF), International Labour Organization (ILO), and the Anti-Slavery Society. UNICEF for instance traces the causes of child labour to financial challenges that plague families, and links child labour to "staggering" consequences that include exploitation and slavery.[1] The ILO's Worst Forms of Child Labour Convention defines child labour as involving the enslavement of anyone under eighteen, and posits that work that is considered to be harmful to the health, safety or morals of a child is considered to be child labour.[2] The Anti-Slavery Society, which is the oldest international human rights organisation in the world, is more explicit in referring to child labour and child trafficking as examples of contemporary slavery.[3]

Scholarship equally examines such exploitation of children in West Africa, finding it to be pervasive,[4] and tying this problem to the fact that in West Africa, labour laws that protect children are not always implemented effectively.[5] Admassie contends that child labourers are "deprived of their freedom" and work in conditions "characterized by low wages, long hours of work under dangerous and unhealthy work conditions, and a lack of physical and social security, all of which might lead to poor physical and mental development."[6] All of these characteristics connect to slavery and slave-like conditions.

For the purposes of this chapter, slavery, as defined by child labour and child trafficking, is structured around exploitation and forced movement, with gestures to underpaid labour, marginalization, and servitude. These features are contextualized by racial inequality and socio-economic imbalances – found on a global scale – that directly influence socio-economic situations in countries like Ghana and Nigeria, where vulnerable groups such as young people suffer inordinately from a mixture of domestic failures and harsh international policies. These countries are also haunted by the transatlantic slave trade, as they acknowledge the atrocity in different ways.

Having been an integral site for the centuries-long transatlantic slave trade, it is inevitable that the West African coastline would reflect effects of the atrocity long after slavery's abolition. These after-effects are visible along the coast of West Africa, along which were dotted several points of departure for those kidnapped in the hinterland. In the region that was known as the Gold Coast and is now the nation Ghana, the Elmina and Cape Coast Castles (built in 1482 and 1653 respectively) were prisons for hundreds of thousands of captured Africans who were tortured before being sent through the Middle Passage to North America, South America, and the Caribbean. The Bight of Biafra in part of what is now the country of Nigeria on the other hand was a site from which more than a tenth of all enslaved Africans were taken away along similar routes to the same destinations.[7]

Centuries after the abolition of the slave trade, aspects of West African culture still bear testament to this legacy of slavery. Obadele Kambon reminds us that the term "legacy" tends to carry a positive connotation (41–43), meaning we have to be mindful of the fact that legacy in this sense is largely negative.[8] Traditionally, names of people and towns, architecture of buildings, greetings, proverbs, and creative work signal the atrocity. While there has been attendant attention paid to these reminders through research, the proliferation of digital media means that two decades into the new millennium, this specific form of slavery is acknowledged in digital spaces such as social media platforms. Despite increasing references to and acknowledgement of slavery via new media, scholarship is yet to catch up with these endeavours.

One such example of contemporary engagement with the slave trade through digital media is a meme that came in the form of a relatively absurd comment that circulated among Ghanaian and Nigerian Facebook users in 2019. The comment stated: "How I found myself in this country isn't my problem, my problem is where was my grandfather when they kidnapped his mates to America." Users who posted this comment were comfortable with the thought of their grandfather being part of the captured group of Africans who were forced to undertake the dangerous journey across the Atlantic Ocean. Obviously, the Facebook post is an exaggeration and could be understood as attempting comedy; nevertheless, it is instructive to note that the possibility of having preceding generations captured and tortured at a slave camp and then in a castle, fort, or camp along the coast before enduring the middle passage, chattel slavery, Jim Crow, and the brutalities of the Civil Rights era among other forms of racial discrimination, was deemed a better option than living in Ghana or Nigeria. The comment was used in different contexts, including a direct response expressing dismay at electoral violence in Ghana, or as a humorous post by a Nigerian Facebook page.

Comments like these support findings by researchers that many Ghanaians and Nigerians desire to leave their country for Western nations, with America typically being the most sought-after destination.[9] Social media platforms like Facebook have become a major means for communication across the sub-region, and in this case, they provide the opportunity to contrast disaffection with their countries with preference for foreign places, as they talk in light-hearted terms about the willingness to suffer slavery in one of its starkest forms. These instances are but a few that underline the fact that slavery continues to occupy the attention of public discourse, even as conversations transition to online spaces.

Apart from social media, other digital platforms reference more modern iterations of slavery in different ways; after all, the transatlantic slave trade is not the only form of slavery that is known to Ghana and Nigeria. There are other forms of subjugation and exploitation that are pervasive in West Africa and are accounted for in digital creative writing. In contemporary times, writers capture these issues by addressing themes related to forced labour, human trafficking, sex trafficking, and servitude; writers also use their creative license to imagine situations that either interrogate the historic slave trade or show how it has essentially been replaced by newer forms of slavery.

Generations after the end of chattel slavery and the transatlantic trade, West African writers continue to harbour sneaking suspicions that white kidnappers are ready to capture unsuspecting Africans and send them across the Atlantic Ocean. These tropes appear in digital media, such as popular short stories that are avidly consumed by West African youth, perpetuating fears of – but also resistance to – new forms of trafficking and labour exploitation that are endemic to the region. In these stories, the writers also respond to these newer forms of slavery, as they construct marginalization and servitude in order to eventually highlight the strategies that the marginalized adopt to deal with problems they face. Ultimately, the authors relate these constructions and concerns to larger structures of radical inequality and forced labour. As such, whether the protagonist is a street-child hawking goods at a busy intersection in contemporary Accra, the capital city of Ghana, amidst the perils of traffic; or an American explorer keen on kidnapping a gifted young boy who is key to the functioning of a small village in pre-independent Nigeria, these stories are parsed through an interplay of isolation and conflict on the one hand, and parody on the other hand, to explore different forms of slavery.

The question that drives this chapter is: in what ways is the legacy of slavery treated on digital platforms by West African writers? I consider this question through an analysis of characters and themes in the short stories "A Rainy Morning in Accra" by Hakeem Adam and Victor Ehikhamenor's "The Iguana Boy with Three Testicles." While the first story was published on *Flash Fiction Ghana*, the latter appeared on *Jalada*. Both websites are high profile outlets for the output of mainly young and amateur African writers who take advantage of digital technology to share their work with wide audiences. *Flash Fiction* Ghana was started in 2012 by Daniel Dzah, a young Ghanaian amateur writer, and curates stories from Ghanaian writers. *Jalada* on the other hand is a Pan-African collective founded in 2014 by young African creative writers from South Africa, Zimbabwe, Uganda, Nigeria, and Kenya, which publishes submissions from Africans both on and off the continent. These contemporary digital media sites frequently publish pieces that reflect on the history, legacy, and contemporary reality of slavery in the West African context.

4.1 West Africa: A Legacy of Slavery

Locations such as the slave bath site at Assin Manso in the south, the Pikworo slave camp in the north, and slave castles and forts dotted along the coast remain prominent reminders of how slavery marked and continues to shape Ghana's relationship with the atrocity of the transatlantic slave trade. The names of towns such as Kormantse (translated from Fante to "You left without telling me") and the architecture of villages like Gwollu are subtle gestures to how indigenes responded to slave raiders. In Nigeria, Yorubaland was one of the most active slave-exporting regions (Ojo, 77), while the Badagry Slave Route and the Bight of Biafra were major sites for events linked to slavery.[10] Modern museums exist in Badagry and Calabar to preserve the memory of the atrocity. Further, Afro-Brazilian descendants of enslaved Africans, who returned from South America in the nineteenth century to settle in Jamestown in Accra and eastern parts of Lagos, serve as reminders of the atrocity. In contemporary times, both countries grapple with child labour and human trafficking.[11]

Beyond physical locations and people, slavery is examined in creative work. Kwakuvi Azasu's novel *The Slave Raiders*, Kwadwo Opoku-Agyemang's poetry collection *Cape Coast Castle*, Ama Ata Aidoo's play *Anowa*, the dance production *Musu: Saga of the Slaves* by Ghana's National Dance Ensemble, and the movie *Sankofa* are representative of genres that have explored the Trans-Atlantic Slave Trade in Ghana, yielding research and public responses. Nigerian creative renditions of the trade include *The Interesting Narrative of the Life of Olaudah Equiano*, one of the oldest personal accounts of a person taken from present-day Nigeria. Other work like Buchi Emecheta's *The Slave Girl* and Ben Okri's *The Famished Road* are examples of literary work that centralize slavery as a theme.

In academia, Naana Opoku-Agyemang analyses how the afterlives of slavery exist in cultural practices among people in Northern Ghana, using Gwollu and Salaga as examples.[12] The edited volume *Slavery and Slave Trade in Nigeria* uses oral tradition and history to present a comprehensive image of slavery in different forms in Nigeria. Laura Murphy's *Metaphor and the Slave Trade in West African Literatures* was the first book-length study of the legacy of the slave trade in written African literature and drew on examples mainly from Ghana and Nigeria.[13] Murphy and Esther de Bruijn further argue that contemporary forms of slavery in cheap popular children's fiction "point to systemic conditions that undergird the entire history of enslavement in West Africa."[14] The prevalence of digital technology in West Africa suggests that an analysis of the thematic concerns reveals ways in which West Africans continue to grapple with the implications of having been a crucial site for slavery in its worst forms. This engagement is seen by exploring new forms of trafficking and labour exploitation that are common mainly in urban centres, where digital literature has become widespread.

Bhakti Shringarpure captures the situation succinctly: "digital literary culture originating from the African continent has exploded." Similar to many African countries south of the Sahara, the Ghanaian and Nigerian literary landscapes are being changed by digital technology. It is common to see people use mobile phones to access stories and poetry via social media, literary apps, and websites. Platforms such as *Brittle Paper*, *Saraba*, and *Okada Books* have become well-known destinations for the latest African digital fiction, with research examining the role that such websites play in forging a new frontier for African literature.[15] *Flash Fiction Ghana* and *Jalada* are also among the best-known platforms and contribute to the new ways that young Africans imagine their environment while sharing their perspectives through short narratives. The link between digital literature and slavery is therefore illuminated through an understanding of these two websites, not least because digital platforms are increasingly the main ways through which writers engage with audiences.

4.2 *Flash Fiction Ghana, Jalada,* and the Advent of Digital Productions

Created in mid-2012 by Daniel Dzah, the website *Flash Fiction Ghana* (https://flashfictionghana.com) has become the foremost venue for flash fiction from Ghanaian writers. This website started with three submissions in July 2012 and started to receive higher numbers of entries mainly from young amateur writers. By the end of 2013, and despite being non-profit in nature while run only by volunteers, *Flash Fiction Ghana* was receiving, vetting, and publishing a handful of stories every month: by the time it took a two-year break in January 2018, the website had curated more than a hundred micro fiction stories that touched on all types of themes and utilized various literary styles. Upon its return in June 2020, the website started to incorporate interviews with writers and continues to publish stories that are a thousand words or less.

Jalada was formed in January 2014 by a group of young Africans spearheaded by Moses Kilolo, their first managing editor. The website is best known for embarking on a project that culminated in the most translated African short story ever: originally a Kikuyu fable entitled "Ituĩka Rĩa Mũrũngarũ: Kana Kĩrĩa Gĩtũmaga Andũ Mathiĩ Marũngiĩ" and otherwise known in English as "The Upright Revolution: Or Why Humans Walk Upright" by Ngugi wa Thiong'o. Translated into more than a hundred languages (with a significant number being African languages), the project led to new ways of viewing African languages in a digital age.[16] *Jalada* also hosts submissions in English, one of which is under this study.

The word "Jalada" is translated from Swahili to mean "archive" in English and has conceptual implications. Processing digital platforms as archives allows for an understanding of these websites as cubicles that serve as repositories for contemporary African forms of digital creative expression. Again, the nature of these websites is such that beyond simply hosting the stories, there is potential for users to engage with the stories through comments. On *Flash Fiction Ghana*, these reader comments are called "Thoughts," signalling a desire to couch responses to the stories as ideas that can extend the work. So far, most of the stories do not receive many responses; nevertheless, the potential to create communities that coalesce around the various stories still remains. One way of harnessing this potential would be to use it as a means to speak to the most obvious feature of short stories, which is the length, or lack of it.

The brevity that characterises short stories can appear restrictive due to the lack of space needed to develop the fundamental aspects of fiction: theme, character, setting, plot, etc. However, this supposed liability rather allows for an explosion of potential extensions of the stories, not least because the reader is implicitly invited to "complete" stories by filling in the many gaps afforded by a story of less than a thousand words. In the two stories selected, the gaps appear in different forms, highlighting suspense, for instance. Put differently, the gaps afforded by the nature of short stories can be seen as untold stories that can be narrated by a reader who takes interest in the uncompleted thread left by the author. While these gaps can also be testament to the currency of short pieces that mark the internet age, for the purpose of this chapter, the inability of the selected writers to speak to these undeveloped literary elements functions as a metaphor for the digital age, where attention spans are short. In the following section, these stories will be looked at to understand the ways through which slavery is imagined in digital spaces.

4.3   Storms Brewing in "A Rainy Morning in Accra"

In Hakeem Adam's "A Rainy Morning in Accra," an unnamed fifteen-year-old street hawker is faced with a series of dilemmas: it has rained and he is hawking in light traffic, meaning he would not be able to make decent sales.[17] He worries about his ability to sell stale plantain chips that are three days old, unlike his competitors who sell non-perishable goods such as shoe polish. And he is battling palpable hunger, having not eaten for a while. These present problems are compounded by his past: he was the product of a rape, and his twin sister was sold into prostitution by the time she was an early teen. People like the protagonist and his sister form the underbelly of West African urban centres like Accra, living on the streets and dealing with tough conditions. This difficult story ends in tragedy when the boy and other hawkers are killed by a fuel tanker that skids on the wet road.

Some of these children are viewed by critics as experiencing contemporary slave-like conditions. Admassie posits that children who work in "marginal economic activities like street trade" risk car accidents and excessive heat. Children like the protagonist are "trapped in slavery and slave-like bondage practices in many sub-Saharan African countries, which are similar to slavery except that the markets are not open."[18]

The story is set in Kaneshie, a popular commercial hub of Accra with a bustling market. Street hawking is a common phenomenon in urban West Africa; heavy-volume traffic lights are usually littered with people selling different wares to drivers and passengers as well as pedestrians. This practice is relatively new: Sam Sarpong and Ibrahim B. Nabubie (2015) note that in the 1980s, it was a "rarity" for noticeable volumes of street trading in Ghana.[19] The novelty of the phenomenon can explain why Ghanaian authorities are yet to come to terms with the situation. With the increased importation of cars and an expanded road network, traffic lights have become a major sales hub for drivers and passengers who find it inconvenient to go to stores to buy desired goods. Heavy traffic and/or bad roads force drivers to slow down, allowing hawkers to make brisk sales. The hawkers at Kaneshie traffic light, like some other places such as the neighbouring Kwame Nkrumah Circle area, have over the years been the sites for clashes between the hawkers and the local government authorities, who have attempted – and failed – several times to move them from the street. The Department of Social Welfare is unable to provide succour for these children as well.[20] Because the practice is not regulated by the relevant authorities, there are a litany of dangers that include the risk of being hit by a vehicle, as occurs in the story. The hustle and bustle at traffic lights is what allows vulnerable people like the protagonist to work at high risk. It is not uncommon to see children like the protagonist hawking at such intersections.

Considering his circumstances, this protagonist is more or less a street child. In 2003, there were 20,000 children estimated to be living and working in the streets of Accra and by 2011, the number had ballooned to be more than 61,000.[21] In "Survival Strategies of Street Children in Ghana: A Qualitative Study," Julie Orme and Michael M.O. Seipel interview thirty-five street children to find that most of these young people were more focused on dealing with present challenges than they were worried about circumstances that forced them into their difficult situations.[22] This attitude is reflected in the protagonist, even though he acknowledges that his background plays a role in his situation. In dealing with his present challenges, he is however unamused by empty positive messages such as those found on trotros, which are a main source of potential buyers.

Trotros are cheap mini-buses that transport passengers along vantage points in mainly urban areas. Like public transport in different African cities across the continent, trotros are famous for their inscriptions that touch on subjects ranging from relationships to religion and everything in between. Such inscriptions include verses from the Bible and the Koran. These inscriptions fall under the latter part of Ato Quayson's stationery and mobile categorization in *Oxford Street* (134) and provide identity to urban centres.[23] They again tell stories and deliver messages, forming a complex web of narrative and communicative tropes that highlight the ways in which the vehicle owners and drivers think about and process issues from their perspectives.

In this story, the three inscriptions mentioned are "E go bee," "God dey," and "Nyame bɛyɛ."[24] While two of these messages explicitly mention God, all three are hopeful in their tone. On the surface, such positive messaging should be met with an equally upbeat attitude, as they seem intent on promoting an optimistic disposition. However, such a response appears to genuflect to privilege, as the inscriptions assume a certain amount of cultural capital and comfort for those that can afford the positive messaging. The narrator informs the reader that these inscriptions are "shoved" in the face of the young boy, signalling the violently exploitative relationship that vulnerable people tend to have with some religious leaders in the country. Attributing positive interventions to God, as is the case of the last inscription, for example, removes responsibility from the person and gives the impression that personal action is not needed to make good things happen. By extension, people are encouraged to hand over their resources to religious leaders who are supposed to in turn unlock doors for prosperity. In popular culture as well as in literature, writers have parodied this issue by portraying religious leaders as charlatans.[25] The overtly religious undertones thus highlight the tendency of some Ghanaians to rely on people other than themselves to progress, thus displacing personal responsibility. More crucially, they signal the exclusion of the boy from access to socioeconomic mobility as presented by religion. This failure appears to be a source of mockery for the boy, hence his anger at religion.

In "Religion on the road: The Spiritual Experience of Road Travel in Ghana," Gabriel Klaeger suggests that religion becomes a fallback option for people because of the failure of institutions; in this case, road users resort to religious interventions due to the bad nature of roads.[26] The attitude of the protagonist thus points to the immediate need for a sociocultural overhaul that can adopt strategies that respond to the needs of vulnerable youth who will not fall into traps such as what the protagonist finds himself in. This vicious cycle is his everyday reality with no tangible exit.

The title of the story adds a quotidian feel, which underlines the lived realities of vulnerable people such as the protagonist and his colleagues. It is not unusual for street hawkers to struggle with making sales while at risk of recalcitrant drivers who in turn have difficulty with poorly constructed roads. The everyday nature of their labour plays into the theme of marginalization by highlighting their isolation from social support. The added burden is that their work is illegal; as such, they are at the mercy of authorities who either overlook them or extort from them. Moreover, these children are unable to attend school, which is supposed to be free for children up until high school.[27] This dire situation is complemented by the circumstance of the protagonist's twin sister.

This sister is sold into prostitution by their mother "to ensure that she survived this life." This act is justified by the mother, who calls it a "good choice." The fact that the twin sister is mentioned in passing can be construed to be a deliberate move to highlight the ephemerality and invisibility of young girls who are trafficked for underage prostitution. In recent times, the Middle East and the European Union have become destinations for these girls, who endure slave-like conditions. These girls are also found in urban areas in Ghana and parts of West Africa and suffer similar experiences. The text does not leave space for the reader to ascertain the location of the protagonist's twin sister. Regardless of whether she is in Ghana, outside Ghana, or even dead, it is likely that her predicament is not encouraging. In any case, dismissing her plight as a "good choice" should not necessarily be seen as insensitive or ignorant; it could equally be a coping mechanism for the mother if we consider her obvious inability to cater for her children.

This coping mechanism is severely tested, as the protagonist's mother is unable to deal with the loss of her child, which she hears about on the radio. Her difficulty with coming to terms with the tragic news is contrasted sharply by a retort from another person who is also listening and hoping that their child is not dead. The radio report itself is presented in a banal way that validates the impression that the lives of these lower-class citizens are not valuable enough to merit much attention. By normalizing this tragedy, Adam critiques the ways in which Ghanaians overlook the problem of child hawking, and indeed, child trafficking.

4.4 Parody and Magic Realism as Agency in "The Iguana Boy with Three Testicles"

While Adam's story is quotidian in feel with a contemporary setting, "The Iguana Boy with Three Testicles" has elements of magic realism and parody, and is set in 1930, at a time when the region now known as Nigeria was a British colony.[28] The transatlantic slave trade had ended several decades prior, but the sociocultural dynamics at play meant that vertical power relations remained stark along racial lines. The story revolves around Dr. Douglas Hurst, an American anthropologist seeking to take pictures of "exotic" Africans to sell to the *National Geographic* magazine. As he witnesses a holy ritual in a village called Ozigono, he is amazed by the sight of a young boy of about twelve years, who levitates high off the ground and throws eggs into a river as a crowd cheers him. What shocks him even more is the fact that the child has three testicles. He wants to embark on an exhibition tour of the United States with the child, recalling the real-life incident of Sarah Baartman, who was paraded around Europe because there was an audience that saw her physical features to be worth paying to view.[29] Accordingly, he tries to convince the boy's family to allow him to take the child to America. The family promptly turns down the request, not least because the boy is integral to the functioning of their cultural ecosystem as high priest of the Ozigono River. Unperturbed, he plots with his local assistant to kidnap the boy and traffic him to the United States. Hurst's plans to monetize the boy by staging an exhibition at a museum in Washington, D.C. go awry when the boy scares the audience as he gyrates amidst loud chanting. In the ensuing chaos, Hurst loses his mind and ends the story falling headlong to the floor, presumably dead like the protagonist in Adam's story.

The legacy of the transatlantic slave trade continues to be a topic that writers grapple with, and creative license allows Ehikhamenor to critique – and sometimes overturn – conventional narratives about the slave trade. Ehikhamenor uses the perspective of the white explorer as a tool to parody aspects of the slave trade experience. For instance, Hurst views the child as a money-making venture. This perspective echoes the hyper-commodification of abducted and enslaved Africans during the transatlantic trade. His boss, who is based in America, even thinks of killing the boy and putting him in a jar to earn more money. Hurst rejects this proposal, as he "still had some strands of humanity left in him." The irony in placing the kidnapper as being more humane than another person extends the mockery, while parsing global capitalism through the lens of dehumanization. The story is coloured by a remorseless intent to profit off Black bodies and Black labour – even to the detriment of those who assist in the success of the kidnap attempt. This intent is seen in the character of Hurst's assistant, Ahwinahwi.

Ahwinahwi is a parody of the local enablers of the historical slave trade. He works assiduously for Hurst, guiding him through unknown territory and running difficult errands for him. He is given "useless gifts" as reward for his endeavours, and he dies on his way home after departing from Hurst. His literal deletion from the text is complemented by narratorial erasure: Hurst intentionally keeps him out of his story concerning how the gifted boy was discovered. Erasure of Black actors from Western versions of African history is not a new phenomenon, and the thankless nature of Ahwinahwi's efforts is not intended to necessarily elicit pity as it is to highlight how disposable such characters are in the scheme of events. In other words, the depiction of this assistant through caricature is an explicit nod to the racial inequality that characterizes global capitalist flows.

Through gestures to the supernatural, there is also the use of magic realism in the story. The connection between magic realism and slavery is explored elsewhere: for instance, in Toni Morrison's *Beloved*, Stephen M. Hart notes that "inner circle" characters are able to take the supernatural for granted in the novel (121).[30] Similarly in this short story, it is only Hurst and the other Americans who are struck by the elements of the supernatural. Contrasted by the Africans who view these elements as part of their worldview, Hurst is subjected to ensuing mockery through his greed.

While the instances of magic realism complement parody, they tend to complicate the perspective of the white explorer. In America Hurst unveils the boy, only to find to his dismay that the place where he had seen the three testicles is "smooth as the small mirror he had offered the iguana boy's parents." The value that Hurst attached to the boy through his offer to his parents turns on its head; he is unable to deal with this change in situation. The boy levitates with chants that are interspersed with proverbs that stress the callousness that informed Hurst's greed. The experience disorients him to the extent of making him unsure of whether he ever saw three testicles, and he starts hearing voices from the village as well. The confusion is settled with his apparent death, which can be construed as a creative way of speaking back to the sustained exploitation of African culture by Western interests.

On the surface, the combination of parody and magic realism appear to make light of a traumatic experience that involves forced abduction and trafficking; on the other hand, these tropes allow the author to reflect on the absurdity of the atrocity. By performing an introspection into the interplay between the sequence of events, theme, and characterization, Ehikhamenor avoids the expected outcome of unchallenged exploitation by underscoring the vulnerability of the oppressors themselves. The agency of the gifted boy is still not meant to detract from the culpability of people like Hurst who contribute to the difficulties that characterize inequality on a global scale.

4.5 Conclusion: Global Capitalist Flows and "The Year of Return"

When Ghanaian and Nigerian users shared on social media that they would prefer their grandfather to suffer through the transatlantic slave trade as sacrifice for them to be living in America, they forcefully threw into sharp relief the disillusionment that they have with harsh realities that inform their current predicaments. People like the protagonist in "A Rainy Morning in Accra" for example have no realistic means of accessing upward socio-economic mobility; the eventual death of this protagonist is an unfortunate possibility that underscores the valueless precarity of their lives. For such a form of slavery to be so pervasive in urban spaces all over West Africa is testament to the weakness of social institutions that are meant to serve as buffers of protection to these vulnerable people against slavery and other forms of exploitation.[31]

What Adam's story does not address directly is the implicit but powerful presence of global capitalism that forces countries like Ghana and Nigeria to remain in positions of subservience to bigger "developed" countries. These countries introduce policies and bilateral agreements that inure to their benefit, but are ultimately detrimental to African countries; sometimes these countries go as far as to strong-arm these countries into kowtowing to their demands.[32] Research shows that on an annual basis, Africa loses up to 60 billion dollars to Western countries – and more recently, China – through the pillaging of natural resources, nefarious deals couched as "partnerships" and "developmental aid," and corruption spearheaded by the political class.[33] Young people typically suffer the most from the outcomes of these developments. The racist undertones of such international relationships are more explicitly highlighted in "The Iguana Boy with Three Testicles" primarily through the characterization of Hurst, who views pre-independent Nigeria as a place to make money, regardless of the means. By letting the story end tragically for the American explorer, Ehikhamenor explores the fragility of the perpetrators of such atrocities while amplifying the agency of one of the grandfathers kidnapped to America.

Even as Ghanaians and Nigerians in their respective countries expressed the wish to be in America online, descendants of those kidnapped and forcibly taken away were coming back across the Atlantic Ocean in person. In 2019, Ghana observed 400 years after the embarkment of one of the first ships of enslaved Africans in Virginia. This massive campaign, known as "The Year of Return," was a year-long commemoration that was intended to facilitate the travel of Diasporic Africans to Ghana in order to visit the places from which their ancestors were forcibly taken. There were high profile visits of Black celebrities to the castles and other sites of slavery, while other Diasporic Africans were granted citizenship at high profile ceremonies attended by the President. This event climaxed in December 2019 with a series of programmes that appeared to redirect the focus from a more spiritual and personal feel to a commercial bent. Nigeria organized a similar series of events but on a smaller scale in 2020 under the title "The Door of Return." The ensuing COVID-19 pandemic meant that planned events were unable to come off. The impact of the Ghana version was nevertheless massively felt both in the country and in the diaspora, with high levels of tourist visits to the country.

The Year of Return resonated worldwide because of the aforementioned history with the transatlantic slave trade, and in this digital age, West African writers continue to imagine contemporary environments that can be tied to slavery, regardless of whether it is the transatlantic trade or more contemporary versions of slavery. By concentrating on modern iterations such as insecurity, vulnerability, agency, and above all, marginalization, these writers show how the institution of slavery, filtered through digital environments, continues to inform the West African sociocultural landscape in intricate ways.

Notes

1 UNICEF. (n.d.) "Child labour." www.unicef.org/protection/child-labour (accessed February 4, 2021).
2 Convention C182 – Worst Forms of Child Labour Convention, 1999 (No. 182). (n.d.). http://www.ilo.org/dyn/normlex/en/f?p=NORMLEXPUB:12100:0::NO:: P12100_ILO_CODE:C182 (accessed February 4, 2021).
3 Anti-Slavery International, "What Is Child Slavery?" (n.d.). www.antislavery .org/slavery-today/child-slavery/ (accessed February 4, 2021).
4 See Ezeibe et al. "From Vulnerability to Sustainability: Implementation of Free Education Programmes and Reversal of Child Trafficking in Nigeria," *Journal of Human Trafficking* 7 (2021): 104–118.
5 A. Foua and W. Diriwari, 'Cultural and Legal Perspectives on Child Protection in the Context of Child Trafficking in Nigeria'; and E. S. Hamenoo et al., "Child labour in Ghana: Implications for children's education and health," *Children and Youth Services Review* 93 (2018): 248–254.

6 A. Admassie, "Explaining the High Incidence of Child Labour in Sub–Saharan Africa," *African development review* 14.2 (2002): 253.

7 G. U. Nwokeji, *The Slave Trade and Culture in the Bight of Biafra: An African Society in the Atlantic World* (Cambridge: Cambridge University Press, 2010).

8 Q. Kambon, "Legacies and the impact of Trans-Atlantic enslavement on the Diaspora," *Journal of Pan African Studies* 8 (2015): 41–61.

9 Various Afrobarometer surveys corroborate this perception.

10 O. Ojo, "The Organization of the Atlantic Slave Trade in Yorubaland ca.1777 to ca.1856," *The International Journal of African Historical Studies* 41 (2008): 77–100.

11 B. N. Lawrance, "From Child Labor 'Problem' to Human Trafficking 'Crisis': Child Advocacy and Anti-Trafficking Legislation in Ghana," *International Labor and Working-Class History* (2010): 63–88 and O. S. Adesina, "Modern Day Slavery: Poverty and Child Trafficking in Nigeria," *African Identities* 12 (2014): 165–179.

12 See N. J. Opoku-Agyemang, "The Living Experience of the Slave Trade in Sankana and Gwollu: Implications for Tourism"; Anquandah, Opoku-Agyemang, and Doortmont, (eds.), *The Transatlantic Slave Trade: Landmarks, Legacies, Expectations* (2007), 210–224. N. J. Opoku-Agyemang, *Where There Is No Silence: Articulations of Resistance to Enslavement* (Accra: Ghana Academy of Arts and Sciences, 2008).

13 L.T. Murphy, *Metaphor and the Slave Trade in West African Literature* (Athens, Ohio: Ohio University Press, 2012).

14 E. de Bruijn and L. T. Murphy, "Trading in Innocence: Slave-Shaming in Ghanaian Children's Market Fiction," *Journal of African Cultural Studies* 30 (2018): 243–262.

15 See representative research such as "The single most translated short story in the history of African writing: Ngũgĩ wa Thiong'o and the Jalada writers' collective" by Moses Kilolo, *African Literature in the Digital Age: Class and Sexual Politics in New Writing from Nigeria and Kenya* by Shola Adenekan, and Stephanie Bosch Santana's "From Nation to Network: Blog and Facebook Fiction from Southern Africa."

16 For an extensive overview of *Jalada*, see M. Kilolo, "The single most translated short story in the history of African writing: Ngũgĩ wa Thiong'o and the Jalada writers' collective." In *The Routledge Handbook of Translation and Activism*, ed. R. R. Gould, and K. Tahmasebian (Routledge, 2020).

17 H. Adam, "A Rainy Morning in Accra," *Flash Fiction Ghana*, 2014. https://flashfictionghana.com/2014/10/03/a-rainy-morning-in-accra-by-hakeem-adam/ (accessed January 8, 2021).

18 A. Admassie, "High Incidence of Child Labour," 257–258.

19 S. Sarpong, and I. B. Nabubie "Nuisance or Discerning? The Social Construction of Street Hawkers in Ghana," *Society and Business Review* 10 (2015): 102–117.

20 N. K. Agyeman, "No Homes, Logistics to Take Child Beggars off Streets', *Daily Graphic*, 2021. www.graphic.com.gh/news/general-news/no-homes-logistics-to-take-child-beggars-off-streets.html (accessed May 24, 2022).

21 J. Orme, and M.M.O Seipel, "Survival Strategies of Street Children in Ghana: A Qualitative Study," *International Social Work* 50 (2007), 489.

22 Orme and Seipel, "Survival Strategies," 494.

23 A. Quayson, *Oxford Street, Accra: City Life and the Itineraries of Transnationalism* (Durham: Duke University Press, 2014).

24 These are respectively translated from Pidgin English as "It will work out," "God is there," and from Akan as "God will do it."

25 Apart from numerous local movies with this theme, Ayi Kwei Armah's *Fragments* includes a scene where the protagonist's mother is scammed by a religious leader.

26 G. Klaeger, "Religion on the Road: The Spiritual Experience of Road Travel in Ghana." In *The Speed of Change: Motor Vehicles and People in Africa, 1890–2000*, ed. , J. Gewald, S. Luning, and K. van Walraven (Leiden: Brill, 2009). https://brill .com/view/book/edcoll/9789047430797/Bej.9789004177352.i-298_011.xml (accessed May 4, 2021).

27 As Admassie points out, "The prevalence of acute poverty and the need of poor households to keep children working to ensure income security makes it impossible for them to invest in their children's education."

28 V. Ehikhamenor, "The Iguana Boy with Three Testicles," *Jalada Africa*, 2015. https://jaladaafrica.org/2015/04/08/the-iguana-boy-with-three-testicles-by-vic tor-ehikamenor/ (accessed May 4, 2021).

29 C. E. Henderson, "AKA: Sarah Baartman, The Hottentot Venus, and Black Women's Identity," *Women's Studies* 43 (2014): 946–959.

30 S. M. Hart, "Magical Realism in the Americas: Politicised Ghosts in *One Hundred Years of Solitude, The House of the Spirits*, and *Beloved*," *Journal of Iberian and Latin American Studies* 9 (2003): 115–123.

31 Adesina, "Modern Day Slavery," 165–179.

32 Upon external pressure, Ghana encouraged the importation of second-hand clothing from America and lead to a sharp drop in jobs within the industry – from 25,000 in 1975 to just 5,000 by the turn of the millennium. (R. Traub-Merz, "The African Textile and Clothing Industry: From Import Substitution to Export Orientation." In *The Future of the Textile and Clothing Industry in Sub-Saharan Africa*, ed. H. Jauch and R. Traub-Merz (Bonn: Friedrich-Ebert-Stiftung, 2006), 17.

33 M. Anderson, "Aid to Africa: Donations from West Mask "$60bn Looting" of Continent," *The Guardian*, 2014.

CHAPTER 5

Enslavement and Forced Marriage in Uyghur Literature

David Brophy

Situated at the meeting point of nomadic and sedentary societies, and frequently contested by rival empires, the region of northwest China known today as Xinjiang has seen forms of slavery and servitude for much of its known history. Some of the oldest surviving documents retrieved by explorers from the sands of the Taklamakan desert – dating to more than a millennium ago – concern the buying, selling, and freeing of enslaved people. With the Tarim Basin's conversion to Islam from the tenth century onwards, local dynasties there acquired humans that they enslaved from surrounding non-Muslim peoples, but the oasis towns strung out around the rim of the Taklamakan desert were themselves vulnerable to ongoing raids from the steppe. The perils of long-distance caravan travel also put Muslims at risk of falling captive to their non-Muslim neighbors, particularly the Mongols who resided to the north of the Tianshan (Heavenly Mountains). Known as Oirats (but to locals as Qalmaqs), these Mongols figure as the non-Muslim enemy par excellence in a range of Central Asian literary traditions and were themselves sold into various forms of military and state service throughout Turkistan.

The presence of enslaved Muslims in Qalmaq hands was a considerable source of anxiety for the region's elites, and to redeem such captives was a meritorious deed. In the fifteenth century, for example, the Naqshbandi Sufi shaykh Khoja Ahrar dispatched one of his disciples from Samarkand to the Tarim Basin "for the sake of releasing the Muslims who are imprisoned in China."[1] Khoja Ishaq Vali, who proselytized in the region in the late sixteenth century, is said to have taken pride in liberating "Muslims who had fallen captive to the Qalmaqs on the road to China and had given up hope of life."[2]

From the point of view of the settled, agricultural population of the Tarim Basin – the people today known as the Uyghurs – the risk of enslavement was heightened from the late seventeenth century onwards, as the local Chaghatayid dynasty (a branch of Chinggis Khan's Mongol empire) went into decline, and a steppe-based Oirat Mongol polity led by the Junghars rose to regional hegemony. Hostage-taking was an integral part of Junghar state-building strategies. As one local historian put it, the Junghar court "became the meeting place for the khans of Piskend, the nobles of Tashkent, and the kings of Badakhshan."[3] With their growing empire centered on the Ili Valley, in the north of what is now Xinjiang, the Junghars also put Muslim captives to work in agriculture and animal husbandry. These became known as 'Taranchis,' from a Mongolian word for 'peasant.' Some were presumably also employed in mines in surrounding regions. Other Muslims who were pressed into forms of unfree labor served as an official merchantry and were known as Bazargan (*bederge* in Mongolian).

Evidence for the growing number of enslaved Muslims in Junghar society can be seen in a decree issued by the Junghar Galdan Khan in 1678 to regulate the affairs of the Taranchi and Bazargan.[4] This was two years prior to Galdan Khan's first full-scale invasion of the Tarim Basin, which led to new deportations. Islamic sources also mention occasions at which Tarim Basin Muslims engaged in raids of their own and were able to free some of these captives, but the net effect of Junghar dominion was a significant redistribution of Muslims to the north of the Tianshan. One estimate puts the total population of Muslims in Junghar service by the middle of the eighteenth century at as high as 17,000.[5] Although visitors from imperial Russia often described these captives as 'Bukharans,' the majority hailed from the Tarim Basin (which was known to Russians as 'Little Bukhara'). Some of these Muslims resided in compact communities with official hierarchies of their own, and which were integrated into the Junghar social structure. Others were assigned to work on the lands of Buddhist monasteries or gifted to Oirat aristocrats residing elsewhere on the steppe. As the armies of the Qing encroached on the Junghar state in the eighteenth century, escapees to the Qing camp testified to the experience of being bought and sold among these Oirat elites.[6]

When a Qing invasion in the 1750s brought an end to Junghar rule, most of these Taranchis returned to the Tarim Basin, effectively depopulating the Ili region. To revive local agriculture in what was now the center of the Qing occupation, Qing officials recruited new cohorts of Muslims to cultivate 'Muslim farms' (Huitun) in Ili. Official sources indicate that these migrations were voluntary, though how the mobilizations were carried out in practice is hard to say: sometimes, local Muslim begs (officials) provided parties of migrants *en bloc* as a way of demonstrating their loyalty to the dynasty. These Qing Taranchis remained tied to the land, either as part of the tax-paying population or as *yanchi* – a term for those who cultivated lands assigned to begs.[7] They were not technically 'slaves' in Qing terms (*nu*). This category was reserved for Muslims who were destined for exile, either for serious criminal offences, or because they were family members of political enemies of the dynasty. While the Ili region served as a destination for such criminals from elsewhere in the empire, initially the practice in Xinjiang was the reverse: enslaved locals were sent to Beijing or to the south of China.[8] This policy shifted in the 1820s, however, in the wake of the uprising of Jahangir Khoja, the first major Sufi-led rebellion to wrest control of the Tarim Basin from the Qing. On the recommendation of Qing officers involved in putting down the rebellion, Muslims who were identified as relatives of its participants were sent to Ili and Ürümchi, where they were given as slaves to officers of the local garrison. As Joanna Waley-Cohen has described, the Qing state retained ultimate responsibility for such individuals: "the master had the use but not the ownership of his slave."[9]

This historical experience of subjugation and enforced migration has been reflected in various forms of literature among the Uyghurs. Here I discuss two such genres: hagiographies that belong to the region's Sufi traditions, and folk literature. In an Islamic society such as this, the depiction of enslavement in hagiographic narratives drew on a rich body of religious legends centered on captivity and deliverance. In that sense, Sufi texts often look backwards in their construction of saintly lives. Folk literature, by contrast, was more responsive to the changing times, with narratives of oppression easily adaptable to new contexts and the construction of a national literary canon in the twentieth century. In the second half of this essay, I explore the evolution of one such story, that of Nazugum, as a vehicle for political imaginings up until to the present day, and the expression of sentiments considered too subversive for more explicit formulation.

5.1   Junghar Captivity in Sufi Hagiography

As a literature of frontier proselytization, the Central Asian hagiographic corpus contains diverse stories and anecdotes of interaction with non-Muslims, with slavery a common theme. The first literary depiction of Junghar captivity is provided by texts from the late eighteenth century, i.e. written in the wake of the Qing invasion. One of these, the *Book of Islam* (*Islamnama*), reflects the point of view of a devotee of the 'White Mountain' khojas, a hereditary lineage within the Nashqbandiyya Sufi order who descended from Khoja Afaq, a seventeenth-century figure whose tomb remains the most prestigious in Kashgar to this day. The hero of the *Book of Islam* is Khoja Afaq's grandson Khoja Ahmad, while Ahmad's two sons also feature towards its end. Both sons grew up in captivity until their release in the 1750s, at which point they led a combined Qing-Muslim army to take possession of the Tarim Basin.

The work's author, Muhammad Abd al-Alim, describes the Junghar raid which carried off Khoja Ahmad (an event dating to ca. 1700) in cataclysmic terms:

> These infidels with tassels on their caps,
> Were heralds of misfortune and mishap.
> Their arrival was a curse,
> People saw their ruinous intent.
> Wherever their steps led them,
> It was nothing less than a dragon's fiery breath,
> Like an alligator advancing with mouth agape,
> It was impossible to escape by flight.
> As they went about their trickery,
> And worked their deceptive ways,
> They conquered these Five Cities,
> And not just these Five Cities, but the entire world.
> They subjugated the people of Islam,
> And caused tears to flow.
> They gave the Muslims no chance,
> Putting them to work (*alban*) night and day.
> All those they took were scattered across the mountains,
> Lost among the falcons and the crows.[10]

The author explains the Muslim community's subjugation in conventional terms as the product of their deviation from "the work of the sharia." It was, in effect, divine punishment. Abd al-Alim's narrative then turns to the tribulations of Khoja Ahmad, who was singled out for captivity by decree of the Junghar khan. Cautioning his fellow Muslims against resisting, Ahmad meditates on his fate, then decides to voluntarily offer himself up – thereby exemplifying the saintly virtue of *tawakkul*, "reliance on God."

> He said to his aggrieved companions:
> "Strategy is no use against fate.
> They are waiting for me,
> Even if I remain safe, it will bode ill for you if I don't go."
> So saying he chose the mountains,
> And entrusted his abode to the care of God.

As they took his freedom into their hands,
He accepted his captivity.
He left straightaway, setting out by the mountain road,
While the people were left lamenting in confusion.
The world dimmed for the Muslims,
As if the sun was hidden from view.
He went and took up residence in Land of the Infidel (*Kāfiristān*),
And lit a candle amid the darkness.
With the coming of his blessed presence,
The Realm of the Infidel became the Abode of Peace (*Dār al-Amān*).[11]

To the chagrin of the Junghars, Ahmad survives the persecution and hardship awaiting him in Ili. They then isolate the shaykh in a mountainous region far from any Muslim settlement, where he is unable to receive well-wishers. Again, Ahmad emerges triumphant from the testing experience, and by his example succeeds in converting his Junghar jailers to Islam.

Dating to roughly the same period, but much less stylized in its depiction of Junghar captivity, is Muhammad Sadiq Kashghari's *In Remembrance of the Saints* (*Tazkira-i Azizan*). Kashghari's narrative centers on a different branch of the Tarim Basin Naqshbandiyya: the family of Ishaq Vali, a saint active in the region in the sixteenth century. While members of this family were often held hostage, on the whole they had a much more collaborative relationship with the Junghars, and it was they who fell victim to the White Mountain khoja invasion of the Tarim Basin in the 1750s. Reflecting this Mongol-Muslim modus vivendi, Kashgari points out that while the Junghars "shipped Khoja Ahmad off like a prisoner and kept him under strict surveillance on the outskirts of Ili, with God's blessing Khoja Danyal [Ishaq Vali's great grandson and a patriarch of the family] lived with dignity and honor in the land of the infidel."[12]

Kashghari's narrative gives a more intimate sense of Junghar captivity, relying far less than Abd al-Alim on the theme of saintly suffering. One important vignette involves a wife and son of Khoja Danyal, who were carried off in a raid and given to a Junghar aristocrat who resided far from Ili. According to the story, the wife was pregnant at the time of her abduction from Kashgar but remained chaste until the delivery. After his birth, her son receives a standard Mongol upbringing until he is seven years old, at which time a traveling merchant encounters the family and brings news of the boy's existence back to Khoja Danyal in Ili. An investigation ensues, and despite a trial that is rigged in favor of the Junghars, a timely request for divine intervention sees the boy eventually reunited with his father and returned to the fold of Islam. Whether by contrivance or coincidence, the story is obviously reminiscent of the Biblical and Quranic narrative of Joseph, or Yusuf – the traveling merchant here playing the role of the passing caravan that frees Yusuf from the pit and takes him to Egypt. The tale seems to have been on the minds of the Muslims at the time as well: after being circumcised and made a Muslim, the boy is given the name Khoja Yusuf.[13]

Captivity was obviously still far from a desirable condition, and Kashgari maintains that the Ishaqiyya khojas were at all times determined to eventually liberate their fellow Muslims from servitude in Ili. There are mentions in the story of members of this Sufi family redeeming captives and bringing them into their employ. At one point in the narrative, for example, Khoja Danyal's son Khoja Jahan berates one of his staff, who has proven unreliable: "Didn't I once buy you from some Qalmaq and set you free?"[14] On various occasions throughout the story, Khoja Jahan's brother, the Junghar-raised Khoja Yusuf, tells of his resolve to "rid the Muslims of this unjust oppression, liberate those various groups of Muslims who were captive in Ili—including the khans, the khojas, and everyone else—and declare Islamic rule openly."[15] But the long anticipated opportunity to throw off Junghar domination never presents itself.

5.2 Nazugum and the Female Heroine in Xinjiang

As mentioned above, while recruiting a new Taranchi peasantry, Qing policy was to send enslaved Xinjiang Muslims to the interior – an experience not depicted in any local sources I am aware of. When the rebellion of Jahangir Khoja was put down in 1828, however, some 1600 family members of participants were identified and deported to Ili and Ürümchi. This was part of a suite of policies designed to restore Qing control in the face of growing influence of the neighboring Kokand khanate. Many of these policies – including a trade embargo – were soon deemed a failure. Emissaries from Kokand demanded the return of any Kokandis who had been enslaved, and by the early 1830s, most captives – foreigners and locals alike – had been freed. In 1835, the Daoguang Emperor received information that only thirty-six remained in Ili, and he decreed that all those who so desired should be able to return to their home south of the mountains.[16]

This amnesty is described in the work of a local historian, Molla Musa Sayrami, writing circa 1900. The author's hometown of Sayram lies just south of the Muzart pass connecting the Ili Valley to southern Xinjiang. In his account, freed slaves returning along this route brought with them a new folksong, entitled "Nazugum." "In the intervening four years [of exile]," Sayrami writes, "some had fallen into Chinese hands and had borne children. When they were delivered from exile and sent back with these children, they were overjoyed at being able to return home, and all alike raised their mournful voices and improvised (*ikhtirā' qïlïp*) the song 'Nazugum! O Nazugum!' As they traveled along the highway, people came from afar to see them, and when they heard their mourning they too were moved to tears."[17]

In its simplest form, "Nazugum" is a short verse, with only vague mention of any political context. The earliest version from the Ili region, recorded by Turkologist Wilhelm Radloff in the 1860s, describes Nazugum as a young woman held captive by a "Chinese infidel" whose advances she resists.[18] Radloff's visit to the region coincided with an anti-Qing uprising, which eventually led to the decade-long Russian occupation of the Ili Valley. During the occupation, Russian official Nikolai Pantusov took down a similar song, describing Nazugum's flight from pursuing Chinese, Qalmaqs, and Solons ('Qalmaq' here refers to local Oirat Mongol members of the Qing garrison in Ili, while the Solons were from Manchuria).[19] Nazugum (meaning 'my slender one') is not identifiable with any historical figure, and these lyrics can probably be seen as adaptations of already existing love songs, in which 'Nazugum' represents an abstract female beloved. Versions of the song from elsewhere in Qing Xinjiang which lack any mention of captivity and flight were also in circulation at this time: Nikolai Przhevalsky recorded one such song in the Khotan region in the 1890s.[20]

As an imperial official on the frontiers of the tsarist empire, Pantusov's literary and ethnographic pursuits complemented his role as an administrator during the Russian occupation. When this occupation ended in the early 1880s, much of the local Taranchi population took the opportunity to migrate westward into Russian territory, laying the foundation for the Uyghur community in today's Kazakhstan. One of Pantusov's main local collaborators in recording this community's literature was a man by the name of Molla Bilal Nazim, who provided Pantusov with a version of the Nazugum story that the Russian eventually published in translation in 1909.[21] Drawing on popular songs he attributed to Nazugum herself, Molla Bilal interspersed these verses with a more elaborate prose account of Nazugum's trials. It is this version of the story that has become best known, with French and Turkish translations following on Pantusov's Russian.[22] Although no manuscript copies of this work are currently available, a modern Uyghur edition of the story was published in the literary magazine *Bulaq* in 1981. This corresponds closely to Pantusov's text, though with some of its more explicitly anti-Chinese wording edited out.[23]

In Molla Bilal's version, Nazugum is deported from Kashgar with her brother Abdullah Khoja, after her husband and son have been executed by Qing troops. Among the Kashgari women sent north to Ili, Nazugum is the prettiest of all, and a Qalmaq official in the village of Chong Yulduz determines to make her his wife. Nazugum resists and flees down the Ili river to Almaliq, in today's Kazakhstan, where she is sheltered by a local family. The Ili Military Governor dispatches a hundred cavalrymen to pursue her, who torture her protectors to force her out of hiding. On this occasion, the Ili Military Governor hands her to a Solon officer. Rather than submit, Nazugum kills her new captor and escapes once again. When she is captured for a second time, Nazugum is publicly executed on the emperor's command.

Writing in 1882, Molla Bilal's interest in expanding and elaborating the story of Nazugum may well reflect the predicament of his Taranchi community at that time. Having revolted against Qing rule a decade earlier, many were now migrating into Russian territory in the face of the returning Qing army – literally following in the footsteps of Nazugum's flight. The emergence of such figures in situations of foreign domination is of course a ubiquitous phenomenon in world literature. The popularity of a militant heroine in a society which tended to frown on female assertiveness seems paradoxical, but rigid gender norms may in fact heighten the salience of this trope. Qing, or Chinese rule represents the failure of Uyghur manhood to perform its appropriate role – the defense of the home against foreign aggression. At many points, Nazugum asks when her father, or indeed any man, might come to rescue her. Communal anxiety as to the loss of land and property naturally extended to the possibility of the generalized theft of women, and with it miscegenation; "All of your children will become Qalmaqs," Nazugum's brother warns her, "and you will become just like these black infidels."[24] The bravery of the unyielding woman thus provides an instructive contrast to less coura- geous male compatriots, and symbolizes the fighting spirit of the entire community. Martyrdom, and its recompense in the afterlife, receives heightened emphasis in Molla Bilal's version: on the eve of her execution, Nazugum comforts herself with the fact that "I'll become an exulted martyr, as the mullas say."[25]

Unsurprisingly, Nazugum was to prove attractive to twentieth-century authors interested in cultivating new national narratives for the modern

Uyghur nation then coming into being. The first of these retellings was produced in the wake of the Russian Revolution by Nezerghoja Abdusémetov, who wrote under the penname 'Uyghur Child' (*Uyghur Balisi*). A native of the town of Zharkent in Semirech'e, Abdusémetov had made links to the pre-revolutionary Russian Muslim world of letters by writing for such reformist journals as *Shura*. In these early works, Abdusémetov's interest had been to construct a historical narrative for the Taranchis, with an abstract, often personified figure of 'Uyghur' serving as a link in their communal genealogy. Some of this Taranchi-centrism remained in his 1922 *Nazugum*, in which he made the heroine a native of Ili, not of Kashgar. This plot change has the effect of removing the themes of punitive enslavement and exile from the story; Nazugum is simply taken as booty (*olja*) one day by a party of 'Manchu-Chinese' hunting in the mountains. At the same time, *Nazugum* also evinces Abdusémetov's post-revolutionary turn towards Uyghur nationalism. The hero of the story is the daughter of a Taranchi herder whose name is 'Uyghur,' and in the middle of the story, Nazugum recites an ode to the glory days of the Uyghur people (*Uyghur éli*) – the Qarakhanids and Idiqut dynasties of a millennium earlier. At its conclusion, as she prepares to face the executioner's block, her last words are an address to the nation: "From tyranny, injustice, and wickedness, and from brutal terror / The days of freedom (*āzād bolush*) are coming soon, may Nazugum rest in peace. / . . . / The Uyghur people will be cleansed of Chinese tyranny / A flag of unity in their hands, may Nazugum rest in peace."[26] One feature of Abdusémetov's text was its identification of a cave as the location where Nazugum took refuge from Qing troops. The cave itself became a place of pilgrimage for Uyghurs in Kazakhstan, who were thereby able to commune directly with the story.

Uyghur literature took large steps forward in Soviet Union during the 1920s and 1930s, as political imperatives, along with growing literacy, widened the field of Uyghur-language publishing. As was typical in the construction of Soviet nations, the Uyghur national history that emerged in this period centered on traditions of struggle against both foreign aggressors and local tyrants. In the 1930s Ismail Sattarov (1916–1944) wrote his own *Nazugum*, which an official history of Soviet Uyghur literature praises for "displaying the spirit of liberation which captured the people's minds, and their high human qualities."[27] The construction of Uyghur history as a national liberation movement stretching back to the eighteenth century received particular emphasis during the 1940s, when Moscow gave its backing to the formation of an East Turkistan Republic in the north of Xinjiang. Ershidin Hidayetov's 1946 article, "Nazugum – A Patriotic Uyghur Girl," published on Soviet soil in the journal *Truth of the East*, exemplifies the rhetoric of this short-lived republic. Here he explains that despite their subjugation by the "Manchu-Chinese empire" in the 1760s, "the Uyghur people never ceased to wage great struggles against the colonizers for their freedom and independence. In our people's history there are many patriotic heroes who have emerged from such freedom struggles, and one of them is the famous Uyghur girl Nazugum."[28]

In the postwar period, Nazugum continued to be a popular theme for Soviet Uyghur authors, with political conditions in the wake of the Sino-Soviet split proving particularly conducive for the expression of anti-Qing, and by extension anti-Chinese, themes. One of the longest versions of the Nazugum tale within this tradition is Hézim Iskenderov's longform verse retelling, published in 1970.[29] During the same period, Q. Hasanov wrote a play version of the story, and provided the libretto for a popular operatic production of *Nazugum* in Russian.[30] Meanwhile, as Xinjiang emerged from the Cultural Revolution in the 1980s, authors there such as Memtimin Hoshur fashioned their own images of Nazugum, with the short story proving the most popular vehicle for doing so.[31]

Uyghur literature and arts have thus shown a sustained interest in the heroic figure of Nazugum, but she is not alone in attracting this attention. Resistance to forced marriage is a common theme in Uyghur folklore, and a range of heroines similar to Nazugum have received modern elaborations. There are also comparisons to be drawn with figures such as Iparkhan, the Kashgari woman who became the Qianlong emperor's concubine in the eighteenth century, and who is known in Chinese tradition as the 'fragrant concubine' (Xiang Fei). As James Millward has described, Uyghur versions of this story provide a counter-narrative to Chinese legends that position the concubine as a symbol of inter-ethnic unity.[32] These Uyghur stories emphasize her determination to remain chaste while in the imperial city, and some modern versions build on this theme to depict her as Uyghur resistance fighter. In Ziya Semediy's play *Iparkhan*, for example, the heroine tries in vain to unite the feuding religious factions of the Tarim Basin in the face of the looming Qing invasion.[33] After her capture, she is shipped to Beijing, where she is kept in a luxurious Islamic-style residence. Not taken in by the emperor's generosity, she declares: "This extravagance is a golden cage for me. The arrogant Qianlong wants to drown me in comfort and pleasure, and make me forget my country and my people, to subdue me and turn me into an emotionless plaything. No, your highness, for a criminal like you, the murderous enemy of my people, I have nothing but outrage and contempt."[34] For her defiance Iparkhan is eventually executed, a fate she welcomes with an impassioned vow:

> You will not silence me. My voice will resound from the Altay mountains to the fields of Khotan, from the Ili valley to the Qumul [i.e. Hami] plain, the Jungharian steppe to the Taklamakan desert! My call will sound in the hearts and minds of my descendants; it will rouse them to struggle. My ideals will burn like a torch, lighting the road to freedom, and leading them to independence.[35]

Whether or not stories like those of Nazugum or Iparkhan themselves reflect historical events, the tensions they embody have at times figured in political events in Xinjiang. We might note, for example, the similarity between these poetic narratives and accounts of the 1931 uprising in the eastern Xinjiang town of Hami, which eventually led to the establishment of the first Eastern Turkistan Republic in Kashgar. Some, though not all, accounts of this uprising cite the lechery of a Chinese officer towards a local woman as the spark for the conflagration. Guomindang official Aitchen Wu, for example, describes how a certain Captain Chang "had no principle of conduct save the satisfaction of his own immediate desires," and "on a day of evil omen . . . laid hands upon a Moslem girl."[36] While Wu says that local religious elites stirred up a mob to take revenge on the Chinese officer, this story, like Nazugum's, has evolved with time. Former chairman of the provincial government Seypidin Ezizi, for example, heightens the drama in his memoirs. Here he tells how local Uyghurs at first went along with the Chinese captain's request to marry the girl and prepared for the wedding festivities. They then took the opportunity to ambush Chang's troops during the party, launching what eventually became a province-wide insurrection.[37] While the event seems to have some basis in reality, therefore, it also seems to have quickly undergone its own folklorization at the hands of authors such as Ezizi. If that is the case, it provides us with some perspective on the formation of the earlier traditions such as Nazugum's.

5.3   Muffled Echoes in Contemporary Xinjiang

The intersection of literary representations and political realities in Xinjiang is equally worthy of consideration in the present day. Since

2016, the Chinese Communist Party has implemented an unprecedented campaign of ideological indoctrination and cultural assimilation in Xinjiang. One of the aims of these hardline policies is to encourage identification with an all-embracing 'Chinese nation' (*Zhonghua minzu*). From that perspective, officials identify the low rate of intermarriage in Xinjiang as something to be remedied. For some time now, various incentives and forms of suasion have been applied to encourage Uyghurs to intermarry with Han Chinese migrants. More recently, activists outside China have circulated video footage of wedding ceremonies that they claim show Uyghurs who have been compelled into such marriages against their will.[38] A second dimension of today's policies that resonates with stories such as that of Nazugum involves forced labor – both within the network of 're-education' camps themselves, and in large-scale labor programs designed to send 'surplus' non-Han labor to factories elsewhere in Xinjiang or in the Chinese interior. The Chinese government insists that such programs are voluntary, but there is evidence of pressure being applied to fill recruitment quotas, and the risk of saying 'no' to party officials must be high. Human Rights Watch is among those who believe these programs meet a definition of enslavement, and on this basis they accuse the Chinese government of committing crimes against humanity.[39]

At the same time, the political environment today sees heightened scrutiny of Uyghur literary narratives and the intellectuals who transmit them. While resistance against the Qing dynasty is in theory something to be celebrated from the Chinese Communist Party's point of view, stories like Nazugum contain a political message that can discomfort paranoid officials. Since a crackdown on cultural nationalism at the end of the 1980s, Uyghur writers have had to be cautious in rendering explicit any such link between the past and present, but such implications have remained palpable. In 2000, one writer in *Bulaq* described the significance of Molla Bilal's story in these terms:

> Through the tragedy of *Nazugum*, the poet emphasizes the importance of not expecting any mercy from the colonialists. The only solution is to take up arms and rise as one with firm unity. No one else will liberate the homeland: one must rely on one's own strength. It is necessary to have faith in one another, and carry on the struggle to the last, just like Nazugum. Only in this case will the blood of freedom fighters such as Nazugum not have been spilt in vain.[40]

Here, praise for the exploits of an anti-Qing rebel carries an indirect, but obvious message for Uyghur politics in the present.

Among the many dimensions of today's security crackdown, a hunt has been on among the Uyghur political and intellectual elite for insufficiently loyal 'two-faced' individuals. As in the Stalinist witch-hunts of the Soviet Union, political blackmarks from earlier periods have come back to incriminate people, and past words and deeds have been reinterpreted in a new, more suspicious, light. One of the most high-profile instances of persecution in this campaign has been the 'case of the textbooks,' which involves a series of Uyghur literature textbooks for primary schools. These were published with government approval in the 2000s but have now been deemed to be replete with subversive 'pan-Turkist' and 'pan-Islamist' messaging. The officials and scholars responsible for these books have received severe sentences, including two suspended death sentences (i.e. life in prison). From available evidence, the material that has incriminated them consists of precisely the kinds of folklore I have discussed here. A propaganda documentary points to the inclusion of the story of the "Seven Maidens" (*Yette qizlirim*), a legend of female martyrs associated with resistance to Qing rule in the 1760s.[41] Online discussion indicates that the story of Nazugum was also cited as evidence of their guilt.[42] New, heavily Sinified Uyghur language textbooks have been printed to replace the offending textbook. Clearly, the party is determined to prevent any possibility that romanticized stories of past oppression might inspire young Uyghurs to reflect on their present. The fact is, of course, that the harsh punishment meted out to these scholars will very likely only serve to stimulate those kinds of comparisons.

Notes

1 Jo-Ann Gross and Asom Urunbaev, *The Letters of Khwāja 'Ubayd Allāh Aḥrār and His Associates* (Leiden: Brill, 2002), 192.

2 Shah Muḥammad ibn Ḥisam al-Din Payravi, *Jalis-i Mushtaqin*. Institut vostochnykh rukopisei Rossiiskoi akademii nauk, A232 (1004/1595-6), fol. 8b.

3 Muḥammad Amin Ṣadr Kashghari, *Aṣar al-Futuḥ*, Abu Rayhon Beruniy Nomidagi Sharqshunoslik Instituti, 753 (1220/1805-6), fol. 124a.

4 S. D. Dylykov (ed.), *Ikh tsaaz / Velikoe ulozhenie: Pamiatnik mongol'skogo feodal'nogo prava xvii v.* (Moscow: Nauka, 1981).

5 Hosung Shim, '*The State Formation of the Zunghar Principality: A Political History of the Last Centralized State of the Eurasian Steppe*', unpublished Ph.D. thesis, Indiana University (2021), 568.

6 See, for example, Zhongguo diyi lishi dang'anguan (ed.), *Yongzhengchao manwen zhupi zouzhe quanyi* (Hefei: Huangshan shushe, 1993), vol. I, pp. 887–888, vol. II, p. 1862.

7 L. I. Duman, 'Feodal'nyi institut iantsii v vostochnom turkestane v xviii veke,' *Zapiski Instituta vostokovedeniia akademii nauk SSSR* 3 (1935).

8 Xinjiang thus features in a range of literary traditions that fall outside the scope of this essay. See, for example, the case of Jahriyya martyrs among the Hui, discussed in Tommaso Previato, "A Neglected Genealogy of the Martyred Heroines of Islam: (Re)-Writing Women's Participation in Jihad Into the History of Late Imperial Gansu," *Journal of Muslim Minority Affairs* 38, no. 3 (2018).

9 Joanna Waley-Cohen, *Exile in Mid-Qing China: Banishment to Xinjiang, 1758-1820* (New Haven: Yale University Press, 1991), 166. For the detailed regulations governing the dispatch of Muslim slaves to northern Xinjiang, see Zhu Qingqi (ed.), *Xing'an Huilan* (Shanghai: Tushu jichengju, 1834), juan 58.

10 Muḥammad Abd al-Alim, *Islamnama*, Institut vostochnykh rukopisei Rossiiskoi akademii nauk, C311 (1190/1776-7), fol. 34b.

11 Abd al-Alim, *Islamnama*, fol. 36a.

12 Muḥammad Ṣadiq Kashghari, *In Remembrance of the Saints: The Rise and Fall of an Inner Asian Sufi Dynasty*, trans. David Brophy (New York: Columbia University Press, 2021), 47.

13 Kashghari, *In Remembrance of the Saints*, pp. 47–51.

14 Kashghari, *In Remembrance of the Saints*, p. 194.

15 Kashghari, *In Remembrance of the Saints*, p. 89.

16 *Daqing Xuanzong Cheng (Daoguang) huangdi shilu* (Taibei: Huawen shuju, 1964), pp. 4700–4701. The exiling of Muslim criminals to the north of Xinjiang is also discussed in Laura Newby, "Bondage on Qing China's Northwestern Frontier," *Modern Asian Studies* 47, no. 3 (2013): 968–994.

17 Molla Musa Sayrami, *Tarikhi Hemidi*, ed. Enver Baytur (Beijing: Milletler Neshriyati, 1986), 154–155.

18 W. Radloff, *Proben der Volksliteratur der türkischen Stämme* (Saint Petersburg: Tipografiia Imperatorskoi akademii nauk, 1886), vol. VI, p. 271.

19 N. N. Pantusov, *Taranchinskiia p'esni* (Moscow: Akademiia nauk, 1890), 7–8, 85–86.

20 Nikolai Mikhailovich Przheval'skii, *Ot Kiakhty na istoki Zheltoi Reki: Izsledovanie severnoi okrainy Tibeta, i put' cherez Lob-Nor po basseinu Tarima* (Saint Petersburg: Tipografiia V. S. Balasheva, 1888), 429.

21 N. N. Pantusov, "Obraztsy taranchinskoi narodnoi literatury," *Izvestiia obshchestva arkheologii, istorii i etnografii pri imperatorskom kazanskom Universitete* 21, no. 2–4 (1909): 49–60.

22 E. de Zacharko and W. Bang, "Contes Du Turkestan," *Le Muséon* 36, no. 1–2 (1923): 101–125; Emel Esin, "'Nâziğim'in Destani," *Türk Kültürü* 73 (1968): 89–97.

23 Molla Bilal binni Molla Yusup, "Nuzugum," ed. Mehemmet Tursun Bahawidin, *Bulaq* 1 (1981): 208–225. Where Pantusov's text has "Chinese" (Kitai), the Bulaq edition has "Manchu."

24 Pantusov, "Obraztsy taranchinskoi narodnoi literatury," 51.

25 Pantusov, "Obraztsy taranchinskoi narodnoi literatury," 58.
26 Uyghur Balasi, *Nazugum* (Almaty: Uyghur kammunistlirining vilayet byurasi, 1922), 28–29. For a modern version in Cyrillic script Uyghur, see Nezerghoja Abdusémetov, *Yoruq sahillar* (Almaty: Zhazushi, 1991).
27 N. Smailov and Q. Tokhtemov (eds.) *Uyghur sovét edebiyatining tarikhi* (Almaty: Akademiia nauk kazakhskoi SSR, 1986), 148.
28 Ershidin Hidayetov, *Ili Uyghurlarning milliy-azatliq heriketliri* (Almaty: Nauka, 1978), 30.
29 Hézim Iskenderov, *Nazugum* (Almaty: Zhazushi, 1970).
30 K. Kuzham'iarov, *Nazugum* (Moscow: Sovetskii kompozitor, 1963). For Hasanov's play, see Smailov et al., *Uyghur sovét edebiyatining tarikhi*, p. 217.
31 For further discussion of the treatment of Nazugum in Xinjiang, see Kara Abramson, "Gender, Uyghur Identity, and the Story of Nuzugum," *Journal of Asian Studies* 71, no. 4 (2012).
32 James Millward, "A Uyghur Muslim in Qianlong's Court: The Meanings of the Fragrant Concubine," *Journal of Asian Studies* 53, no. 2 (May 1994): 427–458.
33 Ziya Semediy, *Mayimkhan* (Almaty: Zhazushi, 1984), 393–439.
34 Semediy, *Mayimkhan*, p. 426
35 Semediy, *Mayimkhan*, p. 439.
36 Aitchen Wu, *Turkistan Tumult* (Oxford: Oxford University Press, 1984), 65. Modern historians take the basic story seriously, e.g. Chen Zhao and Chen Huisheng, *Minguo Xinjiangshi* (Urumchi: Xinjiang renmin chubanshe, 1999), 248.
37 Seypidin Ezizi, *Ömür dastani* (Urumchi: Minzu chubanshe, 1990), p. 183.
38 For discussion, see Darren Byler, "Uyghur Love in a Time of Interethnic Marriage," *SupChina*, 7 August 2019.
39 Human Rights Watch, *"Break Their Lineage, Break Their Roots'" China's Crimes Against Humanity Targeting Uyghurs and Other Turkic Muslims* (2021), 44–45.
40 Abduréshit Hélimhaji, "Vetenperver Uyghur qizi Nazugum toghrisida," *Bulaq* 2 (2000): 90.
41 "Propaganda Films Attempt to Cloak Xinjiang in Disinformation," *China Digital Times*, 6 April 2021.
42 Ruhe pingjia Xinjiang fankong jilupian disibu 'Anliu yongdong – Zhongguo Xinjiang fankong tiaozhan'?" *Zhihu*. https://web.archive.org/web/202105090 93854/https://www.zhihu.com/question/452494324/answer/1815284055.

CHAPTER 6

Consuming Slavery in China's Epic Domestic Novels

Johanna S. Ransmeier

China's most famous novel was written by the grandson of an imperial slave. This grandfather's experience in no way resembles the deprivation we think of when we imagine slavery. Cao Yin, a bondservant to the Kangxi emperor, became a rich man, a powerful man, but all he once possessed he held at the discretion of his master. As textile commissioner in Nanjing, Cao Yin administered a bureau staff of thousands, managing a substantial flow of imperial revenue throughout the empire's silk producing heartland.[1] Yet his position of responsibility meant that he had everything to lose.[2]

Cao Xueqin recreated a world of karma, obligation, retribution, and precarity in *Dream of the Red Chamber* or *The Story of the Stone*. Scholars have grappled for three centuries with the extent to which Cao Xueqin modeled his epic and intimate tale of the once prosperous but inevitably doomed Jia family on his own autobiography and his grandfather's loss of influence. A robust field of "Red Studies" (*hongxue*) draws connections between historical figures from the Cao family and the fictional world of the Jia, delving into *Dream* as a source for understanding the vibrant material culture of Qing era elites. The acquisition of people and consumption of labor was an essential part of that material culture. The Cao family were ethnically Han Chinese who had settled as agricultural colonists in Manchuria during the waning years of the Ming dynasty (1368–1644). When the Manchus gained control over Mukden/ Shenyang in 1621, the Cao clan were enslaved by the Plain White Banner.[3] After the Manchu conquest of China in 1644, the Qing imperial household incorporated these conquered Han families into both administrative and reproductive servitude. (One of Cao Yin's father's wives served as wet nurse to the infant banner prince who eventually became the Kangxi emperor.)[4] Ethnicity does not play a prominent role in the events of the novel, but ruminations on status, romantic and social aspirations, and mutual obligations do.[5]

6.1 The World of Dream

The domestic setting of *The Dream of the Red Chamber* is the adjoining Rong and Ning Mansions, inhabited by the novel's young protagonist, Jia Baoyu, his many cousins, and their numerous attendants. Within these courtyards and gardens, Baoyu comes of age, falls in and out of love, studies (and more often skips class), consumes a great deal of fragrant tea and wine, and absorbs an enormous amount of concern from the women and girls who dotingly surround him. Together, he and his two primary love interests – the erudite and fragile Lin Daiyu, and her pragmatically lovely rival Xue Baochai – struggle poetically, and movingly, with existential questions of how to be in the world. Their adolescent drama is set against the backdrop of growing corruption among the adults in the household and ultimately against the loss of the Jia family fortune.

One form of conspicuous wealth the Jia family possessed was people. Their mansions bustled with pages, cooks, nursemaids, and enslaved girls. These men, women, and children would have been incorporated into the households of the wealthy in diverse ways, bound by different kinds of contracts, employment arrangements, indenture, or outright sales. The Jia family owned several trunks of "property deeds and bonds for household servants."[6] The extent to which any of these arrangements were reversible depended upon many factors, not least – but not solely or even necessarily – the initial terms, whether or not family lived nearby, the type of labor supplied, the judgment of a local magistrate. Gradations of status that may seem bewildering to us amounted to an explicit hierarchical system by which labor, sexual, and reproductive services could be extracted.

When Lin Daiyu arrived at the Jia residence, she brought with her only two attendants, her old wet nurse and a ten-year-old girl. But this was quickly remedied; she, like her other five cousins, was supplied with a personal staff of at least ten.[7] Each of the main characters exists both as themselves, and through a kind of double, in the form of the enslaved domestic servant who attended them.[8] Thus, Zijuan waits attentively upon Lin Daiyu, Ying'er on Xue Baochai; Hua Xiren caters to Baoyu even in his bedroom, and Yuanyang loyally serves the Jia matriarch, Baoyu's grandmother, Jia Mu. Each gains a measure of status from their relationship with their master or mistress, but Yuanyang is the only young enslaved female who manages to deploy that relationship to protect herself from sexual predation. When she wants to rebuff Baoyu's lecherous uncle, Jia She, Yuanyang hails her elderly mistress's displeasure in order to protect her virtue. In the end, however, the matriarch's patronage leaves Yuanyang vulnerable. Her devotion eventually turns to despair; when Jia Mu dies, Yuanyang can see no future and hangs herself. The author depicts Yuanyang's decision to die with what might best be described as unquestioning compassion. "With resolve" and "as if in a trance" she methodically unties her sash and secures it to a beam overhead. The author allows Yuanyang "one last fit of weeping" before describing the slip-knot, the noose, the overturned footstool.[9] His purported empathy rings hollow to a contemporary reader seeking to understand the lived experience of the enslaved, but for the seventeenth-century author and reader, Yuanyang's death appears a languid, measured fate for a slave with no one to serve.[10]

Cao Xueqin portrays mistress, master, servant and enslaved alike with meticulous colorful detail, from the texture and color of clothing, jewelry, hair ornamentations, to mannerisms, tone of voice, and personality. Through physical details Cao Xueqin reveals rivalries, weaves together the relationships, and forecasts the futures of his characters. Xu Baochai's austere, muted clothing and simple coiled braid stand in contrast with the more frivolous spontaneous style of her own attendant, Ying'er. Lin Daiyu's affection for short-lived garden blossoms and delicate silk foreshadow her brief life, while also explaining why Daiyu never quite gets along with either Baochai's Ying'er or Baoyu's Qingwen – their tastes and hasty tempers are too similar. Jia Baoyu's own bedroom companion Hua Xiren so thoroughly resembles Xue Baochai in posture and comportment that at several critical junctures Baoyu confuses the two. Although they suffer occasional bouts of jealousy, the young mistresses themselves generally seem to celebrate their good fortune. Baochai remarks: "Whenever we start gossiping about personalities, we nearly always end up by agreeing what exceptional people you and the other chief maids are. And all exceptional in your own different ways too, – that's what's so interesting."[11]

Despite this jovial and seemingly equitable descriptive treatment, a three-way transaction exists between author, reader, and character. This transaction exploits the social position of the slave characters. We are forced to accept that no matter how compelling the storylines that the enslaved are permitted (and this is an epic tale, so there are many rich and entertaining subplots – confused messages and mis-assignments), in the end the purpose for any enslaved character to exist in the text at all, is to forward the narrative for Baoyu, Daiyu, and Baochai. We find here then, an idealized vision of the role of a slave. Her entire identity, even her precocious or disobedient personality, is put to use, subsumed by the author to service the character who owns her.

Sometimes, what this means is simply that the enslaved character scurries to and fro running errands or delivering messages for master or mistress. It often entailed participating in enforced play, sometimes enjoying the food, wine, and games – partaking in the luxuries of an intimate garden party – but also wiping up mistresses' tears and disposing of their vomit, their sweat-drenched bedding or menstrual clothes.[12] Baoyu's male slave, the young and impudent Mingyan, must not only follow orders, but guard his master's door, anticipate his sexual desires, and – depending upon the needs of the narrator – both lead him into and avert him from folly. Mingyan embodies aspects of Baoyu's lusty sub-conscience, understanding better than Baoyu himself his master's complicated competing desires for Daiyu and Baochai.

To the extent that elite status constrains the behavior of the principal characters, Cao Xueqin dispatches subservient characters to vocalize the things that their masters and mistresses cannot. Baochai is much too shy and proper to tell Baoyu that she carries a golden pendant with a couplet that perfectly matches the verse inscribed on the special jade found under Baoyu's tongue when he was born. But, as he must be told for the story to move on, Ying'er impetuously shares her mistress's secret. Characters like Ying'er are not free, but rather they are "available" to the narrative to make observations.

In later chapters, it is through these characters eyes that the corruption and decline of the family becomes evident. They are perhaps exquisitely more sensitive than their owners to subtle signs that Confucian relations are deteriorating, that their world is shifting. Mistresses plot against their junior concubine rivals, tea party games of competitive poetry writing are eclipsed by gambling, and enslaved people increasingly overstep their assigned bounds. Along the garden pathways and within the courtyards and bedrooms of the mansions, the presence of an enslaved character anticipates the arrival or departure of her mistress. All the characters are moved like chess pieces, in refracting, repetitive, ever-refining patterns – inexorably toward the dénouement of the story. As in Chinese society more widely – though no one in this world is truly free – masters enjoy much greater latitude (and lassitude) than those they enslave.

Patterns of events recur between master and servant: Across 120 chapters, the relationships in the book themselves lock the characters into an elaborate pattern of mirroring, so that, for example, even the first time a master beats an enslaved person, it reverberates upon another pair, and subsequent beatings are sure to ensue.[13] Cao Xueqin, and to a lesser degree his editor, Gao E (whom Hu Shi believed wrote the epic's final forty chapters) created a tightly knit cycle of retribution. But the retribution that Cao Xueqin remains most concerned with is grander than the discipline meted out to individuals; the debt of tears that Daiyu (the earthly incarnation of the Crimson Pearl fairy) owes Baoyu (the reincarnation of a celestial stone),[14] and a public reasoning-through or reckoning-with his own family's loss of imperial favor (through the decline of the fictional Jia family).

The reader is wittingly or unwittingly co-opted into the author's system of slavery, a system of domestic transactions which undergird the entire flow of life in the Rong and Ning mansions. Beneath the personal attendants, companions, concubines, and named serving maids who appear as active participants in the intrigues of the novel, the Jia family mansions also necessarily engaged a vast substructure of enslaved people who ran the household: gardeners, cooks, craftsmen, laundrywomen, entertainers. The sumptuous life enjoyed by the Jia cousins would have required a stunning amount of labor. And yet, we catch only the barest glimpses of these men and women as they plant trees, sweep terraces, hang decorations, prepare and deliver food.

6.2 An Inescapable Hierarchy

When we consider the extent to which slavery is both woven into the world evoked in China's great domestic novels, and yet simultaneously utterly unchallenged, it is perhaps helpful to recall how tenuous even the position of the powerful could be. Slavery and transactions in people shaped Chinese society at every level, and thus cannot be understood as a binary between free and unfree, but rather as a part of a hierarchical continuum. The rise and fall of a lineage like the Cao family provides a context for understanding how precarity worked in Chinese society, yet also shows how the mechanisms of slavery remain obscured, all while operating in plain view. Slavery was so prevalent that it is hard to see. Indeed, China scholars have often gone into great contortions to avoid labeling exploitation and the ownership of people as it persisted in China as "slavery." The Confucian hierarchical logic made slavery seem reasonable, the luxury of the elite world as portrayed in Ming and Qing literature glamorized the consumption of people.

But the transactional mechanisms that made slavery possible were everywhere. As I have written elsewhere, much of Chinese family life was built upon a foundation of trafficking.[15] In domestic literature, readers do not encounter the sale of people as a social injustice. There are isolated instances where the reader is encouraged to view the sale or forced loss of freedom of a character as a *personal* injustice, occurring most often if the identity of the person being sold is constructed by the author as especially morally worthy or upright.[16] To be sure, readers and theatregoers in the Ming and Qing were fascinated and titillated by stories of fallen women, and by the lives of courtesans. Redeeming a sold person was seen as a virtuous act and could help an individual accrue merit. Transactions in people often marked a critical turning point in the plot of numerous Ming and Qing vernacular novellas (*huaben*) and plays. Feng Menglong's "The Oil Seller Wins the Prize Courtesan," first published in Suzhou around 1620 and later reconceived as a play by Li Yu, is but one example. In this story readers encounter a savvy young woman, literally sold into prostitution, who is able to both advise her future husband on sound investments and buy herself out of brothel life.[17] A family forced to sell a beloved daughter to a brothel, might move an audience to tears, but as a tragedy, the event was experienced as in isolation. To save to buy oneself out of slavery required personal gumption and foresight: admirable, but also portrayed in a way that, in essence, legitimated the rights of an owner or brothel keeper. No great novels bemoaned the existence of slavery, pointed out a social ill, or extolled society to remedy its ways. Slavery was not a collective grievance.

Indeed, the idea that it might be perceived in this way was startling. When Harriet Beecher Stowe's *Uncle Tom's Cabin* was translated into Chinese at the end of the Qing dynasty, the novel was received as a revelation.[18] This was no doubt in part because America and its slave system seemed so foreign, so exotic, but it was also because of the way Stowe's novel placed the experience of the enslaved – and the wrong of slavery – at the heart of her story. There was no tradition of the "slave narrative" in China. There was no religiously or politically committed abolition movement. For the most part, the High Qing critique of trafficking came in the form of the literate courtesan or abandoned wife bemoaning her fate in verse. Again, her experience was poignant, and singular. And yet the vast majority inhabitants of the Qing Empire, and virtually all Chinese women, lived under a "Chinese chattel principle" – facing sufficiently dire circumstances, anyone could be sold.[19]

As often as not, however, routine poverty or even an eye toward upward mobility for the rest of the family propelled the kinds of transactions that placed enslaved people in households like the Jia or the Cao. Working in a household, enslaved people themselves were acutely aware of the variations in status definition. Those born into the family received fewer privileges and less respect than new arrivals – among the girls, this likely stemmed at least in part from more restricted potential to promote oneself by attracting the affections of one of the family's young (or older) men; less chance to become a concubine. When Hua Xiren's parents sold her to serve Baoyu, perhaps they already appreciated the Jia household's reputation for treating its elite enslaved "better than girls living outside." Certainly, Xiren later expressed satisfaction with her relative good fortune and the budding sexual relationship with the person who held her in bondage; declining her parents offer to buy her back. Her refusal is revealing, however: "If you were still hard up and wanted to buy me out so that you could raise a bit of money by reselling me, there would be some point in it. But you're not. What do you want to buy me out for? Why don't you just pretend that I am dead, and then you won't need to think about buying me out anymore."[20] She releases her parents from any obligation, but in doing so, also acknowledges that in being enslaved, she is, in some ways already dead. She provides us with a startling example from the world of eighteenth-century Chinese fiction of the applicability of Orlando Patterson's theory that slavery constitutes a form of social death.[21]

Still, her relationship with the man who enslaved her is complicated. Readers hear Hua Xiren balk when the slaveholder expressed interest in another young girl from the Hua family. "Because I have the misfortune to be a slave," she scolds him "does that mean that all my relations ought to be slaves too? I suppose you think every pretty girl you see is just waiting to be bought so that she can be a servant in your household!"[22] The author allows Xiren the chance to offer a critique, but it's of her master's roving eyes, not of the system. She knows how it works. Incensed and jealous, Xiren seizes this opportunity to remind Baoyu that her family has, at least, in theory, a stake in her future. She is, after all, "not one of your house-born slaves."[23]

Merely having arrived from outside the household offered no guarantee of protection or privilege, as a gentle enslaved girl, whom the family would call Xiangling, knew too well. Snatched from her childhood home next to the Bottle-gourd Temple at the age of five, Zhen Yinglian's kidnapper raised her with the express intent of selling her when she reached sexual maturity. Her story appears at the beginning of the novel and helps further illuminate prevailing attitudes toward slavery and trafficking as part of accepted family formation.

Yinglian's situation presents the newly instilled magistrate of Yingtian Prefecture with a moral conundrum, but it isn't her kidnapping itself that bothers him. It transpired that the kidnapper had sold Yinglian twice in the span of just a few days; first promising her to an older gentleman who (despite an established preference for young boys) found Yinglian charming and claimed that he intended to marry her, and then shortly thereafter also taking money from a hot-headed young man named Xue Pan. In the resulting conflict, Xue Pan kills the first buyer. It is this murder – not Yinglian's kidnapping – that catches the magistrate's attention. It appears on his desk as a piece of unfinished business; what looks like an open and shut case left behind by his predecessor. Jia Yucun is on the cusp of forwarding his statement condemning Xue Pan when his more experienced clerk stops him with a rhyme known as "The Magistrate's Life Preserver." This piece of doggerel verse enumerates the wealth of the four most powerful local families and warns against standing in their way. Realizing that Xue Pan comes from one of these clans, Jia Yucun bows to the will of the Xue matriarch and arranges to drop the charge.

Jia Yucun's decision foreshadows the corruption that will run rampant through the family by the novel's end. In the meantime, Yinglian now belongs to Xue Pan. Kidnapping was supposedly illegal under the Qing code, but so, after all, was murder.[24] Xue Pan would be held accountable for neither. The logic of slavery and hierarchy would prevail even over the law. He proves to be an abusive owner, sexually predatory even as his wife lashes out at Yinglian/Xiangling in escalating invidious fits. Although the gentle cultured cousins of the Jia family pity Xiangling, inviting her to join them in composing poetry, offering temporary shelter from her mistress's anger, they again also acquiesce to Xue Pan's irrevocable authority over his property.[25]

Readers of *Dream* entered a world where they too (we too?) must accept the legitimacy of these hierarchies in order to partake in the drama of the story. To feel distraught on behalf of the characters that their world is in upheaval, requires that readers – at least to some extent – empathize with that social order. We are meant to mourn its loss. Cao Xueqin's attention to female characters has led numerous scholars to suggest that an inversion of the household hierarchy implies a feminist or at least anti-patriarchal agenda.[26] Cao himself articulated his own nostalgia in the novel as a paean to the lost girl companions of his childhood.[27] While the novel asks us to identify with female characters, it certainly does not seek their liberation. The celebrated inversion of authority – regardless of dynamic multidimensional female characters – is part of the tragic imperfection, inherent to Jia Baoyu's dreamlike garden existence. His own fatal flaw, after all, is the feminine predilection he revealed from infancy and revels in throughout the novel. The author has created a world destined for corruption; a diaphanous illusion that cannot endure. A steady flow of omens, signs, rhymes, rebuses, allusions and accumulated poetic signals warn readers from the outset that the young love between Lin Daiyu and Jia Baoyu is doomed. By compelling sympathy for the demise of their love, the decline of the Jia household, and the social unravelling that ensues, the novel the reinforces rather than undermines the exploitative patriarchal order of the Qing.

6.3   Precarity in a Persistent Order

Thus, the novel establishes the characters' stake in the established order of things, while simultaneously chastising both characters and readers alike with symbolic reminders that hierarchy itself was a durable structure but could prove impermanent for individuals. The entire premise of the imperial domestic novel is precarity. And yet, whether in *The Dream of the Red Chamber*, or its libidinous Ming dynasty predecessor, *The Plum and the Golden Vase*, the reader experiences the decline of the household and the fall of the male protagonist as inevitable. We are not exactly in suspense. Lin Daiyu must pay her debt of tears, Jia Baoyu lacks the masculinity and moral force (or even attention span) to save his household from ruin, and, in *Plum*, the merchant Ximen Qing's sexual appetites and profligate spending inevitably lead to his expiration.

Under the hand of a dictatorial narrator, even the main characters in these novels are not "free." Instead, they too are bound by cycles of karmic retribution. In the case of *The Plum and the Golden Vase*, the characters are harnessed to a historical allegory that locks their fate to the double imperial folly of the Ming Dynasty Wanli reign (when the text was written) and the Song Dynasty under reign of Emperor Huizong (the historical setting). If it is unclear where autobiography ends and fiction begins for Cao Xueqin, considerably less is certain about the deliberately anonymous author of *The Plum and the Golden Vase*.[28] Drawing upon clues in the novel's preface – the style of which makes clear it came from the same hand as the novel itself –preeminent *Plum* expert David Todd Roy argues that the author was an adherent of the third-century Warring States period Confucian philosopher Xunzi.[29] Roy believes that the author intended to unveil the hypocrisy of Mencius's version of Confucianism, especially in its Neo-Confucian form, which maintained the "complacent assumption that human nature is basically good." [30] Frustrated with the corruption he witnessed in the Late Ming, the author employed as his "vehicle of critique" a Xunzi-inspired Legalist tale that shows man to be as evil as he truly is.

As the novel unfolds, the rapacious merchant Ximen Qing enthusiastically partakes in every vice imaginable; his household becomes increasingly mired in corruption, and the women Ximen Qing has acquired compete for status and for his sexual attention with escalating vindictiveness. After hundreds of pages of carousing, deception, and predation, Ximen Qing finally dies an excruciating death in the priapic throes of an overdose of an aphrodisiac, ejaculating to the point of utter depletion. There is a lot of sexual satisfaction along Ximen Qing's road to retribution.[31]

Ximen Qing's consumption of women may well be unmatched in literature. Early in the novel the narrator informs us:

> Whenever he established a liaison with a woman, even one of good family, he was wont to take her into his establishment; but if she should then fail to please him in any way, however slight, he would call in a go-between and dispose of her without more ado. It was said that he sometimes resorted to the services of brokers as often as twenty times in a single month. As a result, no one dared cross him.[32]

Several things are interesting about this relatively detached and dry observation. First, is the omnipresence and ease with which brokers could be engaged, even for a woman "from a good family." We meet several different kinds of brokers throughout the novel, providing a sense of the range of people who got involved in this business; matchmakers arranging to transfer an inconvenient widow to a new household, traffickers supplying brothels, old men who engage intermediaries to facilitate trading concubines amongst themselves. And this just covers the sexual side of the trade. The *Plum* author was less concerned with describing the physical labor regime that must also have fueled Ximen Qing's life of dissipation.

Second, the narrator suggests an "easy-come, easy-go" attitude, such that we imagine Ximen Qing sending his women and girls away – but as the novel progresses and his appetite continues unabated – women are sexually dispatched, depleted, beaten, but rarely "disposed of." Indeed, on his deathbed Ximen Qing begs his women to remain together. (They don't; instead, each disperses to her own bleak fate.) Third, readers should not expect outsiders to dare to check his behavior. Finally, (and most relevant to my argument) amid all the deviant ecstasy, carnality, voyeurism, sadomasochism, amid a disregard for any norms constraining his sexual behavior, Ximen Qing retains a peculiarly normative need to possess his partners and integrate them into his household.

The Plum and the Golden Vase began circulating over a hundred years before *The Dream of the Red Chamber*, and in many ways set the stage for the development of Chinese novels in which the dramatic intrigue would be constructed around domestic spaces and romantic/sexual tension. The settings are almost claustrophobically confined, the stakes of the rivalries, deadly.

Every one of the women in Ximen Qing's household arrived through brokered transactions. Many were trafficked multiple times. The degree of practical coercion involved in executing such sales is largely obscured by the erotic storyline; subservience or defiance in the ensuing highly unequal sexual encounters serves to heighten the characters' (and likely the readers') arousal. The novel contains an abundance of detail about material life. A profligate spender, Ximin Qing compulsively commissions luxury goods, renovations to his garden and home, purchases exotic sex toys and potions. There is plenty of evidence here for a historian wishing to reconstruct an economic world, and what it cost to buy a girl.[33]

While it is clear that Ximen Qing is no hero, eighty chapters is indeed a long time to wait for a comeuppance. In the meantime, readers are engaged on multiple levels, drawn deeper and deeper into an erotica of delight/disgust. The more we read, the more complicit we are in the sales and sexual exploitation that propel the novel.

This leaves the reader in a paradoxical position with respect to the imbedded Xunzist social criticism proposed by David Tod Roy. Tina Lu has suggested that the novel's sprawling epic form, previously untried in its day, constituted an experiment in genre that allowed the author of *Plum* to "grapple with connections between people of different status" and perhaps even to "theorize slavery."[34] Certainly transactions in people are central to the plot; plenty about the transactional Chinese household can be deduced from both *Dream* and *Plum*. The materialistic focus of the world of the insatiable Ximen Qing offers a clearer accounting of the cost of people. There is significantly more violence in the representation of the lives of sold people in *Plum* than in *Dream*. But *Plum's* violence appears as erotic expression; Ximen Qing routinely beats or threatens to beat the women he beds, often providing apparent sexual satisfaction to a voyeur or a later conquest, and possibly arousing the same in readers. Despite the beatings, the *Plum* author leaves even the most skeptical reader no room to speculate that the sex that follows is anything other than consensual, so enthusiastic are the women who protest that "Daddy" hasn't been paying them enough attention. They, in turn, redirect their aggression on their rivals. Real world counterparts of Ximen Qing's women had little legal space to rebuff violent abuse or sexual demands.[35]

If we accept Roy's assertion that the *Plum* author intended to expose man's irrepressibly worst self, and to criticize the evils of his day, was slavery one of those evils? I don't believe so. More in this text indicates that the author still subscribed to the legitimacy of traditional hierarchies and the transactional mechanisms that enabled them. Much is explicitly marked as deviant in this late Ming novel, but the sales – so very frequent – are not presented as the least bit "remarkable." There is no editorial commentary on the justness or unjustness of selling women. To the extent that judgement occurs, it is about Ximen Qing's excesses, not about the societal process of trafficking or even the entitlements of a master/buyer. Readers may be called upon to witness moral decay, but the human transactions themselves are notably not an explicit site of moralizing.

Looking at these two domestic novels (separated by a century and a dynastic conquest) alongside one another, can we read the first as critique and the second as celebration? No. Although their timbre and motivation differ, each remains heavily invested in a patriarchy grounded in Confucian and Buddhist retributive ethics that assumed – rather than challenged – the legitimacy of transactions in people. *The Dream of the Red Chamber* nurtures a nostalgia for the lost youthful garden world, where Jia Baoyu frolicked with his cousins, all the while benefitting from the devotions of countless enslaved people who made their comfort possible. *The Plum in the Golden Vase* lures readers into the sensual and sexual pleasures of subjugation and the consumption of women. As retributive forces move each master inexorably nearer to the loss of his idyllic world and closer to the collapse of his doomed household, the novels take for granted readers' stakes in that world and their/our acceptance of the precarious and transactional nature of human domestic relationships.

It is no accident that perhaps the most influential novel in China's literary history centers on family life. Nor is it an accident that the author of *The Dream of the Red Chamber* was a descendant of war captives and enslaved people. But it is equally not an accident that no matter how circumscribed by transactions any Chinese novel's characters were, immersed in the opulent world of the Ming and Qing domestic novel, we have been dazzled blind to their imbedded stories of slavery.

Notes

1 Jonathan D. Spence, *Ts'ao Yin and the Kang-hsi Emperor: Bondservant and Master* (New Haven: Yale University Press, 1966). Hu Shi, "Hongloumeng kaozheng." In *Hu Shi wencun* [Collected Essays of Hu Shi] (Shanghai yadong tushuguan, 1930), 185–249.

2 Orlando Patterson, 'The Ultimate Slave,' *Slavery and Social Death* (Cambridge MA: Harvard University Press: 1982).

3 The banner system began as an essential part of Manchu/Jurchen social and military organization, originally as a way of organizing clans into hunting parties and as a means of managing an expanding and mobile steppe population. After the Manchus overthrew the Ming and established the Qing dynasty the Eight Banners remained fundamental to Manchu identity. All Manchu households belonged to one of the banners, often living in close community in their garrison. The "Plain White Banner" was the banner group with the closest ties to the Qing imperial household, and accordingly placed the Cao family in a position of potential influence, but also under considerable obligation.

4 David Hawkes, "Preface" to Cao Xueqin, *The Story of the Stone, also known as The Dream of the Red Chamber*, Volume 1, "The Golden Days," translated by David Hawkes (Penguin, 1973).

5 Banner identity likely played a larger role in the shape of the text than I can explain here. Cao Xueqin's editor, Gao E, who eventually took upon himself the task of completing *Dream*, was also from a Chinese Banner household, and the two men likely shared a similar perspective on Qing society. John Minford, "Preface" to Cao Xueqin, *The Story of the Stone, also known as The Dream of the Red Chamber*, Volume 4, translated by John Minford (New York: Penguin, 1982).

6 Cao Xueqin, *The Story of the Stone, also known as The Dream of the Red Chamber* Volume 5, The Dreamer Wakes, edited by Gao E, Translated by John Minford (New York: Penguin, 1982), 120.

7 Cao, *Dream*, Vol. 1, p. 105.

8 Marsha L. Wagner, "Maids and Servants in Dream of the Red Chamber: Individuality and the Social Order." In *Expressions of Self in Chinese Literature*, ed. Robert E. Hegel and Richard C. Hessney (New York: Columbia University Press, 1985), 251–281.

9 Cao, *Dream*, Vol. 5, p. 209.

10 Upon arriving in the spirit realm, the ghostly Qin Keqing informs Yuanyang that she has been selected to take over Keqing's former position as arbiter of "Fond Infatuation." Suicide provided no escape from the entanglements of the Jia household. Even the masters still living praise Yuanyang for her courage and express gratitude that in death "she has given fullest expression to *our* devotion." Cao, *Dream*, Vol. 5, p. 213. Even her death could not be her own.

11 Cao Xueqin, *The Story of the Stone, also known as The Dream of the Red Chamber*, Volume 2, *The Crab-Flower Club*, Translated by David Hawkes (New York: Penguin, 1977), 261.

12 One particularly overheated scene between Baoyu and Daiyu leaves Ying'er discretely offering up her own handkerchief as Daiyu vomits up a medicinal draught of elshotzia leaves that the fragile young mistress had taken earlier that day. As if unsure what else to do, Ying'er and Xiren both join the master and mistress in overwrought silent tears. Again, their emotions are hostage to their masters. Cao, *Dream*, Vol. 2, p. 89.

13 Wagner, "Maids." In *Expressions of Self in Chinese Literature*, pp. 276–277.

14 Cao, *Dream*, Vol. 1, pp. 53–54.

15 Johanna S. Ransmeier, *Sold People: Traffickers and Family Life in North China* (Cambridge MA: Harvard University Press, 2017), 2.

16 This elision of relative morality as a determining element in whether or not an individual could legitimately be sold developed after the Yongzheng emancipation edicts (1723–1728) as the distinction between *jian* or *liang* – mean person or commoner – shifted from a status identity to a moral identity. Matthew H. Sommer, *Sex, Law and Society in Late Imperial China* (Stanford University Press, 2000).

17 Ariel Fox discusses "The Oil Peddler Wins the Prize Courtesan" 賣油郎獨占花魁 from Feng Menglong's *Constant Words to Awaken the World* (*Xingshi hengyan* 醒世恆言) as well as and other vivid examples of the role of commerce in Ming and Qing drama in Chapter 2 'Every Man a Merchant' of *The Cornucopian Stage: Performing Commerce in Early Modern China*, forthcoming manuscript.

18 The stage adaptation, entitled "A Black Slave's Cry to Heaven" (*Heinu yu tian lu*), first performed by the Spring Willow Society in Tokyo in 1907, inspired still more popular enthusiasm, both in Japan and later in China. Wen Jin, "Sentimentalism's Transnational Journeys: 'Bitter Society' and Lin Shu's Translation of Uncle Tom's Cabin," *Modern Chinese Literature and Culture* 26, no. 4 (Spring 2014): 105–136.

19 Ransmeier, *Sold People*, p. 319.

20 Cao, *Dream*, Vol. 1, p. 388.

21 Patterson, *Slavery and Social Death*.

22 Cao, *Dream*, Vol. 1, p. 385.

23 Cao, *Dream*, Vol. 1, p. 385.

24 Xiaohuan Zhao, "Court Trials and Miscarriage of Justice in Dream of the Red Chamber," *Law and Literature* 23, no. 1 (Spring 2011): 129–156.

25 In one version of the text, Zhen Yanglian dies in childbirth, in another she dies from cruel treatment at the hands of her master.

26 Han Huiqiang, "'Honglou meng' zhong de xing guannian ji wenhua yiyi" ('Sexual concepts and the cultural significance of "Honglou meng"') from *Beijing daxue yanjiusheng xuekan* 1: 77–82. Compiled by Renmin University, Fuyin baokan ziliao "Honglou meng" yanjiu (Copied Materials of Journals and Newspapers on "Honglou meng" Research) 2: 17–22. (Beijing: 1988). R.

Keith McMahon, "A Case for Confucian Sexuality: The Eighteenth-Century Novel 'Yesou puyan'," *Late Imperial China* 9, no. 2 (December 1988): 32–55. Louise Edwards critiques these scholars and others with similar perspectives in "Women in Hongloumeng: Prescriptions of Purity in the Femininity of Qing China," *Modern China* 16, no. 4 (October 1990).

27 Hawkes, "Preface," *Dream*, pp. 20–21.

28 Although, if his identity were ever to be revealed to be one of the prominent author-scholars of his day, then we would suddenly know a great deal. David Todd Roy believed that the prolific playwright Tang Xianzu was responsible for this epic tale. Roy, "Preface" to *The Plum and the Golden Vase or, Chin P'ing Mei*, Volume One: The Gathering, translated by David Tod Roy (Princeton: Princeton University Press, 1993), xliii.

29 The association with Xunzi is made explicit in the preface author's choice of a pseudonym "The Scoffing Scholar of Lan-Ling" that Roy believes specifically refers to Xunzi's hometown. Roy, "Preface," p. xxiii.

30 Roy, "Preface,'" p. xli.

31 As Tina Lu writes, "In the case of the *Jinpingmei*, the text's very length obscures whether its characters are getting their just deserts." From "Slavery and Genre in *The Plum in the Golden Vase*" In "Slavery in Early Modern East, Inner, and Southeast Asia," special issue of *Harvard Journal of Asiatic Studies* 81, no. 1 (forthcoming, expected 2022).

32 *Plum*, p. 53.

33 We even learn what it was worth to matchmakers Ximen Qing employed. "I hope to take out a mortgage on a couple of rooms in a better location than that out-of-way corner in the northern quarter where I'm living now," Auntie Xie explains, as she reminds Ximen Qing that he also owes her several bolts of cloth for helping him purchase a slave girl the previous year. A lusty young widow is worth a couple of rooms; a slave girl, several bolts of cloth. *Plum*, pp. 132–133.

34 Lu, "Slavery and Genre"

35 Archival court records and magistrates' handbooks reveal that both wives and concubines using their limited power to castigate both household staff and children, whether with beatings, scalding water, or withholding food. While women could not always act with the same impunity as men, the Qing legal codes allowed affluent women to remit punishment with a fine. I speculate that for this reason the task of enforcing household discipline was sometimes delegated to the women.

CHAPTER 7

The Language of Slavery in the Mongolian Literary Tradition

Sam H. Bass

Before the advent of mechanical printing and mass production of pamphlets, journals, and books, literary works were widespread through the Mongol literate world of Inner Asia through the transmission of manuscripts and prints pressed from woodblocks.[1] Nineteenth-century travelers remarked that clergy learned to read Tibetan only, so that even among educated Mongols there were many "who do not even know their own Mongol alphabet."[2] However, literacy among the population was higher than these travelers' accounts suggest. Members of the clergy taught non-ecclesial members of their families in informal home schools and the Qing imperial administration maintained schools to teach Mongol and Manchu writing to future scribes.[3] The rate of literacy in pre-twentieth century Mongolia was probably less than 10 percent for men and around 1 percent for women, but partial literacy was high and widespread monasticism meant that the literate population was dispersed through the countryside rather than relegated to urban centers only.[4] This relatively widespread access to the written word meant that literature was more than just the purview of the elite strata in Mongolia before the advent of mass literacy in the twentieth century.

Slavery and servitude are common elements in the Mongolian literary tradition. The terminology of slavery in Mongolia changed over time with political and cultural transformations, and the ambiguities of the terms for slavery – encompassing occupational, gendered, and ethnic concepts – frustrate formalist attempts at translation and analysis. In early literary monuments, the occupational status of *boġol* paralleled the metaphorical use of the word as "slave" in didactic texts. In the early modern period, the ethnic appellation *kitad* or Chinese appeared first in legal texts but then in literary works as well. However, sensitivity to ethnic tensions and changing demographics of Inner Asia in the Qing Empire (1644–1912), of which Mongolia was a vassal or colony, led to the abandonment of the term. By the twentieth century, the ambiguity of the terminology of slavery faded as the political imperatives of understanding slavery either in a dogmatic socialist way or as a metaphor for oppression took precedence in Mongolian literature.

In this essay, I introduce several key terms related to slavery in Mongolian literature and provide some information about their meaning in their literary context. I focus on two literary terms, *boğol* and *kitad*, to demonstrate how the terminology of slavery in Mongolian literature has changed with political, religious, and cultural interactions. As such, this is not an exhaustive survey or list of every term used to indicate slavery and servitude in Mongolian, but a more focused exploration of inter-related terms in the context of Mongolian literature. I draw examples from several important literary works in the Mongolian canon from the earliest known printed works to twentieth-century popular literature. These include works originally composed in Mongolian as well as translated works, primarily from Chinese and Tibetan.

Although slavery is a recurring concept in Mongolian literary works, it was rarely the central conceit of a story or subject of reflection. As Steven Epstein remarks about Italian literature, "these writings are *about* slaves," but are neither slave narratives nor explorations of the nature of slavery.[5] In Walther Heissig's seminal study of Mongolian epic motifs, the enslaved and slavery are common topics but the condition or fact of slavery is unremarked upon both in the works he analyzes and in Heissig's comments, with one exception. Heissig identifies the motif of "estranged enslaved parents." This motif recurs through Mongolian epic literature, for example in the Tibeto-Mongol epic *Geser*.[6] It appears in the Buryat epic poem *The Fifteen-year-old Boy Altai Sümbür Abai* (Mo. *Arban tabun nasutai Altai Sümbür abai köbegün*, recorded in the twentieth century) when the hero disguises himself as an astrologer to find and fight the monster. On his way, the hero discovers that the dung-collector and an old woman are his parents, made slaves (*boğol barluq*) by the monster, fed only filthy water, and made to sleep on thin mats. The hero slays the monster, declaring that he is taking revenge for his parents, and then frees all the people enslaved by the monster and apportions the monster's plundered livestock among them.[7] The condition of slavery in these tales is misery and humiliation, the result of captivity, and usually results in heroic liberation. In the absence of slave narratives or other literary examinations of slavery or the life of the enslaved, the role and significance of enslaved people, the meaning of slavery in an abstract sense, and the terminology employed to describe slavery are the material of the study of slavery in Mongolian literature.

The common terms for slavery in Mongolian literature – *boġol* and *kitad* – are not originally Mongolian words; I discuss their etymologies below.[8] One native Mongolian word for "slave" is *köbüd*, which is a contraction of the word *köbegüd*, meaning "children" but *köbüd* is singular.[9] The contraction is not uniformly used, and sometimes *köbegün* "child, boy, son" was used instead. *Köbüd* and *köbegün* are frequently modified with *ger-ün* "of the tent," or simply "domestic" so that *ger-ün köbegün*, "child of the tent" or "domestic child" became a term for enslaved people regardless of their age and gender. This usage appears in the earliest instance in the medieval *Secret History of the Mongols* (1252, hereafter *SHM*) referring to male and female enslaved domestics.[10] Similarly, the ambiguous term *jalaġu*, meaning both "young man" and "servant" sometimes meant "slave," especially in pre-sixteenth century literature including the *SHM* and the Mongolian translation of the *Guide to the Bodhisattva's Way of Life*. Historical materials from the medieval period to the nineteenth century use all the terms of slavery discussed here and more, but *ger-ün köbegün/köbüd* are most common in administrative documents, and even found their way into Chinese records during the period of Mongol hegemony over East Asia in the form of *qiè lián kŏu* 怯憐□, a phonetic transcription of *ger-ün köbüd*.[11]

In northeast medieval East Asia, the overlapping categories of occupation and status between Chinese and the Mongolic languages of the Kitan khanate or Liao Dynasty comingled and generated new terms of servitude: *boġol*, discussed in the next section. The ethnic term Kitan shifted meaning over the following centuries, and by the late medieval period, *kitad* – derived from the ethnonym Kitan – meant "Chinese" but also "slave" to Mongolian speakers. The meaning and usage of *kitad* as "slave" is clear in literary contexts as discussed below. Unlike the European context, these terms never displaced the native Mongolian terms for slavery and instead mingled in literary and administrative use with *köbüd* and *ger-ün köbegün*. Mongolian authors and translators began using *kitad* as "slave" in the early modern period due to increasing number of enslaved Chinese people, known by the ethnic term *Kitad*, in Mongolian territory, but they stopped using it after the eighteenth century. Official dictionaries published in the Qing Empire do not include the slavish meaning of *kitad*, and in the twentieth century, post-Qing world of Mongolian literature, *boġol* became the standard word for slave, albeit with a narrower definition derived from the Marxist sense of a slave society.

7.1   Slavery in Early Literary Monuments

The term *boġol* derives from a late Kitanese word *bawl* which itself derived from a Chinese word, *pú* 僕/仆, which the eleventh-century Chinese dictionary, *Categories Book* (1067, Ch. *Lèi piān* 類篇) defines as "one who gives service."[12] The Mongolic languages, including Kitanese, used the *–(ġ)ul* ending as a plural marker, so *bawl*/*boġol* meant "slaves" or "servants," but by the thirteenth century and the advent of the earliest Mongolian literary monuments the word was lexicalized to a singular meaning, and the plural form therefore has a double plural ending, *boġol-cud*. In the period of lexical exchange prior to the thirteenth-century Mongol conquests, traders sold enslaved men from the Inner Asian steppe to the Chinese states and brought women and children from the Chinese states to the Inner Asian steppe.[13] Whatever the exact conditions of those exchanges, by the thirteenth century the word *boġol* carried with it the meaning of slavery.

Literary evidence suggests that slavery itself denoted dependency but also subjecthood. In the early and most famous literary monument of Mongolian, the *SHM*, the role of people called *boġol* is ambiguous. The following passage, in which men who joined the early Mongol army give their sons to Chinggis Khan, is typical of the ambiguity present in *SHM* and later historical-literary genres in which the violent language of slavery and violent treatment of the enslaved is, possibly, a euphemistic expression of political loyalty:

> Let these sons of mine be the slaves (*boġol*)
> Of your threshold;
> If they stray from your threshold,
> Cut off their heel tendons!
> Let them be the personal slaves (*emcü boġol*)[14]
> Of your door;
> If they abandon your door,
> Cut out their livers and
> Cast them away![15]

The ambivalence of slavery in the passage depends on contextual information; for example, one of the boys given to Chinggis Khan as a *boġol* was Muqali, later a celebrated general in the Mongol conquests. The ambiguity of slavery in Muqali's case is representative of a central problem of interpreting slavery in medieval Mongolian texts.

The fact that men called *boġol* achieved high status and military valor demonstrates, for some scholars, that *boġol* "were not real slaves," as Duutan Jamsranjav Gerelbadrakh writes:

> This is exactly a case of mechanically adapting the paradigm of slavery from countries where classical slavery developed ... [*boġol*] is what people who were hereditarily subordinated to the authority of an aristocratic or powerful family ... were called.[16]

We must heed Gerelbadrakh's reminder to avoid transplanting concepts of slavery from distant times and places (by "classical slavery" he means Greece and Rome) but his assertion that *boġol* "were not real slaves" is misleading on three counts. First, historical scholarship about slavery does not regard "classical slavery" as a benchmark against which slavery in other places and times must be compared.[17] Secondly, the status and role of *boġol* in medieval texts encompasses high-status people bound to a powerful family as well as low-status, or no-status people – a degraded or base status was not a definitional characteristic of slavery. Third, the meaning of the word *boġol* in Mongolian literary contexts demonstrates that Mongolian translators working the same period as the composition of the *SHM* understood the meaning of *boġol* in the less ambiguous sense that Orlando Patterson includes in his classic definition of slavery as "generally dishonored persons."[18]

Defining slavery in all its facets – the process of enslavement, captivity, vulnerability, exploitation, legal definitions, manumission – for the last nine hundred years of Mongolian history is beyond the scope of the present essay. However, a few generalizations about slavery in Mongolian society are warranted at this point. Slavery in Mongolia took many shapes including chattel or industrial slavery, military or elite slavery, and domestic slavery. The armies of the medieval Mongol Empire captured craftsmen as well as unskilled men and deported them, sometimes en masse, to remote parts of the empire for all types of labor including mining, agriculture, animal husbandry, and domestic work in the palatial tents of the royalty.[19] Outside of periods of conquest chattel slavery was rare. Military or elite slavery, wherein a person called *boġol* was given as tribute to a ruler or taken by force, is redolent of military slavery in the Islamic world, for example the Mamluks, which some scholars trace back to earlier central Eurasian practices.[20] However, during the medieval period translators used the term *boġol* to describe slavery as a degraded condition or the opposite of privilege, so the word encompassed both the elite or military slavery found in the imperial core as well as the more commonly understood of concept of slavery. Domestic slavery is a term of convenience that I use here only to distinguish between the other forms of slavery described above and the most persistent form of slavery in pastoral-nomadic Inner Asia. As Anatoly Khazanov points out, "slavery was characteristic of practically all nomads in the Eurasian steppes" but "the employment of slaves in the pasturing of stock or in domestic work was not usually of any essential economic significance."[21] In early modern Mongolia and presumably earlier periods as well, domestic work included tasks such as milking, sewing, fetching water, and reproductive labor. David Farquhar notes that Mongolian aristocracy and commoners enslaved people but that the enslaved were few.[22] It is imperative to point out that despite Khazanov's designation of slavery in Inner Asia as lacking "economic significance" or Farquhar's assertion that the enslaved "do not seem to have been numerically very important," that slavery was nonetheless widespread. Moreover, the domestic tasks of milking, sewing, fetching water, and reproduction did have economic significance inasmuch as Mongolian society in all its economic complexity would cease to exist without the foundational work of the household economy.

In a study of the relationship between ancient and modern myth and epic in Eurasia, Georges Dumézil traces the literary significance of the theme of slavery from antiquity to the recent past through the "son of the blind man" tales attributed to the Scythians in Herodotus' *Histories*, Armenian legends, Nart sagas, and the Turkic epic cycle of Koruglu. Dumézil proposes interdependence of the themes of captive servility, resistance to an oppressive master, and the reminder of servility in these traditions (Dumézil stops short of arguing that the Scythian story recorded by Herodotus is a prototype).[23] This underlying, mythological stratum of slavery and resistance in Eurasia signals the significance of the opposition of slave and master to the literary traditions of Central Eurasia. After the dissolution of the Mongol Empire in the fourteenth and fifteenth centuries, the Black Sea slave trade was comparable in size to the Atlantic slave trade until the eighteenth century when the Atlantic slave trade swelled to its monstrous peak and the Black Sea trade declined in scale.[24] In the recent recorded past, slavery in Central Eurasia was widespread. Jeff Eden demonstrates that early modern Kazakhs carried out a far-reaching slave trade between Central Asia and the Russian Empire, the impact of which "has gone largely unrecognized, but it can hardly be overestimated."[25]

Slavery and stories of slavery were common enough across the pastoral-nomadic Eurasian steppe that the concept of slavery and enslaved characters found their way into the Mongolian literary lexicon from the earliest examples of written monuments as well as oral epic tradition. That terms of slavery are ambiguous in Mongolian is not a sign that slavery was unimportant, but that the concept and practices of slavery were dynamic. Indeed, as the use of slavery in didactic literature suggests, slavery was an important political and social metaphor for understanding relationships, social position, and power. These metaphors would be meaningless outside of a context in which slavery and the position of enslaved people in society were unfamiliar.

From a literary perspective, the pragmatic ambiguity of slavery terminology – *boğol* is a metaphor for loyalty as well as a type of "real" slavery, an elite status person like Muqali and the nameless person at the bottom of society – means there are multiple, non-exclusive meanings of the terms and ideas attached to slavery and being a slave.[26] Therefore, in twentieth century academic studies of Mongolia focused on ideal models of pastoral-nomadic "social structure" or ethnogenesis slavery resists simple analysis.[27] This ambiguity will frustrate scholars seeking a formalistic analysis of an enslaved person's status in Mongolian history, and its reflection in literature; the purveyors of Mongolian literary tradition employed a variety of terms for slavery both to describe actual enslaved people and for rhetorical devices such as metaphor and allusion.

The earliest monuments of Mongolian literature used *boğol* for slavery in the translation of Chinese and Tibetan terms of servitude. The Mongolian *Classic of Filiality* (the Mongolian title page is lost and unknown) is a translation of the Chinese work (Ch. *Xiào jing* 孝經) introduced to Qubilai (Kublai) Khan in 1244/5.[28] In the eighth chapter, "Governing the People by Means of the Norm of Filiality," the translator of the text chose the phrase "male and female slaves" (Mo. *boğol sibegegcid*) for the Chinese *chén qiè* 臣妾, an archaic term which genders slaves into male (*chén* 臣) and female (*qiè* 妾) types.[29] In Mongolian, it is unclear if *boğol* was gendered as male or was neutral, but *sibeg[eg]cid* exclusively meant enslaved or servant women.

> When an officer administered his household, he did not lose sight of the norm (of filiality) even with regard to slaves and female slaves (Mo. *boğol sibegegcid*), not to mention (his) wife and sons.[30]

Similarly, in translations from Tibetan texts we find that translators in the medieval through the early modern periods used *boğol*, among other related terms of slavery and servitude, to express the meaning of one person being dominated or degraded under the power of another.

Translators of Tibetan texts into Mongolian in this early period also chose *boġol* to translate Tibetan terms of slavery. The celebrated translator of Buddhist literature, Chos-kyi 'Od-ser (fl. 1307–1321) translated Śāntideva's *Guide to the Bodhisatva's Way of Life (Skr. Bodhicaryāvatāra,* Mo. *Bôdhi saïw-a ža ry-a-a a wa ïa a ra orusiba)* from Tibetan in 1312, and the work was carved into wooden blocks for printing and distribution. Enslaved people and slavery appear in the *Guide to the Bodhisatva's Way of Life* as allegory and metaphor, as the work is fundamentally didactic. One feature of the translation of slavery terms is the ambiguity of *boġol* in relation to the Tibetan terms. For example, in the second and third chapters, which comprise a confessional liturgical oath to the Bodhisattva path, the Mongolian reader swears devotion to Buddha by declaring "I am your slave" and that they "may be a bed for those desiring a bed; be a slave for those sentient beings desiring a slave."[31] In both sentences, Chos-kyi 'Od-ser uses the phrase *boġol jalaġu,* translating the Tibetan *'bangs* (subject, dependent) and *bran* (servant, slave) respectively. *Jalaġu* appeared in the *SHM* as a term for a young man or slave, sometimes a personal groom; Chos-kyi 'Od-ser uses *jalaġu* to modify *boġol* in these phrases to indicate a more intimate or personal type of slavery, a positive connotation.[32] In contrast, when saying the state of slavery has negative connotations, he simply uses *boġol,* such as in the phrase, "enemies such as anger and desire have no hands and feet … how do they make me serve as [their] slave (*boġol*)?"[33] The Tibetan text simply reads *bran,* as did the previous quote; Chos-kyi 'Od-ser understood *boġol* as being "slave" with a negative connotation to his readers unless modified with *jalaġu.*

The Mongolian translation of the *Treasury of Aphoristic Jewels* (late thirteenth or early fourteenth century, Skr. *Subhāṣitaratnanidhi,* Mo. *Erdeni-yin sang,* hereafter *Treasury*) is one of the most popular didactic works in Mongolian. Sonom Gara translated the text from Tibetan in the thirteenth century, and since that time scholar-monks produced unique translations of the work in monasteries, from whence it was copied and stored in monastic and temple libraries and private collections across the Mongol-literate world and remained a standard pedagogical text into the early twentieth century.[34] The *Treasury* is especially important for understanding the use of terms over time because the text was initially translated not long after the compilation of the *SHM* and *Classic of Filiality,* but unlike those texts the *Treasury* was distributed widely in Mongolian and Oirat – a dialect of western Mongolian with a unique orthography – through re-translations in the seventeenth, eighteenth, and nineteenth centuries.[35] Thus, the *Treasury* gives a perspective on how the meanings of certain words remained stable or changed over time. Individual translators selected different Mongolian terms to translate identical Tibetan words for slavery and servitude, pointing to the inadequacy of a formalist reading of the terminology.

As a didactic work, the *Treasury* employs short quatrains to impart life lessons, usually through analogy or simile. As metaphor, the work employs slavery to admonish the powerful and correlate the leadership with slave-ownership. For example, in chapter six, "On investigating manners of character," the 204th stanza reads:

> The person who is slack and gives up his efforts,
> even if he is strong, will degenerate.
> Although the elephant is very powerful,
> the little elephant-driver enslaves him and makes him serve.[36]

In Mongolian, the last line translates the Tibetan phrase *bran bzhin 'khol*, "serve as a slave."[37] Nearly all of the translators of the important Mongolian editions of the *Treasury* translated the phrase in this way, with the exception of Caqar Gebsi Lubsangcültem (1740–1810) who offered an interpretive understanding of the final line of the quatrain: "as if being ridden effortlessly by a child."[38]

In other phrases, the translators chose unique ways to express the meaning of slave. The 257th stanza provides a clear example of the different ways the translators chose to translate slavery. In full, the stanza reads:

> A haughty-minded slave,
> a foppish ascetic,
> an emperor who does not act in accordance with the doctrine –
> these three have entered a state of impropriety.[39]

The Tibetan word for "slave" in stanza 257 is *bran g.yog*, wherein both *bran* and *g.yog* are terms of service or slavery. The major Mongolian translators of the *Treasury* used four ways of translating the term.[40] The earliest translator, Sonom Gara, used *boġol jalaġu*. This usage does not contradict Chos-kyi 'Od-ser's use of the same phrase described above: the contrast between the positive connotation of *boġol jalaġu* and "haughty-minded" (*degerügei sedkil-tü*) is purposeful in this sequence of oxymoronic characters. Subsequent translations reflect a change in popular usage. The meaning of slavery implied in *jalaġu* diminished over the centuries to imply servitude or service, for example in the present day it still is used colloquially like the French *garçon* to refer to young service workers. The seventeenth-century Oirat translator Zaya Pandita and eighteenth-century eastern Mongol, Chahar Gebshi Lubsangsültem, translated *bran g.yog* in this stanza as *boġol jaruca* (Zaya Pandita's Oirat equivalent is *bōl zaruca*), reflecting the shift from *jalaġu* as a term of servitude in favor of *jaruca*, "one who serves" or simply "servant" or "slave" rendering the phrase *boġol jaruca* as "slave servant" or simply "slave." The celebrated translator Mergen Gegen (1717–1766) translated the same phrase with *boġol kitad*, literally "slave Chinese." These diverse translations of the same word, even differing within a single century, demonstrate the variability and ambiguity of Mongolian slave terminology. For the reader of these passages, there is not a static image of an enslaved person or static meaning of slavery – the multiple registers of the word are simultaneous, and the multiple Mongolian translations of Tibetan expressions signal a relative status of degradation at the bottom of a social hierarchy as well as a person bought or sold.

7.2 The Early Modern Ethnic Turn

The term *kitad* means "Chinese" in Mongolian, but after the sixteenth century took on the meaning of "slave." The word derives from the plural of the attested Middle Mongolian word *Kitan*, denoting the ethnonym "Kitan," the ruling elite of the Liao (907–1125) and Qara Khitai Empires (1124–1218). While the Kitan spoke a Mongolic language, they ruled over an ethnically and linguistically diverse area in today's north China. After the thirteenth century, Mongols applied the term *kitad* to Chinese speakers in general, so that in the present day *kitad* means "Chinese" people, language, culture, and the country of China.[41] However, during a period of time from which relatively sparse written records remains, *kitad* took on the meaning of slave and servant.

The earliest textual coupling of the notion of "Chinese" with "slave" was the sixteenth century law code of Altan Khan (1507–1582). The term's textual emergence in the realm of Altan Khan is likely related to the influx of Chinese speaking workers and traders in the region, many of whom fled the Ming Empire to work in agriculture or on construction projects in Altan Khan's realm.[42] According to Xiao Daheng, a contemporaneous observer from the Ming:

> The slaves (Ch. *nú pú* 奴僕) who live among the Barbarians are, for the most part, Han Chinese (Ch. *Hàn rén* 漢人), or different Barbarians who

have been captured for that reason. Even their children and their grand-children, from generation after generation, experience no change [in this situation]. If [among the slaves] there is a person who is intelligent, courageous, and capable, it will happen that the administration of affairs is entrusted to him, by which he acquires a dignity equal to that of a chief.[43]

While not all Chinese people living among the Mongols were necessarily enslaved, and according to Xiao, they could rise to a position of promi-nence similar to *boġol* of the earlier period, over the following centuries *kitad* unambiguously took on the meaning of slave while retaining the meaning of "Chinese." In addition to the historical context, we can read the slave meaning of *kitad* out of the literary or historical contexts in which the term appears.[44]

For Altan Khan's legal code, we only have a stilted Tibetan translation of the Mongolian original.[45] In the translation, the scribe used the terms for Chinese (Tib. *rgya*) and slave or servant (Tib. *g.yog*) interchangeably.[46] In some cases the author could be referring to Chinese people, but in other contexts "Chinese" clearly means "slave" or "servant." For example, the first regulation in a sequence of legal prescriptions for master–servant crimes, we find that "if one kills their Chinese slave (*rgya g.yog*) who looks after their belongings, or if they harm [the Chinese slave's] body, they should be fined one five and replace one person."[47] Following regulations read, "if a wicked slave (*g.yog ngan*) kills a person, kill and devastate them," and "if a master's wicked Chinese (*rgya ngan*) kills a Mongol, replace one Chinese."[48] (The meaning of which is unclear.) Without access to the Mongolian original, the Mongolian terminology remains ambiguous, but later texts in the legal and literary traditions unambiguously confirm that "Chinese" meant "slave" during this period.

The word *kitad* appeared in Mongolian literary works from the seven-teenth to the nineteenth centuries. For example, an instruction manual for the recitation of a ritual sacrifice to the hearth-fire from the early 1600s concludes by instructing the reader to request a boon for "the vital energy of the slaves (*boġol*) and dogs of my threshold and the domestics and slave-girls (*kitad-un kegüked*) of my door."[49] It was common for this type of ritual to end with the blessings for the enslaved after blessings for lost animals. As Krystyna Chabros says, referring to more recent texts and ethnographic work, the blessings for the enslaved at the conclusion of the fire-hearth sacrifice "can be regarded as an extension for the wellbeing of livestock" through the order and wording in the ritual.[50] In Mongolian cosmology, humans and animals as *amitan* "living beings" occupy the same sphere of sentience, both having the ability to draw breath (*ami*).

Based on ethnographic work, Natasha Fijn argues that domestic animals in Mongolia are "social" as quasi-members of the household, emphasizing the co-dependent relationship that horses, cattle, goats, and other herd animals enjoy with herders.[51] In these ritual blessings, enslaved people identified as *boġol* and *kitad* were analogous to dogs and livestock as sentient beings belonging to the household, domestic creatures that draw breath but were not on the same plane as humans.

When the *Khalkha Code*, a law code compiled between 1676 and 1709 in central Mongolia, was compiled the word *kitad* was fully lexicalized as "slave." Scholars of Mongolian legal history postulate that Altan Khan's code influenced the *Khalkha Code* in both language and legislation, and we know from the fire-hearth ritual texts that *kitad* as "slave" was already in the vernacular.[52] The *Khalkha Code* also introduced the phrasing "slave of a slave," written as "Chinese of a Chinese." The code reads:

> If a black (a commoner) penetrates a noble-lady, devastate him and then seize his entire family as slaves of slaves (Chinese of Chinese, *kitad-un kitad*) and give them to the subjects of the noble-lady's husband.[53]

The color black denotes "ordinary, low-class" in Mongolian and Turkic cultures, among several other connotations, but not slavery.[54] The phrase "slave of a slave" reinforces the hierarchical notion implicit in early Mongolian social relations which is that everybody was below someone; the hereditary aristocracy referred to their non-enslaved subjects as if they were enslaved and so from their perspective, if one was enslaved in a commoner's household, then they were doubly enslaved.[55] However, the perspective of the aristocracy from which law codes were written is illusory and is an expression of the ambiguity inherent in the terms: *kitad* meant "slave" but like *boġol* and other terms of slavery expressed relative degradation, a *kitad* of a *kitad* was really a person enslaved to a commoner, but from the aristocratic perspective this was a slave (an actual enslaved person) of a "slave" (a person lower in the social hierarchy than themselves, a commoner).

The compilers of the *Khalkha Code* wrote most of the code without imperial oversight – its compilation began prior to Outer Mongolia's submission to the Qing Dynasty. After the incorporation of Outer Mongolia into the Qing Empire in 1691, the *Khalkha Code* remained in effect locally, but a law code originally intended for Inner Mongolia, the *Mongol Code*, was expanded and adapted for use in Outer Mongolia as well.[56] The statute in the later *Mongol Code* equivalent to the one cited above from the *Khalkha Code* includes a harsher punishment typical of the adapted Qing Mongolian law codes, but employs the older word for slave, *boġol* rather than the more recent ethnic term: "If a black has an affair with a noblewoman, kill the man by slicing, kill the woman by decapitation. Enslave (*boġol*) and give away the man's wife and children."[57] Translators, editors, and authors shifted away from the popular usage of the ethnically derived *kitad* and to the occupational-status word *boġol* in Mongolian literary and legal works of the Qing Empire in the late eighteenth century. Writing within the Qing Empire, especially after the eighteenth-century literary projects of the Qianlong emperor, it is little surprise that they avoided potentially derogatory terms in favor of a relatively neutral one. Therefore, this usage of *kitad* never or very rarely appears in Qing-sponsored Mongolian literary works after 1770, including works of Mongolian lexicography, literature, and legal treatises. Although no records explicating the underlying reasons for its absence have been found, the slavish meaning of *kitad* was likely scrubbed from Qing materials as a matter of official policy in deference to the sensitivity with which Qing censors handled ethnic relations as they appeared in printed materials. Scholars have pointed to the imperial censorship of literary works containing or intimating anti-Manchu sentiments (the Manchus being the ethnically distinct rulers of the Qing Empire).[58] The exclusion of *kitad* from post-1770s Mongolian literary works produced with imperial oversight suggests that Qing literary censorship worked in the opposite direction – Mongolian language that harbored anti-Chinese sentiments was subject to censure.

In support of the above supposition, there is an example of *kitad* used as "slave" in pre-1770s Mongolian literature produced in Beijing with imperial patronage. A version of *Geser*, a primarily oral genre of heroic epic with origins in Tibet with many variations, was carved into woodblocks in Beijing in 1716. A popular cult devoted to the eponymous hero Geser existed in the eighteenth century in the Mongol-phone world due to the *Geser* epics widespread popularity.[59] The imperial sponsorship of the printing of the Mongolian *Geser* relates to the Qing court's interest in Geser's role as the god of war. The Qing court associated Geser with the Chinese god of war Guan Yu, the hero of the Chinese epic *Romance of the Three Kingdoms*, whose name replaced Geser's in nineteenth century Mongolian divinatory manuals and newly erected temples.[60] Despite the Qing court's interest in the Mongolian cult of Geser, they did not revise or update the woodblocks on which Geser's tale was told. Throughout the 1716 Beijing *Geser*, the phrase *kitad* and *kitad boġol* are used interchangeably leading to occasional ambiguities in meaning. For example, in the

fourteenth section of chapter one, Joro (Geser's name prior to enthrone-
ment) tricks his unwitting wife-to-be Rombo Goa and surprises her
family by appearing along with her on horseback, as if they were
betrothed. Her father and brother storm out the door while her mother
glances nervously around and shifts things about. The enslaved people in
the house fumble around and prepare a seat incorrectly for Joro in the
house, giving Joro an opportunity to mock their ignorance of horseman-
ship. The text reads:

> the slaves (*kitad*) moved the pot back and forth and spread a saddle blanket
> for Joro but laid it out wrong so that Joro had to sit the wrong way. They
> asked him "why are you sitting the wrong way?" Joro replied, "when you
> ride a horse, which way do you place the saddle?" They had Joro stand up
> and fixed the blanket.

In the above passage *kitad* is ambiguous; it could mean "Chinese servant"
rather than slave. After the 1716 woodblock printing, several variations of
the *Geser* epic of varying length were printed with several chapters added
onto the Beijing *Geser*. One edition includes an episode in which a
Mongolian princess refers to herself as *kitad*. Nayiġulai, the daughter of
Nacin Khan, is twenty years old and unmarried. She receives a miraculous
letter informing her that Geser is coming to marry her, but she must not
tell her parents. In the passage describing her anxiety about what her life
married to Geser will entail, she wonders if she will be "a slave sitting with
a cow (i.e. a milk-maid), a woman-slave sweeping ashes" (*üniy-e saġuqu
kitad, ünesü ġarġaqu sibegcin*).[61] The 1716 Beijing *Geser* was not censored
for potentially anti-Chinese slurs, and subsequent editions were not imperially sanctioned and thus retained the ethnic term *kitad* for slavery.
Official lexical sources, on the other hand, were more comprehensive in
their avoidance of ethnic terms for slave terminology.

The earliest imperially sponsored dictionary of Mongolian, compiled in
1717, explained that "subjects (*irgen*, meaning 'subjects of the empire') are
called *kitad* and *nanggiyad* (a word meaning 'southerner' borrowed from
Chinese *nán jiā* 南家 through the Middle Mongolian and Uyghur
Nangqiyas)," and glossed *kitad* in Manchu as *nikan*, the Manchu ethnonym for Chinese.[62] Subsequent dictionaries, including the massive five-
language lexicon, the *Pentaglot*, retained this gloss of *kitad*, with no trace of
its derogatory meaning.[63] Even as Mergen Gegen translated lines of the
Treasury, the Qing court sponsored the Mongolian translation of the
Sanskrit-Tibetan Buddhist lexical compendium, the *Mahāvyutpatti*, completed in the late eighteenth century.[64] The equivalences for the Tibetan

terms of servitude *g.yog* is *boğol* and for *bran* it is *boğol* and *jarudasun*, a word derived from the verb *jaru-* "to serve" and a cognate of *jaruca*, of medieval antiquity and the same as *boğol.*[65] In the Qing sponsored Mongolian translation of the *Mahāvyutpatti, kitad* appears only as a modifier for plants and herbs, such as *kitad arca* "Chinese juniper."[66] These Qing sources which were used for administrative, literary, and religious texts guided translators away from the popular ethnic term for slavery and towards the neutral and ambiguous *boğol* or *jarudsan.* A Mongolian dictionary produced by a non-Qing subject during the Qing period offers contrast to the dictionaries edited to Qing censorial sensibilities.

The Polish scholar Kowalewski, who traveled through Mongolia and north China during the late 1820s and early 1830s collecting materials for his seminal Mongol-Russian-France dictionary did include *kitad* in his lexicon, with the primary meaning of "Chinese" and a secondary meaning of "slave, captive."[67] His dictionary, compiled from literary materials from the preceding centuries, is one of the only lexicons produced in the early modern period that includes this usage of *kitad.* After the mid-nineteenth century, even dictionaries compiled outside the Qing imperium dropped the "slave" meaning of *kitad.* The explanatory Tibetan-Mongolian dictionary compiled by the Buryat scholar Lubsangrincen (pen-name Sumatiratna) in the late nineteenth century, based partly on the *Mahāvyutpatti* but also on a wide ranging corpus of Tibeto-Mongolian literature, follows the Qing translation methods in translating *bran g.yog* and related terms of slavery as "slaves and servants" (*boğol jarudasun*) and, for *bran mo mchu snyung* "unimportant slave woman" (*sabağ-a ügei nigen sibegcin*).[68] Writing in the 1940s the Reverend Mostaert, a world-renowned specialist in Mongolian studies with more than two decades of experience living in the Ordos region of Inner Mongolia, defined *kitad* simply as "Chinese," with a note the *qara kitad* "black Chinese" was a derogatory term.[69] In popular usage, while *kitad* still carries derogatory implications in Mongolia owing to Sinophobic sentiments, it does not mean "slave," and instead there are other derogatory terms for Chinese which do not bear repeating here. In twentieth-century Mongolian dictionaries, *boğol* and *jaruca* remain as the terms for slaves. The declining use of *kitad* from the late eighteenth century was a result of Qing censorship as well as the decreasing number of Chinese slaves after the incorporation of Inner and Outer Mongolia in the seventeenth century, although the word continued to be legible to readers as evidenced by its use in nineteenth-century literature. However, by the end of the Qing period (1911) and the advent of the twentieth century the term ceased to carry connotations of slavery for Mongolian writers, translators, and audiences.

7.3   Into the Twentieth Century

Slavery plays an important role in twentieth-century Mongolian literature. It appears as a metaphor in nationalistic histories and dramas. In a play put on in the 1930s in the Mongolian People's Republic, the audience witnessed people playing the parts of enslaved characters walk blindfolded onto stage where they were beaten and cursed by a Mongol noble, deceived by a Buddhist monk about salvation through religion, and then a Chinese general came and collected money from the noble and the monk who had oppressed the enslaved. The noble and monk represented the "two feudals" of pre-revolutionary Mongolia, the aristocratic and Buddhist institutions. At that point in the play, a Comintern representative emerges and gives a fiery speech which causes one enslaved man to remove the blindfold. He removes the blindfolds of others, and as the two feudals grew nervous, the Comintern representative tells them "you have weapons in your hands," and the enslaved realize they are holding guns and attack the feudals.[70] In this scene, the Comintern agent as representative of Communist ideology liberates the enslaved people by arming them with the tools to overthrow their oppressors. This twentieth century socialist use of the character of the enslaved is in stark contrast to early depictions of slavery in which the enslaved was totally powerless, for example in *The Fifteen-year-old Boy Altai Sümbür Abai* cited at the beginning of this essay. But, slavery still serves an ambiguous function between metaphor and description. The play is obviously didactic in that it teaches people that they already wield the tools of their emancipation, and so slavery refers to a mental slavery under feudalism. However, the presence of feudals who stand opposed to the enslaved suggests that the oppressed people were, perhaps, supposed to portray actual enslaved people at least in the eyes of the feudals who believed that all commoners as well as those they enslaved were slaves of the aristocracy.[71]

In an essay published in 1964 in the journal *Chinese Literature*, the celebrated writer Malqinhu writes about his visit to Slave Village. Malqinhu reports that he encountered a young man, an orphan named Jamsu, and when Malqinhu inquired about the name of the village, the following conversation transpired:

Jamsu: "...everybody here used to be the slave of some wealthy man or noble."
Malqinhu: "Were you a slave too?"
- "The son of a slave."
- "Both your parents were slaves?"
- "My mother..."
- "Not your father?"
- "I had no father."[72]

The essay continues to describe the depredations suffered by previous generations of Mongols and concludes with an interview with Jamsu's grandfather who explains that "I owe it to Chairman Mao. Thanks to him we've stood up."[73] In Malqinhu's story, the ambiguity is removed. The story is one of real slavery, described in detail by Jamsu. The lesson of Malqinhu's story is also less ambiguous than the play described above; Malqinhu is conveying to his audience the backwardness of pre-revolutionary Inner Mongolia. However, by the twentieth century, certain populations of descendants of enslaved people in Inner Mongolia and Mongolia lived in concentrated populations or villages. For example, the Qotongs of Uws in western Mongolia, originally Turkic Muslims (today's Uyghurs of the Xinjiang Uyghur Autonomous Region), who were forced into agricultural labor by a Mongol prince in the late seventeenth and early eighteenth centuries, or the "hundred households of lamplighters" in Baarin Right Banner, who were originally dowry slaves of a Manchu princess with the hereditary obligation to maintain the princess's tomb and keep her tomb's fire burning.[74] It was this type of concentrated population of descendants of the enslaved people in one village about which Malqinhu wrote, although the implication is that it represented a larger portion of Inner Mongolians. He published the story two years prior to the Great Proletarian Cultural Revolution (1966–1976) and his straightforward admonishment of Mongolia's recent traditional past fit well into the cultural and historical denunciations that characterized the political moment.

In twentieth-century Mongolian literature, the usual terms for "slave" are *boġol* and *jaruca* but in historical fiction terms like *köbüd* occasionally appear as well. For example, in the translation of American literature such as *Uncle Tom's Cabin* from Russian into Mongolian in the 1950s, "slave" was translated interchangeably as *bool* (the Cyrillic spelling of *boġol*) or *jaruca*.[75] In the fourteenth century, *boġol* had an ambiguous occupational meaning ranging from "slave" to something like "subject," but in the twentieth century it came to mean "slave" in a very absolute sense under the influence of dogmatic Communist theories of "slave society" which reduced the ambiguities and nuances of slavery to easy-to-understand binaries of slave and master. Irinchin summarized the problem neatly:

> In modern Mongolian social science writings, bo'ol (*boğol*) means slaves – they are slave owners' chattel without any personal freedom, merely so-called "talking tools." Modern definitions of this word prevent people from precisely understanding its historical meaning; instead, they are led to draw an equal sign between the word bo'ol of the 11th and the 12th centuries and its modern usage.[76]

Irinchin goes on to use exactly the modern definition of slavery that he opposes in the above quotation to conclude that the term *boğol* expresses not a form of slavery but a "serf-like subjected population" unique to Inner Asian historical experience.[77] Irinchin's criticism (and Gerelbadrakh's at the beginning of this essay) is that scholars need to approach the content and terminology of social categories like "slave" carefully in Mongolian history. That is undeniable, but his criticism of using the word "slave" to translate *boğol* relies on a strawman concept of "modern definitions" of slavery; after all, the term "talking tools" was coined by Marcus Terentius Varro (116–27 BC) – not exactly a modern thinker – and scholars of Roman history point out that Varro's definition of a slave was a rhetorical flourish and not an academic exercise.[78] Irinchin's argument makes more sense when placed in the context of twentieth-century Mongolian and Chinese academics treatments of slavery in history and literature. In Mongolia since 1924 and China since 1949, dogmatic Marxist interpretations of slavery limited scholars' breadth of inquiry to questions about slave societies and serfdom as defined by Marx-Engels' paradigm of social evolutionism. Marxist evolutionism is a decidedly Eurocentric model, although scholars in Mongolia and China forced the history of East Asia, sometimes awkwardly, into the mold of "slavery society," "feudalism," and so on.[79] As a result, the meaning of slavery in twentieth-century Mongolia is inextricably tied to the perception of slavery in Greco-Roman antiquity in an unusually tight way. Added to that is the persistent myth in China that slavery as a historical issue was a defining feature of Mongol and Manchu culture but disconnected from Chinese civilization – a stereotype that buttressed racist ideas about the primitiveness or backwardness of Inner Asia.[80] Thus, when Irinchin speaks of "modern definitions" of slavery, those are the definition to which he refers, and the stereotypes with which he contends. That his response is to restate the problem as one of serfdom reflects the limitations of the Chinese academy in 1986, the year of the article's publication.[81]

7.4 Conclusion

Twentieth-century Mongolian and Chinese Communism were and are self-styled abolitionist ideologies – they present themselves as being primarily concerned with the liberation of oppressed people from exploitation. The above examples illustrate how authors inspired by the abolitionist message inherent in Communism employed slavery as a didactic tool to allow people to reflect on or learn about the inequities of a now-bygone past and celebrate the successes of their liberators. It is in this didactic mode of slavery that twentieth-century Mongolian literature resonates with literature dating back as far as the fourteenth century, particularly the salvationist themes of the *Guide to the Bodhisattva's Way of Life* and the didacticisms of the *Treasury*. (The *Treasury* is still popular in Mongolia today, with new translations and deluxe editions regularly filling up bookstore shelves.)

The language of slavery in the Mongolian literary context is complex and employs many phrases, metaphors, and symbolisms. The subject of slavery in Mongolia is understudied partly because scholars in Mongolia and China have rejected the Greco-Roman straw man imposed on them by twentieth-century scholarship. Nonetheless, I have attempted to outline a few of the basic ideas and problems in the study of slavery in Mongolian literature. Foreign scholars of Mongolian literature tend to focus on the formal terminology of slavery and reach a dead end because of the ambiguity of the occupational (*boġol, jarudasun*, etc.), gendered (*köbüd, sibegcin*), and ethnic (*kitad*) words related to servitude and degradation. Showing how these words were used in context and how they changed over time bridges the gap between a purely terminological study and a thematic study. Slavery as metaphor and enslaved people as characters are ubiquitous in the Mongolian literary tradition. The language of slavery in the Mongolian literary tradition reflects the development of Mongolian literature itself, from its origins in the steppe to the Indo-Tibetan influences of Buddhist translation, the impact of centuries of Qing imperial control, and the revolutionary movements of the twentieth century.

Notes

1 György Kara, *Books of the Mongolian Nomads: More than Eight Centuries of Writing Mongolian, Indiana University Uralic and Altaic Series* 171 (Bloomington: Indiana University Research Institute for Inner Asian Studies, 2005).

2 Evariste Régis Huc and Joseph Gabet, *Travels in Tartary, Thibet and China, 1844–1846*, trans. William Hazlitt, 2 vols., The Broadway Travellers (New York: Dover Publications, Inc., 1928), vol. I, p. 178.

3 Phillip P. Marzluf, *Language, Literacy, and Social Change in Mongolia: Traditionalist, Socialist, and Post-Socialist Identities* (Lanham: Lexington Books, 2018), 11–24.

4 Christopher P. Atwood, *Encyclopedia of Mongolia and the Mongol Empire* (New York: Facts on File, Inc., 2004), s.v. "education, traditional."

5 Steven A. Epstein, *Speaking of Slavery: Color, Ethnicity, and Human Bondage in Italy* (Ithaca and London: Cornell University Press, 2001), 40.

6 Walther Heissig, *Erzählstoffe rezenter mongolischer Heldendichtung (Narrative Material of Recent Mongolian Epic Poetry)*, 2 vols., Monographienreihe Zur Geschichte, Kultur Und Sprache Der Völker Ost– Und Zentralasiens 100 (Wiesbaden: Otto Harrassowitz, 1988), vol. II, pp. 582–583.

7 Walther Heissig, *Erzählstoffe rezenter mongolischer Heldendichtung (Narrative Material of Recent Mongolian Epic Poetry)*, 2 vols., Monographienreihe Zur Geschichte, Kultur Und Sprache Der Völker Ost– Und Zentralasiens 100 (Wiesbaden: Otto Harrassowitz, 1988), vol. I, pp. 173–174.

8 Much of the terminology of slavery in Mongolian derives from Mongolian root-words but are less common in literary contexts than *boġol* and *kitad*.

9 In most Mongolian dialects today, *köbegün* is gendered as male, but historically and in some dialects today is gender neutral. The "double plural" form that results from this, *köbüd-ner*, is a common feature in Mongolic languages; see Juha Janhunen, "Proto-Mongolic." In *The Mongolic Languages, Routledge Language Family Series*, ed. Juha Janhunen (London: Routledge, 2003), 13.

10 Igor de Rachewiltz (trans., ed.), *The Secret History of the Mongols: A Mongolian Epic Chronicle of the Thirteenth Century*, 2 vols., *Brill's Inner Asian Library* 7 (Leiden & Boston: Brill, 2006), vol. I, §232.

11 Ch'i-ch'ing Hsiao, *The Military Establishment of the Yuan Dynasty* (Cambridge, MA: Harvard University Press, 1978), p. 199, note 312.

12 Andrew Eric Shimunek, *Languages of Ancient Southern Mongolia and North China: A Historical-Comparative Study of the Serbi or Xianbei Branch of the Serbi-Mongolic Language Family, with an Analysis of Northeastern Frontier Chinese and Old Tibetan Phonology*, Tunguso Sibirica 40 (Weisbaden: Otto Harrassowitz, 2017), pp. 328–329; Sima Guang, *Lei pian (Categories Book)*, (1067), *juan* 8, reprinted in *Qin ding si ku quan shu*.

13 Jonathan Karam Skaff, *Sui-Tang and Its Turko-Mongol Neighbors: Culture, Power, and Connections, 580–800*, Oxford Studies in Early Empires (Oxford: Oxford University Press, 2012), 70, 245, 295.

14 N.b. *emcü* meaning "property, inheritance" and thus "personal slave" in a hereditary sense.

15 de Rachewiltz (trans., ed.), *The Secret History of the Mongols*, §137. N.b. in Mongolian culture in the medieval period as today, "the liver denotes intimacy and close relationship," Francis Woodman Cleaves (trans.), *The Secret History of the Mongols for the First Time Done into English out of the Original*

Tongue and Provided with an Exegetical Commentary, (Cambridge, London: Harvard University Press, 1982), vol. I (Translation), p. 39, note 4.

16 J. Gerelbadrakh, "'Bo'ol – bool' gej khen be? (Who Was a 'Boğol – Slave'?)," *Acta Historica* 10 (2009): 180–181, 187. C.f. Irinchin Yekemingghadai, "Regarding the Mongol Bo'ol in the 11th and 12th Centuries." In *Chinese Scholars on Inner Asia*, ed. Xin Luo, trans. Roger Covey (Bloomington: Sinor Research Institute for Inner Asian Studies, 2012), 315–330.

17 There are volumes of works challenging the paradigm of "classical slavery" as a universal category. Despite its datedness, Patterson's volume on the comparative historical sociology is representative of the critical approach to the subject in academic studies of comparative slavery. See Orlando Patterson, *Slavery and Social Death: A Comparative Study* (Cambridge, MA: Harvard University Press, 1982); more recent surveys include Jeff Fynn-Paul and Damian Alan Pargas (eds.), *Slaving Zones: Cultural Identities, Ideologies, and Institutions in the Evolution of Global Slavery, Studies in Global Slavery 4* (Leiden, Boston: Brill, 2018); Noel Lenski and Catherine M. Cameron (eds.), *What Is a Slave Society? The Practice of Slavery in Global Perspective* (Cambridge: Cambridge University Press, 2018).

18 Orlando Patterson, *Slavery and Social Death*, p. 13.

19 William of Rubruck recounted German miners who the Mongols moved from site to site in Central Asia as well as young men taken into the royal household to smith silver and serve as cupbearers; Willem van Ruysbroeck, *The Mission of Friar William of Rubruck: His Journey to the Court of the Great Khan Möngke, 1253–1255*, Peter Jackson (trans.), (Indianapolis: Hackett Publishing Company, 2009), 144–146, 182–183, 223–224, 246. The Mongol conquests generated the human capital that fueled the Black Sea slave trade, see Hannah Barker, *That Most Precious Merchandise: The Mediterranean Trade in Black Sea Slaves, 1260–1500*, The Middle Ages Series (Philadelphia: University of Pennsylvania Press, 2019), pp. 122–127, *passim*.

20 Christopher I. Beckwith, "Aspects of the Early History of the Central Asian Guard Corps in Islam," *Archivum Eurasiae Medii Aevi* 4 (1984): 29–43; on the meaning of the word Mamluk and the stigmas attached to military slavery despite the high levels of political and military authority, see Koby Yosef, "The Term Mamlūk and Slave Status during the Mamluk Sultanate," *Al-Qanṭara* 34, no. 1 (2013): 7–34.

21 Anatoly M. Khazanov, *Nomads and the Outside World*, 2nd ed. (Madison: University of Wisconsin Press, 1994), 160.

22 David M. Farquhar, '*The Ch'ing Administration of Mongolia up to the Nineteenth Century*' (PhD dissertation, Cambridge, MA: Harvard University, 1960), 8.

23 Georges Dumézil, *Romans de Scythie et d'alentour (Tales of Scythia and Its Surroundings)*, Bibliothèque Historique (Paris: Payot, 1978), 307–326.

24 Dariusz Kołodziejczyk, "Slave Hunting and Slave Redemption as a Business Enterprise: The Northern Black Sea Region in the Sixteenth to Seventeenth Centuries," *Oriente Moderno*, Nuova serie, 25(86), no. 1 (2006), 152.

25 Jeff Eden, *Slavery and Empire in Central Asia, Cambridge Studies in Islamic Civilization* (Cambridge: Cambridge University Press, 2018), 212.

26 Martin Camper, *Arguing over the Texts: The Rhetoric of Interpretation* (New York: Oxford University Press, 2018), 14–42.

27 David Sneath, *The Headless State: Aristocrat Orders, Kinship Society, and Misrepresentations of Nomadic Inner Asia* (New York: Columbia University Press, 2007), 121–179.

28 Igor de Rachewiltz, "The Preclassical Mongolian Version of the Hsiao-Ching (in Memoriam A. Mostaert, 1881–1971)," *Zentralasiatische Studien* 16 (1982): 18–19.

29 Anthony François Paulus Hulsewé, "Supplementary Note on Li Ch'en Ch'ieh," *T'oung Pao* 67, no. 3–5 (1981): 361.

30 N.b. de Rachewiltz translates this phrase as "slaves and female servants," which unnecessarily adds the category of "servant," see "The Preclassical Mongolian Version of the Hsiao-Ching (in Memoriam A. Mostaert, 1881–1971)," p. 44.

31 Boris I. Vladimirtsov (ed.), *Bodhicaryāvatāra Çāntideva mongol'skii perevod Chos-kyi Ḥod-zer'a: I. Tekst*, Bibliotheca Buddhica, XXVIII (Leningrad: Izdatel'stvo Akademii NAUK SSSR, 1929), §§2:8 3:18.

32 Boris I. Vladimirtsov, "Obshchestvennyi stroi mongolov: Mongol'skii kochevoi feodalizm (The Social Structure of the Mongols: Mongolian Nomadic Feudalism)." *In B. Ya. Vladimirtsov: Raboty po istorii i etnografii Mongl'skikh narodov (B.I. Vladimirtsov: Historical and Ethnographic Studies of the Mongolians)* (Moskva: Vostochnaya literatura RAN, 2002), 364.

33 Boris I. Vladimirtsov (ed.), *Bodhicaryāvatāra Çāntideva mongol'skii perevod Chos-kyi Ḥod-zer'a: I. Tekst*, §4:28.

34 Ts. Damdinsüren, *Namtryn khuudsaas: Namtar, dursamj, temdeglel, turshlaga (From the Pages of Life: Biography, Memoir, Notes, Experience)* (Ulaanbaatar: Ulsyn khewlel, 1990); Walther Heissig, *Geschichte der mongolischen Literatur: 19. Jahrhundert bis zum Beginn des 20. Jahrhunderts (The History of Mongolian Literature: From the 19th Century to the Beginning of the 20th Century)*, 2 vols. (Weisbaden: Otto Harrassowitz, 1972), vol I., pp. 13–14.

35 O. Demchigmaa, *"Subashid"-yn Mongol orchuulguudyn galig, ügsiin khelkhee (The Transcription and Index of the Mongol Translation of "Subashid")*, ed. Shagdarsüren, Ts. (Ulaanbaatar: Udam soyol, 2013).

36 James Bosson, *A Treasury of Aphoristic Jewels: The Subhāṣitaratnanidhi of Sa Skya Paṇḍita in Tibetan and Mongolian, Uralic and Altaic Series* (Bloomington: Indiana University, 1969), §204.

37 James Bosson, *A Treasury of Aphoristic Jewels: The Subhāṣitaratnanidhi of Sa Skya Paṇḍita in Tibetan and Mongolian, Uralic and Altaic Series* (Bloomington: Indiana University, 1969), pp. 79, 164.

38 Demchigmaa, O., *"Subashid"-yn Mongol orchuulguudyn galig, ügsiin khelkhee*, §204.

39 James Bosson, *A Treasury of Aphoristic Jewels: The Subhāṣitaratnanidhi of Sa Skya Paṇḍita in Tibetan and Mongolian, Uralic and Altaic Series* (Bloomington: Indiana University, 1969), §257.

130 SAM H. BASS

40 Demchigmaa, O., *"Subashid"-yn Mongol orchuulguudyn galig, ügsiin khelkhee*, §257.

41 Paul Pelliot, *Notes on Marco Polo*, vol. 1, 2 vols. (Paris: Imprimerie Nationale, 1959), pp. 220, 387.

42 Carney T. Fisher, "Smallpox, Salesmen, and Sectarians: Ming-Mongol Relations in the Jiajing Reign (1522–67)," *Ming Studies* 25 (1988): 1–23.

43 Henri Serruys, "Pei-lou fong-sou 北 虜 風 俗: Les coutumes des esclaves septentrionaux de Siao Ta-Heng 簫 大 亨 (Beilu Fengsu, Customs of the Northern Slaves by Xiao Daheng)," *Monumenta Serica* 10, no. Antonio Mostaert, de Studiis in Linguam Mongolicam (1945), 134.

44 For example, Hiroshi Futaki demonstrates that *kitad* was a term of enslavement, meaning people bought, sold, and inherited in the Qing period, see 'Shin dai Haruha Mongoru no dorei kaihō bunsho ni tsuite (Qing Era Khalkha Mongolian Emancipation Documents),' in *Shimada Masao hakase shō toshi kinen ronshū, Tōyō hōshi no tankyū* (Tōkyō: Kyūko shoin, 1987), 21–44.

45 Shagdaryn Bira, "A Sixteenth-Century Mongol Code." In *Mongolyn tüükh, soyol, tüükh bichlegiin sudalgaa (Studies in the Mongolian History, Culture and Historiography: Selected Papers)*, trans. Veronika Veit and Rashidonduk (Tokyo: Institute for Languages and Cultures of Asia and Africa, 1994), 278.

46 The Tibetan *rgya nag* means China or Chinese, and *rgya* is used as an abbreviation, for example "Chinese incense stick" *rgya spos*, "Chinese man" *rgya mi*.

47 B. Batbayar and B. Bayartuyaa, "Altan khany tsaaz (orchuulga, kharitsuulsan sudalgaa) (The Law Code of Altan Khan, Translation and Comparative Study)," *Erkh züi, NUM Law Review* 3, no. 35 (2016): 107.

48 Batbayar and Bayartuyaa, "Altan khany tsaaz," p. 108.

49 Elisabetta Chiodo, *The Mongolian Manuscripts on Birch Bark from Xarbuxyn Balgas in the Collection of the Mongolian Academy of Sciences*, 2 vols., Asiatische Forschungen 137 (Wiesbaden: Harrassowitz, 2000), vol. I, pp. 193, 195.

50 Krystyna Chabros, *Beckoning Fortune: A Study of the Mongol Dalalya Ritual*, Asiatische Forschungen 117 (Weisbaden: Otto Harrassowitz, 1992), 234.

51 Natasha Fijn, *Living with Herds: Human-Animal Coexistence in Mongolia* (Cambridge: Cambridge University Press, 2011), 31–35, 64–80.

52 B. Bayarsaikhan, Ts. Shagdarsüren, and J. Gerelbadrakh (eds.), *Mongγol čaγajin-u bičig: Ekh bichgiin sudalgaa, tergüün dewter (Mongol Code: Textological Study, Volume I)*, Monumenta Mongolica, tomus 4 (Ulaanbaatar, 2004), 8.

53 Dalizhabu (Darijab), *"Ka'erka fagui" Hanyi ji yanjiu ("Khalkha Jirum" Chinese Translation and Research)*, Zhongguo Bianjiang Minzu Diqu Lishi Yu Dili Yanjiu Congshu (Beijing: Zhongyang minzu daxue chuban she, 2015), 220.

54 de Rachewiltz (trans.), *The Secret History of the Mongols*, pp. 265–266. C.f. the argument that slaves, captives, and commoners were "black lineages." However, I have found no evidence that slaves were considered to be black

in the way that commoners were; Sechin Jagchid and Paul Hyer, *Mongolia's Culture and Society* (Boulder: Westview Press, 1979), 283.

55 O. Oyuunjargal, "Sum, khamjlagyg yalgakh shaardlaga: Saishaalt Yerööltiin üyeiin Tüsheet khan aimgiin jisheen deer (The Order to Distinguish between Sumu and Qamjilġ-a: The Case of Tüsheet Khan Province in the Jiaqing Era)." In *Chin uls ba Mongolchuud*, ed. S. Chuluun and Oka Hiroki, CNEAS Reports 13 (Sendai: Center for Northeast Asian Studies, 2014), pp. 109–110.

56 Bayarsaikhan, Shagdarsüren, and Gerelbadrakh, (eds.), *Mongyol čayajin-u bičig (Mongol Code)*, pp. 9–110.

57 Bayarsaikhan, Shagdarsüren, and Gerelbadrakh, (eds.), *Mongyol čayajin-u bičig (Mongol Code)*, §§4.11a.5–8.

58 Alexander Woodside, "The Ch'ien-Lung Reign." In *The Cambridge History of China, Vol. 9 Part One: The Ch'ing Empire to 1800*, ed. Willard J. Peterson (Cambridge: Cambridge University Press, 2002), 289–290.

59 Bayir Dugarov, "Geser Boyda-yin sang: A Little-Known Buryat-Mongolian Sutra." In *Writing in the Altaic World*, ed. Juha Janhunen and Volker Rybatzki, Studia Orientalia 87 (Helsinki: Finnish Oriental Society, 1999), 49–50.

60 Walther Heissig, *The Religions of Mongolia* (Berkeley: University of California Press, 1980), 99–101.

61 Walther Heissig, *Geser-Studien: Untersuchungen zu den Erzählstoffen in den "neuen" Kapiteln des mongolischen Geser-Zyklus (Geser Studies: Investigations of the Narrative Material in the "New" Chapters of the Mongolian Geser Cycle)*, Abhandlungen Der Rheinisch-Westfälischen Akademie Der Wissenschaften 69 (Opladen: Westdeutscher Verlag, 1983), 214–215.

62 *Han i araha Manju gisun i buleku bithe, Qaġan-u bicigsen Manju ügen-ü toli bicig, Man-Meng hebi Qing wen jian ([Ma., Mo.] Imperially Commissioned Manchu Dictionary, [Ch.] Manchu-Mongolian parallel Qing script dictionary)*, Mango bunkenshū, Dai 1-hen, Gogaku hen, reel 4-9, 29 vols., (1717), p. 5-3b.

63 Oliver Corff, Kyoko Maezono, Wofgang Lipp, Dorjpalam Dorj, Görööchin Gerelmaa, Aysima Mirsultan, Réka Stüber, Byambajav Töwshingtögs, Xieyan Li (eds.), *Auf kaiserlichen Befehl erstelltes Wörterbuch des Manjurischen in fünf Sprachen: "Fünfsprachenspiegel:" systematisch angeordneter Wortschatz auf Manjurisch, Tibetisch, Mongolisch, Turki und Chinesisch: vollständig romanisierte und revidierte Ausgabe mit textkritischen Anmerkungen, deutschen Erläuterungen und Indizes (The Imperially Commissioned Dictionary of Manchu in Five Languages: "Pentaglot")*, 2 vols. (Wiesbaden: Harrassowitz, 2013), §1148.4.

64 Alice Sárközi (ed.), *A Buddhist Terminological Dictionary: The Mongolian Mahāvyutpatti, Asiatische Forschungen 130* (Wiesbaden: Harrassowitz, 1995), vi.

65 Yumiko Ishihama and Yoichi Fukuda (eds.), *A New Critical Edition of the Mahāvyutpatti: Sanskrit-Tibetan-Mongolian Dicitonary of Buddhist Terminology, Materials for Tibetan-Mongolian Dictionaries 1* (Tokyo: Toyo Bunko, 1989), §§3823-4.

66 Ishihama and Fukuda (eds.), *A New Critical Edition of the Mahāvyutpatti*, §5790.

67 Joseph Étienne Kowalewski, *Dictionnaire Mongol-Russe-Française (Mongolian-Russian-French Dictionary) (Kasan [Kazan]*, 1844), 2526b.

68 Alice Sárközi, ed., *Sumatiratna: Tibetan-Mongolian Explanatory Dictionary with English Equivalents and Index of Mongolian Words, Classical Mongolian Studies, I* (Ulaanbaatar and Budapest: International Association for Mongol Studies, 2018), 939.

69 Antoine Mostaert, *Dictionnaire Ordos, Seconde Édition (Ordos Dictionary, Second Edition), Monumenta Serica, Journal of Oriental Studies of the Catholic University of Peking, V* (New York, London: Johnson Reprint Corporation, 1968), 267b.

70 Simon Wickhamsmith, *Politics and Literature in Mongolia (1921–1948), North East Asian Studies* (Amsterdam: Amsterdam University Press, 2020), 71–73.

71 Oyuunjargal, "Sum, khamjlagyg yalgakh shaardlaga (The Order to Distinguish between Sumu and Qamjilġ-a)," pp. 109–110.

72 Malqinhu, "A Visit to 'Slave Village.'" In *On the Horqin Grassland, Panda Books* (Beijing: Chinese Literature Press, 1988), 131–132.

73 Malqinhu, "A Visit to 'Slave Village,'" p. 136.

74 Magdalena Tatár Fosse, "The Khotons of Western Mongolia," *Acta Orientalia Academiae Scientiarum Hungaricae XXXIII*, no. 1 (1979): 6–7; Wei-chieh Tsai, *"Mongolization of Han Chinese and Manchu Settlers in Qing Mongolia, 1700–1911"* (PhD dissertation, Bloomington, Indiana University, 2017), 192–199.

75 Garriet Bicher-Stou (Harriet Beecher-Stow), *Tom awgyn owookhoi (Uncle Tom's Cabin)* (Ulaanbaatar: Ulsyn khewleliin khereg erkhlekh khoroo, 1962).

76 Irinchin, "Regarding the Mongol Bo'ol in the 11th and 12th Centuries," p. 315.

77 Irinchin, "Regarding the Mongol Bo'ol in the 11th and 12th Centuries," pp. 328–329.

78 Juan P. Lewis, "Did Varro Think That Slaves Were Talking Tools?," *Mnemosyne* 66 (2013): 634–648.

79 Yang Haiying (Coġtu Oġonos), *Wenming de youmu shiguan: Yi bu nizhuan de da Zhongguo shi (The Nomadic Historical Perspective of Civilization: A Contrarian Work of Great China History)*, trans. Cheng T'ien-en (New Taipei City: Baqi wenhua chubanshe, 2019), 59–64.

80 Pamela Kyle Crossley, "Slavery in Early Modern China." In *The Cambridge World History of Slavery, Volume 3: AD 1420–AD 1804* (New York: Cambridge University Press, 2011), 210–211.

81 Yilingzhen, "Guanyu shiyi shier shiji de bowole (Regarding Bo'ol of the Eleventh and Twelfth Centuries)." In *Yuan shi lun cong*, vol. III, ed. Yuan shi yanjiu hui (Zhonghua shuju, 1986), 23–30.

PART III

Legacies and Afterlives

CHAPTER 8

Slavery and the Virtual Archive: On Iran's Dāsh Ākul

Parisa Vaziri

In the opening scene of the Iranian filmmaker Masʿūd Kīmīāyī's *Dāsh Ākul*, a series of unthinkably quick shot reverse shots fuels a founding antagonism: "Everyone in Shiraz knew that Dāsh Ākul and Kākā Rustam would shoot each other's shadows."[1] These lines, lifted from the opening of the famous short story by the modernist writer Sādiq Hidāyat, appear during the opening credits of Kīmīāyī's film of the same name. The famous, beloved story chronicles the rivalry between a village hero, Dāsh Ākul, and his foe, Kākā Rustam, while pronouncing two archetypal models of masculinity reproduced and spectacularized by Iranian film in the mid-twentieth century.[2] By unexpectedly bringing to the fore a detail that was abandoned in Hidāyat's literary vision of a legend supposedly constructed from fact, Kīmīāyī's film virtualizes a historical element of the Shirazi legend of Dāsh Ākul. This historical element presents us with an unexpected testimony – a testament to the history of slavery in Iran. However, in *reviving and distorting* simultaneously, the film's recursive gesture reveals an aberrancy at the heart of the history of slavery in Iran and its archival foundations. Archival virtuality, or the virtual archive, exposes an original historiographical perversion.

A recent topic of investigation among historians, literature on the subject of slavery in Iran unfolds in spite of, and in avoidance of this perversion that corrupts historiography's claims to truth. By contrast, drawing upon the enigmatic case of Dāsh Ākul and its literary, cinematic, and virtual adaptations, I argue that it is not possible to narrate a history of slavery, nor reckon with slavery's ambiguous legacy in the Indian Ocean context, without engaging the fundamental distortion that occurs when fact is dissociated from experience. This is not simply a matter of the inevitable and usual distortions that occur in the process of articulating experience into language, of assimilating the nonsensical into sense. Nor is it a matter of the possibilities lost to the sometimes unrational course of a historian's choice-making that arranges language, and therefore historical meaning, into narrative.³ Rather, the *experience* of slavery is *fundamentally distortive*. Slavery is an experience of annihilation, and an annihilation of experience. If the history of slavery is a history rooted in fact, it is also the case that the nature of (historical) fact is to conceal, by presuming, the conditions of possibility for consensus about its existence. History's consensus ties truth to materiality and inscription, ignoring the incommensurable gap between inscription and experience when, as under slavery, the category of experience loses all claims to self-evidence and coherence. The virtual possesses unique resources for illuminating aporias both produced and concealed by the hierarchies of disciplinary authority that elevate the historian's inevitable positivism to an untenable, even injurious position.

Sometimes categorized as part of a genre of commercial action movies known as jāhilī (roughly, "tough guy" films), on first analysis, Kīmīāyī's *Dāsh Ākul* would appear to have little to do with slavery's history in Iran. Not only was the history of slavery little discussed, even an irrelevant topic in the 1970s when *Dāsh Ākul* was made and in the 1930s when it was written, but the film's plot is on the surface entirely disconnected from such a history. About a revered lūtī (loosely, chivalrous rogue) in the Sarduzak neighborhood of Shiraz who reluctantly gains charge of an old companion's estate (Hājī Samad's) upon the latter's death, "Dāsh Ākul" is a story of the unrequited love between Dāsh Ākul (played by the filmfārsī star, Bihrūz Vūsūqī) and Marjān (played by Mary Apik), the young daughter of Hājī Samad put under the hero's guardianship. It is also a film about the infamous rivalry between Dāsh Ākul and Kākā Rustam, the neighborhood lūtī and the neighborhood lout, a cosmogonic story of good and evil representative of the broader filmfārsī (pre-revolutionary Iranian film) commercial mode, and comparable to the dichotomous character types of American Westerns. As one commentator aptly puts it, it is a typically Iranian story in which light battles dark.⁴ Male rivalry bookends the film, which begins and ends with physical altercations between Rustam and Dāsh Ākul, as it subordinates the narrative's romance to its preoccupation with masculine codes of honor, which are in turn politically colored by the sociocultural context of Muhammad Reza Pahlavi Shah's modernization campaign.

8.1   Glitch as Trace

The shot-reverse-shot sequence that initiates Dāsh Ākul and Kākā Rustam's first altercation is a ubiquitous technique in Kīmīāyī's film and collects excitement in scenes of action, playing up the contrast between Dāsh Ākul's heroism and Kākā Rustam's villainism. (In the remainder of this text, I will refer to Bahman Mufīd's character as Rustam. Like Dāsh, a contraction of dādāsh, brother, Kākā is also invoked as a term for brother in Shirazi Persian; however, it is simultaneously invoked as a strong racial epithet for black people. Kākā Rustam holds this perverse doubled meaning.) The sequence's *unthinkable* quickness signals the precarious status of the film's material existence. For, like most degraded or fully expired pre-revolutionary Iranian films, we inherit Dāsh Ākul's legacy only through digitized form.

The unthinkability of Kīmīāyī's shot-reverse-shot sequence derives from the unnatural, too-automated, almost metaleptic quickness of the frame movements, which do not mimic a plausible real-time movement of the eyes as the traditional shot-reverse-shot technique does. In indicating an area of the stock where breaks in the film may have been repaired through retroactive frame splicing, or more likely, simply a deterioration of tape, the sequence also suggests a disruption of editing once clearly ordered around the rational logic of a spatiotemporal event (a physical duel). This false speed thus opens up, on the one hand, the temporal layering sub-sumed under the category of memory, and on the other, an event on the order of non-eventuality, or virtuality. Something is amiss in the image, communicating its aberrancy through a doubtful speed, moving the viewer to pause at an uncomfortable kinesthesia. In the film's opening scene, the hero and anti-hero prepare for their physical duel with a linguistic brawl, enacting Hidāyat's citation. Rustam invites Dāsh Ākul's ire with an assault on a young child. After insulting the boy's mother, Rustam forces wine down the boy's throat, lifts him and spins him on his shoulders in the center of a crowd of aghast onlookers, as the camera's point of view whirls into that of the raised spinning boy. Dāsh Ākul approaches, and Rustam dares him to strike. Hurling insults, Dāsh Ākul responds in turn, mutter-ing about Rustam's illegitimate birth, a bastard from a line of adulteresses ("ay jadan dar jad zinātkār"). The allusion to Rustam's lineage is almost irrelevant in the context, subsumed by the general deluge of verbal affronts. In the prose story version, Dāsh Ākul mocks his name, accusing him of being a fake Rustam ("ma'lūm mīshah rūstam sūlat va ifindī pīzī kīst.") Rustam is the name of the valiant and celebrated Persian hero [pahlavān] of Firdawsi's tenth-century *Shāhnāmah, Book of Kings* epic, "a central moral core of the Persian imperial order."[5] Combined with the hyperquick series of shots that focuses on Dāsh Ākul, and then on Rustam's blackened face, the charges of bastardism (in the film) and, more indirectly, of ersatz identity (in the story) together acquire a particular meaning: a black Rustam couldn't possibly be a real Iranian paladin. This

impossibility is connected to the "real" Rustam's biography upon which
Sādīq Hidāyat's story was originally based.

When Kīmīāyī's *Dāsh Ākul* was released in theaters in 1971, Rustam's
blackface makeup would not have caused viewers the slightest pause. The
practice of blackface in films was more or less ubiquitous by the 1970s[6]
and Bahman Mufīd, the actor who played Rustam, was well known for his
blackface acting. However, in light of *Dāsh Ākul*'s complex history of
adaptation, it is worth reflecting on the signifier of blackface, which
reactivates an original detail from the Shirazi legend of Dāsh Ākul that
had been effaced from its literary stage. This is the detail of Rustam's
Africanness and of his enslavement, eclipsed from the film due to inad-
vertent acts of censorship, and from the short story version for even more
ambiguous reasons. At only two moments in Kīmīāyī's film do such details
emerge. First, in this initial altercation when Dāsh Ākul calls him a bastard
and in a later brawl in an alleyway when, attacking Dāsh Ākul during the
hero's drunken stupor, Rustam reveals, in muffled, nearly inscrutable
words, his own family history: "They threw my parents in the water in
the black of winter right before my eyes. Yes, my dad was a slave [ghūlām].
They did it to make me obedient. But instead of learning obedience,
I learned force."

Rustam's words are barely audible, absorbed by the thickness of his lout
accent and his chronic stutter, and therefore, his personal story is nearly
undetectable in the film. According to an interview between the film
historian Hamid Naficy and Bahman Mufīd the choice of blackface was
deliberate and connected to other changes the filmmaker had made in light
of research on the original legend. The choice to clothe Rustam in
blackface was made after the actors, in the process of researching the
Dāsh Ākul legend through conversations with Shirazi elders, learned that
the biographical Rustam was in fact a black man. He was the child of
enslaved Africans who had been killed by the wealthy Shirazi Qavām
family after a member of the family had assaulted Rustam's mother. We
do not know the details of Qavām's sexual advance, only that "One cold
winter night, when his father had refused to grant Qavām sexual access to
his wife, they were thrown out into the courtyard as punishment."[7] The
people enslaved by the Qavām family – Rustam's parents – froze to death
"in the black of winter right before [Rustam's] eyes."

What the film historian names a "backstory" to Dāsh Ākul thus contains
a trace from Iran's history of slavery, that, in characteristic fashion,
dissolves in its abstraction to legend, fiction, and then film. I want to
reflect on this recursive function of adaptation and remediation, and in

particular, on blackface in the cinematic *Dāsh Ākul*. On the one hand, Rustam's blackface references the Africanness of the real-life enslaved child Rustam, thus appearing to reacquire a historical dimension previously dissolved in the creative act of literature. At the same time, Mufīd's blackface practice also assimilates into the ubiquitous practice of Persian sīyāh bāzī (black play) that continues to be denied historical referentiality. In its digitized preservation, Dāsh Ākul suggests that the history of slavery is itself a virtual history, that is, a history of a different order than the one upon which a binary of reality and unreality can be safely structured. At the same time, it therefore destabilizes historiography's competence in comprehending, adjudicating, archiving, guarding this history.

As literature and film scholars point out, the digital does not produce the category of the virtual. Rather, cinema has long taken recourse to a certain thought of the virtual through (ancient) anti-realist techniques meant to conjure the fantasy world of dreams. These are also literary techniques; formal properties of language can produce the experience of potentiality.[8] The musical genre's dream or song sequence fulfills the function of a distinction between real and imaginary as disparate registers that produce and reinforce one other.[9] Melodrama achieves anti-realism through the most banal narrative elements – for example, the ubiquitous heterosexual romance. In *Dāsh Ākul*, the adult male's fixation on the fourteen-year-old daughter of Hājī Samad, Marjān, punctuates the film with moments of fantasy that are colored by desemanticized, evocative music. Dāsh Ākul first sights Marjān's face at Hājī Samad's funeral in the woods. Wailing herself near to unconsciousness, Marjān's mother implores Dāsh Ākul to find water to calm her. As he dutifully returns with bowl in hand and lifts her face veil, he is arrested, indeed overpowered by what he glimpses momentarily under the niqab. Symphonic music with distinct melodic flute phrases rises out of the new shot-reverse-shot sequence – this time, of Dāsh Ākul and the girl-child Marjān, as Dāsh Ākul shakes droplets from his fingertips onto Marjān's closed eyelids, each hand jerk punctuated by the string of a tar, emphasizing the cryptic (and creepy) eroticism of this arousal to conscious-ness. In the tamer, fiction version of the story, Dāsh Ākul first glimpses Marjān through a curtain, not a facial veil.

Marjān's veil is a uniquely fetishistic symbol of the larger enigma that heterosexual desire comes to stand for in *Dāsh Ākul*, reflecting a similar theme in Hidāyat's *The Blind Owl* (*Būf-i Kūr*). The cinematic *Dāsh Ākul* narrative follows the hero's resistance to a desire that becomes his only reason for living – on the one hand, because the desire for Marjān is energizing, powerful, life-giving; on the other, because Dāsh Ākul's humanness depends on rejecting Marjān, or saving her from the dangerous vitality of his desire. Humanness, here, is masculinity itself – the simultaneously quaint, and terrifying masculinity (lūtīgarī) that *Dāsh Ākul* celebrates, and which opposes itself to the animalistic masculinity, the false lūtīgarī of the black lout who does not deserve the name Rustam. "There is only one thing dearer to Dāsh Ākul than Marjān, and that is his pride, status [manā 'at]."[10] (This contradiction or tension between general moral duty [vazīfah-yi akhlāghī] and personal tendencies defines the jahilī, or tough-guy filmfarsi genre).[11]

To the extent that Rustam's black makeup is also a kind of fetishistic veil, it too suggests a hidden but prosthetic depth whose exposure must at all costs remain repressed. If fiction partially accomplishes this repression, cultural transmission reveals the impower of the literary gesture – its inherent instability. The first encounter that illustrates the antagonism between Rustam and Dāsh Ākul, the first shot-reverse-shot duel results from an affront that precedes Rustam's assault of the child. The boy's mother, veiled identically to Marjān with a black chador and white face covering, calls out to Rustam as he is harassing someone in the gathering. He reaches for her face to grab and lift her rūband, but is stopped in his tracks by her son, who spits in Rustam's blackened face. The narrative cannot tolerate Rustam's unveiling, neither his own unveiling – that is, the unveiling of his black mask – nor of the unveiling of the meaning of the veil itself, its unconquerable mode of presentation, its stabilization of legitimacy and authority.

8.2   Nonracial Blackface, Nonracial Slavery

I have mentioned the unremarkability of Mufid's blackface practice in *Dāsh Ākul*. Sīyāh bāzī refers to the Persian popular improvisatory theater tradition which focalizes a male character who has blackened his face with soot or vegetable fat and who improvises scenarios through self-deprecation, vulgarity, and insolence toward his master (arbāb), or another figure of social rank. As a tradition without written scripts, the origin of sīyāh bāzī is challenging to track, though commentators suggest its documentation since at least the Safavid period (c. sixteenth century), thereby antedating the American tradition of blackface minstrelsy.[12] Because of its ambiguous origins, to this day, both individual scholars and public citizens continue to debate, in all seriousness, the racism of the sīyāh bāzī tradition. Scholars, public figures, and those who blindly submit to the false authority of academics concoct sinuous genealogies to dissociate sīyāh bāzī from any probable reference to a history of African enslavement, conjoining it to a range of mythical origins, from mourning rituals during the Sumerian Festival of Dumuzi, to vague Zoroastrian fire worshipping practices.[13]

To trace modern forms of blackface practice to ancient history is to indiscreetly dissolve any characterization of sīyāh bāzī as racial, as it is to segregate and protect this practice from the history of African slavery with which, as its description suggests, it undeniably communicates, separately from any conjecture about its origins. The insistence on a form of "non-racial" black caricature that cannot even be properly translated into English mirrors the tendency of scholars to dissociate the history of African enslavement in the Indian Ocean from the history of racial blackness (as it most pronouncedly unfolds in an Atlantic context) in general. Rather than affirm this self-reproducing distinction unreflectively, I want to draw attention to one specific dimension of the comparative logic, which is too often treated as a casual, disposable fact. In an essay published over a decade ago, one historian contemplated the dearth of slave narratives in the Middle East and North Africa, wondering about its consequences for historians' ability to reconstruct a history of slavery in general: "The slaves themselves seem to have left no traces, either written or genetic."[14]

What would it mean to honestly confront the impasse created by a *lack* of trace? Unsurprisingly, the paucity of materials produced by the enslaved themselves has not deterred historians from proceeding to produce histories of slavery in the Middle East and North Africa. In the absence of slave testimony, there are nevertheless ways, acts of "decipherment" through which to recognize the character and importance of the institution of slavery in Southwest Asia and North Africa. The historian must not consign herself to silence, even in the face of the silence of the enslaved, nor must she, paradoxically, cover over the enslaved's silence with her own voice. The formulation is familiar, but also tautological. Obviously, a silent historian is no historian at all. That silence kindles the historian's urge, even necessity of speech is self-evident. The more challenging question is whether historiography has the capacity to *listen* to silence; or, more precisely, whether silence exists on the order of eventuality that is the terrain of historiography. Historians would not "understand a world grounded on the destruction of that which is their very essence," that is, the destruction, as well as the absolute impossibility of the archive.[15]

In their research for *Dāsh Ākul*, Kīmīāyī's film crew did not have access to slave testimonies – neither of Rustam's, nor of his parents. Instead, they interviewed community elders who lived contemporaneously with the events that conditioned Dāsh Ākul's original rivalry with Rustam. From their stories, we learn that Dāsh Ākul, and not Rustam, violated the lūtī code of honor and was killed for his betrayal of the Qavām family. Unlike the fictional self-abnegating Dāsh Ākul, who renounces his love for the fourteen-year-old Marjān out of awareness of the impropriety of abusing his position of guardianship, the legendary Dāsh Ākul endangers the daughter of the Qavām family who is put in his care. The *Dāsh Ākul* film crew learned of a story that was quite distinct from Hidāyat's version. Years after the murder of Rustam's parents, a Qavām elder put Dāsh Ākul in charge of his estate while embarking on a pilgrimage to Mecca. Dāsh Ākul's male lover "impregnated Qavām's daughter through an illicit relationship." According to the interview's language, it is ambiguous, though likely, that this "illicit relationship" was in fact a rape; "tartībish-u dād," says Bahman Mufīd.[16] "Dāsh Ākul was placed in front of a tree and killed with a machete by the next person in line to become the neighborhood's luti. . . Kākā Rustam."[17]

If the detail of Rustam's enslavement to the Qavām family, and the violent death of his parents are part of the "authentic" Dāsh Ākul legend, these details did not survive in Hidāyat's version of the story, which both made it famous, accessible to a broad reading public, and served as the subtext for Kīmīāyī's popular and award-winning film decades later. Without Hidāyat's story, it is unlikely Kīmīāyī's film would have been made in the first place; in turn, Kīmīāyī's film revitalized Hidāyat's story and widely expanded its reception beyond the limited scope of an elite reading public. But this non-survival of detail is different than total disappearance. For in fact, the details do survive, as distortions, like a glitch in the image, a break in the film stock, arresting the suspension of disbelief. Two rapes, Rustam's mother's and Marjān's, are contorted into virtual elements; on the one hand, into Rustam's blackness, and on the other, into the transcendental desire for Marjān's purity, kept sacred by the veil that protects its blinding source.

It is indisputable that certain aspects of the original legend of Dāsh Ākul were jettisoned in the name of fiction. And of course, such is the prerogative of fiction writers; anyone who does not claim to be a historian ought not to be held to the standards of one. But Hidāyat was not only a famous fiction writer. Also considered by some to be the father of Iranian anthropology, Hidāyat's collections of traditional folklore (*Nayrangistān; Awsānah*), the first of their kind, forged the intimacy between modernist literature and Iranian tradition, an inherently fraught relation between Culture as a realm of spiritual and civilizational existence [farhang] and culture as a body of tradition, ritual, and superstition [adāb va rusūm], reflective of the hierarchical dynamics of the global surrealist tradition by which Hidāyat was very much influenced. By enveloping the raw material of (lower-case) culture, adāb va rusūm, inside of itself, Culture, farhang, both distinguished itself as a morally superior sphere of being and defined, while validating norms according to supposedly proper modes of Persian behavior.

Dāsh Ākul's lūtīgarī symbolizes an ancient code of masculine honor, while the ersatz Rustam suggests the despotism and force that has corrupted Iranian culture.[18] Black Rustam's ultimate victory over Dāsh Ākul expresses the completed process of a long genealogy of perceived Iranian alienation and injury, first by Arabs and their supposedly corrupting Islamic religion, and then by Western modernity, a degeneration metonymized by the ruthlessness of the streets under the aggressively pro-modernist regime of Muhammad Reza Shah Pahlavi. After Dāsh Ākul's major defeat, Marjan's betrothal to a man even older and uglier than he, the hero returns to his favorite square in Sarduzak and watches people pass: "compared to the past, this place had deteriorated, people seemed in his eyes to have changed, just as he had changed." Importantly, this realization of Sarduzak's degradation coincides with Dāsh Ākul's final defeat at the hands of Rustam, at the syntactic and thematic levels. The sentence that continues to describe Dāsh Ākul's waning vitality merges with Rustam's sudden infiltration of lexemes and his literal hovering: "[Dāsh Ākul] became dizzy" (literally, "his eyes went black [chishmish sīyāh mīrāft])," "his head hurt, suddenly the shadow of darkness appeared and came toward him." Hidāyat, "Dāsh Ākul," 51–2.

What, precisely, is the nature of the *loss of history* that occurs as the legend of Dāsh Ākul is transformed into the modernist story, Dāsh Ākul, given that the so-called original legend is itself a fiction modeled on anonymous testimony? For certainly, the story itself was never told in the first person by Rustam, nor his mother who was sexually assaulted and then killed by her master. We are unlikely to ever learn more about the details of the sexual violation. And certainly, we will never learn about the experience of her death. To the extent that slavery is itself a form of death, however, at the very least, historically a substitution for death, what kind of testimony is possible as slavery is lived and in its wake? The loss of history demonstrated by these series of leaking transcriptions suggests, perversely, uncomfortably, that perhaps the most faithful engagement with the facts that one does not and cannot know is *not* manifestation, not representation, but rather, incubation.

The legend of Dāsh Ākul and its aesthetic expressions constitute a set of objects whose charged intrarelations exemplify the challenge to historiography, and more generally, to full facticity that *is* the context of Indian Ocean slavery history. Although Hidāyat's story twists the details of the original story – some of which Kīmīāyī's film partially revises – it is also the case that Hidāyat's story, which effaces the fact of slavery, and distorts Rustam's life, is a necessary step in the legend's preservation. The abstraction of truth that thus occurs from fact to legend is heightened by the transition from legend to short story, an ongoing process of abstraction that culminates only when its film version is literally virtualized, digitized. But, just as the digital process must recomposit numbers back into an image once they have been converted and filed, Dāsh Ākul's compounding abstractions are in turn necessary to its culmination in a new form. This form retroactively illuminates some prior factual loss: namely, the fact of blackness, of slavery as a form of annihilation.

8.3   The Archive as Annihilation

It is an unthinking truism for scholars who write and research about it, that Indian Ocean slavery is qualitatively distinct from Atlantic World slavery. The ubiquitous, if sometimes confusingly implicit and self-evident comparative logic is anchored in the emblematic name of the Atlantic slave, in contrast to whose extreme abjection stands the well-treated enslaved domestic of a more archaic, kinder world. In her 2017 monograph on slavery in Iran, the first of its kind, Behnaz Mirzai doubles down on the good-treatment thesis, drawing (reasonably) upon the limited available sources: chronicles, travelogues, geographical treatises, observations of the British Foreign Office, correspondences between government officials. (Because the British had interests in ending the slave trade in the Ottoman Empire and Persian Gulf in the nineteenth century, their presence, and perspective, in the form of bureaucratic *document*, is overrepresented in modern studies of slavery). Under such circumstances, slave testimony becomes the effect of a position that can be said to be fully outside of the experience of slavery, even if it is not entirely outside of the event of slavery – that is, if slavery can be said to constitute an event. From these monodirectional sources, Mirzai repeats the conclusions of historians of slavery in the Middle East that precede her: we lack "anything resembling the traumatic American experience of slavery."[19] To sit with this uncontroversial and predictable conclusion, we must then, too, be able to express, with at least some degree of coherence, the status of our facts in their independence from experience. This status is uninteresting for the historian to the extent that it undermines her entire practice, as well as her, though in truth more often his, stature as gatekeeper of the past's reality.

In the presence of particular kinds of evidence, consensus is established in a particular way. This means that, logically, the presence of new kinds of evidence can sway consensus; the fact that new evidence is always possible means that it is the nature of history to change, to not only tolerate, but exist as its own possibility of transformation. The expansion of the archive (and it is also the nature of the archive that it must always remain open to its own future) means that, in theory, consensus is never stable. However, *in the absence of evidence*, there is no way to disrupt consensus. "The very limited documentation of the sea voyage" from East Africa to Asia, lamented an early scholar of Indian Ocean slavery, "results, no doubt, from the fact that the Arab dealers and crews did not keep many records of the slave trade, certainly not on the more inhumane aspects of it."[20]

All archives have their limitations; it is in fact the very impossibility of storing everything (and the fact that everything can and likely will be destroyed) that defines the archive's finitude and its reason for existence. There would be no need for solicitous protection from the elements, or from theft, in the institution of the museum, the office bureau, the cordoned archaeological site, without this limitation. There would be no archive without the natural annihilation that is forgetting, without a radical finitude.[21] But the writing of historiography through the limitations of its own archives does not just produce limited or faulty historiography. Because the humanist underpinnings of historiography imbue the materiality of the archive with spiritual life, historiography sacralizes contingency, dissimulates contingency as irrefutable fact.[22] It is thus that the grave limitations of the archive can nevertheless authorize social memory in the name of historical truth. I am suggesting that contemporary historiographies of slavery in Southwest Asia inherit an unjust, unjustified authority. Against the domineering stature of the document, against the confident testament of the material archive, silence cannot defend itself; absence is meaningless. And though not quite unreal, the virtual is not only not yet real; it is and will *never* be real, is defined by this liminal suspension. The virtual remains unrecognized by the metaphysical norms of the present.

The legend of Dāsh Ākul contains no slave testimony. This is not only because Dāsh Ākul's legacy remains only in the form of fictions that have evacuated its truth, nor because slave testimonies are entirely nonexistent. Rather, as I have suggested, it is the essence of slavery to annihilate experience, just as it is the essence of the archive to obliterate itself. Slavery annihilates experience. Rustam's parents are left in the cold of winter to freeze when Rustam's father attempts to protect his wife from rape. If Dāsh Ākul's humanness depends on his dignity, just as the modern Persian subject's humanness depends on his cultured being [farhang], his capacity for proper speech and knowledge, Rustam's father has no standing to preserve. Not only is he not a subject *of* culture (a cultured subject); he cannot even be included as the digested element of farhang. (For example, as the folktale of Dāsh Ākul is metabolized by Hidāyat's modernist vision and as lūtīgari is consumed by modern Persians as an admirable, authentic but antiquated form of being.)[23]

Black Rustam, too, is not human. Both Hidāyat and Kīmīāyī emphasize this through Rustam's chronic stutter [luknah]. Rustam's broken relation to Persian syntax evokes the mutated, mutilated speech of the sīyāh [black] in sīyāh bāzī, who confuses consonants and mangles lexemes; his solecisms produce humor for Persian-language audiences. In both Persian and Arabic humanist thought, proper speech [sukhan; bayān] is a condition for civilized being and opposed to ignorance [jahl].[24]

Rustam's father's act of resistance was abhorrent, monstrous, murder-worthy, because he is excluded from, the proper code of (masculine) humanness in the fictional world of Dāsh Ākul. As the enslaved attendant of Qavām, Rustam's mother (who, like Rustam's father, remains nameless, anonymous) had no ownership over her own experience. The experience of her body belonged to her master, Qavām, who believed himself authorized to kill the body that refused to serve as a surrogate of his own (sexual) experience and pleasure. No consequences would ensue from this murder. What do we learn from this accidentally transmitted, possibly even specious story which is not ours? If the legend of Dāsh Ākul is a typically Iranian legend, as its commentators claim, then maybe it is, too, typically Iranian in that it represses the unspeakable story that it cannot but carry. The unspeakable story of the annihilated maternal body is muttered quickly, inscrutably, under the blackface actor Bahman Mufid's breath, only once the story is transcribed to film, as if not to be heard, not to be disseminated.

In the absence of the experience of the enslaved – which, as the Qavām murder and its subsequent erasure-as-distortion suggests, is *impossible* – historians fill in the dead space of absence with the claim of an echo that is in truth written from the perspective of the annihilators. Is the historiography of slavery, then, the extension of an annihilation of what it purports to present to us as fact? What if fact itself could be a distortion, a form of destruction? If Rustam's story is an anomaly, then surely, we have enough testimonies to prove it, testimonies that tell a different kind of story. After all, the point about the relevance of slave narratives to the historiographical project is that, as Ralph Ellison suggested, experience repeats itself. Thus, the study of slave narratives may discover repetitions and coincidences which amount to a common group experience: "We tell our individual stories so as to become aware of the *general* story."[25] But where are these many individual stories that pattern a general story? The lack of a general story is dissimilated through the substitution of some stories the historian happens upon, the document that is accidentally preserved and that thereby constitutes her contingent archive (it is unnecessary to add that it also constitutes her professional well-being, her institutional standing).

The destroyed experience suggested by the nonexistent testimony of Rustam's mother is exposed to the future in the form of art. But as the term too plainly suggests, "backstory" indicates a story behind or elsewhere than the one we read, see, celebrate and transmit. The backstory is a virtuality, to the extent that it indicates an unmanifest dimension that is concealed by the spectacle and automatism of tradition. It also suggests that the palpable story represses *as* it transmits itself. Hidāyat's "Dāsh Ākul" preserves and even publicizes the legend, releases Dāsh Ākul to common knowledge, as it virtualizes its strangest and *most historical* details. And it is only through the continuation of its transmission, in particular, its translation across media, across geographical boundaries, across generations, that this repression is activated, if only to partially exteriorize what cannot become manifest in the facial inscription of a mask. What Dāsh Ākul's remediation suggests, no less than contemporary historiographies of slavery in the Middle East, is that the condition of transmission is itself a kind of repression, that the archive's preservation is also a concealment and dissimulation, an annihilation of annihilation.

Notes

1 Sādigh Hidāyat, "Dāsh Ākul." In *Sih Qatrih Khūn* (Tihrān: Chāpkhānah-yi Zībā, 1932), 38.

2 On the paradoxical modernism of these "ancient" models of masculinity, see Pedram Partovi, *Popular Iranian Cinema before the Revolution: Family and Nation in Filmfarsi* (Abingdon, Oxon: Routledge, 2017).

3 This by now well-known relation between historiography and narrative was foundational to the sometimes symptomatic polemics between historians, literary theorists and philosophers in the 1980s.

4 Īlmīrā Dādvar, "Dāstān-i dāsh ākul: pāsukhī bih baynāmatnīyat va āfuq-i intizār," *Nāmah-yi Farhangistān* 12, no. 1 (2011).

5 Hamid Dabashi, *The Shahnameh: The Persian Epic as World Literature* (New York: Columbia University Press, 2019), 130.

6 Ghūlām Haydarī, *Trājidī-yi Sīnamā yi Kumidi-i Īrān* (Tihrān: Fīlmkhānah-'i Millī-i Īrān, 1991), 97.

7 Hamid Naficy, "Iranian Writers, Iranian Cinema, and the Case of 'Dash Akol,'" *Iranian Studies* 18 (1985): 244.

8 Katherine Biers, *Virtual Modernism: Writing and Technology in the Progressive Era* (Minneapolis: University of Minnesota Press, 2013), 3–5; Marie-Laure Ryan, *Narrative as Virtual Reality: Immersion and Interactivity in Literature and Electronic Media* (Baltimore: Johns Hopkins University Press, 2003).

9 D.N. Rodowick, *The Virtual Life of Film* (Cambridge, MA: Harvard University Press, 2007), 5.

10 Parvīz Davā'ī, "Dāsh Ākul." In *Majmū'ah-i maghālāt dar naqd va mu'arrifi-i āsār-i Mas'īd Kīmīyāyī*, ed. Zavān Qūkāsīan (Tihrān: Āgāh, 1985), 219.

11 Hamid Naficy, "Gūnah-yi fīlm jāhilī dar sīnamā-yi īrān: barrisī-yi sākhtārī-yi fīlm-i dāsh ākul," *Iran Nameh* 10, p. 543.

12 Muhammad Bāqir Ansārī, *Namāyish-i rūhawzī: zamīnah va 'anāṣir-i khandah'sāz* (Tihrān: Shirkat-i Intishārāt-i Sūrah-Mihr, 2008), 44.

13 For more on the details of this history see Parisa Vaziri, "Antiblack Joy: Transmedial Sīyāh Bāzī and Global Public Spheres," *TDR: The Drama Review* 66, no. 1 (2022), 62-79.

14 Eve Troutt Powell, "Will that Subaltern Ever Speak? Finding African Slaves in the Historiography of the Middle East." In *Middle East Historiographies: Narrating the Twentieth Century*, ed. Israel Gershoni, Amy Singer, and Y. Hakan Erdem (Seattle: University of Washington Press, 2006), 243.

15 Marc Nichanian, *The Historiographical Perversion* (New York: Columbia University Press, 2009), 41.

16 Mufid, Bahman. Interview by Hamid Naficy. Tape Recording. Los Angeles, September 11, 1984.

17 Naficy, "Iranian Writers," p. 245.

18 Naficy traces the code of lūtīgarī back to Mitraism, though his reference to the speculative linguist Mihrdad Bahar undermines the veracity of this claim ("Gūnah-yi Fīlm Jāhilī dar Sīnamā-yi Īrān," p. 541).

19 Behnaz Mirzai, *A History of Slavery and Emancipation in Iran: 1800–1929* (Austin: University of Texas Press, 2017), 3.

20 Joseph Harris, *The African Presence in Asia: Consequences of the East African Slave Trade* (Evanston: Northwestern University Press, 1971), 33.

21 Jacques Derrida, *Archive Fever: A Freudian Impression* (Chicago: University of Chicago Press, 1996).

22 Arjun Appadurai, "Archive and Aspiration." In *Information Is Alive: Art and Theory on Archiving and Retrieving Data*, ed. Arjen Mulder and Susan Charlton (Rotterdam: NAI Publishers, 2003), 15.

23 For Hidāyat's digestion of culture, see Sādiq Hidāyat, "Fuklur yā farhang-i tūdeh." In *Farhang-I Amīyānah-yi Mardūm-i Iran* (Tihrān: Chishmah, 1999).

24 Yasir Suleiman, *Arabic in the Fray: Language Ideology and Cultural Politics* (Edinburgh: Edinburgh University Press, 2013), 51–89.

25 Maryemma Graham and Amritjit Singh (eds.), *Conversations with Ralph Ellison* (Jackson: University of Mississippi, 1995), 372.

CHAPTER 9

Impossible Revolutions? The Contemporary Afterlives of the Medieval Slave Rebellion of the Zendj

Martino Lovato

In his novel *Rose noire sans parfum* (1998), Jamel Eddine Benchecikh gives voice to a wealthy man of the city of Basra living in the late ninth century, during the bloom of the Arab-Islamic golden age. As he witnesses the fall of the city, set on fire by the insurgent enslaved black people, the Zendj, captured in eastern Africa and brought to desalinize the marshes of lower Iraq, this patron of the arts nostalgically enlists the names of those famous Arab poets and essayists nurtured by city's refined ruling class, and wonders: "which of these poets, or of their successors, will ever talk of the revolt of the black slaves, if not to curse it?."[1] More than a thousand years later, the late twentieth and early twenty-first centuries have seen poets emerge who are willing to celebrate the rebellion of the Zendj, considered as the greatest servile insurrection of the medieval Islamic world.[2] Situated at the margins of the contemporary global industry of slave and neo-slave narratives, Bencheikh's novel and Tareq Teguia's film *Révolution Zendj* (2013) similarly establish "parallels across time, seeking to understand the present as an unfolding of a past not yet laid to rest."[3] Both *auteurs* reflect the complex postcolonial relationship between Algeria and France in the global age. A university professor of medieval Arabic literature at the Sorbonne University, Bencheikh wrote *Rose Noire sans parfum* in French, infusing in the novel his knowledge as a scholar and his talent as a poet.[4] Considered as a "thematic and stylistic exception" in contemporary Algerian cinema, Teguia participates in the recent wave of *cinema d'auteur* in the country.[5] Funded by several institutions in Europe and the Arab World, the film's production also reflects the nature of an artistic project transversal across countries and audiences. Conscious of its relevance in the global history of slavery and racism, both Bencheikh and Teguia engage with the medieval rebellion of the Zendj beyond the centuries long controversy between Christian-European and Arab-Islamic authors on the "embarrassing institution" of slavery.[6] They retell the story of the Zendj rebellion as "double critiques," as the Moroccan critic

Abdelkebir Khatibi defines works expressing biographical trajectories between France and the Maghreb that engage critically with European and Arab audiences.[7]

The Zendj rebellion took place between 865CE/255H and 883CE/ 270H, and has been described by the poet Adonis as among one of the first attempts to forge a new form of egalitarian consciousness in the history of the Arab-Islamic world, beyond the tribalism and racial distinctions traced between the Arabs and the other nations during the first two centuries of Islam.[8] The Zendj were one of the black populations living on the coasts of Eastern Africa. The medieval Arabic sources of the time have employed the term "Zendj" to designate the specific ethnic group of the Zendj, but also to denote black Africans in general, and the black African subjects captured in Africa and sold in Iraq.[9] Although the precepts of the Qur'an and the Traditions of the Prophet speak generally in favor of removing the status of slavery,[10] the growth of Baghdad as a capital of an empire extending across Africa, Europe, and Asia, heightened the new ruling classes' demand for enslaved laborers in the domestic, manufacturing and agricultural fields. In the marshes of lower Iraq, an inhospitable region contended between the sea and the land, the Zendj enslaved men were employed to remove the nitrous topsoil to render arable land: "they were penned up in working gangs of 500 to 5.000 men, and clumped there permanently with only a few handfuls of meal, semolina and dates."[11]

The rebellion was led by a free man of Arab descent, Ali ibn Mohammed, a courtier, a poet, and a political adventurer who had previously attempted two uprisings in Bahrein and Basra. Emphatically referred to in the chronicles as the "Master of the Zendj" (*ṣaḥib al-zinj*), to increase his reputation among his followers he claimed to be a direct descendant of Ali ibn Abi Talib, the nephew and son-in-law of the Prophet. Without undermining the idea of rebellion for freedom and against oppression, a scrutiny of the goals of the Zendj rebellion speaks against the modern, romantic idea of a rebellion made in the name of abolishing slavery itself. Claiming to be a prophet charged by God to fight the corrupted power of the Caliphs, Ali ibn Mohammed promised to emancipate the enslaved black men and to award them their own slaves in return for their services. By pillaging the neighboring cities, and seizing the commercial convoys headed to Baghdad from Africa and the Indian ocean, the insurgents established a state with its own administration, tribunals, and currency. For fifteen years, it extended around its newly founded capital al-Mokhtara in the region between contemporary southern Iraq and Iran; including the cities of Basra, Abadan, al-Ubullah, and al-

Ahwaz. It took ten years for the grand vizier al-Muwaffaq, brother of the Caliph al-Mu'tamid, to gather the imposing army necessary to engage against the rebels in a land suitable for guerrilla warfare, and five more to wipe the Zendj state off the map. The main source of information about the rebellion is the monumental *Book of Prophets and Kings* by Muhammad ibn Jarir al-Tabari, an authoritative historian who wrote a detailed chronicle of the events.[12] No written record, however, has been preserved that presents the point of view of the Zendj or of their leader. Al-Tabari represented the point of view of the Caliphal power, and refers to Ali ibn Mohammed with epithets such as dissolute (*fājir*), traitor (*khā'in*), and profligate (*khabīth; fāsiq*). He presented the Zendj's as a rebellion (*thawra*), an imposture (*ḍalāl*), an apostasy, an "exit" (*khurūj*) from the Muslim community.[13] Reflecting on the religious character of the upheaval and its relation with racial and economic exploitation, both Bencheikh and Teguia creatively interrogate the historical silence of the Zendj: as they witness to the current crisis of secular national projects in Algeria and across the Arab World, they trace analogies between past and present upheavals, responding across the centuries to the Zendj's cry for liberation against oppression.

9.1   Jamal Eddine Bencheikh's *Rose noire sans parfum*

In *Rose noire sans parfum*, Bencheikh provides a "philological reconstruction" of the insurrection, as Umberto Eco has described narratives in which the representation of the events emerges from a precise investigation of the historical subject.[14] The accurate reconstruction of the historical events flows in the novel with the author's work of introspection on the subjective developments of the characters' psychology during the different phases of the rebellion:

> I haven't, at any moment, imagined people or places. I kept close to the facts as they are reported by the chroniclers, but I submitted them to the scrutiny of reflection and nothing can contradict what I inducted from them. I did not disguise anything, I just read silences. They are sometimes more explicit than speech.[15]

The author's claim to historical accuracy should not be mistaken for an old-fashioned claim to absolute "historicity": it rather emerges from the author's awareness of the interpretative challenges and of the limits of our knowledge on the "historical" rebellion of the Zendj. The narration is conducted by the voice of a narrating "I" whose identity imperceptibly changes, from one chapter to another. As in his chronicle al-Tabari mainly focuses on the actions of the two military leaders, so Bencheikh's narrating "I" is mostly that of Ali Ibn Mohammed himself. The fall of Basra, however, is suggestively narrated by the frightened bourgeois of the city. As the arc of rebellion starts bending towards its failure, al-Muwaffaq himself narrates how he crushes the state of the Zendj by subduing their cities one by one. Playfully caught between being the voice of a historical character and a creation of the author, the voice of the narrating "I" occasionally breaks the mimetic conventions of the historical novel, providing a nuanced postmodern feature that allows the character of Ali ibn Mohammed to provoke the reader with references made to modern history and to the present world.

Written in a refined style rich in poetic imagery, the black rose's lack of perfume mentioned in the novel's title alludes to the silence to which the enslaved Zendj themselves have been reduced by the Arab chroniclers. In the novel's prelude, the author pays homage to the Zendj by having them speaking as a choral voice: "we are reduced to be nothing but a mass, object of your fantasies; our language will have no more chances to liberate itself from the books that speak about us. We, who never learned how to write, exist only in those writings that mutilate us."[16] Bencheikh thus comments on this choice:

> I give the first words to the slaves as to clearly underscore the oblivion into which they are kept, the scorn of which they are the object, even on the part of their rebel leader. Once this voice is granted in the prelude to the novel, we will not hear from them anymore. Their actions will suffice. Nothing underscores their condition more than their silence.[17]

As his "I" speaks to the reader, Ali ibn Mohamed reveals himself to be a pragmatic opportunist, making use of religion to feed – to his own advantage – on the enslaved's dream of liberation: "Since I wanted a lineage, I chose an ancestor. I pretended to be the sixth descendant in the direct line of Ali, cousin and son-in-law of the Prophet ... Besides, why am I saying 'I pretended to be,' ... history is chosen and taken, and since I had a chance to be believed, I first believed in it myself."[18] The author engages with the personality of Ali ibn Mohammed, intending to restitute intact to the audience the complexity and contradictory facets of this revolutionary leader. His "I" speaks as a political and military leader in the process of making history, whose life and success are interdependent and always at stake. As he exploits religion and prophetic visions to motivate and manipulate the credulous or fanaticized subjects he leads, he sincerely hopes that God is on his side, and takes his victories for as many signs of divine favor. As the rebellion progresses, he himself becomes more and more persuaded of his own prophetic mission. The pages devoted to his identification with al-Hussain in the martyrdom of Karbala reach a touching, mystical hue that shows Bencheikh's depth of exploration into the character.

Though it is never mentioned in the novel, in an interview the author explains that he completed the novel "under the pressure of the massacres" perpetrated during the Algerian civil war,[19] in which the tragic confrontation between the authoritarian Algerian state and the Islamic Salvation Front (FIS) plunged the country into a spiral of violence leading to some 200,000 casualties between 1992 and 2002.[20] The author's psychological engagement with the personality of the "Master of the Zendj" reflects his examination of the similarities between upheavals distant in time, yet so similar in their dynamics, in which religion is invoked to respond to the needs of a despairing people, both as an agent of liberation and hope and as a justification for coercion and violence. Bencheikh does not sympathize with the historical character of the Zendj leader *per se*, nor idealize the Zendj or their leader by hiding or erasing how the rebellion was fought and then repressed. As he reports the cruelties perpetrated by the Zendj under their leader's command, as well as those committed by the Caliphal power, such as beheadings, crucifixions, pillages, capture of women, he makes of the novel a reflection on "war, and violence, power and its arbitrariness, revolt and its deadlocks, injustice and absence of communication" between the two fronts at war.[21]

What the author sympathizes with is the idea itself of the Zendj slaves' rebellion against oppression. By inserting two quotations reporting the supposed intellectual "deficiencies" of the Zendj from medieval classic authors such as al-Mas'udi and al-Kindi, Bencheikh consciously inscribes the Arab-Islamic culture of the time within the uninterrupted history of racial prejudices that, from Ptolemy to Galenus, has been transmitted to the medieval sciences of both Europe and the Arab-Islamic world.[22] This is part of a parallelism traced, in the novel, between past and present empires, where medieval Arabs and Muslim oppressors are brought together with modern French and Western ones. Both become part of the broad "vous" against whom the protagonist addresses his invectives. As he presents Ali's cynicism, Bencheikh challenges the reader to question the inequalities that make "impostors" like himself appear: "these men, did they follow me because I appeared, or did I appear because they had to follow?"[23] The cursive references he makes throughout the novel to the modern history of European colonialism, to Marx, to the Vietnamese general Giap, or to the

1991 Gulf War and Saddam Hussein – referred to as tyrant who, like himself, received a prophet in a dream before "invading the 19th province of his own country"[24] – trace meaningful analogies between past and present forms of oppression:

> My Zendj come back, keeping in their teeth the heads of the vanquished. [...] While the night falls [...] around the lighted fires, the revolted slaves share, to crown their victory, the flesh still warm of their enemies. Horror? Abomination? Yes. We are not yet, it's true, in your civilized twentieth century [...] And these victims at the end of the century in Sre... bre... how was it? Oh, nica. Read again your world: *thousands of men executed over a whole day and a whole night, and thrown in a mass grave; hundreds buried alive, mutilated; children killed in front of their mothers; a grandfather nailed to a tree and forced to eat the liver of his grandchild...* it's written down in the indictment of an international tribunal![25]

In the first line of the quotation, the author reports the words of al-Tabari,[26] then allowing the narrating "I" of Ali ibn Mohammed to comment on the horrors occurred during the rebellion, so similar to those he witnesses in the 1995 massacre of Muslims in Srebrenica. As these invectives accumulate, this second aspect of Bencheikh's narrating "I" emerges as a sort of timeless presence, a voice that from the past speaks to the present and is in all ages ready to inflame sentiments of rebellion and unrest among the hopeless and the dispossessed.

The episode of the fall of Basra culminates the sense of empowerment Bencheikh wants to give to the Zendj slaves. Here the "I" of the quiet bourgeois of Basra, for whom Islam is order "and everyone has a place in this order,"[27] witnesses the breaking of the social chain of power on the eve of the sack, when even the highest in command do not respond to a hopeless call to arms by the governor, trying instead to save their lives in the imminent fall of the city. The aghast bourgeois describes the Basrians and the Zendj as belonging to two different worlds finally coming together. The death of learned grammarian Zayd al-Faradj al-Riyashi is emblematic of the incommunicability between them:

"To him, a Zendj asked while putting a sickle under his throat:

"Where is your money?"

> And he, the eighty years old eminent professor, who lectured at the great mosque, to whom one could speak only after having kissed his shoulder and his hand, did not understand."

> The weak eye lost, the mouth trembling in feeling this blade over his throat, did not understand what this black slave wanted, who turned him upside down on the ground. ....

He, the great al-Riyashi, who would look indignantly to a misplaced vowel,
angered on an unrefined verse, and got incensed by a duteous attribution!
Which money did he want, this man he could hardly distinguish amidst the
cries and the smoke? What did he want, exactly?

His throat opened as a ripe fruit."[28]

This reversal of the social order, however, is only temporary. The third
and final part of the novel narrates the fall of the Zendj state at the hand of
Caliphal army until the final siege to al-Mokhtara, bringing the world back
to its unjust order, and the surviving Zendj back into subjection. Al-
Muwaffaq describes in minute details the laborious tactics he deploys to
recover the lands under the control of the rebels, thus bringing the
narration back to the version of history produced by the winner. As al-
Tabari's chronicle reports the uncertain identity of the head recognized by
al-Muwaffaq's soldiers as being that of the Zendj's leader, the novel ends
with the protagonist's surviving the fall of al-Mokhtara. Wounded to
death, unrepentant, Bencheikh allows the reader to see the last moments
of the character's life, ready to die in order to haunt the future ages with
the spirit of rebellion: "I am going to meet my death, to submit myself to
the lies of the victors, but I will be an unextinguished amber, a firebrand
exposed to the wind."[29] Through this fading away into history, the author
completes the character's presentation as an active, living force in the
unconcluded struggle of the Zendj across the centuries.

9.2   Tariq Teguia's *Révolution Zendj*

Whereas Bencheikh offers in his novel a historical reconstruction of the
rebellion, Teguia's *Révolution Zendj* is rather its retelling in the present, a
visual journey across the contemporary Arab World through which the
director conveys to the audience those feelings of impotence and rage that
first animated the historical rebellion of the Zendj. By opting to render in
the film's title as "revolution" rather than "rebellion" the Arabic word
thawra, which denotes both meanings, Teguia consciously opts for an
empowering rendition of the original Arabic word, inviting the audience to
question its open meaning after the 2011 "Arab spring" and its "revolu-
tions." The film's narration proceeds independently from that of the Zendj
rebellion, but its narrative is similarly structured on the pattern of rise and
fall, and halfway through the film a symbolic act of revolt against empire
alludes to the events of the rebellion itself. Configured as a quest for the
"ghosts" of the Zendj across the contemporary Arab World undertaken by

the protagonist, the journey of an Algerian journalist (evocatively named Battuta after the famous medieval traveler) becomes instrumental to inform the spectator about the medieval rebellion itself and to bring to the screen the current forms of oppression and disempowerment he witnesses in Algeria, Lebanon, and Iraq.

As Jacques Rancière remarks, Teguia's cinema creates a space of dissent outside the dominant discursive logics of representation, by which "beauty and fiction are for the rich, and sad reality and the dry gaze of the documentary is for the poor."[30] His films "aestheticize" the suffering of the dispossessed, focusing on marginal or forgotten sites, inviting the audience to rethink the way in which they look at the globalized world. Reduced to their essential structure, the plots of his films are like single act plays in which one sudden decision of the protagonist may, as in *Gabbla (Inland)* and *Révolution Zendj*, drastically change the course of events. Within this simple narrative structure, much goes on within the camera frame, where space is perceived from car windows, aerial views on desert tracks, large advertising billboards that stimulate the audience's reflexivity. The length of still or panning shots sets a specific *tempo* tuned to the characters' reflective stillness, a slow pace symptomatic of a world experience perceived from the Global South. In *Révolution Zendj*, the choice of marginal sites such as the region of the M'zab, in the Algerian South, and the very marshes of Lower Iraq in which the Zendj rebellion took place, resist an easy codification of space. Teguia erases the exotic and ethnographic distance of the people living in these regions, to directly impact the spectator with the current reality of their struggles.

The point of departure of Battuta's quest is the city of Ghardaïa, the capital of the M'zab, at the doors of the Saharan desert. Here Battuta is confronted by a group of angry young men with covered faces and stones in their pockets: they are unemployed, explains one of them, despite the large resources of natural gas extracted from underneath the region's soil: "the jobs have been taken by those of the north – Who do they think we are, Zendj?" The spectator will not see the faces of these young men – a feature through which the director visually alludes to the anonymity of the medieval Zendj – and will be confronted with their rage against an unequal distribution of wealth in their own country. The immediacy of this visual challenge does not provide further explanations; only an interested spectator will find out that in the last decade the M'zab became the center of riots and violent demonstrations against the lack of employment and shortages of all kinds, together with violent clashes between the Sunni and Ibadi religious communities living in the region.[31] Is the director here establishing a parallelism between the slave rebellion and the current unrest in post-civil war Algeria? Are the attacks against the Ibadi, considered heretics by the Sunni, as we see in the following sequence, the connection the director intends to establish with the religious aspects of the Zendj rebellion; a reflection upon the contemporary curbing, across the Arab World, of secular national projects into sectarian clashes between ethno-religious communities? Teguia does not answer these questions: he is interested, rather, in raising them, inviting the audience to look at the contemporary world from the perspective of the subjects he represents.

Battuta's investigation on the Zendj rebellion begins after this initial episode. Once back to Algiers, he ponders the young man's use of the word "Zendj." He would now like to do a reportage on contemporary Iraq: here sectarian violence has become an everyday reality after the 2003 US-led invasion in the country, and the establishment of a political representative system based on ethnic and religious quotas (*muhasasa*). However, his chief editor Nassera diverts his quest to Beirut, where he is sent to interrogate the failures of the Arab World. Teguia's retelling the original narrative of the Zendj rebellion is structured by a logic of displacements and substitutions, in which Beirut is given a role as a crossroads linked to the whole Arab World and to the global network of empire. The city is celebrated in the film as a place of encounters, perplexity, desires, where the wounds of the civil war fought in Lebanon between 1975 and 1990 have not been completely healed; it is perhaps the earliest and greatest example, in the recent history of the Arab World, of an inclusive secular project collapsed into sectarian violence between ethno-religious groups.

In Beirut Battuta soon meets the female protagonist, Nahla, the daughter of Palestinian refugees who left Beirut in 1982 and settled in the Greek city of Thessaloniki. The sequence filmed in Greece, in which she and her friends, with their faces covered, write messages on the walls inviting the people to class struggle and revolution, creates a European equivalent to the angered Algerian youth Battuta met in Ghardaïa. She carries a donation from her group of Greek Anarchists to the Palestinian refugees in Beirut, residing in the camp of Shatila. This camp provides a site of memory through which Teguia traces analogies with the medieval Zendj, where in 1982 thousands of Palestinians civilians were massacred by Christian militias backed by the Israeli army. The director makes the audience witness to the condition of disempowerment experienced by the Palestinians in the camp, at once incapable to return to their homeland and living secluded within the Lebanese society. Meanwhile, Battuta's quest for the "ghosts" of the Zendj leads him to meet university professors, discontented young Marxists, and an antiquities dealer who guide him through the black market of the coins minted by the Zendj, and found in the proximity of al-Mokhtara during the 1990s.

His and Nahla's trajectories gradually unfold and merge, to becoming part of what could be called the "contemporary" Zendj staged by Teguia in the film. This group is progressively structured in two distinct ways. First by affinity through the friendship between Battuta, Nahla and Rami, a young Palestinian refugee living confined with his family to an unfulfilling life between the camp and the city: the character through which the director establishes the analogy between this group and the Zendj; then, by the contrast with a group of American investors working for the U.S. government, living in the hotel across the street from where Battuta is hosted. A father and his son waiting in Beirut for a bank transaction vital to their business, we first see them walking around military training camps in Iraq. They are neither caricatures nor simplistically stigmatized as evil agents of the empire. Teguia provides an ideological portrait of them as actors and interpreters of the American wars in the Middle East; the opening lines of Walt Withman's *Song of the Open Road*, quoted by the son while standing in the twilight on a sand dune, is suggestively employed by the filmmaker to underscore the sense of omnipotence they feel while walking on the land of the subdued country. Through the contrast between the two groups, Teguia distinguishes between power and impotence, to shape the contemporary/historicized struggle between the Zendj and empire. Battuta's sudden intrusion into the American businessmen's hotel room, where he takes away a bag full of money destined to finance their operations in Iraq, is the sudden action that changes the course of the plot and establishes the film as a symbolic reenactment of the Zendj rebellion. Through this guerrilla act, similarly to the medieval Zendj, Battuta appropriates a small portion of an endless empire, projecting these "contemporary Zendj" beyond the sense of impotence pervasive in the first part of the film. Whereas Battuta is now free to continue his quest in Iraq, Nahla tries to smuggle Rami into Greece. They use their share of the money to pay for this risky, clandestine journey through which Teguia brings the audience to witness the despair of contemporary migrants attempting to reach the European shores across the Mediterranean.

This last phase of the film introduces, by the parallelism created between the medieval and contemporary stories of the Zendj, the final narrative phase: when the lands conquered by the Zendj start being retaken by the empire. In this last segment, Battuta leaves Beirut heading to the marshes of lower Iraq, where he overcomes the diffidence of a group of workers in the oil sector who first found the coins of the Zendj near al-Mokhtara, and let him participate in the nocturnal funeral of their leader, a unionist female engineer. Her story recapitulates that of union workers after the invasion of Iraq, who have been defending the oil resources of the country against the interests of the major multinational companies, becoming over the years the target of murderous attempts and raids. They have been kidnapped, detained, tortured, and killed; their offices have been repeatedly bombed or looted by foreign private contractors, occupying forces, the Iraqi national army itself, terrorist organizations, and competing ethno-religious sectarian militias.[32] Through this last shocking fragment of the contemporary social conditions in contemporary Basra, Teguia structures a direct parallelism between the past and present condition of oppression in the place where the rebellion took place, and a latitudinal equivalence between Ghardaïa and Basra, which holds 71 percent of the oil resources of Iraq but has been similarly the theater of revolts against the shortage of food, water, and electricity in the past years.[33] Dramatic is the simultaneous narration, through a series of extremely long still shots, of how Rami is caught by the Greek border police, while Nahla is able to escape: the slow pace of this dramatic sequence parallels the funerary sequence involving Battuta, to create the tragic ending of the Zendj's attempt to free themselves from subjection.

As in Bencheikh's novel, in the film's finale, Teguia underscores the unconcluded nature of the Zendj's struggle in the contemporary world. Brought to the place where the Zendj coins have been found, here Battuta discovers that the worker who brought him to this empty spot, his own face covered, is a black man. His body appears as a tangible sign that the ghosts Battuta was looking for are still alive in the present world. Through Nahla's final dissolve into a demonstration, followed by the original footage of a violent street protest in Greece, the director sends a strong, final exhortation to the audience to join the Zendj's contemporary struggle against oppression.

9.3   Conclusions as Open Endings?

It is perhaps not surprising that reading *Rose noire sans parfum* in 2021 gives the astonishing impression of reading the chronicle of the rise and fall of the Islamic State of Iraq and the Levant (*daesh*, IS, or Isis). Bencheikh published his novel in 1998 and didn't witness the growth of Isis during his lifetime. The analogies between the medieval and the contemporary world Bencheikh shows in his novel are striking, but the silent parallel traced between the Zendj rebellion and the Algerian civil war is perhaps the most relevant to understand his engagement with the personality of Ali ibn Mohammed, and with his use of religion as a channel to challenge power: to raise the hope of the dispossessed, and as a justification for violence. The traumatic experience of the civil war gave to Algeria the role of antecedent for the season of unrest that spread across the Arab World after 2011.[34] Working a few years after Bencheikh, Teguia takes the spectator across different contemporary sites, from the Algerian South to the refugee camp of Shatila, and finally to the marshes of Basra, to interrogate the causes of oppression and unrest among the peoples in these regions; they are either national, or related to the external agency of international actors. Teguia questions obliquely, across Arab and Western audiences, the present curbing of inclusive national projects in the region. From the unequal division of resources in Algeria, to the impossibility of Palestinian refugees to return to their homeland, from the foreign military intervention in Iraq to the contemporary condition of migrants attempting to cross the Mediterranean, the present injustice and inequalities he retells as analogs to the suffering of the medieval Zendj are approached in the film as a double critique symptomatic of a global, interconnected age. Similarly, the "vous" that Bencheikh's Ali ibn Mohammed addresses in his invectives is both medieval and contemporary. It emerges as a "historical presence" that connects Europe and the Arab World across space and time, from the medieval Zendj rebellion to the contemporary massacre of Srebrenica, as a shared history of slavery, racism, and oppression.

Against these evils, the open ending of Bencheikh's novel makes of Ali ibn Mohammed an active living presence rather than just a character of the past. In a similar way, by showing that the medieval Zendj are alive in the present world rather than just "ghosts" of the past, Teguia wants to urge contemporary audiences to rebel against the present inequalities and imbalances of the global age. As the medieval oppression of the Zendj provides them the opportunity to denounce the injustice of the present, so too is their rebellion, after more than a thousand years, presented as a meaningful example to follow in order to redress it.

Notes

1 Jamal Eddine Bencheikh, *Rose noire sans parfum* (Algiers: Barzakh, 2009), 81.
2 A first wave of narratives on the Zendj rebellion emerged among Marxist Arab intellectuals in the 1970s. Among them, relevant is Muʿin Bsisu's theater play

Thawrat al-Zendj (1970). See Walid Mahmoud Abu Nadi, *Al-fikr istidʿāʾ al-tarikh fī masraḥiyyat "thawrat al-zinj" lil-kātib "Muʿin Bsisu": rūʾiyat naqdīyat muʿāsirat / Thought and Recalling History in Muaeen Bsisoʾs "The Nigro Revolution"* (*Critical Vision of Contemporary*. 2016. Islamic University of Gaza, online version accessed March 2018).

3 Yogita Goyal, *Runaway Genres: The Global Afterlives of Slavery* (New York: New York University Press, 2019), 8–9.

4 Born in Morocco from an Algerian family, Bencheikh (1930–2005) moved to Algeria after the independence, and then to France in late the 1960s. Together with essays on medieval Arabic literature, he published several collections of poetry and a new translation, with André Miquel, of *The One Thousand and One Nights* into French. See Mohamed Barrada, "J.E.D. Bencheikh et l'imaginaire arabe." In *Paroles, signes, mythes: Mélanges offerts à Jamel Eddine Bencheikh*, ed. Floréal Sanagustin (Damascus: Institut français de Damas, 2001), 31–33.

5 Born in 1966, Teguia grew up in Algiers and currently lives between Algeria, France, and Greece. *Révolution Zendj* is Teguia's third long-feature film, after *Rome plutôt que vous* (2006) and *Gabbla* (*Inland*) (2008). The film was awarded the 2013 Grand Prix Janine Bazin at the Festival Entrevues de Belfort, and the Prix Scribe pour le Cinéma Indépendant in the same year. See Latifa Lafer, "Les films de Tariq Teguia: l'exception esthétique et thématique des années 2000," *Esprit Bavard* (2017): 75–78; and Anna Victor, "Experimental Cartographies in Tariq Teguia's Inland," *Journal of African Cinemas* 8, no. 3 (2016): 267–281.

6 Orlando Patterson, *Slavery and Social Death: A Comparative Study* (Cambridge, MA: Harvard University Press, 1982), ix; William Gervase Clarence-Smith, *Islam and the Abolition of Slavery* (Oxford: Oxford University Press, 2006), 1–6.

7 Abdelkebir Khatibi, *Plural Maghreb: Writings on Postcolonialism* (New York: Bloomsbury Academic, 2019), 117–123.

8 Adonis, *Al-Thābit wa al-mutaḥawwal*, 2 vols. (London: Dar al-Saqi, 2003), Vol. I, p. 69.

9 Muhammad Abdul Jabbar Beg, "The 'Serfs' of Islamic Society Under the Abbasid Regime," *Islamic Culture* 49, no. 2 (1975): 255.

10 Walid Arafat, "The Attitude of Islam to Slavery," *Islamic Quarterly* 10, no. 1–2 (1996): 14.

11 G.S.P. Freeman-Grenville and Alexander Popovich, 'al-Zandj.' In >*Encyclopaedia of Islam, Second Edition*, ed. P. Bearman, Th. Bianquis, C.E. Bosworth, E. Van Donzel, W.P. Heinrichs (Leiden: Brill, 1960–2005). See also Faisal Al-Samer, *Thawrat al-Zinj* (Damascus: Al Mada, 2000), 22–34.

12 For a detailed reconstruction of this turbulent historical period, and on the historiographical aspects of the rebellion, see M.A. Shaban, *Islamic History: A New Interpretation. Volume 2: A.D. 750–1055 (A.H. 132–448)* (Cambridge: Cambridge University Press, 1976), 100–111; Al-Tabari, David Waines (ed.), *The History of al-Tabari: The Revolt of the Zanj A.D. 869–879 A.H. 255–265*,

40 Vols. (New York: State University of New York Press, 1991), Vol. XXXVI, p. 38; Murray Gordon, *Slavery in the Arab World* (New York: New Amsterdam Books, 1989), 105–127.

13 Al-Tabari, David Waines (ed.), *The History of al-Tabari*, p. 410.

14 Umberto Eco, "Dreaming of the Middle Ages." In *Travels in Hyperreality* (New York: Harvest Books, 1986), 71.

15 Christiane Chaulet Achour, "Entretien avec Jamel Eddine Bencheikh," *Algérie Littérature / Action*, no. 17 (January 1998): 50.

16 Bencheikh, *Rose noire sans parfum*, p. 16.

17 Chaulet Achour, "Entretien avec Jamel Eddine Bencheikh," p. 51.

18 Bencheikh, *Rose noire sans parfum*, p. 28.

19 Chaulet Achour, "Entretien avec Jamel Eddine Bencheikh," p. 50.

20 James, McDougall, *A History of Algeria* (Cambridge: Cambridge University Press, 2017), 290.

21 Christiane Chaulet Achour, "... J'ai refait mes aïeux de mes mains ...," *Algérie Littérature / Action*, no. 17, January (1998): 48.

22 Bencheikh, *Rose noire*, pp. 60–61.

23 Bencheikh, *Rose noire*, p. 30.

24 Bencheikh, *Rose noire*, p. 32.

25 Bencheikh, *Rose noire*, pp. 111–112.

26 Al-Tabari, David Waines (ed.), *The History of al-Tabari*, p. 141.

27 Bencheikh, *Rose noire*, p. 79.

28 Bencheikh, *Rose noire*, pp. 87–88.

29 Bencheikh, *Rose noire*, p. 190.

30 Jacques Rancière, "Inland de Tariq Teguia," *Trafic 80: 20 Ans 20 Films* (Winter 2011): 76.

31 See Chérif Bennadji, "Algérie 2010: l'année des mille et une émeutes," *L'Année du Maghreb*, VII (2011): 263–269; Naoual Belakhdar, "'L'éveil du Sud' ou quand la contestation vient de la marge: Une analyse du movement des chômeurs algériens," *Politique africaine*, no. 137 (March 2015): 27–48.

32 Benjamin Isakhan, "Protests and Public Power in Post-Saddam Iraq: The Case of the Iraqi Federation of Oil Union." In *Informal Power in the Greater Middle East*, ed. L. Anceschi, G. Gervasio, and A. Teti (London: Palgrave, 2014), 121.

33 Saudad Al-Sahly, "Iraq protests threaten to 'paralyze' oil industry in Basra," *Arab News*, July 10, 2018.

34 Lin Noueihed and Alex Warren, *The Battle for the Arab Spring: Revolution and Counter-Revolution in the Making of a New Era* (New Haven: Yale University Press, 2012), 263.

CHAPTER 10

Slavery and Indenture in the Literatures of the Indian Ocean World

Nienke Boer

Article 16: If he, prisoner, sharpening the knife on the doorframe of the kitchen, did not say: "Yes, knife, you will stab into my soul, or into another soul"?

Answer: Yes, I did say that, in despair.

Interrogation of Alexander van Couchin [Kochi] at the Cabo de Goede Hoop, 1741.[1]

Slavery in the Indian Ocean has a complex, inter-imperial history, starting well before the rounding of the southern tip of Africa by Portuguese vessels in the late fifteenth century, which inaugurated the age of European interventions in the Indian Ocean world. One of the earliest literary texts from the Indian Ocean, the c. tenth-century *Book of the Wonders of India* (*Kitāb 'Ajā'ib al-Hind*), a compendium of tales collected by Buzurg ibn Shahriyār, mentions slavery in several of the vignettes that make up the book.[2] European settlement and trading networks, however, significantly expanded upon and altered earlier systems of debt bondage and enslavement. The relatively late entry of the British Empire into Indian Ocean slave trading meant that other European powers, specifically Portugal, France, and the Netherlands, had a larger impact on the legal and procedural structures that shaped the experience of enslavement in the Indian Ocean. Theorizations of slavery in the Indian Ocean world have drawn upon the work done on the more familiar literature of enslavement in the anglophone Black Atlantic world, in ways that have been productive in thinking about continuities between systems of unfree labor migration across oceans. In what follows, however, I focus mainly on the ways enslavement in the Indian Ocean diverged from Atlantic models, and the implications this has had for the literatures of slavery.

Literary reflections of slavery in the Black Atlantic have been shaped by the existence of a small but significant number of exemplary autobiographies by formerly enslaved individuals. In the Indian Ocean world, however, there is no Olaudah Equiano, Quobna Cugoano, Ignatius Sancho, or Phillis Wheatley to provide a glimpse into the world of the enslaved. On the other hand, scholars of Indian Ocean slavery under the Dutch East India Company (*Vereenigde Oostindische Compagnie*, or VOC) trade empire, as well as the French Empire, have substantial legal archives to draw upon, unlike scholars of the anglophone Atlantic world.[3] In Dutch legal systems, the enslaved were tried by the same courts as the other inhabitants of VOC settlements, and those who were enslaved could testify in cases involving their fellow enslaved, slaveholders, or other officials and settlers. We thus have records of interrogations (like the one above, of Alexander van Couchin), witness statements, and sentences, in which the enslaved are seen to be speaking. In the French Mascarene Islands (Mauritius and Réunion), too, records of criminal procedures included the testimony of the enslaved. If the anglophone Black Atlantic, then, is a sphere of autobiographical speech and legal silence, the Indian Ocean world of enslavement can be seen as one of autobiographical silence, but legal speech. The rich heteroglossia of the Indian Ocean legal records stand in contrast to portrayals of the Atlantic Ocean slave trade as a process of silencing and erasure, its archive "a place of lack, absence, silence and violence."[4] This is not to ignore the innate violence of imperial legal records, but to reflect on the differences produced in subsequent representations of the enslaved by their absence – or presence – as speaking figures in legal archives. The existence of these legal records affects how the enslaved are represented in later, fictional narratives of slavery, which, while taking a variety of forms, share an interest in voice, testimony, and the law.

After a brief summary of the historical contexts of slavery in the Indian Ocean world, this chapter turns to an examination of the representations of enslaved voices in the Indian Ocean legal archives (with a focus on Dutch legal sources), followed by readings of some of the fictional works representing Indian Ocean slavery. Indenture, a more recent form of coerced labor migration that was overseen by the British Empire, sometimes overshadows discussions of enslavement in the Indian Ocean world. The final section of this chapter thus takes on the question of whether we can consider indenture as simply a "new system of slavery" by more closely examining selected Indian Ocean literatures of indenture.[5]

10.1 Historical Contexts

The Indian Ocean world is, in historian Sugata Bose's terms, better described as an "interregional arena" rather than a system: "Tied together by webs of economic and cultural relationships, such arenas had flexible internal and external boundaries ... where port cities formed the nodal points of exchange and interaction."[6] This arena is often studied in two temporal phases: before significant European expansion, when the Indian Ocean was predominantly the space of trade and exchange facilitated by monsoon winds between the Arabian peninsula, the eastern coast of Africa, the South Asian subcontinent, and ports and settlements in Southeast Asia; and later periods of increasing European influence on the region, starting at the turn of the sixteenth century. European conquest and trade networks meant that southern Africa and Australia were increasingly incorporated into the Indian Ocean arena. As Bose, Michael Pearson, and others have convincingly argued, however, there is more value in seeing the links and connections between these two periods in the history of the Indian Ocean than in separating them. In order to understand later systems of chattel slavery and indenture, we thus need to keep in mind both the interactions between European and non-European powers in the Indian Ocean world and the shifting dynamics between different European empires.[7]

Indigenous and other precolonial forms of slavery in the Indian Ocean world were incredibly varied. Islamic, South Asian, and African systems of bondage and enslavement predated European interventions in the region, and these networks continued to form part of the supply of people sold into slavery after European powers largely seized control of the slave trade in the region.[8] Focusing on the Dutch Indian Ocean slave trade, Kerry Ward defines the difference between these earlier systems of slavery and VOC chattel slavery by arguing that "[t]he VOC was the first political entity to introduce a form of slavery whereby slaves were purchased or born as Company property, devoid of the directly personal, religious, and/ or judicial connections that characterized indigenous forms of bondage in the Indian Ocean."[9] In *Testimonies of Enslavement*, a compilation of court cases from the Dutch Council of Justice at Cochin (Kochi, on the Malabar Coast in southwest India), the authors demonstrate, however, that pre-European systems of enslavement played a substantial role in shaping Dutch understandings of slavery, "with the slave trade drawing from and affecting local regimes of bondage based on social, religious, caste and ethnic differences."[10]

Indian Ocean enslavement regimes differed from that of the Atlantic Ocean in that the slave trade was multidirectional: "forcing enslaved from Southeast Asia into South Asia, and vice versa, while forcing enslaved from East Africa and Madagascar into South and Southeast Asia; from all these regions, the enslaved in turn also ended up in South Africa."[11] Indian Ocean slavery thus expands our notions of enslavement away from the Atlantic understanding of modern slavery as inevitably involving individuals from sub-Saharan Africa, as the enslaved in the Indian Ocean were often not African in origin. The Cape of Good Hope, for example, served only as a destination, not a point of embarkation, for enslaved from elsewhere in the Indian Ocean: South and Southeast Asia, East Africa, and Madagascar.[12]

From the sixteenth to the nineteenth centuries, many of the coastal regions on the Indian Ocean rim were implicated in European slaving networks.[13] Under the VOC, the enslaved were transported between the Indonesian archipelago, the South Asian coast, Ceylon, Madagascar, eastern Africa, and the Cape of Good Hope. Under the French, enslaved persons were brought from Madagascar and eastern Africa to the Mascarene islands. The Portuguese transported enslaved persons between Mozambique, South Asia, and the Philippines. Eventually, British territorial expansion and conquest within the Indian Ocean at the turn of the nineteenth century included the transportation of enslaved persons from Mozambique and eastern Africa to the Cape of Good Hope and Mauritius.

10.2 Enslaved Figures in the Legal Archives

Given the rich legal archives of the Indian Ocean enslaved world, I start this exploration of the literature of enslavement in the legal archives of the Dutch Councils of Justice based at various VOC outposts. These legal records are, I argue, worthy of literary analysis, as their depictions of the enslaved allow for textual nodes of opacity – ambiguity, heteroglossia, untranslatability – to be recorded in the archives, alongside accounts of overt forms of resistance, such as arson, escape, and violence against slaveholders.

Legal records from the Dutch settlement of Cochin on the Malabar Coast (today Kochi, in the state of Kerala) demonstrate the importance of understanding the interactions between pre-European indigenous understanding of slavery and European enslavement. The court cases from the Cochin Council of Justice collected in Rossum et al's *Testimonies of Enslavement* focus on the concept of *slaafbaarheijd* or enslaveability – who can be enslaved, by whom, and how – which the Dutch attempted to adapt from preexisting patterns of enslavement. Thus, when an enslaved person is sold, the seller has to produce an *ola* testifying to the enslaveability of the person: demonstrating that the seller is the legal owner of the enslaved, whether through inheritance or purchase.[14] By focusing so rigidly on the existence of this tangible proof of enslaveability, Dutch officials can circumvent larger questions about their imbrication in the slave trade. We see, in several of these court cases, prosecutors producing philosophical statements about the horrors of wrongful enslavement (illegal enslavement or human theft (*menschen dieverije*) is punishable by death, and both the seller and the buyer is held culpable, if the buyer did not ask for a *slaafola*), without the system of slavery itself ever being questioned.

One of these cases, the 1757 case against a Malabari Christian, Thome, for the illegal sale of another local man named Ittamen to a VOC sailor Lourens Seret from Leiden, shows the hypocrisy of the Dutch fiscal (prosecutor), who begins the case by detailing how freedom is a gift of nature, such that even animals suffer if not freed, and "the course of water strives to be free, such that there is no barrier or resistance that it will not overcome to achieve a free flow."[15] Similar powerful rhetoric in defense of freedom can be found in several of the cases collected in this volume, suggesting the importance to the Dutch – who shared power with other authority figures (the kings of Cochin, Travancore, and Calicut, and the head of the St Thomas Christian church) in a carefully negotiated web of legal jurisdictions based on territory and religion – of maintaining the impression of protecting the right to freedom of those who had not been enslaved in ways seen as legally binding.[16]

The words of Ittamen, who was almost sold into slavery, as recorded in his interrogation are particularly striking. The Council asks why he accompanied Thome to Cochin even though he did not know him well: "[T]he deponent was then asked how he could have been so stupid to leave his wife and children so easily and follow the prisoner based only on his promise and pure-sounding words. Answer: Because of my poverty and in my ignorance [*om de wille van mijn armoede en in mijn onnoselheit*]."[17] Ittamen's plaintive response here holds space for and highlights the silences of the enslaved who did not get a chance to contest their freedom in court, who were transported across the ocean to labor, until their deaths, under new names. His testimony also raises another question though: "And finally, he was asked whether if he, the deponent, had in this way fallen into eternal slavery, it would not have been his own fault. Answer: Yes, to an extent, but I did make my objection known, but was not heard."[18] These records are remarkable in seeming to bring to life the words, however contingently and perhaps inaccurately recorded, of these subaltern figures. However, we should also ask to under what circumstances we are capable of "hearing" their words: even though these interrogations convey the impression of truth and immediacy, their context – the power imbalance between the Dutch officials and those questioned – means that our access to these worlds is still limited to what the powerful allow us to hear.

Following across the Indian Ocean an individual possibly from Cochin who, unlike Ittamen, did not escape enslavement, I now turn to Council of Justice records from the Cape of Good Hope.[19] As indigenous inhabitants of the Cape could not be enslaved, legal questions of enslaveability do not feature in these records, which deal with other matters deemed criminal. The Council of Justice relied on the inquisitory procedure, whereby the accused had to confess their crime before they could be found guilty. If the accused did not initially confess, they were interrogated by delegates from the Council of Justice, using a list of questions drawn up by the fiscal based on evidence collected. The following extract is from the interrogation of Alexander van Couchin, accused of threatening a slaveholder, Daniel van der Lith, in 1741:

Article 8: Where he, the prisoner, obtained the knife, and with what intention he returned to the kitchen with it?
Answer: I found my old knife on the windowsill of the sitting room, and with it in my hand along with a plug of tobacco went to the kitchen to carve the latter. . . .
Article 11: If when he, the prisoner, entered the kitchen, his master did not say to him "Go to bed and sleep, you just came from the Cape and are tired;" and if he, the prisoner, did not answer "I do not want to do that"?
Answer: My master instructed me, since I did not want to go to sleep, that I should fetch a basket of peaches from Miss Cloete, upon which I answered, "Yes sir that is good," which happened in the presence of the slave of Master Cloete, named Isacq.
Article 12: If he, the prisoner, after his master told him the second time that he should go to bed, did not say again "I do not want to do that," and then sat down on a chest in the kitchen?
Answer: I do not know about that.
Article 13: If he, while speaking to his master, did not advance upon his master?
Answer: No.
Article 14: If he, the prisoner, did not do this in order to, with the knife he had, harm the same?
Answer: No, that I did not do.

Article 15: If he the prisoner, shortly after leaving the kitchen the first time, did not return with a knife in his hand?
Answer: Yes, with the old knife and a plug of tobacco.
Article 16: If he, prisoner, sharpening the knife on the doorframe of the kitchen, did not say: "Yes, knife, you will stab into my soul, or into another soul"?
Answer: Yes, I did say that, out of despair [*uit mismoedigheijt*].[20]

The interrogation format, as we see here, takes the form of rather stilted leading questions, prefaced by "if," and usually simply requiring a yes/no answer. This language is invested in the formulaic and scripted. These interrogation performances stage the power imbalance between the questioner, who is in charge of steering the conversation, and the accused.

However, Alexander van Couchin, as much as is possible, refuses to fall in with the narrative that has been prepared for him. He inserts a different narrative, one in which a plug of tobacco and a basket of peaches play as central a role as the knife the interrogator repeatedly mentions. The form of the interrogation allows the reader to see the power dynamic at work, but also allows for surprising revelations. In this case, the proclamation by Alexander, "yes, knife, you will stab into my soul, or another soul," is read by the court as a threat, but Alexander reframes it as a cry arising out of despair. For the contemporary reader, this is a poetic moment, perhaps revealing a glimpse of interiority even when multiply mediated by the language and context of the court.

We can see how the prosecutor's questions work to create a narrative of rage and threatening behavior (one that even contradicts itself, since Alexander van Couchin seems to be both sitting on a chest in the kitchen and advancing upon Van der Lith threateningly at the same time). The magistrate called for the death sentence for Alexander van Couchin, calling him an "enraged person" [*verwoedend mensch*], but this recommendation was overturned by the Council of Justice. While this was not always the case in these courts (more often than not, the enslaved received disproportionately brutal sentences), here Alexander's counter-narrative may have been convincing enough to cast doubt upon the accusation.

When the British take over the Cape of Good Hope, first in 1795 and then after a brief period of rule by the Dutch Batavian Republic from 1803 to 1806, they choose not to change the existing Roman-Dutch legal system extensively, though they do outlaw torture and some of the more brutal forms of capital punishment. This means that they inherit a legal system in which the enslaved may testify in court, and even testify against

Europeans, which is highly unusual in British colonies. The works of fiction from South Africa I examine in the next section can thus also draw on nineteenth-century anglophone legal records in which the names and testimony of the enslaved are documented.

In the absence of autobiographies, these legal records from various outposts in the Indian Ocean serve as windows into the experiences of enslavement and slavery, and should be read, not only for their content, but for the form these narratives take: how the various individuals are depicted, and to what extent they are represented as speaking. Later, fictional works on Indian Ocean slavery are influenced by these records, which often serve as the sources for historical fiction set in the region. These fictional works demonstrate a tension between drawing upon these sources in dialogue with an understanding of slavery and abolition that is borrowed from the more well-known Atlantic world. While we should be careful not to read these legal records as accurately depicting the words of the enslaved, never losing sight of the inherent violence of the legal and archival processes at work, it is worth reflecting on how latter-day imaginaries of slavery have been influenced by these earlier depictions of the enslaved in the archives.[21]

10.3 Fictional Imaginaries of Slavery

During the European imperial period, as historian Rila Mukherjee has suggested, the cartographic and the historical category of the Indian Ocean was "slow to capture the European imagination," which also may explain why literary depictions of the various systems of slavery in the Indian Ocean did not proliferate in the same way that those of the Atlantic slave trade did.[22] One important fictional source in the francophone literary tradition is the 1788 French novel *Paul et Virginie* by Jacques-Henri Bernardin de Saint-Pierre, in which slavery plays an important role. Anglophone antislavery literature from the nineteenth-century Cape Colony reveals the influence of the British abolitionist movement on literary depictions of the Cape Colony. The most well-known such anti-slavery texts are by Scottish abolitionist Thomas Pringle, who published a report dated 1826 on "Slavery at the Cape of Good Hope" in the *Anti-Slavery Monthly Reporter*, and a number of antislavery poems, including "The Bechuana Boy," "The Captive of Camalú," "The Slave Dealer," and "To Oppression."[23] There are also a few obscure novels from the nineteenth-century Cape Colony which reference slavery (*Makanna; or the Land of the Savage* (anon., 1835); *The English Boy at the Cape* (Edward

Augustus Kendall, 1835); and *Governor van Noodt's Revenge, 1727* (Thomas Mcintosh McCombie, 1887)).[24]

Later South African novelists, however, discovered in the legal archives of the eighteenth- and nineteenth-century Cape rich sources for crafting their fictional imaginaries of slavery – texts which, understandably given the sources, are interested specifically in questions of speech and law. In twentieth-century apartheid South Africa, for example, André Brink used legal and other records from the colonial Cape Colony to write thinly veiled allegories for contemporaneous injustices. One of his novels, *A Chain of Voices* (originally published in Afrikaans as *Houd-den-Bek* in 1982), is based on British court records following an 1825 slave uprising led by an enslaved man, Galant.[25] The Afrikaans title refers to the name of the farm where Galant lived, which literally translates as Shut-Your-Mouth, and the novel is structured as a sequence of different first-person narrations telling the story of this uprising, thereby imaginatively refusing the injunction to keep quiet. The novel acts as a critique of the contemporaneous Afrikaner ruling party and its segregationist policies, as the concluding sentences in the voice of Galant make clear: "The eggs of the Lightning Bird remain in the earth for a long, long time: but one day they'll hatch and bring the fire back over these mountains without beginning or end, where my footprint remains forever proudly trodden in the stone. I'm going down now. In a way I suppose I'm burnt out. But the fire: the fire remains."[26] Slavery thus becomes a way to read the present into the past, mapping the racial injustices of the 1980s onto the historical figures of the enslaved.

Post-apartheid novelists in South Africa have also drawn upon the rich archives of enslavement from the region to reimagine larger oceanic worlds, moving beyond the binaries imposed by apartheid-era protest writing. Some of these novels include Rayda Jacobs' *The Slave Book* (1998), Dan Sleigh's *Eilande* [*Islands*] (2002), and André Brink's *Philida* (2012).[27] *Cargo* (2007) is an innovative collaboratively written performance piece (directed by Mark Fleishman) incorporating the archives of slavery, and Nadia Davids' play, *What Remains* (2019), also engages the afterlives and historical traumas of slavery. One of these post-apartheid novels, Yvette Christiansë's *Unconfessed* (2006), is based on the trial for infanticide of an enslaved woman, Sila van den Kaap, at the Cape in 1823. *Unconfessed* exemplifies how authors have engaged with, and troubled, representations of the voices of the enslaved in the legal archives.

The novel describes the farm where the protagonist grew up in 1806:

> There was Philip from Malabar ... Philip spoke a language that none of us
> understood ... Amerant came from Batavia. She worked in the house.
> Perhaps it was because they had no-one else from their lands that she and
> Philip kept close together. Some days I would hear them talking, each in his
> or her own tongue, laughing ... And then there were those of us who are
> called Mozbiekers. We all came in ships and we never got that rolling world
> out of our ears because, on some days, one of us would stumble and the
> others knew the ocean was sending us a message.[28]

Christiansë focuses on uniquely Indian Ocean circumstances of enslavement, where the enslaved come from various different VOC settlements
and trading posts: in this case, Malabar in India, Batavia on the island of
Java, and Mozambique. Philip and Amerant form a bond where their
shared laughter transcends the different languages they speak. VOC court
records showcase the multilingualism of the contemporaneous Cape society: the Council of Justice allowed witnesses to testify in their language of
choice, and the languages listed in the records include Bugis, Arabic,
Chinese, Javanese, Malagasy, Portuguese, Malay, German, Dutch, and
English. Although the records are all transcripts of the Dutch translations,
names, exclamations, interjections, and phrases from almost all of these
languages make it into the final recorded versions. Christiansë's Sila
suggests that the shared experience of transportation across the Indian
Ocean unites these individuals, regardless of their origins and languages,
such that the afterlife of this oceanic journey viscerally haunts them: "we
never got that rolling world out of our ears." Oceanic displacement thus
speaks a new language into their ears, and their stumbling communicates
this message to others – a language, however, that could not be transcribed
into the legal records of the Council of Justice. This passage speaks to both
the realities of the multilingual slave society at the Cape, and also imagines
forms of communication that goes beyond the linguistic. The novel draws
on the legal records of the Cape, but in a way that focuses on what is
not heard.

Christiansë encountered Sila van den Kaap's case in the archives, where
she was struck by a neologism, *heartsore*, from the Dutch word *hartzeer*:

> That the Prisoner, supposed to be between Thirty and Thirty Five years of
> age, having left her Master's place situated in the District of George, about
> three o'clock on the 24th December last year, repaired to the place of
> Hendrik Van Huysteen, Field Cornet of the land behind said Bay, she
> there, in presence of a certain Carel Schaffer, acquainted the Field Cornet,

at the same time delivering him a Clasp Knife and shedding some Tears, that she, through Heartsore and Grief, had cut the Throat of her Child named Baro with that knife because she, as well as the Child, were ill treated both by her Master and Mistress.[29]

Christiansë describes this word as erupting from the testimony: "Even so, she [Sila] remains largely unknowable, the bearer of unbearable knowledge, the keeper of secrets, including, most powerfully, the meaning of a word that erupts in testimony, the word *hartzeer*."[30] The novel thematizes the distance between Sila's life as recorded in the archives and the secrets that remain undisclosed. Regarding the scene recorded above, Sila says:

> What he [the field cornet] sees is what he puts into words for the *landdrost*, like feet into shoes because the ground has thorns. But he can say it all in polite words – is it true?
>
> I told him, *hertseer*. It is like wind blowing against a closed door. *Pffmph*. I told him on that day. I tell them what must be told and the truth is like a leaf in a big wind.
>
> Is it true, that on the twenty-fourth day of December eighteen and twenty three, you took your son, Baro. . .
>
> Leaves fall.[31]

The truth claims embedded in the legal language of the confession (as recorded by the field cornet, in terms of dates, times, names, and locations) is shown to disintegrate into first, an untranslatable word (*hertseer*) and then, an inexpressible sound, the sound of wind blowing against a closed door. "The truth is like a leaf in a big wind . . . leaves fall," she reflects, the two halves of the simile separated by a line of interrogation, suggesting the power of the authoritative legal voice to dispel the fragile, inexpressible truth of any such experience. If the persistence of the neologism of heartsore/*hertseer* can perhaps preserve some truth of her statement (the "closed door" temporarily blocking the wind, allowing Christiansë to see Sila briefly erupting from the legal records), this protection is not strong enough to survive her later court interrogations. This reminds us of Ittamen's statement discussed earlier, where he says "I did make my objection known, but was not heard" – the fictional Sila here reflects on how the historical Sila's words may have been recorded, but the truths embedded in them were not heard.

Unconfessed draws on a trope familiar from the Black Atlantic literary tradition, the talking book, but in the particular legal context of the Cape, this takes on a new meaning. As discussed by Henry Louis Gates, Jr., the talking book in early Atlantic slave narratives refers to the enslaved's struggle with literacy, figured through an encounter with a speaking/silent Bible: "Literacy, the very literacy of the printed book, stood as the ultimate parameter by which to measure the humanity of authors struggling to define an African self in Western letters."[32] Sila van den Kaap's talking books do initially refer to her attempts to learn to read, and read the Bible specifically: "the Bible lessons, scratching on slate that spoke when you pointed at it and said what the missus said it said, and which then took on its chalk body."[33] Later in the novel, however, the talking book increasingly refers to Sila's existence within legal records: "why was I seeing that time all over again when this was the day that *Oumiesies'* paper would speak and make the governor himself listen?," Sila asks, referring to her manumission, supposedly recorded in the slaveholder's will.[34] In contrast to this will though, she is listed in a slave registry as property attached to the farm: "She made my name come out of that book like a crazy thing lost in a big wind when everything is thrown up in the air and spins around. There we all were, the cows and you and me and Carolina and Camies and Pieter."[35] At one point, Sila believes that she is working to earn her freedom, "[b]ut all along, the pages of the books were rubbing against each other and whispering things I did not know."[36] The talking book thus becomes a figure for the legal documents which form the backdrop of Sila's life, and which allow Christiansë to follow her traces through the archives, but also act as the "big wind" which scatters the truth of her experience. While the novel partakes in conversations familiar from slave and neo-slave narratives in the Atlantic world, Christiansë's attention to legal records, as well as to the heteroglossia of the Cape slave society, thus shifts the center of gravity of this novel to the Indian Ocean context.

The novel ends inconclusively: "You want to know. What happened to her? Well, some say she left the island, but there is no agreement on how. Some say it was on the center of piece of paper that she rode like a bier – not a young woman anymore."[37] Sila disappears from the legal archive, such that this novel itself becomes, perhaps, a new written bearer testifying to her life. Christiansë's decision to not write an ending to Sila's story, to leave her suspended between Robben Island and Cape Town, between living and dead, demonstrates the power of the fictional narrative to not foreclose and classify, thereby refusing to reinscribe the violence of the archives onto the lives thus commemorated.[38]

10.4   Indenture as a New System of Slavery?

In this short final section, I briefly touch upon the history and fictional afterlife of indenture in the Indian Ocean world. Following the emancipation of the enslaved in the British Empire in 1834, more than 1.3 million Indian subjects of the British Raj migrated to Mauritius, the West Indies, Suriname, Fiji, East Africa, and South Africa under indenture contracts, which bound them to work for a specific employer for a clearly defined period of time, in return for wages and the cost of passage.[39] The first ship containing indentured laborers from British India arrives in Mauritius in 1835. "'Tell Mr Burnham that I need men. Now that we may no longer have slaves in Mauritius, I must have coolies, or I am doomed,'" states the planter M. D'Epinay in Amitav Ghosh's novel *Sea of Poppies* (2008), neatly summarizing one view of indenture as simply a "new system of slavery" (the title of Hugh Tinker's influential 1974 study of indenture).[40] While the continuities between slavery and indenture are striking, especially in the callous treatment of indentured laborers, contemporary researchers on indenture have pursued lines of inquiry that also focus on discontinuities between the two systems. Forms of indenture that predate emancipation, return journeys undertaken by indentured laborers after the conclusion of their contracts, and voluntary re-indenture by laborers to the same or new locales, are all practices which challenge the notion that indenture is simply slavery under a new name.[41] While both indenture and slavery are concerned with the movement and control of labor power, slavery is intended to continue throughout the life of the enslaved, and there is no expectation of a return journey. Indenture, on the other hand, with its insistence on contracts and repatriation, is concerned with time – the time of indenture is understood to be limited, an interruption of the biographical lifetime, as opposed to being identical with it. This temporal constraint has various effects on how indenture is depicted in fiction: the relatively short-lived nature of the indenture contract means that it can be elided in fiction, and the precarity associated with the indenture contract can foreclose autochthonous claims of belonging.

   We do not have many sources, literary or autobiographical, written by indentured laborers themselves, though their descendants have enriched the literary canon of the Indian Ocean, as well as other regions of the world. Vijay Mishra, for example, identifies what he calls a "*girmit* ideology" within the literatures emerging out of South Asian indenture, which focuses on mourning (and the impossibility of mourning), travel and translation, and trauma.[42] Such a transoceanic indenture canon would include the autobiographical writings, originally in Hindi, of Totaram Sanadhya (*My Twenty-One Years in the Fiji Islands* [*Fiji Mein Mere Ekkis Varsh*]) and Munshi Rahman Khan (*Jeevan Prakash: Autobiography of an Indian Indentured Labourer*) about Fiji and Suriname respectively, as well as novels by Jan Shinebourne (Guyana), V.S. Naipaul (Trinidad), Satendra Nandan (Fiji), Sam Selvon (Trinidad), and others.[43] In this section, however, I will focus on literature from the Indian Ocean.

Ghosh's *Sea of Poppies*, part of the *Ibis* trilogy (*Sea of Poppies, River of Smoke* (2011), and *Flood of Fire* (2015)), has been widely read as representative of a new canon of Indian Ocean writing that is centered in the lives of subaltern actors, including lascars, convicts, and indentured laborers.[44] The central figure of the first part of the trilogy is Deeti, who flees Bihar following her husband's death to seek a new life as an indentured laborer on Mauritius, traveling on the *Ibis* from Calcutta to Port Louis. The novel ends before Deeti and the other laborers reach Mauritius though, and we never see them while under their indenture contracts. The second novel, *River of Smoke*, picks up on Deeti's life in Mauritius, but many years later, when her contract has expired: we thus never see her perform any indentured labor. *Sea of Poppies* is, instead, interested in bringing indenture and slavery together.[45] It does this through the character of Zachary Reid, the son of a former enslaved woman from Maryland serving on the *Ibis*, as well as the *Ibis* herself, a former "blackbirder" refitted to transport opium rather than enslaved humans. I suggest, however, that the lines of continuity that Ghosh wants to stress between slavery, and specifically Atlantic Ocean slavery, and the system of indenture, work to overshadow the specificities of the latter. The short-term nature of the contract here allows actual indentured labor as a practice to be rendered invisible.

Indenture is, in fact, often erased from fictional narratives, due to the precarity associated with the contract. For South Asian would-be settlers in other parts of the Indian Ocean world, whether they are descendant from indentured laborers or other migrants, the specter of the indenture contract is one of transience, rather than permanence and putting down roots. In both apartheid-era writing by Indian South Africans, such as Ansuyah R. Singh's *Behold the Earth Mourns* (1960), and writing by East Africans of South Asian descent, such as M.G. Vassanji's *The Gunny Sack* (1989), there is a tendency by authors to focus on South Asian merchants who did not migrate under indenture contracts.[46] In the post-apartheid period, new kinds of South African Indian writing emerge, some of which, like Praba

Moodley's *The Heart Knows No Colour* (2003), Aziz Hassim's *Revenge of Kali* (2009), and Joanne Joseph's *Children of Sugarcane* (2021), explicitly address the experiences of indentured laborers.[47]

The island where Ghosh's Deeti settles, Mauritius, also proves to be an exception to the tendency to downplay indenture as a vehicle of migration and settlement, perhaps partly because Indo-Mauritians form the majority of the population. The Mauritian poet Khal Torabully writes extensively about the legacy of indenture, coining the term *coolitude* – a more positive description of the creative afterlife of indenture than Mishra's girmit ideology – as a blending of *négritude* and *créolité*.[48] In his poem, "[Coolitude: petites mains des colonies]" (1992), the speaker begins by reflecting on the shared legacy of Mauritius as an island that received both enslaved and indentured individuals: "Coolitude: worker bees of the colonies; you have been the merchandise and we, the merchandising, or vice versa."[49] The poem continues by stating: "Coolitude: because I am Creole by my rigging, I am Indian by my mast, I am European by the yardarm, I am Mauritian by my quest and French by my exile./I can only be elsewhere within myself because I can only imagine my native land. My native lands?"[50] This final questioning note reflects one of the central themes animating creative works about indenture: how to negotiate multiple or conflicting sources of identity. Torabully's poem suggests a sense of belonging originating not in autochthony or a rootedness in the soil, but in the oceanic journey itself, naming the various parts of the ship, and its ambiguous purpose (quest or exile?), as the parts making up a sense of self.

Both the discomfort around the legacy of the indenture contract seen in South Asian African writing, and the more robust engagement with the experience and afterlife of indenture in Mauritius, suggest that simply collapsing the differences between slavery and indenture (as Ghosh's *Sea of Poppies* risks doing) fails to do full justice to either system of labor transportation.

In this reflection I have focused on both the importance of a longue durée perspective on slavery and indenture in the Indian Ocean, and the specific influences that legal forms – testimony, the contract, the report – have had on the literatures emerging from these systems of bondage. These are, however, just some of the many rich threads to pursue in examining how the literatures of the Indian Ocean expand our understanding of slavery and bondage on a global scale. Inherently inter-imperial and transnational, the literatures of slavery and indenture in the Indian Ocean world offer a productive viewpoint from which to study the Global South in both its historical and contemporary dimensions.

Notes

1 Nigel Worden and Gerald Groenewald (eds.), *Trials of Slavery: Selected Documents Concerning Slaves from the Criminal Records of the Council of Justice at the Cape of Good Hope, 1705–1794* (Cape Town, ZA: Van Riebeeck Society for the Publication of South African Historical Documents, 2005), 194. My translation.

2 Buzurg ibn Shahriyār, *The Book of the Wonders of India: Mainland, Sea and Islands*, trans. Greville Stewart Parker Freeman-Grenville (London/The Hague, East-West Publications, 1981). For more on this work, see Suhanna Shafiq, *Seafarers of the Seven Seas: The Maritime Culture in the Kitāb 'Ajā'ib Al-Hind (The Book of the Marvels of India) by Buzurg Ibn Shahriyār (d. 399/ 1009)* (Berlin: Klaus Schwarz Verlag, 2013).

3 For example, Diana Paton, writing on eighteenth-century Jamaica, explains that very few legal records regarding slave crimes survive from Jamaica and other British Caribbean societies, since the slave courts failed to keep accurate day-to-day records, and newspaper accounts of court proceedings only start appearing in the 1780s. In Dutch, Spanish, and French Atlantic colonies, more extensive legal records were produced. Natalie Zemon Davis offers an excellent description of legal pluralism in Dutch Suriname, "Judges, Masters, Diviners: Slaves' Experience of Criminal Justice in Colonial Suriname," which largely focuses on links between African justice systems and the enslaved experience of Dutch justice. Scholars such as Herman Bennett and Ana Hontanilla have also examined Spanish colonial legal records to understand the experience of slavery in the so-called New World, and a recent book by Sophie White examines French legal records from Louisiana. Diana Paton, "Punishment, Crime, and the Bodies of Slaves in Eighteenth Century Jamaica," *Journal of Social History* 34, no. 1 (2001): 923–954; Natalie Zemon Davis, "Judges, Masters, Diviners: Slaves' Experience of Criminal Justice in Colonial Suriname," *Law and History Review* 29, no. 4 (November 2011): 925–984; Herman L. Bennett, *Africans in Colonial Mexico: Absolutism, Christianity, and Afro-Creole Consciousness, 1570–1640* (Bloomington, IN: Indiana University Press, 2003); Ana Hontanilla, "Sentiment and the Law: Inventing the Category of the Wretched Slave in the Real Audiencia of Santo Domingo, 1783–1812," *Eighteenth-Century Studies* 48, no. 2 (Winter 2015): 181–200; Sophie White, *Voices of the Enslaved: Love, Labor, and Longing in French Louisiana* (Chapel Hill, NC: University of North Carolina Press, 2019).

4 Brian Connolly and Marisa Fuentes, "Introduction: From Archives of Slavery to Liberated Futures?," *History of the Present* 6, no. 2 (2016): n.p.

5 Hugh Tinker, *A New System of Slavery: The Export of Indian Labour Overseas, 1830–1920* (Oxford, UK: Oxford University Press, 1974).

6 Sugata Bose, *A Hundred Horizons: The Indian Ocean in the Age of Global Empire* (Cambridge, MA: Harvard University Press, 2006), 6. For more on Indian Ocean studies, see, amongst many, Edward Alpers, *The Indian Ocean*

in World History (Oxford, UK: Oxford University Press, 2013); Kirti N Chaudhuri, *Asia before Europe: Economy and Civilization of the Indian Ocean from the Rise of Islam to 1750* (Cambridge, MA: Cambridge University Press, 1990); Thomas R. Metcalf, *Imperial Connections: India in the Indian Ocean Arena, 1860–1920* (Berkeley, CA: University of California Press, 2007); Michael N. Pearson, *The Indian Ocean* (New York, NY: Routledge, 2003); Nile Green, "The Waves of Heterotopia: Toward a Vernacular Intellectual History of the Indian Ocean," *The American Historical Review* 123, no. 3 (2018): 846–874; and Pamila Gupta, Isabel Hofmeyr, and Michael Pearson (eds.), *Eyes across the Water: Navigating the Indian Ocean* (Pretoria, ZA: Unisa Press, 2010).

7 Laura Doyle makes a compelling case for such inter-imperial (including non-European empires) approaches to understanding both history and literature in *Inter-imperiality: Vying Empires, Gendered Labor, and the Literary Arts of Alliance* (Durham, NC: Duke University Press, 2020). Lisa Lowe's *The Intimacies of Four Continents* (Durham, NC: Duke University Press, 2015) demonstrates the value of such an approach.

8 See the various case studies found in these edited volumes: Anthony Reid (ed.), *Slavery, Bondage & Dependency in Southeast Asia* (Brisbane, AU: University of Queensland Press, 1983); Gwyn Campbell (ed.), *Structure of Slavery in Indian Ocean Africa and Asia* (London: Frank Cass, 2004); Gwyn Campbell and Alessando Stanziani (eds.), *Bonded Labour and Debt in the Indian Ocean World* (London: Pickering & Chatto Publishers, 2013); Indrani Chatterjee and Richard M. Eaton (eds.), *Slavery and South Asian History* (Bloomington, IN: Indiana University Press, 2006); Edward Alpers, Gwyn Campbell and Michael Salman (eds.), *Slavery and Resistance in Africa and Asia* (London: Routledge, 2005); as well as Pier M. Larson, *History and Memory in the Age of Enslavement: Becoming Merina in Highland Madagascar, 1770–1822* (Portsmouth, NH: Heinemann, 2000).

9 Kerry Ward, *Networks of Empire: Forced Migration in the Dutch East India Company* (Cambridge, UK: Cambridge University Press, 2009), 81.

10 Matthias van Rossum, Alexander Geelen, Bram van den Hout, and Merve Tosun (eds.), *Testimonies of Enslavement: Sources on Slavery from the Indian Ocean World* (New York, NY: Bloomsbury Academic, 2020), 4.

11 van Rossum et al., *Testimonies of Enslavement*.

12 The Dutch West India Company held slave-trading posts in West Africa, but these enslaved individuals were transported across the Atlantic, and, due to competition with the VOC, were not (except in very rare circumstances) sold at the Cape of Good Hope or other VOC-held settlements along the Indian Ocean.

13 For more on the history of Indian Ocean slavery under European empires, see, especially, Richard B. Allen, "Satisfying the 'Want for Labouring People': European Slave Trading in the Indian Ocean, 1500–1850," *Journal of World History* 21, no. 1 (2010): 43–73. Other sources include Nira Wickramasinghe, *Slave in a Palanquin: Colonial Servitude and Resistance in*

Sri Lanka (New York, NY: Columbia University Press, 2020); Megan Vaughan, *Creating the Creole Island: Slavery in Eighteenth-Century Mauritius* (Durham, NC: Duke University Press, 2005); van Rossum et al., *Testimonies of Enslavement*; and Markus Vink, "'The World's Oldest Trade': Dutch Slavery and Slave Trade in the Indian Ocean in the Seventeenth Century," *Journal of World History* 14, no. 2 (2003): 131–177. For slavery in the Indian Ocean during the nineteenth century, see Robert Harms, Bernard K. Freamon, and David W. Blight (eds.), *Indian Ocean Slavery in the Age of Abolition* (New Haven, CT: Yale University Press, 2013).

14 The word *ola* comes from the Tamil word for a palm leaf manuscript, but comes to refer to any form of written proof, say of a transaction. A *slaafola* refers specifically to a document testifying to a person's enslaved status.

15 "The Value of 'Freedom,'" van Rossum et al. (eds.), *Testimonies of Enslavement*, p. 282 (my translation throughout).

16 For more on the complexities of Dutch rule on the Malabar coast, see van Rossum et al. (eds.), *Testimonies of Enslavement*.

17 van Rossum et al. (eds.), *Testimonies of Enslavement*, p. 291.

18 van Rossum et al. (eds.), *Testimonies of Enslavement*, p. 292.

19 The toponyms ("van Couchin") attached to the names given to enslaved persons at the Cape did often, but not always, reflect their countries of origin – in some cases, they merely reflected the port of embarkation. For more on slavery at the Cape, see A. J. Böeseken, *Slaves and Free Blacks at the Cape* (Cape Town, ZA: Tafelberg Publishers, 1977); Robert C-H Shell, *Children of Bondage: A Social History of the Slave Society at the Cape of Good Hope, 1652–1838* (Hanover, NH: Wesleyan University Press, published by University Press of New England, 1994); Robert Ross, *Cape of Torments: Slavery and Resistance in South Africa* (London: Routledge and Kegan Paul, 1983); and John Edwin Mason, *Social Death and Resurrection: Slavery and Emancipation in South Africa* (Charlottesville, VA: University of Virginia Press, 2003).

20 Worden and Groenewald (eds.), *Trials of Slavery*, pp. 189–201. My translation preserves the long sentences and repetitive structure of the archaic Dutch.

21 Hershini Bhana Young performs an exemplary literary analysis of the afterlife of one of these court cases, that of Tryntie/Tryntjie van Madagascar, in historiography and fiction, which demonstrates some of the dangers of reading the court records as accurately representing the inner lives of the enslaved. Young, *Illegible Will: Coercive Spectacles of Labor in South Africa and the Diaspora* (Durham, NC: Duke University Press, 2017), 73–108.

22 Rila Mukherjee, "The Indian Ocean: Historians Writing History," *Asian Review of World History* 1 (2013): 299.

23 Thomas Pringle's writings on slavery have been published as appendices to Sara Salih (ed.), *The History of Mary Prince: A West Indian Slave* (London: Penguin Books, 2004), 89–98; 104–115. Author Zoë Wicomb has recently published a novel on Pringle: Wicomb, *Still Life* (New York, NY: The New Press, 2020).

24 See David Johnson, "Literature and Cape Slavery," *Imagining the Cape Colony: History, Literature, and the South African Nation* (Edinburgh: Edinburgh University Press, 2011), 140–57.

25 André Brink, *A Chain of Voices* (London: Faber and Faber Limited, 1982). The full record of Galant et al.'s trial can be found here: G.M. Theal (ed.), "Records held before His Honor Sir J. A. Truter, Chief Justice, and the Members of the Worshipful Court of Justice at the Cape of Good Hope and the Dependencies thereof, in the Criminal Case of His Majesty's Fiscal, Prosecutor for the Crown, versus Galant et. al.," *Records of the Cape Colony: Copied for the Cape Government, from the Manuscript Records in the Public Record Office, London,* vol. 20 (London: William Clowes and Sons, Limited, 1904), 188–341.

26 Brink, *A Chain of Voices*, p. 509.

27 For more on these novels, see David Johnson, "Representing Cape Slavery: Literature, Law, and History," *Journal of Postcolonial Writing* 46, no. 5 (2010): 504–516; and Jessica Murray, "Gender and Violence in Cape Slave Narratives and Post-Narratives," *South African Historical Journal* 62, no. 3 (2010): 444–462.

28 Yvette Christiansë, *Unconfessed* (New York, NY: Other Press, 2006), 155.

29 Cited in Johnson, "Representing Cape Slavery," p. 511.

30 Yvette Christiansë, "'Heartsore': The Melancholy Archive of Cape Colony Slavery," *The Scholar and Feminist Online* 7, no. 2 (Spring 2009): n.p.

31 Christiansë, *Unconfessed*, p. 234.

32 Henry Louis Gates, Jr., *The Signifying Monkey: A Theory of Afro-American Literary Criticism* (New York/Oxford: Oxford University Press, 1988), 131.

33 Christiansë, *Unconfessed*, p. 10.

34 Christiansë, *Unconfessed*, p. 174.

35 Christiansë, *Unconfessed*, p. 246.

36 Christiansë, *Unconfessed*, p. 295.

37 Christiansë, *Unconfessed*, p. 341.

38 For further reflections on *Unconfessed*, see Meg Samuelson: "'Lose Your Mother, Kill Your Child': The Passage of Slavery and Its Afterlife in Narratives by Yvette Christiansë And Saidiya Hartman," *English Studies in Africa* 51, no. 2 (2009): 38–48; and Murray, "Gender and Violence."

39 For more on the historical contexts of indenture, as well as some possibilities for using it as a framework for approaching the Global South, see Nienke Boer, "Indenture," *Global South Studies: A Collective Publication with The Global South* (2019). https://globalsouthstudies.as.virginia.edu/key-concepts/indenture (accessed May 27, 2022).

40 Amitav Ghosh, *Sea of Poppies* (New York, NY: Picador, 2008), 21.

41 See, for example, Sugata Bose, "Blackbirders Refitted? The Journeys of Capitalists and Labourers in the Indian Ocean, 1830s–1930s." In *Indian and Chinese Immigrant Communities: Comparative Perspectives*, ed. Jayati Bhattacharya and Coonoor Kripalani (London: Anthem Press, 2015), 3–12.

42 *Girmitiya*, from agreement, was one of the terms by which these indentured laborers became known, and one they frequently used for themselves. *Vijay Mishra, The Literature of the Indian Diaspora: Theorizing the Diasporic Imaginary* (New York, NY: Routledge, 2007), 22.

43 Totaram Sanadhya, *My Twenty-One Years in the Fiji Islands and The Story of the Haunted Line*, trans. John Dunham Kelly and Uttra Kumari Singh (Suva, Fiji: Fiji Museum, 1991); Munshi Rahman Khan, *Jeevan Prakash: Autobiography of an Indian Indentured Labourer*, trans. Kathinka Sinha-Kerkhoff, Ellen Bal, and Alok Deo Singh (New Delhi: Shipra Publications, 2005). For larger comparative surveys of the literatures of indenture, see Mishra, *The Literature of the Indian Diaspora*; Mariam Pirbhai, *Mythologies of Migration, Vocabularies of Indenture: Novels of the South Asian Diaspora in Africa, the Caribbean, and Asia-Pacific* (Toronto: University of Toronto Press, 2009); and Véronique Bragard, *Transoceanic Dialogues: Coolitude in Caribbean and Indian Ocean Literatures* (Bern et al.: Peter Lang, 2008).

44 See, for example: Mark R. Frost, "Amitav Ghosh and the Art of Thick Description: History in the Ibis Trilogy," *The American Historical Review* 121, no. 5 (December 2016): 1537–1544; Clare Anderson, "Empire and Exile: Reflections on the Ibis Trilogy," *The American Historical Review* 121, no. 5 (December 2016): 1523–1530; Antoinette Burton, "Amitav Ghosh's World Histories from Below," *History of the Present* 2, no. 1 (Spring 2012): 71–77; Ravi Ahuja, "Capital at Sea, Shaitan Below Decks? A Note on Global Narratives, Narrow Spaces, and the Limits of Experience," *History of the Present* 2, no. 1 (Spring 2012): 78–85; Anupama Arora, "'The Sea Is History': Opium, Colonialism, and Migration in Amitav Ghosh's *Sea of Poppies*," *Ariel: A Review of International English Literature* 42, no. 3–4 (2012): 21–42.

45 For more on the *Ibis* trilogy as linking indenture and slavery, see Gaurav Desai, "The Novelist as Linkister," *The American Historical Review* 121, no. 5 (December 2016): 1531–1536; Greg Forter, *Critique and Utopia in Postcolonial Historical Fiction: Atlantic and Other Worlds* (Oxford, UK: Oxford University Press, 2019); and Françoise Lionnet, "Shipwrecks, Slavery, and the Challenge of Global Comparison: From Fiction to Archive in the Colonial Indian Ocean," *Comparative Literature* 64, no. 4 (2012): 446–461.

46 For South African Indian writing in relationship to indenture, see Nienke Boer, "Settlers and Laborers: The Afterlife of Indenture in Early South African Indian Writing," *Research in African Literatures* 47, no. 4 (2016): 21–35. For East African Indian writing, see Gaurav Desai, *Commerce with the Universe: Africa, India and the Afrasian Imagination* (New York, NY: Columbia University Press, 2013); and Gaurav Desai, "Asian African Literatures: Genealogies in the Making," *Research in African Literatures* 42, no. 3 (Fall 2011): 5–30.

47 Other post-apartheid South African Indian authors include Ishtiyaq Shukri, Imraan Coovadia, Achmat Dangor, Shamin Sarif, Farida Karodia, and

Beverley Naidoo. *Pallavi Rastogi's Afrindian Fictions: Diaspora, Race, and National Desire in South Africa* (Columbus, OH: The Ohio State University Press, 2008) examines these authors and works as part of the canon of South African Indian writing from the 1970s onwards.

48 In Mauritius, Torabully's voice is one amongst several reflecting on the experience and legacy of indenture, including Nathacha Appanah, Ananda Devi, and Amal Sewtohul. Theorists like Véronique Bragard, Françoise Lionnet, and Françoise Verges take the literature of the Mascarenes as a starting point for theorizing diaspora and creolization. See, for example, Marina Carter and Khal Torabully, *Coolitude: An Anthology of the Indian Labour Diaspora* (Anthem Press, 2002); Véronique Bragard, "L'Empreinte des kala pani dans la littérature caribéenne et mauricienne: une comparaison transcoloniale," *L'Esprit Créateur* 50, no. 2 (Summer 2010): 86–94; Lionnet, "Shipwrecks, Slavery;" and Françoise Vergès, *Monsters and Revolutionaries: Colonial Family Romance and Metissage* (Durham: Duke University Press, 1999).

49 Khal Torabully, "[Coolitude: petites mains des colonies]," trans. Nancy Naomi Carlson, *The Southern Review* 54, no. 2 (2018): 286–287.

50 Torabully, "[Coolitude: petites mains des colonies]."

CHAPTER 11

Rehearsing the Past
The Terrestrial Middle Passage in Uwem Akpan's
"Fattening for Gabon"

Supriya M. Nair

When Toni Morrison published *Beloved* in 1987, the paradoxical inter-diction repeated in the novel – "this is not a story to pass on" – ironically launched a virtual industry of neo-slave narratives or, as some prefer, contemporary narratives of slavery, largely set in the Americas.[1] In *Praisesong for the Widow*, a novel published in 1983 but set in the 1970s, Paule Marshall drew an earlier historical arc in a modern spectral version of Morrison's "rememory" of the U.S. history of slavery.[2] Marshall's African American protagonist, Avey Johnson, experiences an intensification of the seasickness that begins during her tourist cruise from the United States, and she hallucinates the retching of enslaved bodies while crossing the Caribbean Sea on a local trip. The collective agony, while illusory, fuels Avey's rediscovery of her diasporic identity by surfacing her forgotten origin story of the Middle Passage, although the oceanic rim remains in the Caribbean and the physical space of Africa is only an apparition like the enslaved people Avey conjures up on the boat. These literary excursions into the physical spaces and psychic imaginary of what Paul Gilroy labeled the Black Atlantic were not, of course, restricted to the eighties.[3] They were preceded by earlier heritage discourses of black consciousness and Black Power in North America and the Caribbean, which inspired multiple forays into black transatlantic genealogies or contemporary narratives of slavery such as Alex Haley's *Roots*,[4] Charles Johnson's *Middle Passage*,[5] Andrea Levy's *The Long Song*,[6] Marlon James's *The Book of Night Women*,[7] and Yaa Gyasi's *Homegoing*,[8] among many others. Rather than laying the ghost of Beloved, the publication of slave narratives and neo-slave narratives proliferated for several decades, culminating in Mat Johnson's mutinous declaration of his boredom with the subject of slavery.[9] Whatever the vaunted exhaustion with the topic on this side of the Atlantic, narratives of contemporary slavery in Africa have reversed direction from the Americas as the primary site of slavery and drawn attention to its specific trajectories within the continent today, even as they raise the spectral past of the transatlantic Middle Passage.

While Johnson's self-reflexive critique of implied literary overproduction is deliberately provocative, slavery as an academic topic continues to be immensely generative. A new domain of slavery studies has expanded the topic to global dimensions, multiple forms of subjugation, and different temporalities. Contemporary slavery across the world is gaining increasing scholarly attention across disciplines and in institutional and international human rights activism. Indeed, as Laura Murphy cautions, the contemporary human rights industry may promote packaged scripts of new slave narratives.[10] Meanwhile, other scholars worry over the inflatability of slavery, which was once exceptional and primarily specified by the transatlantic slave trade, but now encompasses a vast range of human rights abuses and exploitative labor. As Joel Quirk protests, maximalist interpretations of slavery lead to all kinds of problems with data collection, prevention, and solutions when the "trafficking gravy train," for instance, ignores sex work as involving some degree of choice and paints all participants as hapless enslaved victims, triggering ultimately obstructive reactions and moral panic.[11] Similarly, atrocity narratives about sex slavery, kidnapped children, or labor bondage in Muslim countries provide grounds for Islamophobia and trigger "humanitarian" interventions that hinder rather than help.[12]

At the same time, UNICEF admits that "all Africa's 53 nations reported human trafficking, spurred by poverty, armed conflict, and instability, as well as traditional practices, such as early marriage."[13] Women and children from Kenya, Ghana, Malawi, Togo, and Zimbabwe, the report notes, were trafficked for sex work in Europe and the Middle East; girls as young as eight were bought for their "purity" from AIDS; children were forced to labor in tea, cotton, cocoa plantations, and in mines on the continent; and others were sent abroad to labor as household servants. In some cases, children were then sent to recruit others. Meanwhile, African countries, struggling with social and economic problems that exacerbated the vulnerability of their citizens, had been slow in ratifying international conventions outlawing human trafficking. Despite the wariness of many of the scholars cited here, the link between contemporary slavery and human trafficking is not unwarranted. As opposed to the reluctance to expand slavery as a term that applies to contexts other than traditional chattel slavery, some scholars insist that there are varying forms of slavery and the term can no longer be restricted to the eighteenth-century slave trade.[14]

The slave narrative is now a global, cross-cultural genre that incorporates multiple experiences of human bondage and coerced labor.

African writing, which had once largely skirted the thorny subject of transatlantic slavery, addresses contemporary slavery within the continent more directly, even if it does not invoke the term as such. Yogita Goyal notes that postcolonial studies typically circumvent race whereas the global slave narrative forces us to confront the racism undergirding its progenitor of transatlantic slavery.[15] But conversely, it must be noted, the transatlantic ur-text of slavery tends to make race the master narrative and does not venture too deeply into the African interior. Murphy argues that memories of the African slave trade were not so much suppressed as repressed in Anglophone West African literature, since an earlier generation of African writers tended to allude metaphorically to the transatlantic slave trade.[16] The West and Central African performative dance traditions that mimic raids on villages which populated the coffles driven into slave ships for transatlantic migration and plantation labor suggest that Africans have not forgotten the internecine involvement in the trade. Zadie Smith's acerbic account in *Swing Time* of the trauma tourism involving the slave trading ports and monuments in Africa targets multiple constituencies, including the locals, for exploiting the memory of the Middle Passage, even as they attempt to venerate it.[17] The very settlement of these monuments and commemorative rites along the coasts, however, elide the events in the hinterland that actually initiated the inland capture and forced marches to the coasts before the oceanic passage onward.

Using Uwem Akpan's novella "Fattening for Gabon" as my focus in this essay, I explore how contemporary African writing about slavery binds together old and new forms of bondage, suggesting a continuum between past and present rather than a historical rupture between them.[18] The story is one of a collection that exposes the precarious lives of children in a range of national contexts, and is related from the first-person adult perspective of Kotchikpa, who is haunted by a tragedy from his past. The narrative tracks how Kotchikpa, then ten years of age, gradually realizes that his uncle and foster father Fofo Kpee plans to sell him and his five-year-old sister Yewa to traffickers. Since the jovial and caring Fofo Kpee deceives the children into believing they will be voyaging across the Atlantic to be adopted and educated by benevolent Americans, the unraveling of the deception by the unknowing but increasingly uneasy children takes up most of the story. After Fofo Kpee repents and is murdered by the vengeful trafficking cartel, Kotchikpa escapes from his captors but his sister Yewa is

SUPRIYA M. NAIR

left behind as his secret plan to run away with her misfires. Akpan's story draws attention to new modes of slavery in Africa but strikingly restricts it to national borders rather than pursue the diasporic shipboard voyages as in some of the texts mentioned above or follow the Afropolitan trend of contemporary African literature of migration projected as the fantasy to these children. In not crossing the ocean in his story, he acknowledges the monumental trauma of the Middle Passage but primarily dwells on contemporary social realities in Nigeria. His choice not to go all the way to the coast and revisit the voyages across the ocean implicitly critiques the resounding focus on the outward routes of the Middle Passage and Afropolitanism to the global North, emphasizing local contexts and the internal diasporas of forced migration *within* the African continent. Akpan's tale of contemporary slavery suggests a more explicit mapping of the interior origins of the Middle Passage.

Such a return to specific African sites signals a more open recognition of internal complicity and culpability, however coerced, in the slave trade as against placing the onus solely on white European and American iniquity and racism. Akpan's references to the Nigeria and Benin locations draw attention to the internal cross-border realities which underlie human trafficking in Nigeria and other African countries. While the earlier slave trade is invoked in his narrative, it is not where he leaves us. In metaphor-ically rehearsing but also reinventing the path to the Middle Passage, "Fattening" emphasizes local and contemporary particularities across dif-ferent timelines and contexts. By constantly alluding to the sea but not actually crossing it in the story, Akpan reverses the Middle Passage and discloses other contextual, temporal, and physical locations of slavery. The Passage figures, then, as a portal between the past and present, and the ominous ending of the story projects an ambivalent futurity suspended in flight, which is a stock trope of the slave narrative. Unlike the resilient, even triumphant, closures of most previous and contemporary slave nar-ratives, however, Akpan's uncertain ending, riddled with guilt for the child who escapes and horror for the child left behind, is a somber reflection on the enduring and unresolved prevalence of slavery.

The fact that none of Akpan's child figures in the collection of stories fits conventional stereotypes of childhood may be attributed to the loss of innocence in abject conditions of poverty and exploitation, but perhaps the mawkish ideal of children's stories anywhere is far less common than we imagine it to be. "The child is the specter of who we were when there was nothing yet behind us," Kathryn Stockton observes in her study of queer(ed) children.[19] She estranges the category of the "normative child,"

188

arguing that they are endowed with an innocence that is denied to many children. Despite saccharine literary and artistic portrayals which stimulated reforms in Western law in the past couple of centuries, they offer unsustainable models of ingenuous purity and virtue. While the war children of Africa stereotypically represent the polar extreme of the impossible Anglo-American ideal, the paradigm of "safe" and "safeguarded"[20] children has always been complicated in ancient fairy tales and folklore from across the world, in modern children's literature, and in contemporary child psychology. Akpan's juvenile subjects in "Fattening for Gabon" present a spectrum ranging from innocent naivete to critical awareness and agency, inciting outrage and fear over the fate of vulnerable children without reducing them to contrived types.

Like Stockton, Kate Manzo interrogates the supposedly universal perception of childhood as a customary period of security and comfort, noting that even the timeframe of what constitutes childhood is dominated by its Western idealization, which is not shared by all cultures, even legally for work or marriage, especially in conditions where not just poverty but civil war and disease accelerate the child's introduction to adult responsibilities. The controversy and media hype over the "slave ship" *Etireno*, which was said to have held enslaved children but revealed no evidence of it when inspected, reveal the complex social and cultural perceptions of child trafficking.[21] Manzo discourages the interchangeability between slavery and trafficking and insists on a more careful calibration of terms to maintain their force and precision as analytical categories. However, Akpan, whose novella may well have been inspired by this notorious traffic between Benin and Gabon and even by the *Etireno* scandal in 2001 when there was a spate of rumors – as well as realities – about child trafficking by boat between these regions, weaves the two terms together, even as he is primarily concerned with the contemporary setting.

The "African Gothic," as Goyal reminds us, has long been annexed to the reactionary cause of justifying European colonialism on the continent.[22] It is invoked in racist discourses that cross and recross the Atlantic from representations of unimaginable violence in Africa to the rhetoric of black criminality in metropolitan inner cities. Such portrayals have been used to vindicate perceptions of "failed" postcolonies, inexorably continuing their descent into the heart of darkness despite exposure to Western civilization. They have also rationalized excessive police violence against black populations in the United States in pathological discourses of racialized ontology. The bloodthirsty warlord, the "Voodoo"-worshipping psychopathic Big Man who is incapable of rational governance, the

relentless civil wars, the rapine of land and rapes of women, the kidnapping
of schoolchildren are familiar characters and episodes in hackneyed illus-
trations of African dysfunctionality. That Akpan runs the risk of cement-
ing this discourse in the entire collection of tales is evident when
interviewers ask him about whether his collection confirms negative stereotypes of Africa.[23] Akpan's response varies from insisting on the reality of
the tragedies he presents to casting himself as a spokesman for children,
which accumulates other risks of speaking for the subaltern. However, his
characters are generally nuanced, and his children are elusive figures who
are not easily appropriated.

The cover photo of *Say You're One of Them*, the collection in which
"Fattening" appears, shows a barefoot, close-shaven child running along an
unpaved road lined by greenery. Apart from the white frock and bow,
there is no indication of the gender of the child, who is facing – running –
away from the reader. While the sunlight on the road casts a deformed
shadow (of the child and of the swirling dress cloth) that looks like a bird
in flight, and although the position of the feet suggests hasty long strides
rather than a leisurely run, there is no sign that the child is in deadly peril.
Even the partial image of the child's eye on the book's spine, looking
intently away from the reader, gives no hint of the child's point of view,
what lies ahead for the child in the photo – or in the stories. Ultimately,
the recurrent emplotment of flight or attempted flight and the unbearable
tension in the stories reveal that this is not a carefree sprint but a solitary,
hazardous rush for freedom.

The opening lines of "Fattening" further implicates the reader from the
likely cause of the child's flight to the potential perpetrator of the crime:
"Selling your child or nephew could be more difficult than selling other
kids. You had to keep a calm head or be as ruthless as the Badagry-Seme
immigration people" (39). As we find, the blame and culpability extend to
Kotchikpa, the one who escaped and is now the older narrating-I of the
story behind his solitary flight. Rather than simply inviting the reader to
identify with the child who is to be trafficked or even the (usually white
and First World) savior, the opening lines disconcertingly force the reader
to inhabit the position of the trafficker, whom the child must flee. The title
of the collection is ambivalent, unclear about what constitutes the "you" or
the "them," and about whether the act of speech implies solidarity or
complicity, empathy, or threat.

The palimpsestic coastal town of Badagry harkens back to its significance from the eighteenth to the nineteenth centuries as the seminal point
for the transfer of African captives from the Nigerian hinterland to

European traders located at the coast. The dangerous intimacy of the family unit signals both the allegorical betrayal of natives sold by their own people to outsiders centuries ago as well as the literal reality of older family members engaging in child trafficking and sex slavery, sometimes unwittingly or in desperation. Kotchikpa reveals in the very first paragraph that his uncle, Fofo Kpee, had been planning to sell him and Yewa for three months. But both children are unaware of the plan for much of the story, and while the reader understands, because of the initial plot give-away and frequent elements of dramatic irony, that the children are to be trafficked, their own devastating apprehension of their endangerment occurs just before the denouement of the male narrator's escape. The title "Fattening for Gabon" gains increasingly disturbing meaning as it offers the sinister motive of raising children to be sacrificial lambs in a context of dire poverty and few options for survival.

"Food horror" is as elemental an aspect of children's literature as the sensuous pleasures and joys of children's food fantasies. The fear of being eaten adds frisson to many children's fairy tales and the fear of going hungry so eloquently expressed by Oliver Twist's plaintive request for "more" haunts tales of childhood across cultures. As Lorna Piatti-Farnell claims, the "Gothic horror element [of food] – together with its common tropes of alienation, liminality, and torture –" demonstrates that "food and consumption [are] . . . conducive metaphors for the 'horrors' of society."[24] A Google search on how to fatten lambs for slaughter brings up suggestive threads that I cannot follow here, but the feast and famine bitter paradox in Akpan's story illuminates his choice of title. Online tips for "fattening lamb nutrition," "feeding slaughter lambs for profit," "reducing lamb days to slaughter," "fatten[ing] up a sheep fast," and the more delicately worded but chilling "harvesting" of lambs provide robust how-to manuals that seem ironic in the biblical context of the phrase "gentle lamb led to the slaughter" (*Jeremiah* 11:19). The innocence and trust of the hapless animal are conferred on unprotected children but also symbolize a Christ-like suffering and sacrifice, the connotations to which Akpan, as an ordained Franciscan priest, would have been attuned.

Kotchikpa and Yewa are reduced to tradeable commodities by their uncle primarily because of the poverty that leads him to his previous choice of occupation as a border smuggler, an *agbero*, a tout for clandestine migration at Badgary, the site of an earlier traffic in humans. Trafficking in children, even his own family members, seems the logical next step as Kpee desperately seeks ways to make money. The children, meanwhile, are largely clueless about his schemes, not even aware that their parents in the village have died of AIDS, another example of systemic breakdown and structural violence, rendering them orphans wholly at the mercy of their uncle. The metaphor of fattening the children in preparation for their fostering by first their black and then their white "godparents" who will give them a "better life" not only reveals the historical conditions of how and why children get trafficked, it charts a vast network of criminality and collusion that involves local Nigerian figures, transnational middlemen, and the international trafficking cartels that fund and organize the system abroad. No wonder, then, that the cover photo shows the individual child running away from the reader, fleeing the treacherous societal carceral for an uncertain future.

Although those imprisoned on board in the Middle Passage were brutalized and subject to inhumane treatment leading to high mortality, the slave traders' concern over physical health and the force-feeding of the captives who refused to eat were motivated by the need to keep transported bodies in optimal shape for the pending rigors of slave labor. In the several grotesque episodes of eating in the story, the anxiety that fuels the feasts is not over maintaining fitness for the plantation routine, but over the belief that these children must not conform to the starving African poster child. Their bodies are to be nourished for sexual profit, a different kind of slavery that demands a different physical requirement. Yewa especially is targeted for sustenance: "We must fatten her for de trip [to Gabon]" (99). This is not to say that chattel slaves, conjugal slaves, and kidnapped children conscripted into various civil wars were not routinely subject to rape and assault, but here the children are not headed to plantations or to militarized killing fields but to U.S. brothels. The banquet they are fed in the introduction to their first adoptive family (the godparents and the other "siblings" who will accompany them to Gabon) is an obscene masquerade for the children who, given their poverty, subsist on far leaner fare. The table is heaped with dishes of "crab soup, mounds of *akasa* wrapped in fresh leaves, macaroni, cous-cous, and stew. A pot of pepper soup . . . with chunks of bush meat . . . . Coke, Maltina, La Place beer, and Chivita orange juice" (83).

Initially resistant to her renaming, Yewa is, as in cautionary children's stories of temptation through gluttony, seduced by the feast, guzzling large amounts of Coke and gobbling food "like a hungry dog" (86). While Paul, one of the other children, rejects the food and vomits, a foreshadowing of what will await the children on the boat that will take them to and out of Gabon, Yewa thereafter only wants "Gabon food" and idealizes Mama as a benevolent and trustworthy parent figure. But as the two children begin to realize the danger they are in, the food takes on repulsive qualities such that Yewa's later act of stuffing herself at the risk of choking is stimulated by her terror of the men who chase them down and prevent them from escaping with their uncle in the first abortive flight. When she subsequently empties her bowels, the smelly room that is their prison becomes a surrogate for the slave ship hold, where enslaved men and women were forced to endure the effluvia discharged in conditions of stress, fear, and seasickness (153).

As was common in slave narratives, references to their chattel status signify the varying approaches to ensnaring children. Big Guy sees them as little more than "chickens in Badagry open market" (78) and becomes increasingly menacing as he reveals himself to be not Kpee's immigration officer friend but a middleman for the trade. Mama, on the other hand, intent on seducing the children into leaving for Gabon for the overseas phase of the trafficking itinerary, treats them like they are her "precious vulnerable pet[s]" (82). Indeed, feeding them is both part of the seduction scenario as well as the hard-headed fattening *modus operandi* for a more profitable sale. Through the gendered stereotype of caregiving and by inducing them to believe that the excessive amounts of food and drink she brings are signs of her affection, Mama beguiles them into obedience just like seemingly humane "madams" coax their subjects into sexual service by inviting them to be part of their "family." Like slaves, they are given new names, Pascal and Mary, and also as in domestic slavery, where the veil of intimacy could be ripped apart at any moment by the master and mistress, the paternalism and maternalism of the "godparents" are ultimately abandoned by their violent henchmen who openly terrorize the children once the latter realize what lies behind the mask of adoption and promise of a better future abroad.

Although Akpan is borrowing from the template of transatlantic slavery, he also provides new narratives and images that indicate significant differences. Rather than simply replicating the traditional model in this story of contemporary child trafficking and sex work, Akpan departs from the original to emphasize the different circumstances of this commerce. The children do not embark on the notorious slave ships nor do they even make it to the sea, although it increasingly dominates the stage quite literally when the iterative "rehearsals" crossing that the children are subject to throughout the story includes drinking salt water to prepare them for the impending sea voyage. Beginning with Kpee's "Repeat after me" "*owhèntition*" sessions (106–109), reinforced by Big Guy's queries (126–127), and finally the unnamed guard's "*repetez après moi*" exercise

(155), the children are regularly coached into false family narratives in preparation for suspicious immigration officials at various borders. The adults provide the various scripts in different languages, which, for the most part, the children meekly repeat, rather like a catechism, reinforcing duty and obedience to elders as their religious obligation. The breaking point both for Kpee and Kotchikpa, however, is the physical rehearsal for sex work. Kpee suggests that they get comfortable with the nakedness of their benevolent "godparents" abroad who allegedly run a charitable NGO "Grace Earth" and do good work for children, extending this family romance into a larger kinship network. "You go see white people, colored people, tourists who support de work of your godparents. Do whatever dem want–go beach wid dem, go hotel wid dem . . . ," he ominously advises, even warning them not to be shocked by the nakedness of other children on the boat with them (117). But it is not until he exposes himself to the children and invites them to "*touchez moi*" that they recoil, particularly Kotchikpa, who begins to grasp the stakes of their "adoption."

Following that night of horror, both a repentant Kpee and a fearful Kotchikpa decide to escape from their captors. Kpee, who is not above quoting the scriptures like the devil when he wants the children to lie, undergoes a conversion and admits, "I no fit sell you and Yewa to anybody, like de slaves of de Badgary slave-trade tales. *Iro o*, I no fit allow dem ship you across dis ocean to Gabon. If you reach dat Central African country, *c'est fini*. You no go smell dis West Africa soil again" (135).[25] Kpee's confession rewrites both the script of transatlantic slavery, when kin, strangers, and enemies were sold, and the contemporary one, when he "no fit allow" the betrayal of selling the children he fosters. Symbolically, he begins to break apart the shack that he had initially buttressed to prevent his precious possession, the Nanfand motorcycle he had accepted as a preliminary bribe, from being stolen. He later transforms the place into an airless prison to house children who will be trafficked, including his nephew and niece and perhaps their siblings. His fortified shack mirrors the hold of the slave ship, one room with small porthole-like openings on the walls and another completely sealed. As they sweat in the unbearable heat, Kpee tells them, "Sometimes, de vessel to Gabon hot *pass* dis place . . . just manage" (103). His dismantling of the structural prop is a tacit refusal to follow the stage directions or rehearse the new script of slavery, but his redemption comes at a high cost when he is murdered, and his gravediggers are given the cherished motorcycle as payment.

Kpee's murder accelerates the pace of the story as Kotchikpa plots and carries out his nail-biting escape from his captors, a critical plot element in traditional and contemporary slave narratives that end on a high note. The foreboding at the end of this story suggests that Akpan does not subscribe to triumphalism, even if the children are not passive characters. Conventional gender stereotypes of protecting the girl result in the catastrophic decision made by Kpee and Kotchikpa not to reveal to Yewa the magnitude of the deception and entrapment. Consequently, when Kotchikpa finally alerts her to the possibility of escape, Yewa refuses, causing her older brother to push her out of the way and flee, pursued by the sound of her keening wails as she is left behind (172). His casting off the padlock and key that imprisoned them as he flees into the bush has limited symbolic potential for the victorious flight motif, both because his young sister is abandoned to her fate and because he admits that his sister's screams will forever haunt him: "I ran and I ran, though I knew I would never outrun my sister's wailing" (172). The ending pushes back against the hard-won freedom of many slave narratives, so that rather than the empathetic reader or the finally free slave, the emphasis is on incomplete and fragile freedom and on the work that still needs to be done for slavery to be vanquished in its entirety and not just in an individual's life. Like Kotchikpa, we cannot outrun those left behind.

Unlike the cover images of many contemporary slavery books, which feature the resolute face of the freed protagonist now involved in activist work, the child in the cover photo of Akpan's collection is viewed from the back. Rather than neatly turn the page or reach the final goal post, the past, present, and future follow a continuum, a long passage with no beginning and no end like the chronotopic road that stretches on in the cover photo. Eleni Coundouriotis draws attention to "improbable figures" in what she calls "fictions of insecurity." In her reading of the chronotope, which is "the space of the new in insecurity," she argues that the improbable figure who miraculously survives signifies a dynamic moment of "history making, of social change."[26] She would see, therefore, in the open future that lies ahead for Kotchikpa, a bracing ray of hope. Turning to Murphy, however, this open road could stand for the "not-yet-freedom" narrative, the turn away from a full recovery and rehabilitation not only for the trapped Yewa but also for the remorseful Kotchikpa.[27]

Akpan is not alone in invoking the traditional patterns and iconography of slavery to critique and expose contemporary trafficking. As Fuyuki Kurasawa argues, "anti-slavery advocacy seeks to draw on the past to acquire moral weight in public spheres in the present, while avoiding the suggestion of an easy moral and structural equation of the present with this past."[28] Confronted by a global predicament of ceaseless calamity and realizing the limits of international fatigue with such a scenario, anti-slavery writing galvanizes public consciousness by borrowing the tropes and conventions of transatlantic slavery, which has, through centuries of research, accumulated a substantial archive of visual and narrative material to draw from. The history of the transatlantic slave trade has received such widespread publicity that it sparks immediate condemnation of any practice of slavery, even if some are uneasy about loose equivalence and terminology. To ease such concerns, Kurasawa notes, modern writers "operate via a logic of symbolic analogy" that draws parallels between the modes of slavery then and now rather than conflate them into identical practices.[29] In some ways, repurposing the older narratives achieves a necessary degree of similarity, since sex trafficking is not always accepted as a form of slavery. Thus, as Murphy points out, the resonance of the earlier slave narrative helps make slavery in newer contexts more "legible." "Later in the 1990s," she explains, "a diverse set of cultural and political actors emerged who designated the experience of coerced sex work, debt bondage, conscripted military service, and other forms of forced labor as 'slavery.' The slave narrative was quickly mobilized as a major vehicle for circulating that shift in understanding."[30]

However, the indexicality of the borrowed symbols (in Akpan's story, for example: the lock, the airless prison, the slave ship hold, the salt water, and the sea), Kurasawa acknowledges, runs the risk of "desacralizing" the unspeakable horrors of the Middle Passage and watering down their undeniable differences. Goyal addresses the resistance of Afro-pessimism to claiming any analogy for the transatlantic experience of slavery, especially when assumed by non-black people. While acknowledging the critique of loose analogy, she believes that the literary device can enable scrupulous connections without erasing the differences. In Akpan's case, his subject is still black and, at least by some definitions, also enslaved, but his analogy encourages, I would agree, "a new comparative literacy across past and present, then and now."[31]

As contemporary slavery studies establishes its independent archive, previous history becomes a usable past for current critiques of slavery, however different they may be in practice and origin. While Akpan seeks a through line from the tragedy of the Middle Passage to continuing human rights abuses within the continent, he does not absolve the participants on either the African or non-African side of trafficking in contemporary contexts. Rather, he arrests the narrative before the coastal voyage and grounds the action within the terrestrial location, since Gabon is never arrived at. Although there are echoes and resonances, these histories are not restricted either to the oceanic journey from the African slave-trading coasts that gave the Middle Passage its name or the Final Passage to the plantations of the Americas. Instead, Akpan inspires us to reconsider the First Passage before the loading of slave ships in order to confront the continuing conditions and aftereffects of colonialism and slavery on the continent rather than in its transatlantic diasporas.

Notes

1 Toni Morrison, *Beloved* (New York: Vintage, 1987).
2 Paule Marshall, *Praisesong for the Widow* (New York: Plume, 1983).
3 Paul Gilroy, *The Black Atlantic: Modernity and Double Consciousness* (London: Verso, 1993).
4 Alex Haley, *Roots* (New York: Doubleday, 1976).
5 Charles Johnson, *Middle Passage* (New York: Scribner, 1990).
6 Andrea Levy. *The Long Song* (New York: Farrar, Straus, and Giroux, 2010).
7 Marlon James, *The Book of Night Women* (New York: Riverhead, 2009).
8 Yaa Gyasi, *Homegoing* (New York: Vintage, 2016).
9 Mat Johnson, Mat, *Pym* (New York: Spiegel and Grau, 2011). For a fuller discussion of this statement, see Aida Levy-Hussen, "Boredom in Contemporary African American Literature," *Post* 45, no. 2. https://post45 .org/2019/04/boredom-in-contemporary-african-american-literature/ (accessed May 27, 2022).
10 Laura Murphy, *The New Slave Narrative: The Battle Over Representations of Contemporary Slavery* (New York: Columbia University Press, 2019), 48.
11 Joel Quirk, "When Human Trafficking Means Everything and Nothing," *Contemporary Slavery: Popular Rhetoric and Political Practice*, edited by Annie Bunting and Joel Quirk (Vancouver: University of British Columbia Press, 2017), 75.
12 For an account that struggles with religious tensions and the conflicted presence of slavery in Islamic contexts, see Samuel Cotton's *Silent Terror: A Journey into Contemporary African Slavery* (New York: Harlem River Press, 1998).
13 Fiona Fleck, "Children are main victims of trafficking in Africa." *BMJ (Clinical research ed.)* vol. 328,7447 (2004): 1036. doi:10.1136/ bmj.328.7447.1036-b. See also UNICEF Innocenti Research Centre "Trafficking in Human Beings, Especially Women and Children, in Africa" at www.unicef-irc.org/publications/pdf/trafficking-gb2ed-2005.pdf (accessed May 27, 2022).
14 Laura Murphy, *Survivors of Slavery: Modern-Day Slave Narratives* (New York: Columbia University Press, 2014), 3–4.
15 Yogita Goyal, *Runaway Genres: The Global Afterlives of Slavery* (New York: New York University Press, 2019), 4.

16 See Laura Murphy, *Metaphor and the Slave Trade in West African Literature* (Ohio: Ohio University Press, 2012).
17 Zadie Smith. *Swing Time* (UK: Hamish Hamilton, 2016), 314–317. See also Laura Murphy, Chapter One, "Against Amnesia: Metaphor and Memory in West Africa." In *Metaphor and the Slave Trade in West African Literature.*
18 Uwem Akpan, "Fattening for Gabon." In *Say You're One of Them* (New York: Back Bay Books, 2008), 37–172. All references in the essay are from this edition.
19 Kathryn Bond Stockton, *The Queer Child, or Growing Sideways in the Twentieth Century* (Durham: Duke University Press, 2009), 30.
20 Stockton, *Queer Child*, p. 30.
21 Kate Manzo, "Exploiting West Africa's Children: Trafficking, Slavery and Uneven Development," *Area* 37, no. 4 (2005): 396. The *Etireno* was accused of trying to ship over two hundred child slaves to Gabon, but when it reached a port and was searched, only a few dozen children were found. For a critique of sensationalist accounts of child trafficking and slavery (as in "slave chocolate" narratives that inspire bursts of activism abroad but largely leave conditions within African cocoa plantations unchanged), see Joel Quirk and Darshan Vigneswaran, "Human Bondage in Africa: Historical Legacies and Recent Innovations." In *Slavery, Migration, and Contemporary Bondage in Africag*, ed. Joel Quirk and Darshan Vigneswaran (Trenton: Africa World Press, 2013), 1–35.
22 Goyal, *Runaway Genres*, p. 90.
23 See "Author Gives Voice to Plight of African Children." Interview of Uwem Akpan by Michel Martin. *Tell Me More*, NPR, 2008.
24 Lorna Piatti-Farnell, "Ravenous Fantasies and Revolting Dinners: Food and Horror in Children's Literature." In *The Routledge Companion to Literature and Food*, ed. Lorna Piatti-Farnell and Donna Lee Brien (New York: Routledge, 2018), 50.
25 For a nuanced reading of Kpee, who is not the conventional sex-trafficking monster figure, see Thando Njovane's "Trauma, (Mis)Perception and Memory in Uwem Akpan's 'Fattening for Gabon,'" *English Studies in Africa* 55, no. 2 (2012): 102–112.
26 Eleni Coundouriotis, "Improbable Figures: Realist Fictions of Insecurity in Contemporary African Fiction." *Novel: A Forum on Fiction* 49, no. 2 (2016): 237.
27 Murphy, *The New Slave Narrative*, p. 25.
28 Fuyuki Kurasawa, "Show and Tell: Contemporary Anti-Slavery Advocacy as Symbolic Work." In *Contemporary Slavery: Popular Rhetoric and Political Practice*, ed. Annie Bunting and Joel Quirk (Vancouver: University of British Columbia Press, 2017), 161.
29 Kurasawa, "Show and Tell," p. 161.
30 Murphy, *The New Slave Narrative*, p. 11.
31 Goyal, *Runaway Genres*, p. 10.

PART IV

Metaphors and Migrations

CHAPTER 12

Itineraries of Arabic across Oceans and Continents
Edward Wilmot Blyden and Muslim Slave Writing in the Americas

Jason Frydman

In 1851, after spending his youth as a freeborn person of African descent in the slave port of Charlotte Amelie, St. Thomas, Danish West Indies, Edward Wilmot Blyden settled for the remainder of his life in West Africa. There, he became President of Liberia College, a candidate for president of the Republic of Liberia, and one of the nineteenth century's most respected scholars and commentators on African history and culture. A foundational thinker for Pan-Africanism, Blyden worked to correct the fallacious representation of Africa as a place of savagery and backwardness. Through his mastery of classical and Semitic languages, he demonstrated the cosmopolitan grandeur of African history, notable not only for continental achievements in the arts and sciences, but also for the continent's participation in the great trends and movements of world history. This correction turned him away from an Atlantic perspective to one oriented around the Mediterranean Sea and the Indian Ocean. Blyden's personal itinerary, with extensive travel throughout Africa and the Ottoman Empire, replicated his historiographical shift from the Caribbean and Atlantic to the Mediterranean and Indian Ocean worlds.

For Blyden, Islam formed a crucial context for apprehending African cosmopolitanism. His encounters in West Africa with the mid-nineteenth-century Islamic world of the Sahel inspired him to learn Arabic and travel throughout the Ottoman Empire. Blyden interpreted Islamic history attuned to the opportunities it afforded for African agency and social mobility, opportunities foreclosed or severely restricted within the domain of Atlantic chattel slavery. He emphasized how education in Arabic and Islamic traditions provided a passport from one end of the *umma* to the other, enabling African participation and achievement across what after Bandung in 1955 would be called Afro-Asia. Yet Blyden did not neglect the hemisphere of his birthplace. Drawing upon his own research, travel, and relationships, Blyden conveyed to his nineteenth-century peers on both sides of the Atlantic how Arab-Islamic education propelled African geographical and social mobility, which in turn helped shape attention to African Muslims in the New World. Blyden's arguments about Black social mobility within the Islamic world durably frame Muslim slave narratives in the Americas, revealing their protagonists' lived and ongoing connection to a world outside the dehumanization of Atlantic slavery. With African Muslims cast as Afro-Asians *avant la lettre*, Muslim slave writings in the Americas emerge as bids to reclaim a sacred, cosmopolitan subjectivity, a pious solidarity, across the rupture of the Middle Passage.

The catastrophic mobility of the transatlantic slave trade wrenched many Muslims, as with all the enslaved, from their native religious communities. The records they left, in the form of narratives, letters, amulets, and manuscripts in Arabic script, attest to persistent efforts to maintain their traditions and rejoin their communities. Held in bondage and surrounded by hostile Christians, stolen from an Afro-Asian world where Blackness did not exclusively connote servitude and servitude did not connote social death, Arabic literacy offered multiple ways to shape their destinies and reclaim their faith. The Mandingo Society of Port of Spain, Trinidad opened their early nineteenth-century petitions to King George IV and Queen Victoria for repatriation to Africa with a formulaic Islamic incantation and concluded by signing their names in Arabic. Job ben Solomon, abducted into slavery in the early eighteenth century and in flight from his cruel master, set his remarkable journey back to Africa in motion by covering his jail cell with Arabic writing. From the Georgia Sea Islands to Jamaica to Brazil, Muslims precariously re-established textual traditions and networks by writing letters in Arabic and transcribing sacred texts from memory. Bearing witness to their rich and cosmopolitan educational backgrounds, African Muslims in the New World used Arabic literacy to literally and figuratively overthrow the chains of slavery. They narrated as well as propelled their itinerant diasporic histories through literary and epistolary models, from Scheherazade to al-Hariri, studied in the markets and madrasas of Africa and the Ottoman Empire.[1]

12.1 Encountering Islam in the Sahel

When he set off on his own diasporic trajectory from Charlotte Amelie, Blyden knew little about the African Muslims of the Americas. All this changed with his emigration to Liberia at the behest of Presbyterian missionaries who encountered his astounding intelligence and gift for languages when he was a teenager. Blyden took his degrees and ordination from the Presbyterian missionary institution of Liberia College and later

joined the faculty as a Professor of Greek and Latin. Notwithstanding his
own work as a Christian missionary, Blyden soon took a deep interest in
the Islamic culture of the Sahel. Encounters with this culture were commonplace in nineteenth-century Liberia and Sierra Leone, as in the following account:

> It was, indeed, an inspiring sight a few weeks ago, while walking the streets,
> to meet those stalwart men, with flowing robes and majestic tread, from
> every important city in Nigritia for a thousand miles from the sea. The
> streams poured into the settlement, sometimes hundreds a day, from the
> golden hills of Boure, the shining plains of Wasulu, the pasture grounds of
> Futah, and the populous districts of Bambarra, from Timbuctoo, from
> Jenne, from Sego, from Kankan. And we heard, on every hand, the same
> vocal sounds which may be heard in the streets of Cairo and Alexandria, of
> Morocco and of Tunis.[2]

This account typifies Blyden's regard for the Sahel's Arab-Islamic culture:
its regal subjects ("stalwart" and "majestic"), its romantic geography
("golden hills" and "shining plains"), and its cosmopolitanism echoing
"the streets of Cairo and Alexandria, of Morocco and of Tunis."

Already adept at Hebrew, the study of which he began with the
Sephardic Jewish community during his childhood in Charlotte Amelie
and continued with his Protestant theological studies, Blyden devoted
himself to its Semitic cousin, Arabic. He investigated the history and status
of Islam in Africa, and in 1866 traveled to Beirut to study Arabic with the
circle of Syrian intellectuals and Anglo-American missionaries gathered
around the Syrian Protestant College, later the American University of
Beirut. In works ranging from *The People of Africa* (1871), *From West
Africa to Palestine* (1873), and *Christianity, Islam and the Negro Race*
(1887), Blyden demonstrated his deep knowledge of Islam in Africa and
Africans in the Islamic world. Despite his own Protestant missionary work
and institutional commitments, Blyden offered a positive view of Arab-
Islamic history and culture vis-à-vis "the Negro race." He suffered no little
censure in Protestant and Orientalist periodicals for this view. As Blyden
biographer Hollis Lynch writes, in the British press, reviewers of
Christianity, Islam and the Negro Race "took violent exception to
Blyden's high praise of Islam."[3] By contrast, the book was "acclaimed in
the Muslim world; the journals and newspapers of Damascus,
Constantinople and Beirut, carried highly complimentary reviews of it,
and gleefully reported the controversy which the book had generated in the
British press."[4]

Blyden's attitude to Islam discomfited Anglo-American and European readers by presenting the religion as a dynamic force in African history that, unlike Christianity, propelled the development of an autonomous yet worldly African culture. Basing his assessment on his decades of mission experience, his extensive travels, as well as erudite study in multiple languages (Blyden knew Greek, Latin, Hebrew, Arabic, French, German, and Spanish, and he was conversant in various West African vernaculars including Sierra Leone Creole), Blyden exposed how Atlantic chattel slavery and colonial conquest undergirded Anglo-American and European discourses on Africa and Islam, providing material incentives to view Africans as enslaveable and Muslims as obstacles to the "civilizing mission" that covered up Western hunger for African plunder. In fact, Blyden condemned European-led missionary work from the inside, arguing that it is:

> more and more apparent that an enterprise which requires so much and such continuous foreign aid and oversight – such an apparatus of alien training and directing agencies – is ill-adapted to compete with that energetic and cosmopolitan system from Arabia, whose agents are indigenous and stand on their own legs, pursuing methods, which, if under the inspiration of the Koran, are "racy of the soil."[5]

The scant number of Black missionaries to attain leadership positions in their organizations revealed to Blyden a continuous deferral, a permanent state of tutelage, "requir[ing] so much and such continuous foreign aid and oversight – such an apparatus of alien training and directing agencies," contrasting poorly with the history of Islam in Africa.[6]

Integrated into the "cosmopolitan system from Arabia," Africans maintain their cultural integrity while joining a complex global community linked by faith, language, and trade. Blyden writes:

> The native missionaries – Mandingoes and Foulahs – unite with the propagation of their faith active trading. Wherever they go, they produce the impression that they are not preachers only, but traders; but, on the other hand, that they are not traders merely, but preachers. And, in this way, silently and almost unobtrusively, they are causing princes to become obedient disciples and zealous propagators of Islam. Their converts, as a general thing, become Muslims from choice and conviction, and bring all the manliness of their former condition to the maintenance and support of their new creed.[7]

This "manly" nexus of religion and mercantilism will play a key role in the apprehension of enslaved Muslims in the Americas, many of whom – such as Job ben Solomon, or Ayuba Suleiman Ibrahima Diallo – were, as Philip Curtin describes them, "Muslim clerics with mercantile interests."[8] This status girded many African Muslims in the Americas with persuasive narrative and economic tools, as witnessed by the successful efforts of Job ben Solomon, Abdurrahman ("Prince"), Lamine Kaba, and Abu Bakr as-Siddiq to write and recite their way home from Maryland, Mississippi, South Carolina, and Jamaica, respectively, by enchanting Anglo-American audiences, from statesmen to financiers to amateur Orientalists, with dazzling displays of storytelling, Arabic scholarship, and enticements to the riches of the African interior. Having lived through epic, transoceanic tragedies of captivity and loss, yet deft in the Scheherazadian art of suspenseful narration and steeped in the genres of classical Islamic biography, these men applied their mercantile and religious educations to moving their readers and listeners to sponsor their desires for repatriation.

12.2 Education and Mobility in Islamic Afro-Asia

Blyden contrasts the stagnant apparatus of Christianity in Africa with the dynamic mobility of Islam, which has crucial importance for the perception of African Muslims in the New World. He seizes the language of Protestant capitalist propaganda and reassigns it to what he dubs the "healthy amalgamation" of African and Islamic culture. He surveys the "numerous Negro Mohammedan communities and states in Africa which are self-reliant, productive, independent."[9] If on the one hand these "Negro Mohammedan communities" seem to embody the Protestant spirit of capitalism, on the other hand "wherever Christianity has been able to establish itself" resembles a sort of "Oriental despotism" where "foreigners have taken possession of the country, and, in some places, rule the natives with oppressive rigour."[10]

The "self-reliant" dynamism of Islam spoke precisely to Blyden's often thwarted ambitions and those of his Black peers in Anglo-American missionary work, so many of whom had been denied admission to institutions of higher learning, reaching glass ceilings in the ministry. Blyden recognized himself as an outlier in his world, "an African who has enjoyed exceptional opportunities of travel and observation in the Eastern and Western hemispheres – in Central Africa, in Egypt and Syria, in Europe, in North and South America, and in the West Indies."[11] Yet this sort of cosmopolitanism is the *unexceptional* birthright of African Muslims.

Muslim slave narratives in the Americas represent the alienation from that cosmopolitanism as one of the gravest injuries of slavery.

More than anything else, Arab-Islamic education paves the way for this cosmopolitanism, as Blyden documents over and over again, and acts out himself by carrying a portfolio of "Arabic manuscripts written by natives of West Africa" on his travels from West Africa to England, throughout the Ottoman Empire, then with him across the Atlantic on lecture tours of North America. Within West and Central Africa, "Hausas, Foulahs, Mandingoes, Soosoos, Akus, can all read the same books and mingle in worship together, and there is to all one common authority and one ultimate umpirage."[12] Not only does Islam unify West and Central Africa through the Qur'an, but it links this geography to the wider continent:

> Indeed, throughout Mohammedan Africa, education is compulsory. A man might now travel across the continent, from Sierra Leone to Cairo, or in another direction, from Lagos to Tripoli, sleeping in a village every night, except in the Sahara, and in every village he would find a school. There is regular epistolary communication throughout this region in the Arabic language – sometimes in the vernacular, written in Arabic characters.[13]

Given the abysmal state of literacy in the European colonies, and the denial of Africans from getting even that scant education, the contrast between Christian educational neglect and Muslim compulsory education stands out all the more. Blyden also highlights how education frames networks of mobility and communication in Africa, conjuring the itinerant African Muslim traveler who will find a school in every village he passes through, perhaps on his way to the Holy Land, as Blyden documents on his own pilgrimage in *From West Africa to Palestine*. In the Valley of Jehoshaphat, he records:

> We passed by the mosque of the West Africans, where I saw natives from Senegambia at prayers possibly from Futah and the neighbourhood of Sierra Leone, as it is no uncommon thing for Mohammedans from the west coast of Africa to find their way across the continent to Egypt, Arabia, and Syria, on pilgrimage.[14]

Blyden insists over and over again on the peripatetic impulse in Islam, propelling adherents to depart their homelands for pilgrimage and study, a feature of Islamic life commemorated in and encouraged by classical Arabic writing, from the *maqamat* tradition founded by al-Hamadhani and al-Hariri to the travel (*rihla*) narratives of figures such as Ibn Battuta and Ibn Jubayr, standard parts of the West African curriculum. These literary precedents, often invoked by Blyden through his familiarity with the curriculum of the Sahel, shape the Muslim slave narratives of the Americas as well, as we will see below.

Before reaching Palestine, Blyden had spent the summer months of 1866 in Beirut and Mount Lebanon studying Arabic. Dr. Henry Harris Jessup, an American Presbyterian missionary and a founder of the Syrian Protestant College, escorted Blyden to the steamer to Jaffa. By way of farewell, he told Blyden: "'You may henceforth write 'Hajj'-pilgrim under your name,' said the hospitable Dr. Jessup, as he took leave of me on the wharf at Beirut; 'and for years to come you will be the only living referee in your country on matters relating to the Holy Land.'"[15] Blyden's writings would discreetly correct Dr. Jessup's ignorance of African Muslim mobility throughout the Islamic world, featuring not only his attunement to African travelers in Egypt and Palestine, but right under Dr. Jessup's nose in Beirut: "When I was at Beirut, in 1866, there was a celebrated 'rawi,' or minstrel, from the Soudan, of jet black complexion, drawing crowds every evening by the eloquence of his recitals."[16]

Perhaps this *rawi* recited the beloved epic of Antar, the quintessential hero-poet of pre-Islamic Arabia, "the pattern of Arabic chivalry,"[17] one of the many Black figures, Blyden notes, celebrated in Arab-Islamic culture, and including also Bilal, an Abyssinian slave, early convert to Islam, companion of the Prophet, who, with his beautiful, powerful voice, became the first *muezzin* to call the faithful to prayer.[18] For Blyden, this story illustrates the great social mobility of the Islamic world: "The slave who embraces Islam is free, and no office is closed against him on account of servile blood."[19] In this spirit Blyden recounts the story of Kafur:

> "a Negro of deep black colour, with a smooth, shining skin," who rose to be Governor of Egypt, from the position of a slave. He had shown himself equally great as a soldier and a statesman. His dominion extended not only over Egypt, but Syria also; and public prayers were offered up for him, as sovereign, from the pulpits of Mekka, Hijaz, Egypt and the cities of Syria, Damascus, Aleppo, Antioch, Tarsus, &c.[20]

Around the Mediterranean, the Ottoman Empire, and the Indian Ocean, the mark of slavery did not condemn one, not even Black Africans, to a state of social death. Like their Albanian and Circassian peers throughout the region they experienced a "continuum of various degrees of bondage rather than a dichotomy between slave and free," often rising, like Kafur, to the highest ranks of social, military, political, and economic power.[21]

12.3   Remembering New World African Muslims

Blyden's research into the relationship between Africa and Islam reoriented contemporaneous Anglo-American discourses about Blackness and Muslims in Afro-Asia and the New World. In the second half of the nineteenth century, the British were consolidating their naval dominance of the Mediterranean and the Indian Ocean, linked in 1869 by the Suez Canal. Muslim merchants along the Swahili coast, often Omani Arabs under the Sultan of Muscat and Zanzibar, posed obstacles to this dominance, and fueled naval and propaganda campaigns against them. Historian Lindsay Doulton explains:

> The Royal Navy's sustained attempt to suppress the so-called Arab slave trade during the last three decades of the nineteenth century was prompted to varying degrees by a combination of renewed British abolitionist zeal, perceived religious responsibility, and political and economic self-interest.[22]

Casting Arabs and Islam as the enemy of Africa allowed Britain to project itself as "the great emancipator,"[23] in spite of the familiar irony of expeditionary maritime imperialism that "British purchases of cloves and ivory from East Africa stimulated increase in both slavery and slave trading at the very time the British were campaigning to end the Indian Ocean slave trade."[24] Ignoring this irony, missionary journals and British print culture at large, according to Dolton, spread "vital propaganda" about freeing Africans "from the influence of the perceived archaic customs of Islam."[25] Blyden's message about the positive impact Islam had on Africa, his complication of the Atlantic world's racialized relationship between bondage and freedom, slavery and social status, flew in the face of this "vital propaganda," earning the enmity of many missionary and secular commentators.

On the other side of the Atlantic, Blyden's writing on Islam and Africa entered a different field of Orientalist prejudices and desires. As scholars such as Philip Curtin, Timothy Marr, and I have argued, American attitudes toward Islam, and especially African Muslims, typically relied on a fabulous exoticism.[26] In fiction, African Muslims from Harriet Beecher Stowe's *Dred, A Tale of the Great Dismal Swamp* (1856) to Joel Chandler Harris's *The Story of Aaron, So Named, the Son of Ben Ali* (1896) robed the "noble savage" in the finery of an enchanted East. Blyden's work with the American Colonization Society (ACS) and the American Ethnological Society (AES) positioned him to influence some of the most important commentators on African Muslims in the Americas, including Theodore Dwight, a founder of the AES. The ACS played a determining, if cynically racist, role in supporting the Republic of Liberia, arranging for the resettlement of African Americans in West Africa. Liberia, and Blyden in particular, offered the ACS, as well as the AES and the American Oriental Society, a direct connection to a population fluent in Arabic. This served these Societies well, as Arabic manuscripts kept turning up in the New World, piquing their "gentlemanly" interest. Blyden's work contextualizes these texts as something other than exotic curiosities composed by unlikely scribes such as Omar ibn Sa'id (1770–864), an enslaved Muslim of Futa Toro resident in North Carolina.

Nicolas Said in Alabama, Abu Bakr as-Siddiq in Jamaica, Job ben Solomon in Maryland, Omar ibn Sa'id in North Carolina, Sheikh Sana See in Panama, and Bilali Mahomet in Sapelo Island were all African Muslims who left behind textual trails in Arabic of their exile and enslavement in the New World. These writings, and others besides, testify to the social and geographical mobility of African Muslims, and they represent gestures to recapture their interrupted participation in that dynamic, cosmopolitan world. Ranging from narratives and personal letters to recapitulations of classical learned texts, they inscribe their drafters in the *umma* as a respite and refuge from their captivity. A breakthrough edited volume in American Orientalism, *The People of Africa* (1871) assembles Blyden's research on Africa since antiquity, along with a companion piece, among others, by Theodore Dwight on enslaved African Muslims, and represented an effort of the American Colonization Society to publicize Blyden's revisionist perspective on Islam in Africa. Turning away from the exotic, *The People of Africa* instead aims to correct, in Dwight's words, the "erroneous impressions which prevail in the civilized world respecting the condition of the Negro race in Africa."[27] Dwight's essay seeks to do this by compiling a record of enslaved African Muslims in the United States, from Job ben Solomon in the eighteenth century to Abdurrahman ("Prince"), Omar ibn Sa'id, and Lamine Kaba ("Old Paul") in the nineteenth, and attending to their education in West African religious schools. While valuable, what Dwight's vindication of African educational institutions misses are precisely the affective cadences of his subjects' textuality. Blyden, on the other hand, enables us to apprehend the dynamic cosmopolitanism of the Afro-Asian *umma*, where "African Moslems are continually crossing the continent to Egypt, Arabia, and Syria"[28] while "brilliant Arab youth[s], from the schools of Bagdad [make] missionary visits to the Mohammedans"[29] of Sierra Leone. The manuscripts composed by African Muslims in the Americas, then, poignantly reconstitute this ambulatory republic of letters.

12.4   Arabic Literary Legacies in the African Diaspora

Literary genre markers often reveal this poignant reconstitution of an Islamic republic of letters.[30] In 1873, during the post-Civil War Reconstruction period in the United States, a small publishing house in Memphis put out *The Autobiography of Nicolas Said, a Native of Bornou, Eastern Soudan, Central Africa*. Born Mohammed Ben Ali Said to a military commander of Kouka, in Bornou (currently the Central African Republic), Said's mastery of languages ("Kanouri (my vernacular), Mandra, Arabic, Turkish, Russian, German, Italian and French"[31]) and lifetime of travel rival Blyden's, though headed in the other direction. Said's narrative confirms the fluid nature of unfreedom in the ambit of the Ottoman Empire, where we find, as Edud Toledano writes, that "continuum of various degrees of bondage rather than a dichotomy between slave and free."[32] Said's text manifests a lifetime of education provided first upon the death of his father in his native Bornou and later by the high-ranking Turkish pashas and Russian princes in whose households he dwelled.

Key Arab-Islamic genre markers demonstrate his ongoing auto-inscription in the *umma* even after Said began self-identifying as a Swedenborgian mystic. He would have begun his early encounters with Islamic letters in his years of study with "Malam Katory [who] was well versed in the Arabic, Turkish, and Persian languages, besides possessing mental endowments of a very superior character in other respects, and, in our country was esteemed almost as highly as the king himself."[33] Said approaches the task of recounting his life through a notion of edification specifically rooted in his African Muslim origins. A vindicationist element also runs through Said's text, responding most likely to the spirit of Reconstruction in his adopted homeland: "My motive in this publication I believe to be good: a desire to show the world the possibilities that may be accomplished by the African, and the hope that my humble example may stimulate some at least of my people to systematic efforts in the direction of mental culture and improvement."[34]

Prior to his travels in Europe and North America, Said, like Blyden, found the geography of Ottoman rule congenial to "his people." After crossing the Sahara with his Tuareg captors, the Turkish tobacco merchant Hadji Daoud bought him and installed him as an apprentice in his shop in the city's principal bazaar. Like his other Turkish masters, "Hadji Daoud treated me with extreme kindness and, in this connection I feel constrained to say, that of all the nationalities of people I have seen in my life, I like the Turks the best."³⁵ Said's motivation extends beyond mere personal experience:

> During my stay in Tripoli, the garrison was relieved and the troops sent home to Turkey, their place being supplied by a force from Gallipolis. In this new garrison there were several black officers and privates among the Turkish soldiers. There seems to have been no prejudice among the Turks on account of complexion.³⁶

Throughout his servitude in the Ottoman Empire, Said noted precisely that "continuum between bondage and freedom" where Circassian and Abyssinian, fair- and dark-skinned, occupied a range of positions in household, social, religious, military, and political hierarchies. From Tripoli to Egypt, from the Hajj to Istanbul, Said enjoyed uninterrupted physical safety and intellectual growth.

Said frames these "edifying" travels through classic tropes of *adab*, an Arabic concept entailing not only artful and eloquent language, but also that which provides useful knowledge and guides proper conduct. Thus, for example, his journey (*rihla*) from Benghazi to Cairo proceeds through a series of marvels, *aja'ib* in Arabic, invoking "a genre of literature" that, according to Roy Mottahadeh, "accounts for the diversity of things that are sometimes considered wondrous and marvelous according to the various taste of the medieval authors ... which also makes clear the role of '*ajab* as a source of *adab*."³⁷ Sometime in the 1860s, Said's first voyage by sailboat, whose "main-mast was twice struck by lightning" on the third day out, gave way to his first view of a steamship which towed them to Alexandria. From Alexandria, he and Hadji Daoud boarded "the then new railroad" to Cairo. He comments wryly:

> I cannot say I was much surprised at the novel conveyance I then saw for the first time. Truth told, I had seen so many wonderful and unexpected sights within the few previous years, that I think my organ of marvelousness had gone to sleep from sheer surfeit and exhaustion, and I took everything as a matter of course. In fact I don't think my pulse would have been quickened had I been transported from one part of the country to another in an aerial car, or shot across a river from a bomb mortar.³⁸

Pushing the literature of *aja'ib* to its limit, Said's narrative enters a domain of prescient, speculative Afro-futurism.³⁹

His journey in Egypt, perennial land of wonders, provides other invocations of Arab-Islamic *adab*. As they travel down the Nile into Upper Egypt, past the Pharaonic remains of Philae, they encounter "the ruins of another town, built (so said Hadji Daoud) by the Arabs in the days of

Caliph Omar."[40] Thus Said finds himself standing before the ruins, *al-atlal*, reenacting one of the most fundamental gestures of the Arabic literary tradition, with its roots in pre-Islamic poetry. "Here the antiquarian might spend many profitable hours," Said continues, "exploring and examining the crumbling monuments of primeval grandeur."[41] Said's reflections are consonant with the Islamic tradition of gazing upon the ruins of ages past. As the scholar Elliot Colla comments, such ruins "gestured beyond normal human scales of time and toward the eternal and divine" while their "ruined state suggested the vanity of human endeavor in this world."[42] Said's perspective incorporates this bifurcated gaze with an eye toward the "profitable hours" it provides.

After completing the Hajj and returning to Tripoli, Said learns that a fire has swept through the Turkish bazaar and destroyed Hadji Daoud's tobacco shop. These circumstances force the latter to sell Said at the slave market of Smyrna, where he is purchased by Fuad Pacha, the Minister of the Interior of the Ottoman Empire, to serve as a *tchiboudji*, or pipe (narguileh) cleaner. With frequent visits to the Sultan's palace, Said "had excellent opportunities of seeing and learning many things in regard to the Turkish etiquette and mode of living in the highest circles."[43] He passed into the household of Fuad Pacha's brother-in-law, Reschid Pacha, who, "like every Turkish master I had, treated me very kindly, giving me holidays, almost every day, from breakfast to noon, and furnishing me with small sums of money to spend in my own gratification." Reschid Pacha's "intimate associates" were "the French Ambassador M. De Montholon, the English Minister Lord Stratten de Ratcliffe, and the Envoy Extraordiniary or Minister Plenipotentiary of Russia Prince Anatole Mentchikoff." This latter became so taken with Said that Reschid Pacha conferred Said into his possession, and so began Said's European sojourn. Prince Mentchikoff also presented Said to his brother-in-law, one Prince Troubetzkoy, with whom Said made a grand European tour of cities and holiday towns. These travels made Said homesick, and Prince Troubetzkoy granted Said three hundred pounds sterling and one year to make the long journey from England to Bornou and back. However, Said was offered the opportunity to enter the paid service of one Mr. Rochussen, "then lately from Paramaribo (Dutch Guinea)" in undertaking "a bridal tour through the West Indies, the British North American Provinces, and the United States."[44] Said's "fondness for travel asserted its supremacy," and he acquiesced. Eventually, Mr. Rochussen deceived Said, leaving him penniless in Canada. Said then began a peripatetic journey from Canada down to the Southern United States, finally settling in Alabama, where he dedicated himself to teaching in a small "Negro school." He ends his narrative by emphasizing the importance of education, merging the "edifying" ethos of his Arab-Islamic education with the uplift ideology of Reconstruction:

> My honest and ardent desire is to render myself useful to my race wherever it may be. I have no aspirations for fame, nor anything of the sort. But I shall always prefer at all times to find myself in the midst of the most ignorant of my race, and endeavor to teach the rising generation the advantages of education.[45]

Said's narrative testifies to the fluid continuum of bondage and freedom in the Islamic world of the Ottoman Empire and its environs that Blyden recognized as enabling a boundless, if still subordinated, African mobility. As he negotiated his itinerant status around the world, Said hewed to the fundamental literary principles of *'ajab* and *adab*, maintaining ties to his earliest studies in Bornou that deepened with the intellectual support of his Turkish masters through North Africa, Egypt, and Istanbul. Arriving in the United States after emancipation, he carried this legacy of Arab-Islamic learning into a small Alabama schoolhouse and disseminated it in writing and in lectures to a population struggling to emerge from centuries of chattel slavery.

12.5   Fragmented Assemblages of African Islamic Memory

Said's tale, then, differs from many of the other Muslim slave narratives penned in the Americas. Unlike Job ben Solomon, Lamine Kaba, or Omar ibn Sa'id, Nicolas Said did not endure the Middle Passage on a slave ship, yet his story helps corroborate Blyden's feel for the African Muslim's cosmopolitan possibilities. These foreclosed possibilities emerge with poignant force in the texts of other African Muslims in the New World. Theodore Dwight, seeking to vindicate the misrepresentation of African educability through finding enslaved Muslims literate in Arabic, became an important liaison for the reconstitution of those lost cosmopolitan networks of the Sahel. Dwight conducted extensive interviews with "Lahmen Kibby," a name that would now more commonly be rendered as Lamine Kaba (though he was renamed by the white Southerners who enslaved him as "Old Paul"). Freed in 1835 after forty years of bondage in South Carolina and Alabama, Kaba had worked before capture in Africa as a teacher in a coeducational madrasa in Futa Toro, a region now part of Senegal. Recruited by Dwight to work for the American Colonization

Society, Kaba returned to Africa in 1836. Before he left, however, he provided Dwight with extensive information on African Muslim education that Dwight published in *The American Annals of Education and Instruction* in 1835.

Through Dwight's intercession, Kaba began a correspondence in Arabic with Omar ibn Sa'id of Fayetteville, North Carolina, who reached the New World in 1807, the year of the abolition of the transatlantic slave trade. Like Kaba, Said had extensive religious schooling in Futa Toro, rising also to the rank of teacher. Contemporaneous with the 1834 correspondence in Arabic brokered by Richard Madden in Jamaica between Timbuktu-native Abu Bakr as-Saddiq and Mahomed Caba,[46] their correspondence recapitulates what Blyden called the Sahel's "regular epistolary communication throughout this region in the Arabic language." Ibn Sa'id sent Kaba an 1831 Arabic manuscript containing extensive citations of the Qur'an that preface a recounting of his life. Notably, like as-Saddiq in his missive to Caba, Ibn Sa'id also provides his *'ijaza*, a testimony of the names of his Quranic teachers, "I sought knowledge under the instruction of a Sheikh called Mohammed Seid, my own brother, and Sheikh Soleiman Kembeh, and Sheikh Gabriel Abdal."[47] Through this *'ijaza* and the preceding Quranic citations, ibn Sa'id shores up, against his "weak eyes" and "weak body," his connections to his Arab-Islamic past at a time when he has "much forgotten my own, as well as the Arabic language. Neither can I write very grammatically or according to the true idiom."[48] Yet for a moment this act of inscription activates totemic powers of blindness and Quranic memory, as well as the epistolary networks under the aegis of the Qur'an that constituted among the Muslims of West Africa, as Blyden writes, "one common authority and one ultimate umpirage."

Whereas after four years this 1831 letter finally found an addressee capable of deciphering it, ibn Sa'id had also composed a letter in 1819 to James Owen, who enslaved him, which embeds a single request, "I wish to be seen in our land called Afrikā, in a place [on] the river called K-bā / K-b-y," in extensive citations from the Qur'an and other learned texts of Islam. Despite ibn Sa'id's later 1831 praise for Jim Owen as a "good man" ("During the last twenty years I have known no want in the hand of Jim Owen"[49]), it is hard not to read these citations as invocations of divine intervention and righteous judgment. For example, before expressing his wish, ibn Sa'id cites the second sura of the Qur'an, Surat al-Baqarah (the Cow), imploring: "O our Lord, do not burden us with what we have no strength to endure, and pardon us and forgive us and have mercy on us. Thou art our Lord, so aid us against the unbelievers."[50]

The applicability of this verse to ibn Sa'id's predicament emerges clearly: stolen away into captivity in middle age, ibn Sa'id had gained some minor celebrity due to his Arabic literacy, first demonstrated on the walls of his jail cell (like Job ben Solomon) after he had run away from a cruel master. The "novelty" of an African Muslim had been covered in a variety of newspapers in the region and beyond. Jim Owens had been appealed to to manumit him, and though under Owens "I have no hard work to do," Owens refused to release ibn Sa'id from bondage. Ibn Sa'id's participation in the Presbyterian congregation of the Owens family notwithstanding, it is not hard to imagine Owens interpellated as an "unbeliever" in the 1819 letter.

For whom did Omar ibn Sa'id compose this Arabic letter, then? Why inscribe in Arabic a request denied in English? Similarly, why did Belali Mahomet of the Georgia Sea Islands inscribe a tenth-century legal treatise in Arabic and Pulaar? Or Sheikh Sana See of Panama an excerpt from a meditative text of the Qadiriyya Brotherhood? Perhaps a clue resides in a small five-cornered star ibn Sa'id drew just before expressing his wish to return to Africa in 1819. As John Hunwick reports:

> It is in fact a very powerful talismanic symbol, the pentacle, said to be the "seal of Solomon", and the first of seven "seals" that are frequently found in talismans or inscribed over doorways of buildings to protect them. It was no doubt drawn by 'Umar in this spot to invoke God's power. It is said to represent the secret 100th name of God and to have miraculous powers.[51]

In Islamic lore, King Solomon conquered the heretical jinn, who like the series of slave dealers and slaveholders that perpetrated "saltwater slavery,"[52] were callous and whimsical arbiters of life and death for the Muslims caught in their power. In punishments resonant against the nautical landscape of the Middle Passage and the American South's orchards of strange fruit, Solomon imprisoned these jinn in the trunks of trees and in chests at the bottom of the sea.

And yet perhaps more than just the pentacle constituted a talisman. Perhaps the whole text, and Arabic script itself, constituted for these African Muslims in the Americas a talisman with miraculous powers. On the one hand, Arabic inscription had the power to subjectively reintegrate those severed cosmopolitan networks of study, prayer, and remembrance (*zikr*) that bound Islamic Afro-Asia together and constituted the birthright of those "African Muslims [who] are continually crossing the continent to Egypt, Arabia, and Syria."[53] On the other hand, the script itself, bearing the language of the Qur'an, offered "divine help and protection,"[54] according to Sylviane Diouf: from the Islamic amulets (*bolsas de mandinga* [mandingo purses or grisgris]) worn by African Muslims throughout the Caribbean, Spanish America, and Brazil; to the one hundred Qur'ans sold every year to the enslaved men – many illiterate – of Rio de Janeiro by the French booksellers Fauchon et Dupont;[55] to the one-hundred-page manuscript of Quranic verses and prayers in Arabic and an African vernacular "found in a pouch hanging around the neck of a dead insurgent"[56] of the 1835 Bahia Slave Rebellion. Through this materiality of the Word in Arabic, in ink, on paper, enslaved Muslims in the Americas – like Blyden himself, Pan-African visionary of an Africa for the Africans, who seemed never to travel without his packet of Arabic manuscripts from West Africa – remembered communities both earthly and divine.

Notes

1 For more on the literary heritage of African Muslims in the New World, see Jason Frydman, "Scheherazade in Chains: Arab-Islamic Genealogies of African Diasporic Literature." In *The Global South Atlantic*, ed. Kerry Bystom and Joseph R. Slaughter (New York: Fordham University Press, 2017), 65–80.

2 Edward Wilmot Blyden, *Christianity, Islam and the Negro Race* (London: W.B. Whittingham & Co., 1888 [1887]), 236.

3 Hollis R. *Lynch, Edward Wilmot Blyden: Pan-Negro Patriot, 1832–1912* (New York: Oxford University Press, 1970), 75.

4 Lynch, *Blyden*, p. 77.

5 Lynch, *Blyden*, p. vii.

6 Emphasizing Blyden's missionary objectives, largely dismissed by the end of his life, Jacob Dorman insists that "Blyden's view of Islam was far more Orientalist and far less positive than most accounts portray," taking issue in particular with Richard Brent Turner's *Islam in the African-American Experience* (Bloomington: Indiana University Press, 2003). See Jacob S. Dorman, "Lifted Out of the Commonplace Grandeur of Modern Times: Reappraising Edward Wilmot Blyden's Views of Islam and Afrocentrism in Light of His Scholarly Black Christian Orientalism," *Souls* 12, no. 4 (2010): 398–418.

7 Lynch, *Blyden*, p. 12.

8 Philip Curtin, ed., *Africa Remembered: Narratives by West Africans from the Era of the Slave Trade* (Madison, WI: University of Wisconsin Press, 1967), 37.

9 Blyden, *Christianity*, p. 11.

10 Blyden, *Christianity*, p. 354.

11 Blyden, *Christianity*, p. ix.

12 Blyden, *Christianity*, p. 8.

13 Blyden, *Christianity*, p. 360.

14 Edward W. Blyden, *From West Africa to Palestine* (London: Simpkin, Marshall, & Co., 1873), 180.
15 Blyden, *Palestine*, p. 191.
16 Blyden, *Christianity, Islam*, p. 262.
17 A.O. Stafford, "Antar, the Arabian Negro Warrior, Poet and Hero," *The Journal of Negro History* 1, no. 2 (April 1916): 153. See also Rachel Schine, "Conceiving the Pre-Modern Black-Arab Hero: On the Gendered Production of Racial Difference in Sīrat al-Amīra Dhāt al-Himma," *Journal of Arabic Literature* 48, no. 3 (2017): 298–326.
18 Blyden, *Christianity*, p. 264.
19 Blyden, *Christianity*, p. 202.
20 Blyden, *Christianity*, p. 281
21 Ehud R. Toledano, "The Concept of Slavery in Ottoman and Other Muslim Societies." In *Slave Elites in the Middle East and Africa: A Comparative Study*, ed. Miura Toru and John Edward Philips (London: Kegan Paul International, 2000), 164.
22 Lindsay Doulton, "'The Flag that Sets us Free': Antislavery, Africans, and the Royal Navy in the Western Indian Ocean." In *Indian Ocean Slavery in the Age of Abolition*, ed. R. Harms, B.K. Freamon, and D.W. Blight (New Haven: Yale University Press, 2013), 102.
23 Doulton, "The Flag," p. 103.
24 Harms, "Introduction" to *Indian Ocean Slavery*, p. 6.
25 Doulton, "The Flag," p. 108.
26 Curtin, *Africa*; Timothy Marr, *The Cultural Roots of American Islamicism* (New York: Cambridge University Press, 2006); Frydman, "Scheherazade."
27 Theodore Dwight, "Condition and Character of Negroes in Africa." In *The People of Africa*, p. 44.
28 Edward W. Blyden, "Mohammedanism in Western Africa." In *The People of Africa*, p. 96.
29 Blyden, *Christiantiy*, p. 263.
30 Muhsin J. al-Musawi, *The Medieval Islamic Republic of Letters* (South Bend: University of Notre Dame Press, 2015).
31 Nicolas Said, *The Autobiography of Nicolas Said, a Native of Bornou, Eastern Soudan, Central Africa* (Memphis: Shotwell & Co., 1873), vii.
32 Toledano, "The Concept of Slavery," p. 164.
33 Said, *Autobiography*, p. 36.
34 Said, *Autobiography*, p. v.
35 Said, *Autobiography*, p. 68.
36 Said, *Autobiography*, p. 69.
37 Roy P. Mottahadeh, "*Ajaʿib* in *The Thousand and One Nights*." In *The Thousand and One Nights in Arabic Literature and Society*, ed. Richard Hovanissian and Georges Sabagh (Cambridge: Cambridge University Press, 1997), 30.
38 Said, *Autobiography*, pp. 78–79.

39 To my knowledge, this is the first linking of Nicolas Said with Afrofuturism. For more on Afrofuturist origins in this period, see W. Andrew Shephard, "Afrofuturism in the Nineteenth and Twentieth Centuries." In *The Cambridge History of Science Fiction*, ed. Gerry Canavan and Eric Carl Link (Cambridge: Cambridge University Press, 2019), 101–119.

40 Said, *Autobiography*, p. 82.

41 Said, *Autobiography*.

42 Elliott Colla, *Conflicted Antiquities: Egyptology, Egyptomania, and Egyptian Modernity* (Durham: Duke University Press, 2008), 75.

43 Said, *Autobiography*, pp. 120–121.

44 Said, *Autobiography*, 187.

45 Said, *Autobiography*, 212.

46 Richard Robert Madden, *A twelve month's residence in the West Indies, during the transition from slavery to apprenticeship; with incidental notices of the state of society, prospects, and natural resources of Jamaica and other islands* (Westport, CT: Negro Universities Press, 1970 [1835]), 246–248.

47 John Franklin Jameson (ed.), "Autobiography of Omar ibn Said, Slave in North Carolina, 1831," ed., *The American Historical Review* 30, no. 4. (July 1925): 792.

48 Jameson, "Autobiography of Omar ibn Said," p. 792.

49 Jameson, "Autobiography of Omar ibn Said," p. 795.

50 John Hunwick, "I Wish to Be Seen in Our Land Called Afrika: 'Umar B. Sayyid's Appeal to Be Released from Slavery (1819)," *Journal of Arabic and Islamic Studies* 5 (2003–2004): 76.

51 Hunwick, "I Wish to Be Seen in Our Land Called Afrika," pp. 73–74.

52 Stephanie E. Smallwood, *Saltwater Slavery: A Middle Passage from Africa to American Diaspora* (Cambridge, MA: Harvard University Press, 2008).

53 Edward W. Blyden, "Mohammedanism in Western Africa." In *The People of Africa*, p. 96.

54 Sylviane A. Diouf, "African Muslims in Bondage: Realities, Memories, and Legacies." In *Monuments of the Black Atlantic: History, Memory and Politics*, ed. Maria Diedrich and Joanne M. Braxton (Hamburg: Lit Verlag, 2004), 81.

55 Alberto da Costa e Silva, "Buying and Selling Korans in Nineteenth-Century Rio de Janeiro," *Slavery & Abolition* 22, no. 1 (2001): 72.

56 Diouf, "African Muslims," p. 82.

CHAPTER I3

Apartheid's Ghosts
Slavery in the Literary Imagination
Kirk B. Sides

In 1915, South African writer and translator Sol T. Plaatje published *Native Life in South Africa*, which describes the disastrous effects the 1913 Natives Land Act had upon Black life in South Africa. Plaatje's now famous opening line charts some of the space, and proximity, between different modes of racial control, slavery, segregation, and apartheid, which will be discussed below. Plaatje also gives detail to the ways in which what Achille Mbembe refers to as the colonial "fantasy of separation" (segregation) is enshrined in one of the earliest pieces of formal scaffolding leading to apartheid in South Africa.[1] Plaatje writes that, "Awaking on Friday morning, June 20, 1913, the South African Native found himself, not actually a slave, but a pariah in the land of his birth."[2] Plaatje's structural comparison is important for how he positions slavery as a critical lens or metric through which to read the delineated landscape of segregationist policy. Plaatje's assessment also reveals how already, thirty-five years before it would be formally codified into national policy, the segregationist plan that would become apartheid was set to evolve along a rhetorical axis extolling "separate development." He writes that the "Bill was going to set up a sort of pale – there was going to be a sort of kraal in which all the Natives were to be driven, and they were to be left there to develop on their own lines."[3] In a clear reference to chattel slavery, Plaatje's comparison inverts southern African economies of wealth associated to cattle by showing how segregationist policy dehumanized the Black peoples of South Africa through commodification and racial enclaving. The "kraal," rather than the central spatial configuration of economic and cultural wealth, is ominously rendered here as a prison for containment that Plaatje associates closely to slavery.

In her recent book *Runaway Genres: The Global Afterlives of Slavery*, Yogita Goyal writes that part of accounting for the "global afterlives of slavery" is "a recognition of the semiotics and the geopolitics of US empire, including a consideration of how these relate to or depart from earlier

219

European imperialisms."[4] This is an incredibly important move in thinking about the virulent reach of white supremacy transmitted through
various ecosystems of colonial control. I want to depart from this departure
in order to think about how slavery and the post-slavery history of
segregation in the United States informed the subsequent moments of
high empire leading into and through the middle of the twentieth century.
There is an underexplored trajectory within the larger one charted by
Goyal, moving from the history of enslavement and Jim Crow
Segregation in the United States as precursors and precedents to the
development of segregation and apartheid in South Africa. Such a connection relies on a similar set of methodological approaches[5] as those laid
out by Goyal, who argues that "Focusing on slavery – as perhaps the most
momentous global event the world has seen – demands a dialogue across
the disciplines of postcolonial and African American studies, connecting
US minority populations to those in the Global South."[6] This chapter is
also interested, at least in some small way, in the stakes, or perhaps the
politics, of comparison and what it might mean to think about the legacies,
or "afterlives" of the policies and ideological structures that emanated from
the histories of slavery in the southern United States and how these
traveled as markers of both precedent and caution to other nations, and
especially in this case South Africa. In other words, the chapter will posit
that the ideological and legislative trajectory that runs from the segregation
of the early twentieth century through to formal apartheid for the rest of
the century in South Africa be read as one of the "transnational afterlives of
slavery" that Goyal outlines.

Most of the critical literature on the development of South African
segregation policies has historically centered around the triangulated relationship between rapid industrialization, economics, and racial policy as
response to the first two. The evolution of the argument from Martin
Legassick to Harold Wolpe to Shula Marks and Saul Dubow has tended
towards useful and needed critiques of the functionalist nature of segregation as a safety net set up by the South African state for the continued
accumulation of white capital. From a political and economic perspective
this is certainly the case, but these nuances of the debate do not figure in
this study, as it is far more interested in the *circulation* of racist and
segregationist ideas and ideologies between the United States and South
Africa. In pointing to a few instances of historical connection and resonance around issues of race and racial policy, the chapter departs from
earlier comparative scholarship on the United States and South Africa,
which as critic Leigh Anne Duck argues was interested primarily and solely

in mapping "similarities and differences" between the two countries and their histories.[7] Instead, I want to demonstrate a genealogy which looks at the development of apartheid as one of the "afterlives of slavery" to which Goyal gestures. I also want to make clear any anxieties of conflation: the plantation economies of enslavement in the United States are not identical to forms of forced labor elsewhere in the colonial world (and there is much literature to this point); nor is Jim Crow segregation the same as segregation as it was practiced in South Africa, whether pre-1948 or through the more unified and expansive platform of apartheid. But this chapter is not looking for equivalencies, and, rather, will explore instances where ideas about race, and colonial/colonizing technologies that sought to "control" it, developed out of a post-slavery America, whose formalizing of segregationist policy in the late nineteenth century provides something of a template, if also a cautionary tale, for other colonial nations.

There is an archive of South Africans persistently looking towards the United States and its history of slavery and subsequently Reconstruction and Jim Crow Segregation, from early South Africa traveler and author on race in the United States, Maurice S. Evans, all the way to the "architect of apartheid," Hendrik Verwoerd. The latter not only traveled and studied in the United States, but in his academic career, which preceded his political one, was revered as an expert in American sociology. I am interested here in reading examples of this circulation from a literary critical perspective and as a way to think about how the global afterlives of slavery come to figure prominently in the history of technologies of racial control, especially in the development of apartheid. Not only how slavery travels as a critical metaphor, as in the case of Plaatje whose comparison opened this chapter, but also for the ways in which segregationist discourse wrote an imaginary landscape, a common ground of sorts to chart a flow of racial technologies of control moving from the United States to South Africa. One of the ways of thinking about the "transnational afterlives of slavery" is to reposition the United States as a test case; a laboratory for the testing and development, and subsequent dissemination to the larger colonial world of racial/ist technologies designed and implemented around the enslavement of Black peoples.

Further to this idea, it is not only the policies around slavery, but also those of post-Emancipation Jim Crow segregation which served as templates to various theatres of racial rule across the imperial world, including in the post-1910 Union of South Africa. While there have been quite a few explorations of how slavery at the Cape, as well as resistances to it, continue to shape the South African literary imaginary,[8] there has been

less attention paid to how the experience of transatlantic slavery in the
United States might be seen to have traveled and impacted the racialist
infrastructure and imaginaries of a space such as (pre-)apartheid South
Africa. This repositioning goes a long way towards helping us see the ways
in which not only was the United States a practitioner of colonial rule
around the world, from the Pacific to the Caribbean, but this viewpoint
also stresses the precedential nature of technologies of racial control
designed in and exported from the United States. Consequently, this study
will work towards some critical ground clearing in which to think about a
genealogy of southern African literature which grapples with the legacies
and afterlives of the histories of U.S. slavery. A genealogy which we could
posit stretches back at least as far as the early years of the twentieth century
with a writer such as Sol Plaatje.

Of course, transatlantic slavery was not unique to the United States,
though the plantocracies of the ante-bellum southern United States do
have their historical specificities (of which much has been written and
exceed the bounds of this chapter). However, what seems to be the greatest
export of the United States was not the economic structures (plantation
economies) of slavery itself, but rather the political and ideological mechanisms of racial rule. In other words, perhaps the U.S.'s strongest and most
violent imperial legacy is one of historical precedent for the colonial world
outside its borders. In this way, we can see a particularly poignant example
of the ways in which, as Goyal explains, "The postcolony . . . appears as the
site for the manufacture and revival of obsolete racial paradigms."[9] Perhaps
too it reminds us of Mahmood Mamdani's comparison in which he argues
that "inserted in the history of colonialism, America appears less as
exceptional and more as a pioneer in the history and technology of settler
colonialism. All the defining institutions of settler colonialism were produced as so many technologies of native control in North America . . . The
American 'reservation' became the South African 'reserve.'"[10] I want to
argue that Mamdani's claim is both true but not quite that straightforward.
It seems that in trying to draw a direct line between the United States and
South Africa, between reservations and reserves, one must look first to the
post-slavery histories of segregation in the United States for how they serve
as template and caution to nations such as South Africa.

13.1 The Language and "Logics of Analogy"

In this chapter, I want to pose a question: What spaces of comparison are
opened up by seeing the development of apartheid in South Africa as an
extension of the racial technologies of slavery and segregation in the US? In

the critical literature on this topic, this seems to be a recurrent focal point of anxiety. I want to argue that it is precisely analogy that we need in order to understand better the global reverberations of racism such as those formalized under the names of apartheid and segregation. This is made imminently clearer in light of the global rise of ethno-nationalist right-wing movements, which arise in a web of influence and resonance; even more so in those instances where there has been explicit claiming of one set of cultural markers of white supremacy, etc. from one context to another.

When it comes to the post-slavery institution of Jim Crow segregation and "native segregation" or "separate development" in South Africa, George M. Frederickson writes that "Despite some superficial similarities ... the differences between [them] are too great, in terms of both underlying structures and patterns of historical development, to sustain elaborate comparison based on analogy."[11] Countering this refusal of an "elaborate" basis for analogy, I argue that despite missing many of the structural similarities, what sustains a common ground for thinking about the historical development of racial/ist technologies from the United States to South Africa (and elsewhere) are the concepts of precedent and influence. This is based upon the idea that the exercising of the racist controls of white supremacy in one place invigorates and emboldens those in another, and offers a specific example of what Mbembe means when he claims that "the principle of separation lay at the root of the colonial project."[12] White supremacy at the turn of the twentieth century was, and indeed until today still remains, a planetary project; a kind of collective or shared "fantasy of separation."[13] It is this influence, this less tangible conversation on race and racial/racist technologies between the United States and South Africa that I am focusing on in this chapter. In other words, these are entwined tales of racial violence and resistance. They bear upon one another. Both contexts are evidence of the ways in which "Colonialism ha[s] to a large extent consisted in a constant effort to separate," as well as to offer further example to the idea that when slavery was formally abolished in the United States it did not disappear, but rather transmitted across racist ecologies of colonial control.[14]

13.2 Transcolonial Ecologies: Segregation's Global Reach

Many critics argue that in South Africa much of the success of segregationist discourse in the first quarter of the twentieth century had to do with its malleability. Saul Dubow writes that "The very flexibility of segregationist discourse added to its attraction. It provided a ready vocabulary which spoke to different interests within the dominant classes ... [and] Thus segregation commanded the effective consent, if not always the active support, of a very wide range of political constituencies."[15] Dubow notes that for South African, "English-speaking intellectuals ... Howard Pim, Maurice Evans, Charles Templeman Loram, and Edgar Brookes were amongst the most important exponents of segregationist ideas in the first two decades of the twentieth century."[16] It is important to note here the proximity and intimacy that many of these segregationists had with race policies in the United States, having traveled and spent considerable time there.

For instance, C.T. Loram's extensive study, based on travel in the United States, is representative of how South African "liberals" adopted and invested segregationist ideology with an aura of the scientific. Chronicling various ideological-political approaches to the so-called Native Question in South Africa, Loram first describes the positions of "Repressionist" and "Equalist," and then moves on to "Segregationist." The latter platform, Loram tells his readers,

> would attack the problem in a scientific fashion. It would have exhaustive inquiries made into the social, political, and economic progress of the race in the past. It would seek the advice of anthropologists, ethnologists, and psychologists in its endeavor to obtain a thorough knowledge of the people. With this knowledge, and the facts culled from investigations into race problems, it would endeavor to give the Bantu race every assistance to develop on the lines of its racial genius.[17]

Both Loram and Maurice Evans also repeatedly applaud the U.S. examples of Hampton and Tuskegee as models for "Bantu education" in South Africa, and both do so as an articulation of a "middle way," or a balance between what Loram maps out as three schools of thought on the "native question," namely the "Repressionists," the "Equalists," and the "Segregationists."[18] Moreover, for Evans, more than being simply a liberal "middle ground," segregation had the potential to act as a synaptic network pulling together an ecosystem of more local approaches to policies to do with race. For Evans, and indeed for the South African Native Affairs Department itself, segregation was seen as a malleable and "natural synthesis of different regional approaches to native administration, each of which contained something of value."[19]

13.3   Slavery Past and Segregation to Come: Maurice S. Evans's Study of the Southern States and Warnings for South Africa

It is this same Maurice Evans who is unequivocal in his framing of the U.S. South and South Africa as the two globally prominent places where the machinations of segregation were being most keenly felt in the first quarter of the twentieth century. Evans's work *Black and White in the Southern States* is based on his extensive travel through and ethnographical study of the U.S. South, and methodologically echoes his earlier work *Black and White in South East Africa* (1913). Evans frames his opening chapter, "The Question of the Century" – by which he means the question of race (racial rule) – by expounding on what he sees as similar historical provenances of each place. He continues to spend much of his study waxing melancholic on the emotional landscape of similarity he finds he is able to access while in the United States. While Evans writes that he can feel the Atlantic receding and "Africa was before me," his true concern above and beyond this nostalgia (itself perhaps symptomatic of a recognition of structural similarities), is the future of how race relations will be managed in both the United States and South Africa.[20] To other areas of the colonial world he is far less concerned, dismissing the relations between "East and West" as a matter of "international relations" or, in other words, the negotiations of nation-states roughly in parity with one another, and to which he predicts a "mutually satisfactory" outcome. To the tropical colonial holdings of Europe, where the "white man cannot make a home," but is determined to rule at this moment of high empire (1915), Evans predicts that "The genius of the European peoples will probably enable them to govern their tropical dependencies with justice and consideration, and adjust their methods to suit the development and changing needs of the governed."[21] The condescension of the passage, not to mention its blatantly white-supremacist ethic, fortunately can be seen in retrospect to have offered a fundamentally flawed prognosis; within thirty-five years this predication would already be shown to be utterly and spectacularly crumbling under the weight of global decolonization movements.

However, I am more interested here in Evans's diagnosis of this moment in which he deemed these two specific spaces, the southern states of the United States and South Africa, to carry with them a common key to understanding and approaching racial rule across the colonial world. More than other areas of the colonial world, to which Evans give us only passing remarks, it is the American South and South Africa, which for him provide the precedential experience for answering what he deems to be "the question of the century."[22] Evans writes that "Where white and black have each their permanent homes and live intermixed, as in South Africa and the United States, the problem is much more complex and difficult. The events of the nineteenth century have accentuated and increased these difficulties. It is the problem of the twentieth century to discover a basis of adjustment."[23] There are two important things to point out about this passage for our purposes here. The first is that by "events of the nineteenth century" Evans most surely means slavery, its end, and the period of Reconstruction – to which he repeatedly returns. This historical trajectory of slavery and, more importantly, the political and legislative aftermath of it, from Reconstruction to Jim Crow Segregation, Evans believes has made the United States a harbinger (if not also often a warning) for the larger colonial world about how technologies of racial control are to be handled according to a strictly segregationist model which he prescribes for South Africa. And here lies the second important feature of this passage: the description of a set of circumstances diagnosed as both similar and reso-nant with one another, as providing an example, or a model for the colonial world globally, and perhaps even more specifically as a template for settler-colonialist world-building and social structuring. If apartheid is to be read as an afterlife of slavery, then it must be for how the former incorporated the spirit of segregationist social engineering which followed on from slavery in the United States, and did so as an applied technology of racial control for South Africa. For Evans there is a direct line leading from the history of slavery in the United States, through Reconstruction and Jim Crow, to the development of a segregationist ideological and political platform in South Africa, which in turn would develop into the apartheid regime of the second half of the twentieth century.

A preoccupation for Evans is the white political landscape of the South at the turn of the twentieth century, which he sees as haunted by the specter of the Black vote. However, by the time Evans writes (in 1915), there was very little actual political power held by a Black constituency, but the "threat" of it continued to shape and direct Southern (white) politics. It seems that Evans stresses this threat for its possible commensurability to the South African context, especially at this moment of close historical proximity to the political struggles around enfranchisement emanating from the Union of 1910 in South Africa. Evans writes that "And yet the Negro, voteless and voiceless in political affairs, is the one force that makes Southern politics what they are ... It is the Negro who has made politics in the South what they are; speechless and voteless he yet prevails."[24] This unfair and libelous accusation towards Black peoples and would-be voters of the South is still important for how Evans's diagnosis – of a South that is politically stagnant for its inordinate fear of Black enfranchisement, a fault to be placed squarely within in the psychology of white anxiety – this diagnosis can be read in some ways as Evans's prognosis for a white South Africa that would become reified politically by overly focusing on the singular question of Black enfranchisement. Published in 1915 Evans's study of the United States comes only five years on from the consolidation of white political rule as it was enshrined in the Unification of South Africa in 1910. The unification also provided a legislative safety-valve to regulate the liberal racial politics of the Cape Colony, which at that time still made provision for the Black vote. While Evans feigns support for "keen interest and discussion" rather than "torpid indifference" in the realm of politics, it is clear that what he reads in the American political landscape as the danger of a history of a single-issue political imagination bears weight for the future of the nascent white South African political body.

For Evans, his many months traveling through and studying the southern states is structured in this diagnosis–prognosis way, alternating between assessment of the racial, political, and social landscapes of the southern United States and employing these metrics in the articulation of a theory of sorts, a speculative projection for South Africa. As we see again and again in his study, the theory which Evans wishes to be further enshrined in policy and practice in South Africa is one of segregation, even when he advocates for a greater easing of – notably only social and economic – segregation for the southern United States. After a long chapter on what Evans refers to as "The Great Opportunity," in which he offers an overly optimistic assessment of the economic possibilities open to would-be Black farmers across the South, Evans rails against "a movement [that] has been started among the whites to prevent him [potential Black land owner] acquiring in areas that are at present mainly in the hands of the whites."[25] Evans notes that in the United States a greater amount of legislation would be required at this moment (1915) to "legally secure segregation or separation in the rural areas" and "in South Africa this doctrine of the separation of the races is held by a majority of the Europeans to be the true policy."[26]

Noting the recent passing of the 1913 Natives Land Act in South Africa, which Evans sees as "engaged in provisionally demarcating the areas which it is intended shall eventually be white and black respectively," he states unequivocally that "With this policy *in South Africa* I am in accord."[27] However, for the United States, Evans writes that "I am not . . . in favour of such a legal territorial separation in the South land."[28] The reasons Evans lists for this difference of direction are many and, in his words, include – somewhat generically – differences in "land and people, history and custom."[29] Evans's main concerns seem to be firstly with securing an "economically independent" Black population in the South as "the great opportunity" of which he speaks. Without it, he predicts, the Black individual in the South "will remain a helot, not bound by the material shackles that bound his limbs in slavery times, but as much a slave as though those fetters remained."[30] Note the structural resonance here to Plaatje's earlier-cited metaphorical metric of slavery in South Africa. Moreover, this is also where the more sinister reasonings behind Evans's diagnoses and prognoses are made more explicit. For the United States, an increasing of segregationist policy would, for Evans, reverse a course he saw as already set in motion through slavery. For Evans the presumed "civilizing" and, perhaps more importantly, the assimilatory effect of slavery on the social, cultural, and demographical landscapes of the United States – and especially in the South – meant that increased segregation would be tantamount to "an arrested development." However, this is where Evans turns from sociological diagnosis to segregationist prescription.

For Evans the issue and the reason for variations in policy has to do with how he grounds his recommendations in a racist metrics of measurement and proximity to ideas of modernity. Evans implores his readers to "remember that the Negro in America has been in intimate contact with the white race for nearly three hundred years, speaks the language of the country, and in customs, religion, and aims has, perforce, adopted those of the white man."[31] To attempt to legislate away the amount of assimilation that Evans sees as already pervasive would, he believes, be reckless and dangerous. However, for South Africa, he argues that this is largely not the case, and as such, presents the newly formed Union with a possibility, a chance to heed what he says is the "warning" being offered by "the experience of the South." Evans gives voice to this experience, rhetorically embodying a Southern (white) man who would offer council to a (white) South Africa:

> Too late it may be for the South, but I feel that if some of her best men, who are at present filled with doubts as to the future, and with their tragic experience ever before them, could counsel us, *they would say* that on such lines [segregation], and not in the way that was forced upon them by the conquering North [assimilation] lies our hope for the future in South Africa.[32]

The South, and here because of a cultural and economically colonizing North, did not do enough to shore up the racial mixture of its Black and white populations. And so, integration seems to be the only, if "tragic" for Evans and these "best men of the South," course of action left available. Evans is categorical about the negative example set out by the United States (and thus the lesson to be learned by South Africa) when he writes that "The great sin of the white man against the black lay not in slavery, nor in economic exploitation, but in the debauchment of the race by illicit sexual intercourse."[33] Evans feels that he has provided something of a "chart or compass" to South African politicians who he otherwise characterizes as "voyagers ... on an unknown sea." But as with other technologies of racial control and colonial infrastructure, America is looked to here for precedent, as a harbinger, and producer and exporter of colonialist, world-organizing systems.

For Evans and others, J.E. Holloway notably, the blame for racial assimilation was placed not solely on the liberal approach of the North, but importantly on slavery. Slavery was seen as the engine of racial mixture to such an extent, Evans argues, that to try and undo this process through greater segregation in the United States would result in widescale revolt. The example set by the United States, and laid out here by Evans, is part of why he becomes – even after his death – one of the prominent voices in the further construction of segregationist discourse in South Africa. The final line of Evans's book makes clear that segregationism in South Africa must learn from the preceding experiments performed in its name. He writes of South Africa that: "The present is full of menace. The United States fifty years ago tried the experiment of giving to Africans the full franchise, and the result has been disastrous. The same course is impossible in South Africa. But it's the first duty of South Africa to find a better way."[34] Segregation for South Africa according to Evans was then to be a refinement of sorts to the examples set with slavery in the United States: all the supposed civilizing gains of modernity without the unwanted side effects of assimilation.

13.4 Verwoerd's American Affinities: Social and Racial Engineering

While Hendrick F. Verwoerd is well known for his political career as "the architect of apartheid," what is less known is his early life as an academic and as a Professor of Psychology and Sociology. It is perhaps here, in his earlier life, that we can see a clear triangulation of spaces from which some of his ideas on race and separate development grew into the more formalized policies of nationalism and segregation under the banner of apartheid. It has been argued that Verwoerd's decision to turn down a fellowship to Oxford for postgraduate study in favor of studying in Germany is a possible source for Verwoerd's later articulations of white supremacy and anti-Semitism. Nor is Verwoerd alone here, being part of a long line of young South African intellectuals and would-be politicians who flocked to the intellectual centers of Germany for most of the first half of the twentieth century. Most notably before him are both Werner Eiselen, the anthropologist and linguist known as the "intellectual architect of apartheid," as well as N.J. Van Warmelo, Government Ethnologist for the Native Affairs Department from 1930 to 1969 and responsible for the intellectual foundations of the apartheid Homelands policy.[35] If many of the National Party politicians and ideologues denied political affiliation with Germany, especially after the rise of the Third Reich, the intellectual link between Germany and South Africa – and mostly in areas of anthropology and linguistics – is undeniable, and Verwoerd's study in Berlin and Hamburg certainly mark him as part of this tradition.[36]

However, as Roberta Miller argues, while Verwoerd's time in Germany may have been infused with the popular spirit of neo-Fichtean nationalism and a reverence for the *volk*, it was Verwoerd's short trip to and intellectual intimacy with the United States that proved the more foundational to his later thinking. Initially trained in psychology, Verwoerd's tour of American psychology departments was "far more important to his intellectual development than was his much longer stay in Germany."[37] In 1932, when Verwoerd was tasked with heading the newly created Department of Sociology and Social Work at Stellenbosch University, the American influence of "social engineering" in Verwoerd's approach waned somewhat in exchange for a more individualized reading of how to deal with questions of (mostly white) poverty. However, the social engineering influence would return later with the advent Verwoerd's political career. Before this, however, "Verwoerd became recognized not only as an expert in American social science but also as a proponent of American social welfare systems, and his department at Stellenbosch was known as the place where one could learn about American social welfare."[38] Whatever the reason, there is indeed a marked shift in Verwoerd's outlook and ideology from his earlier academic career, where he is in line with more liberal notions of racial equality (if still adamant about various metrics of difference) and an outspoken supporter of Anglo–Afrikaner collaboration, to the later moments where he becomes the political proponent of a virulent ethnic nationalism and architect of a national engineering scheme based on racial difference and separation.

Verwoerd gave a speech to open the Transkei Territorial Authority in 1957, a first and major step in the building of the apartheid Homelands infrastructure. Titled "Separate Development: The Positive Side," Verwoerd's speech takes the time to define separate development, saying that, "Separateness means: Something for oneself . . . the other word refers to what is bigger still, viz. 'development,' which means growth."[39]

Verwoerd continues by elaborating on an ecological metaphor whereby separate development looks like an agricultural program designed by the state to promote well-being along lines of ethnic and racial identity. Separate Development – or apartheid – Verwoerd claims is "a tree, a fruit tree which this government gave the Bantu of South Africa. It planted the tree, but the tree must be tended in order to grow."[40] Not only is the role of the nation as racial policy infrastructure builder clear in Verwoerd's metaphor of separate development, but his attention to ideas of oneness and ownership strongly suggest that by this point he has come around to a belief in the importance of the idea of the *volk*, whether out of ideology or pragmatism. At the helm of the apartheid national project, Verwoerd is also clear about the transatlantic origins of much of what is collated under the political ideology of apartheid, even if the rougher edges of institutionalized, state-sponsored racism are attempted to be smoothed over with a slogan like "separate development." As T. Dunbar Moodie notes, it

> irritated Verwoerd that American criticism of apartheid ignored the fact that much early apartheid legislation, defining racial groups and enforcing racial separation, was lifted straight from the law books of Alabama, Georgia and Mississippi – sometimes word for word. Not that Verwoerd suggested changing those laws. His point was that institutionalized racism was not unique to South Africa. What made South Africa different was that high apartheid claimed to be "separate development."[41]

Returning to the Transkei Authority speech as a culminating moment in Verwoerd's career, we can begin to see how apartheid discourse was developing through the entanglement of rhetorical strains of American social welfare, linguistic and anthropological theories of ethnic and racial difference, all harnessed into the articulation of national-scaled projects of policy infrastructure. It is also worth noting what has been said about the history of labor management in the United States as an influence here. Writing about the contexts of post-slavery in which labor management, especially its articulations as scientific management in the Taylorist school, Esch and Roediger argue the important connection that "Managers . . . were never outside of the US racial system and, in many ways, created that system. Further, the degree to which factory-management understood itself as possessing racial knowledge links it to, rather than distinguishes it from, the management of work under slavery."[42] The connection to a still rapidly industrializing South Africa becomes even clearer in Esch and Roediger's analysis of the United States when they write that, "As members of both a white-settler and a slaveholding society, Americans developed a sense of themselves as 'white' by casting their race as uniquely fit to manage land and labour, and by judging how other races might come and go in the service of that project."[43] If the national-level control of labor in tandem with a national project to define and segregate races captures some of the animating forces of apartheid, these aspects have both precedent and resonance across the Atlantic in the United States.

13.5   Conclusion

If the analysis of the origins of apartheid is expanded beyond the economical and the structural then it is fairly clear how apartheid did not develop solely as an endogenous system of racial control. Rather, as an ideological platform, apartheid was informed and formed by discourses circulating through a transcolonial ecosystem of racial policies and technologies of racial control, and these in turn made up the metrics and machinations of what Mbembe calls the "fantasy of separation" employed in the development of apartheid. The histories of slavery and segregation in the United States were a prominent coda around which segregationist discourse in South Africa revolved, from at least the turn of the twentieth century, and served as both example and caution in the development of a national plan of racial segregation, labor controls, and uneven land distribution. Often underacknowledged, the United States was a pioneer in the racial technologies of settler colonialism informing the development of apartheid in South Africa. These influences of policy and precedent traveled along the vectors of a global and synaptic network of white supremacy, and reified and ossified differently in different spaces, but can be seen as part of a virulent planetary network of colonial machinations. As a transnational afterlife to the histories of slavery in the United States, apartheid can be seen to grapple with the legacies of racial control such as segregation, employing the racialized landscapes of the post-slavery American South as metrics and templates for the articulation of segregationist platform that would lead to formal apartheid by the mid-twentieth century. Slavery did not create apartheid, but the transcolonial circulation of technologies of racial control did mutually inform and structure the national and cultural landscapes of spaces such as the American South and South Africa. As such we should remain attentive to how these transatlantic and transcolonial negotiations with the legacies of slavery informed and continue to inform the literary and cultural imaginaries of a place like South Africa. Post-apartheid culture in South African can in this way be said to participate in a global reckoning of what post-slavery has meant in the United States.

Notes

1 Achille Mbembe, *Necropolitics* (Durham and London: Duke University Press, 2019), 46.
2 Sol. T. Plaatje, *Native Life in South Africa, before & since the European War & the Boer Rebellion* (New York: Negro Universities Press, 1969; London: P.S. King & Son., 1969), 17.
3 Plaatje, *Native Life in South Africa*, p. 34.
4 Yogita Goyal, *Runaway Genres: The Global Afterlives of Slavery* (New York: New York University Press, 2019), 30.
5 There is not necessary space in this study to go into some of the epistemological questions around how "slavery is now the site for the reinvention of form," and Goyal and others, such as Achille Mbembe, Laura Murphy, Ato Quayson, and Simon Gikandi, have already traced many productive variants of this relationship. While I will be concerned with the transdisciplinary nature of what it means to think about the networks of travel and influence that racial/racist ideologies travel through, for brevity I will be less focused on the question of form.
6 Goyal, *Runaway Genres*, p. 30.
7 Leigh Anne Duck, "Apartheid, Jim Crow, and Comparative Literature," *Safundi: The Journal of South African and American Studies* 8, no. 1 (2007): 38.
8 For instance, see: Pumla Dineo Gqola, *What Is Slavery to Me: Postcolonial/Slave Memory in Post-apartheid South Africa* (Johannesburg: Wits University Press, 2010); Gabeeba Baderoon, *Regarding Muslims: From Slavery to Post-apartheid* (Johannesburg: Wits University Press, 2014); Serah Kasembeli, "*The Ghosts of Memory: Literary Representations of Slavery in Post-Apartheid South Africa*," unpublished PhD dissertation (Stellenbosch University, 2018).
9 Goyal, *Runway Genres*, p. 30.
10 Mahmood Mamdani, "Settler Colonialism: Then and Now," *Critical Inquiry* 41, no. 3 (2015): 13.
11 George M. Fredrickson, *White Supremacy: A Comparative Study in American and South African History* (New York: Oxford University Press (1981), 250.
12 Achille Mbembe, *Necropolitics*, p. 46.
13 Achille Mbembe, *Necropolitics*.
14 Achille Mbembe, *Necropolitics*.
15 Saul Dubow, *Racial Segregation and the Origins of Apartheid in South Africa, 1919–1936* (Oxford: Macmillan, 1989), 9.
16 Dubow, *Racial Segregation*, 6.
17 Charles T. Loram, *The Education of the South African Native* (New York: Longmans, Green, and Co., 1917), 23.
18 See Dubow, *Racial Segregation*, p. 28. See also J.E. Holloway, "The American Negro and the South African Abantu – A Study in Assimilation," *The South African Journal of Economics* 1, no. 4 (1933): 421–432.
19 Dubow, *Racial Segregation*, p. 26.

20 Maurice Evans, *Black and White in the Southern States: A Study of the Race Problem in the United States from a South African Point of View* (London: Longmans, Green & Co., 1915), 4.

21 Evans, *Black and White*, pp. 2–5.

22 It has to be pointed out that there is an obvious, if unacknowledged by Evans, direct reference to W.E.B. Du Bois's own characterization: "The problem of the twentieth century is the problem of the color line." Of course for Du Bois and for Evans the "question" or the "problem" were not the same, nor where their remedies. For Du Bois it was greater racial equality, and for Evans the question was to how greater segregation and separation between races could be achieved.

23 Evans, *Black and White*, p. 5.

24 Evans, *Black and White*, pp. 152–153.

25 Evans, *Black and White*, pp. 257–258.

26 Evans, *Black and White*.

27 Evans, *Black and White*, p. 258; emphasis added.

28 Evans, *Black and White*.

29 Evans, *Black and White*.

30 Evans, *Black and White*, p. 259.

31 Evans, *Black and White*, p. 268.

32 Evans, *Black and White*, p. 270.

33 Evans, *Black and White*, p. 281.

34 Evans, *Black and White*, p. 283.

35 See Andrew Blank, "Fathering Volkekunde: Race and Culture in the Ethnological Writings of Werner Eiselen, Stellenbosch University, 1926–1936," *Anthropology Southern Africa* 8, no. 3/4 (2015).

36 See, for instance, John Sharp "The Roots and Development of Volkekunde in South Africa," *Journal of South Africa Studies* 8, no. 1 (1981); Robert Gordon, "Apartheid's Anthropologists: The Genealogy of Afrikaner Anthropology," *American Ethnologist* 15, no. 3 (1988); T. Dunbar Moodie, *The Rise of Afrikanerdom Power, Apartheid and the Afrikaner Civil Religion* (Berkeley: University of California Press, 1975); Sara Pugach, *Africa in Translation: A History of Colonial Linguistics in Germany and Beyond, 1814–1945* (Ann Arbor: The University of Michigan Press, 2012).

37 Roberta B. Miller, "Science and Society in the Early Career of H.F. Verwoerd," *Journal of Southern African Studies* 19, no. 4 (1993): 640.

38 Miller, "Science and Society in the Early Career of H.F. Verwoerd," p. 646.

39 Hendrik F. Verwoerd, *Separate Development: The Positive Side* (Pretoria: Information Service, Department of Native Affairs, 1958), 4.

40 Verwoerd, *Separate Development*.

41 T. Dunbar Moodie, "Separate Development as a Failed Project of Social Engineering: The Flawed Logic of Hendrik Verwoerd," *South African Historical Journal* 69, no. 2 (2017): 153.

42 Elizabeth Esch and David Roediger, "One Symptom of Originality: Race and the Management of Labour in the History of the United States," *Historical Materialism* 17 (2009): 4.

43 Esch and Roediger, "One Symptom of Originality," p. 8.

CHAPTER 14

African Boat Narratives, Disposable Bodies, and the New Native Survivor

Subha Xavier

African boat migration, from the slave ships of the sixteenth century onwards to the "left-to-die boat" of 2011 and those that follow, is a harrowing story of human survival that is rarely individuated to recount the experience of a single person. Instead, their imagery alone, whether in old drawings or the photographs that populate our newsfeeds today, show migrants amassed atop a flailing vessel at sea, bodies so close to one another that they resemble the mythical sea creatures that overturned ships, barring human entrance into secret underworlds. The most recent rendition of these images, mainly taken by drone photography, once more betray the perspectival vision of destination countries intimidated by overcrowded boats full of bodies threatening, or so the story goes, to overtake their borders. Even the dead among them do not deter the accompanying narrative from its foreboding account of human invasion by those escaping war and poverty on one continent to jeopardize peace and security on the other. A humanitarian counter-narrative of migration reminds us of the story of poverty and loss where boats full of migrants become a tragic embodiment of human despair and the will to survive. African boat narratives, however, tell still another story. One that is deeply emmeshed in histories of slavery and forced sea crossings, but recast within the economic disparities brought about by the global exploitation of resources and climate change. In the pages that follow, we will reconsider chattel slavery's legacy in contemporary stories of migration, highlighting the inadequacies of reading these works through memories of the Middle Passage alone, while analyzing the insidious new forms of enslavement that African boat narratives expose. When read through the prescient work of Frantz Fanon, these stories present us with nothing less than revolutionaries of the crossing; those whose resounding "yes to life," in the words of Fanon,[1] is a deafening rejection of European anti-blackness, challenging border logic and the political machinations of inhospitality for a world in crisis. Migration, especially in today's climate crisis, is above all else a human impulse that challenges the logic of inequality that slavery and colonialism have cast upon Black lives, offering up movement as the dynamic imperative of life today.

2015 was a watershed year in the global consciousness of migration across the Mediterranean Sea as European countries sounded the proverbial alarm and tightened their immigration policies, closing their borders to the boats full of migrants seeking asylum on their shores. Images of overcrowded boats dominated the news cycles since the two tragic shipwrecks of 2013 off the coast of the island of Lampedusa in Italy and the subsequent launching of the Missing Migrants Project by the International Organization for Migration.[2] The accompanying narrative alluded only to realities of war and poverty, neglecting to signal climate change's catalytic role in the political conflict and economic crises that drive scores of African migrants Northward each year, risking a perilous journey across the Mediterranean. Though 2015 saw a spike in European political awareness around migration, boat crossings from Mauritania, Morocco, Algeria, and Libya did not peak during that time, with the turn of the century perhaps still marking the most significant number of crossings by African migrants. Water migration from the African continent towards Europe and even the Americas is comparatively far less frequent than internal land migration within the African continent itself. African migration has long been mostly internal to the continent, with immigration to Europe accounting for only 32 percent of all migration.[3] The risky business of clandestine travel by sea is even less frequent, often a last resort since most migrants elect to enter Europe by air. Those who take to the seas, with its many perils that await, do so knowingly, calculatedly, in a collective act of decision-making that draws on the resources of many. When one recasts the act of boat migration as a collective action that is shouldered by the financial and emotional investment of a community, rather than the risk-laden resolve of a young person alone, the political valence of the outcome changes. It is difficult to dismiss individual migrant deaths – by drowning, dehydration, and starvation – as the inevitable cost of foolish choices, or assign death-defying agency to the young migrants themselves, when they most often take on boat migration in the name of their families and entire communities. This sociocultural reality requires a reframing of migration through a different set of political and ethical prerogatives, something that boat narratives from Africa in particular, when considered transversally across the globe and historically across time, bring to light in telling ways.

In 2008, Senegalese writer Abasse Ndione published *Mbëkë mi. À l'assaut des vagues de l'Atlantique*, his third novel and one that joins the ranks of other boat narratives detailing the Vietnamese and Haitian exodus, the mass migrations over the Mediterranean from Morocco, Algeria, Tunisia, and Libya through the last several decades and one other Senegalese boat narrative by Omar Ba.[4] To consider African migrant boat narratives in relation to neighboring ones from the global South is both to give these refugee stories their rightful place within a global history of migration and to engage the racial institutional biases that reassign asylum, denying it to many who are most in need. In today's political landscape, these narratives perform the crucial tasks of recasting boat migration through tropes such as the boat immemorial and the *bildungsroman* or journey of the human spirit. They also expose its intimate ties to global economics, labor, and markets in the age of scarcity and climate change, where certain bodies become disposable, condemned as the wretched of the sea. Borrowing and redeploying Fanon's famous words for the cause of boat migrants is to read them as Frantz Fanon's new native underclass, in order to unveil their revolutionary potential.

14.1   The Boat Immemorial

The history of the boat as a trope of great political reach has been theorized poetically and powerfully by thinkers such as Edouard Glissant, Paul Gilroy, and Marcus Rediker who retrace its roots to the Middle Passage and reinterpret global modernities through its lasting legacy.[5] Michelle Wright, on the other hand, argues that histories of the Middle Passage tend to include only a fraction of the viewpoints and struggles faced by Black identities across the world. Wright warns against our overuse and misuse of a Middle Passage epistemology that promotes a static understanding of today's diasporic complexities.[6] To Wright's cautioning against the linear progress narrative in which Middle Passage epistemology takes its place, let us add the narratives of Western modernity that are constructed around the agency of the very same few and the passive receptivity of a great many others. That is to say, that no matter what story is spun around the spatiotemporality of modernity from a Western standpoint, its key players remain the same – they are European and white – while everyone else is subjected to the whim and fancy of the select few. The legacy of the boat as eternally linked to the slave trade continues such a violent distortion of histories. I am not disputing the critical importance of the Middle Passage in the narrative redeployment of the boat today, but looking rather to draw its literary and political potency from histories – both real and mythical – that came before, during, and after the

transatlantic slave trade. What if the boat, beyond "chronotope" as Gilroy
puts it, or "relational experience of the abyss" in the words of Glissant, or
"formative institution of slavery and modern capitalism" according to
Rediker, is a harbinger of the immemorial? By immemorial, I mean the
histories both remembered and unremembered, those that our history
books contain and those that they do not. Most importantly, the immemorial extends beyond the reach of memory, records, and traditions,
summoning a trace of other lives, worlds, ecosystems that are deeply
emmeshed with our own.

In Ndione's *Mbëkë mi. À l'assaut des vagues de l'Atlantique*, the boat, or
in this case the fishing pirogue used as a makeshift crossing vessel,
undergoes an imaginative transformation through a narrative that grows
it into mythical proportions. Kaaba – one of the novel's two protagonists –
convinces his fellow co-pilot Baye Laye that their pirogue is indeed strong
enough to withstand a sea voyage because it is made of neem bark from
Casamance.[7] Neem is a tree that originates in India and was brought over
to Senegal at the time of independence to make up for deforestation that
resulted in increased droughts.[8] Neem trees grow with very little water and
are not confined to certain types of soil. They are robust, drought resistant,
and grow quickly into considerable biomass that is able to provide protection from the wind and regenerate leached soils into fertile land. Indeed,
they are nature's "supertree," with a variety of medicinal properties derived
from the bark, leaves, and seeds, neem trees have spread across the planet
today.[9] The hollowed-out bark of the neem tree is then the quintessential
vehicle for the migrant, its metonymic purchase offering migration as the
needed remedy for shortages of all kinds. In fact, Kaaba contrasts their neem
wood pirogue to that of others made of assembled planks, "Elle est beaucoup
plus résistante"[10] [it is far more resistant] he assures. When he is pressed
again about the lack of life vests on the boat, he confirms, "Elle est très
solide, très résistante, son fonds est formé par le tronc d'un neem constituant
un seul bloc, elle ne se brise pas, ne se renverse pas"[11] [it is very solid, very
resistant, its bottom is formed out of the trunk of a neem tree constituting
just one piece, it does not break, it does not turn over]. Indeed, his words
will ring true later in the novel, when their pirogue will remain intact even as
they mourn the dead and contemplate the wreckage of other boats. Kaaba
will not survive the crossing, but their neem-wood boat does, safeguarding
the remnants of human life until most of its cargo is returned to safety.

This mythical aggrandizement of the boat occurs in the migrant narrative of Haitian Canadian writer Émile Ollivier too, whose 1991 novel
Passages recounts the perilous voyage of Haitian immigrants across the

Caribbean Sea. The novel's hero Amédée and his crew construct a sailboat that "sera à toute épreuve"[12] [won't fail][13] with three masts and a hull made of cedarwood from Lebanon. Lebanese cedar is another prized wood for its fine grain and long history of use in the Middle East. Ollivier's character Derville Dieuseul will go "as far as Port-de-Paix where he was sure he would find cedar wood imported by a Syrian he knew."[14] Cedar figures in the biblical and Quranic traditions and marks the constructed vessel with its fabled durability. Ensuring the wood's Syrian origin is to recognize the migratory path Northward of Lebanese cedar trees which have climbed to higher altitudes for their survival and growth in changing climate zones.[15] When the storm shatters the boat, throwing its human cargo overboard, the surviving twenty-two of Ollivier's original sixty-seven passengers drift on the wreckage of the boat's cedar hull.

The Spanish word *patera* as deployed in Europe "has come to mean 'little boats,' named 'boats of death,' 'boats of shame,' 'pateras of despair,' and 'floating tombs,'" Hakim Abderrazak tells us in his work on clandestine migration from North Africa,[16] but migrant boat narratives invite an alternative reading of their sea vehicles tapping into a history of human survival and migration. The material construction of the boats signals a connection to a larger ecosystem, where diasporic trajectories link people through inventiveness – but also sturdiness, resilience, unbreakableness, survival – and the migrant imaginary. Boats attain mythical dimensions because they are built to the size of the human life they carry, their metonymic function far outweighing their actual capacity. More than markers of the "possible" or the "unknown," they carry futurity in the immemorial. They are boats that carry life and death through treacherous seas and to other coasts. Vessels of migration that whilst evoking mythical boats across planetary time and space, reach into the abyss of history, summoning slave ships, but also the cedarwood arks of the Quran, Torah, and Bible. The specter of Homer's Odysseus building his raft hovers over these migrant narratives, just as the faint trace of shipbuilding Phoenicians sailing the Mediterranean for their livelihood lingers within. To read boat narratives through these multiple histories, real and imagined, corrects the overuse of the Middle Passage as the dominant interpretive lens of African boat stories, but also hones in on its devastating reversal of the emancipation narrative. Overdetermined memories of slave ships dawdle back through time and into the work of Ndione, as it does in Ollivier, but they do not constitute the work's overarching framework. African boat migration today is not just a contemporary form of forced migration, it is also, as we shall see, an elected crossing into other worlds.

14.2   A Journey of the Human Spirit

The passengers of the pirogue named *Adja Astou Wade* in Abasse Ndione's
Mbëkë mi, just as those of the sailboat *La Caminante* in Ollivier's *Passages*
and the boat named *Agwéton* in Haitian writer Néhémy Pierre-Dahomey's
debut novel *Rapatriés*, published in 2017, all embark on their boat journeys as a pilgrimage of sorts. These are today's *bildungsromans*, young
would-be heroes taking fearlessly to the sea to pursue a quest that is as
spiritual as it is economic. While the decision to leave is sparked by failing
local economies, the journey is taken on in a spirit of combativeness and
pursuit that moves away from the narrative legacy of Middle Passage
epistemology, into the realm of a divinely inspired mission. Kaaba and
Baye Laye's pirogue is named after a Senegalese woman. Wade is a
common last name in Senegal, but "Adja," from the Arabic "Hadj" is a
Wolof rendition of pilgrimage, while "Astou" from the Arabic "Aïssatou'"
is a variation on "God saves" or another form of Aïcha who was "Mother of
the believers." Likewise, Ollivier's *La Caminante* from the Spanish verb for
walking refers to a walker or traveler, and Pierre-Dahomey's *Agwéton* refers
to Agwé, the loa and great vodoun admiral of the seas. Ndione's pilot
carries a talisman with him on his voyage, seeks the blessings of his Imam
before setting sail and follows the explicit instructions of his mother-in-
law's marabou to ensure his safe return home one day. His wife Kiné pours
water on the footprints he leaves as he departs their courtyard, accom-
panies this purification with a series of invocations and blessings, and he
breaks seven eggs before definitely departing the neighborhood. Before
each of the migrants enters into his pirogue, Baye Laye insists that they
perform a ritual of absolution, say the Bismillāh, and only then step in very
deliberately with their right foot.[17] Every difficulty encountered in travel is
interpreted as a test of faith, of strength and resilience. Ollivier's voyagers
even sing and dance an invocation to their old African Gods when the
storm clouds appear. In Pierre-Dahomey's *Rapatriés*, a little girl named
Fréda disappears into the sea during a stormy night. Her mother later
explains this loss as a sacrificial reunion of the loa of love after whom she
was named – Fréda Erzulie, also known as La Sirène, the mermaid – with
her loa husband Agwé after whom their boat is named. The boat narrative
folds in on itself to recount loss not as the journey's failure, but as its
horrific center of tribulation and despair wherein a spiritual quest finds its
true actualization. It is perhaps here that African boat narratives delve deep
into the legacy of the Middle Passage to at once connect with and reverse
its necropolitical impulse. Necropolitics, in Achille Mbembe's articulation

of the term, alludes to "the work of re-organizing the political order in such a way that make human life precarious, expendable, and unprotected by the liberal democratic order."[18] Abasse Ndione's work, like that of writers like Tahar Ben Jelloun in *Partir*, for example, both acknowledge this longstanding oppressive order and rethink its violence from the perspective of those who choose, against all odds, to fight against it with their lives. Those who perish in the crossing are then at once victim and hero, and perhaps most importantly of all, they are those who expose the necropolitical structures that make migration a penalty worthy of death.

The decision to leave is also realized in Ndione's novel not so much with designs to become rich abroad in some imaginary El dorado, but because as the title suggests, *mbëkë mi* is the only option. The Wolof expression captures the sense of hopelessness that sparks a sudden disposition to risk everything in the most costly crossing imaginable. And the inevitability of choice is expressed in much the same way globally, across this type of literature. Vietnamese Canadian Kim Thúy's debut novel *Ru*, published in 2009, recounts a sudden departure as experienced by a ten-year-old child. Thúy's narrator Nguyên An Tịnh recounts her mother's unwavering decision to leave Saigon in much the same way, like a strong conviction that can only be acted upon with the utmost urgency and resolve. Everywhere, it is described time and time again, in language akin to a leap of faith, especially when mothers step into unsound boats or ill-equipped ships with infants in their arms and children tugging at their sides. Pierre-Dahomey's Belliqueuse Louissaint is one such mother, who abandons everything to step into a boat with her baby boy and young son in tow. When she and her older child drift to safety on the boat's wreckage, despite the death of the infant, she is only strengthened in her resolve to leave by other means. The destination is very strangely absent from many of these narratives, as it is in *Mbëkë mi*. The professed goal is only that the migrants will earn enough money to send back home so that their families and villages can continue to subsist. When Ndione's passengers get their first glimpse of lights across the Mediterranean, they exalt, shouting in Wolof "Dinaa téeki! Dinaa téeki!"[19] translated in a footnote as "Je réussirai! Je réussirai!" [I will succeed! I will succeed!], but in the text only as the feeling of "connaître un meilleur avenir" [knowing/experiencing a better future]. While many migrant African novels decry the lack of opportunity in Europe, boat narratives are generally far less invested in that reality as anything more than a place where, as the French translations of "dinaa téeki" attest, life can be conjugated in its future tense. Migration, despite its many perils, is driven only by the possibility of extending a human life that sees no future for itself where it exists. In contrast, the legal definition of asylum grants protection only to those who can prove persecution at the hands of a government or institution. While the boat narrative pleads for an understanding of asylum as a simple human right to futurity or a future time.

Indeed, time on the boat is suspended in the boat narrative that is described as a series of endless days and nights. While every effort is deployed to account for each passing day at the beginning of the journey, time quickly blurs into a haze of sunrises and sunsets. The first week at sea in *Mbëkë mi* is described as a beautiful rhythm of contemplative reflection, communal meals, and conversation, until a disruptive storm empties the pirogue of its rations, fuel, and sends a man to his death. With the boat adrift and soon heading in the wrong direction, time all but stops. Despair and illness set in as Mor Ndiaye, the Imam's nephew, decries his loss of faith and later attempts to rape the boat's only female passenger. Sadio, another migrant, violently hallucinates that his village is on fire. In timeless drift, each passenger looks into the abyss of dehumanized existence in a boat filled with vomit, sweat, urine and feces. Some retreat into prayer and recitation while others settle into "un état de torpeur, de délire ou de mutisme"[20] [A state of numbness, delirium, or silence].

In a recent presentation, author Kim Thúy likened the trajectory of the refugee to that of a "superhuman," a simile that can be interpreted as the transformation of someone who is able to achieve extraordinary feats in ordinary time and space after having experienced horror in suspended time and space.[21] *Mbëkë mi*, just like *Ru* or *Rapatriés*, paints the portrait of the human spirit in exactly such terms. When they are finally rescued aboard a ship from the Red Cross, Ndione describes the haggard, famished, and emaciated survivors as beaming with the glow of relief in their eyes, "une lueur de soulagement brilliant dans les yeux,"[22] [a glimmer of relief shining in their eyes]. Even if they were deported back to Senegal, there is little doubt that many will attempt the crossing again. That is also the lasting image of this literature: the journey is cyclical and constitutes many repeated attempts to cross or at least to leave, as is possible. Failure is measured not by return, but by the crushing of the will to depart, the annihilation of "mbëkë mi" that might reset the course of time. African boat migrants defy the death wish that is cast upon them by Western liberal democracies in a determined effort to break through borders that deny them a future. In so doing, their narrative becomes one of emancipation that builds out of the chronotope of the slave ship and beyond

Middle Passage epistemology, into a will not only to survive, but to thrive in a time that can only come through migration.

14.3   Abject Bodies

Against the tropes of the boat immemorial and the crossing as journey of the human spirit, however, lie the floating bodies – "balloons" as Moroccan writer Mahi Binebine's 1999 novel *Cannibales* describes them – that wash up on Mediterranean shorelines.[23] Images of body bags or corpses bloated and unrecognizable prevail on Spanish television, as Binebine recounts. Novels about illicit boat crossings always replay stories of individuals amidst the mass of fleeing bodies, some of whom will never emerge from their watery grave. Kaaba's drowning in *Mbëkë mi* is barely mourned, no ritual will follow his untimely death when everyone else is struggling to hold on to what is left of life. Vietnamese boat narratives such as that of Kim Thúy particularly dwell on the lack of burial rites for those who perish on the seas, doomed to wander as "hungry ghosts" or "specters" with no family to usher them into the world of ancestral spirits.[24] This destiny alone is enough to reinvigorate the starving and weary body still alive on a makeshift raft awaiting rescue, or restore the resolve of a weakened passenger on a drifting boat. Vietnamese narratives will go as far as to suggest anthropophagy as the only possible alternative. Linde Lê's short story "Vinh L." from her collection of short stories *Les évangiles du crime* and Kim Thúy's third novel *Vi* uncover this gruesome reality.[25] Anthropophagy in the work of Linda Lê, and as the case of Senegalese writer Omar Ba attests, nonetheless, is also a critique of the boat narrative itself that feeds on human misery and death for its existence.[26] Omar Ba, Professor at Gaston Berger University in Saint-Louis, and author of the autobiographical boat narrative *Soif d'Europe: Témoignage d'un clandestin* published in 2008, has been since accused both in Senegal and France of imposture, his novel denounced as false testimony.[27] This type of anthropophagy is not far from what Mahi Binebine calls cannibalism; that is, the way European bosses feed on Black and brown bodies for cheap labor in neoliberal economies that survive on immigration. African migrant texts in French like those of Alain Mabanckou (*Bleu Blanc Rouge*, 1998; *Black Bazar*, 2009), Fatou Diome (*La Préférence nationale*, 2001; *Le Ventre de l'Atlantique*, 2003), or Gauz (*Debout-payé*, 2014) – to name only a few – specifically address the exploitative work conditions that African immigrants face in France. Because they are recruited from an underclass of

asylum seekers who are awaiting papers, these migrant workers have no
legal recourse to combat their unfair treatment and dehumanization at the
hands of stingy employers. Instead, they form a new slave-like class of
laborers (janitors, groundskeepers, babysitters, nannies, caregivers, security
guards). Meanwhile, there is a literary feeding frenzy for migrant texts that
recount the difficult experience of migration, which boat narratives like
that of Omar Ba expose in the most disturbing way.

Contemporary African migration's links to colonial systems of oppression are also undeniable. Frantz Fanon's *Wretched of the Earth*, in which he
explores the psychiatric effects of the dehumanization of colonized peoples
is thus helpful in understanding the boat migrant's political and ethical
predicament. Fanon's title to his famed work comes from Eugène Pottier's
1871 left-wing anthem "L'internationale," where the opening line beckons
"Debout les damnés de la terre" [Stand up wretched of the earth]. It is a
proletariat call to arms, an underclass he calls "foule esclave" [crowd of
slaves], "peuple" [people], "ouvriers" [laborers], "travailleurs" [workers],
held under the tutelage of "les rois de la mine et du rail" [the kings of
mining and railways], "ces cannibales" [these cannibals]. As Miguel
Mellino reminds us, Fanon's redeployment of Pottier's anthem is mediated
through Aimé Césaire and Jacques Roumain, to suggest a different proletariat from the one implied by Western Marxism's modernist subjectivities.[28] Indeed, the wretched or *damned*, to remain faithful to Fanon's
original language, are those who inhabit a zone of nonbeing, those whose
lives are relegated to a ground zero of human subjectivity out of which they
can emerge as revolutionaries unthought by Western modernism. The
literary images in Abasse Ndione's African boat narrative, when considered
in contrast to those of Omar Ba's scandalous *Soif d'Europe*, suggest that the
new "wretched" are those condemned to anthropophagy and abjection at
sea. Ndione's novel, unlike the film by Moussa Touré it inspired, grants us
not one dead body to contemplate as it makes its way into the watery
abyss. Kaaba simply disappears, falling overboard on a stormy night while
trying to secure down the boat's gasoline tanks. His loss is expressed in the
initial shock and consternation of his fellow travelers, and later in the
despair of his co-pilot. Kaaba, "disparu sans laisser de trace" [disappeared
without a trace] and "perdu à jamais" [29][lost forever] are all the narrator
will say about this death. Baye Laye confirms his friend's fate twice, "Kaaba
est mort!" [Kaaba is dead!], spliced with the Quoranic ritual verse "*Innalil
Laah, wa inna illeyhi raadjioune*" [We belong to Allah and to Allah we shall
return].[30] That night the young boy Talla thinks he sees Kaaba's body
afloat, only to discover that it is the wreckage from another pirogue whose

eighty-five passengers were certainly all lost to the ocean. Here again, Ndione's text gives us no macabre description of cadavers at sea, only the assurance that "aucun être humain n'aurait pu resister à la furie de l'océean" [no human being could have resisted the fury of the ocean].[31] Ndione's prose actively defies the familiar images of migrant deaths on the Mediterranean, refusing to conjure up for us a sight that is today all too common. This in opposition to Omar Ba's text, where the author-narrator professes he was the sole survivor of a boat carrying a human cargo of fifty migrants, ten thrown to sea in an effort to lighten the vessel and others choosing a watery grave over starvation and dehumanization. If the imagined suicide of over thirty young Black men did not tip off Ba's readers to the inventiveness of his supposed testimony, his unlikely accounts of detention in holding camps in Italy, Libya, Ceuta, and Melilla did. Narrativizing the abjection of Black bodies at sea is to give over his text to the anthropophagy of these mostly young Black male bodies, those that scholar Suvendrini Perera reminds us in her critique of EU and Australian migration policies, have become "disposable lives tossed in the tidal movements of global labor."[32] In many ways, Omar Ba's work thrives on this historical link to slavery that Perera translates for our times, while Abasse Ndione both engages that history of a disposable labor force, but also disengages its prevalence on today's migrant story. Though the slave ship might haunt contemporary African boat narratives, it must not become the single lens by which this new literature is read and understood.

14.4 Fanon's New Native

Fanon's third category of native, what in a Marxist-driven system, he termed the lumpenproletariat underclass, is thus closest to what African boat migrants have become today. Abasse Ndione, just like Senegalese film director Moussa Sene Absa's 2010 documentary *Yoole, The Sacrifice*, point to the desperation of African youth – not only in Senegal but in Guinea, Mali, Sierra Leone, and Ivory Coast – who experience an increasing distance with the political and business elite who are unable to come to the aid of unemployed young people from rural parts of their countries. Ndione's novel begins with the state-mandated end of the peanut farming industry in Senegal and the need for each village to rely on the patronage of ten of its children clandestinely sent abroad using the collective funds of the community. Kaaba and Baye Laye, also turn to "mbëkë mi" because their artisanal fishing trade is all but dried up due to overfishing in the region. An alarming trend that the Food and Agriculture Organization of the UN noted affects 90 percent of the country's fisheries, which are either "fully fished or facing collapse."[33] The crisis is further "exacerbated by European and Asian fleets prowling the seas off West Africa."[34] Artisanal fishing has been destroyed by European and Asian fishing trawlers that "often drag nets across the ocean floor and damage once-plentiful breeding grounds" to feed "growing appetites for seafood in Europe and Asia."[35] The European Union's fishing subsidies thus drive Senegalese fisherman on a migrant sea voyage across the Mediterranean almost every day.[36] What Ndione's novel does not explain is also the ways in which climate change has affected the agricultural yield of the country. Food insecurity is a growing concern in the region and this entire reality is obliquely exposed in the opening pages of *Mbëkë mi*. This new underclass of migrants is perhaps suited, as Fanon once theorized, to resort to violent resistance, but they are mostly the targets of Mauritanian and European coastguards who intercept them or more recently are leaving them to die through draconian turn-back policies. As recently as October 2020, the deadliest migrant shipwreck in recorded history resulted in the loss of another 140 lives.[37] In the face of so much loss, it is difficult to read contemporary African emigration and asylum seeking as anything but a tragic extension of an age-old story of Black oppression.

Perhaps we need to understand Fanon's thought here through that of Lewis Gordon, who warns us that theory is coded as white and experience as Black.[38] White intellectuals have been quick to dismiss Fanon's use of Black reason to justify the exercise of force. Though film director Moussa Sene Absa poeticizes young Black migrant bodies as a spiritual sacrifice in times of crisis, texts like *Mbëkë mi* present us with a new type of resistance by young migrants that is no less violent than that which Fanon imagined. Confronting the abyss of history, in small fishing boats, armed only with the global literary imaginary of human migration, theirs is a violent entry onto Mediterranean shorelines and a distortion of national border configurations with the power of nothing but the human body. Dead, decomposed, and floating in abjection, or starved, exhausted, and witness to human volition, they are soldiers in a new war, no longer against colonialism, but in the global competition for the planet's limited resources. Lewis Gordon's writing on Fanon reminds us of the ways in which Fanonian reasoning has been obscured in interpretative work that refuses to comprehend the native in anything beyond its national conceptualization. Yet Fanon's corpus, from *Black Skin White Masks* to a *Dying Colonialism* and *The Wretched of the Earth*, has sought to extract reason from its colonial and racist power structures, returning it to a universal usage that just might allow us to reconsider the work of African writers like Abasse Ndione, a retired Senegalese nurse who still lives in the Senegalese fishing village-turned-suburb of Rufisque, as the purveyor of new models for thinking the boat migrant. Migration defies and overturns a logic of inequality that remains the enduring post-slavery, postcolonial reading of Black lives at sea.

In *Black Skin White Masks*, Fanon wrote "L'homme est mouvement vers le monde et vers son semblable"[39] ["Man is motion toward the world and toward his like,"][40] words that have been analyzed in every possible way for what they mean to Black consciousness, but not what they mean for the study of migration. Because this sentence is followed just a few lines later by what Fanon will call the "ultimate stage," that is "ethical orientation," perhaps the ethical turn in our current political/economic conjecture lies in human movement. To rid ourselves of racist power structures is to return migration to its dynamic human imperative, to think not in terms of flight but in terms of the Wolof expression "mbëkë mi," pointing to that sudden, inevitable impulse to leave that can only be quietened in movement.

Notes

1 Frantz Fanon, *Black Skin White Masks*, trans. Charles Lam Markmann (New York: Grove, 1967).
2 See "Missing Migrants: Tracking Deaths Along Migratory Routes," *International Organization for Migration (IOM)'s Missing Migrants Project*.
3 Dhruv Ghandi, *Brookings*, June 7, 2018. www.brookings.edu/blog/africa-in-focus/2018/06/07/figures-of-the-week-internal-migration-in-africa/ (accessed May 27, 2022).
4 Novels in French about the crossing from Haiti include Frankétienne's 1968 novel, *Mûr à crever* (2004); *Marie-Thérèse Colimon's Chant des sirènes* (1979); Claude Dambreville's *Un goût de fiel* (1982); Anthony Phelp's 1983 poem 'Même le soleil est nu . . .' (1992); Jean-Claude Charles's first novel dedicated to the phenomenon, *De si jolies petites plages* (1982); Émile Ollivier's *Passages* (1991); Louis-Philippe Dalembert's *L'autre face de la mer* (1998); Marie-Célie Agnant's *Alexis d'Haïti* (1999) and *Alexis, fils de Raphaël* (2000); Maryse Condé's *Haïti chérie* (1991) and *Rêves amers* (2001); Néhémy Pierre-Dahomey's *Rapatriés* (2017). In English, see Felix Morisseau-Leroy's poem "Boat people." In *Haitiad & Oddities* (1991); Edwidge Danticat's novel, *Breath, Eyes, Memory* (1994), her collection of essays, *Create Dangerously: The Immigrant Artist at Work* (2010), and short stories, "Children of the Sea." In *Krik? Krak!* (1996) and "Without inspection" (2018) www.newyorker.com/magazine/2018/05/14/without-inspection (accessed May 27, 2022). Novels in French about boat migration from Vietnam include Kim Thúy's *Ru* (2009) and *Vi* (2016); Linda Lê's *Les Évangiles du crime* (1992). While

English language works include Mary Terrell Cargill and Jade Quang Huynh (eds.), *Voices of Vietnamese Boat People: Nineteen Narratives of Escape and Survival* (2000); Carine Hoang (ed.), *Boat People: Personal Stories from the Vietnamese Exodus 1975–1996* (2013); Nam Le's collection of short stories, *The Boat* (2008), which was also adapted into an interactive webcomic by Matt Huyhn, *The Boat* (2015) www.sbs.com.au/theboat (accessed May 27, 2022); Viet Thanh Nguyen's collection of short stories, *The Refugees* (2017). Novels in French from North Africa include Mahi Binebine's *Cannibales: Traversées dans l'enfer de Gibraltar* (1999); Youssouf Amine Elalamy's *Les Clandestins* (2000); and Tahar Ben Jelloun's *Partir* (2006). Omar Ba's *Soif d'Europe: Témoignage d'un clandestine* (2008) is the only other novel about boat migration written by a sub-Saharan novelist in French, although there are now several African films on the subject, including Mostefa Djadjam's *Frontières* (2001) and Moussa Touré's *La Pirogue* (2012) that was based on Abasse Ndione's novel.

5 See Edouard Glissant, "La Barque ouverte." In *Poétique de la relation* (1990); Paul Gilroy, *The Black Atlantic* (1993); Marcus Rediker, *The Slave Ship: A Human History* (2007); and Marcus Rediker, Emma Christopher, Casandra Pybus (eds.), *Many Middle Passages: Forced Migration and the Making of the Modern World* (2007).

6 See Michelle Wright, *Physics of Blackness: Beyond the Middle Passage Epistemology* (Minneapolis: University of Minnesota Press, 2015).

7 Abasse Ndione, *Mbëkë mi. À l'assaut des vagues de l'Atlantique* (Paris: Gallimard, 2008), 18.

8 See Opender Koul, "Neem: A Global Perspective." *Neem: Today and in the New Millennium* (Dordrecht: Springer, 2004), 1–19.

9 See H. Schmutterer (ed.), *The Neem Tree: Azadirachta Indica A. Juss. and Other Meliaceous Plants: Sources of Unique Natural Products for Integrated Pest Management, Medicine, Industry, and Other Purposes* (New York: VCH, 1995) and National Research Council. *Neem: A Tree for Solving Global Problems* (The Minerva Group, Inc., 2002).

10 Ndione, *Mbëkë mi. À l'assaut des vagues de l'Atlantique*, p. 19.

11 Ndione, *Mbëkë mi. À l'assaut des vagues de l'Atlantique*, p. 43.

12 Emile Ollivier, *Passages* (Paris: Serpent à plumes, 1991), 121.

13 Emile Ollivier, *Passages*, trans. Leonard W. Sugden (Victoria, BC: Ekstasis, 2003), 96.

14 Ollivier, *Passages* (2003), p. 71.

15 See Lara Hajar, Louis François, Carla Khater, Ihab Jomaa, Michel Déqué, and Rachid Cheddadi, "Cedrus libani (A. Rich) Distribution in Lebanon: Past, Present and Future," *Comptes Rendus Biologies* 333, no. 8 (2010): 622–630 and Anne Barnard, "Climate Change Is Killing the Cedars of Lebanon," *New York Times*, July 18, 2018. www.nytimes.com/interactive/2018/07/18/climate/leba non-climate-change-environment-cedars.html (accessed May 27, 2022).

16 Hakim Abderrezak, "Burning the Sea: Clandestine Migration Across the Strait of Gibraltar in Francophone Moroccan 'Illiterature,'" *Contemporary French and Francophone Studies* 13, no.4 (2009): 464.

17 Ndione, *Mbëkë mi. À l'assaut des vagues de l'Atlantique*, p. 49.
18 Achille Mbembe, *Necropolitics* (Durham: Duke University Press, 2019), p. 92.
19 Ndione, *Mbëkë mi. À l'assaut des vagues de l'Atlantique*, p. 63.
20 Ndione, *Mbëkë mi. À l'assaut des vagues de l'Atlantique*, p. 78.
21 "'Textual Drifting': A Roundtable with Kim Thúy," *Écrivains d'aujourd'hui*, Department of French and Italian, Emory University, Atlanta, April 18, 2018.
22 Ndione, *Mbëkë mi. À l'assaut des vagues de l'Atlantique*, p. 83.
23 "On voyait des policiers ramasser des corps gonflés comme des ballons..." [We saw policemen collecting bodies bloated like balloons]. Mahi Binehine, *Cannibale* (Paris: Fayard, 1999), 214.
24 Alexandra Kurmann and Tess Do, "Children on the Boat: The Recuperative Work of Postmemory in Short Fiction of the Vietnamese Diaspora," *Comparative Literature* 70, no. 3 (June 2018): 225.
25 See Linda Lê, "Vinh L." In *Les évangiles du crime* (Paris: Christian Bourgois, 1992), 171–227 and Kim Thúy, *Vi* (Montreal: Liana Levi, 2016).
26 For a more in-depth analysis of the boat narrative as anthropophagy, see Subha Xavier, "Wretched of the Sea: Boat Narratives and Stories of Displacement." In *Contemporary Fiction in French,* ed. Anna-Louise Milne and Russell Williams (Cambridge: Cambridge University Press, 2020), 184–198.
27 Senegalese writer Bathie Ngoye Thiam was among the first to question the veracity of the autobiographical account in an opinion piece that appeared two months after the novel's publication: "Soif d'Europe: L'imposture d'un immigré,"*Le Soleil,* July 17, 2008, www.seneweb.com/news/News/diouf-revele-un-scandale-dans-la-taniere_n_17507.html. Since then, *Le Monde*'s Benoît Hopquin took up the investigation in "Contre-enquête sur un affabu-lateur," *Le Monde,* July 7, 2009, www.lemonde.fr/societe/article/2009/07/07/contre-enquete-sur-un-affabulateur_1216190_3224.html and "Un 'impos-teur' repéré par la diaspora sénégalaise," *Le Monde,* July 7, 2009, www .lemonde.fr/societe/article/2009/07/07/un-imposteur-repere-par-la-diaspora-senegalaise_1216191_3224.html#ens_id=1216285. With increased scrutiny and pressure, Ba first recanted parts of the novel before admitting to creating all of it from the experience of others. Philippe Peter's article in *L'Humanité* captures the anthropophagic nature of the novel: "Un imposteur joue du malheur des clandestins sénégalais," *L'Humanité,* August 21, 2009, https:// philippepeter.wordpress.com/category/lhumaniteils-ont-ose-le-faire/ (all web-sites accessed May 27, 2022).
28 See Miguel Mellino, "The Langue of the Damned: Fanon and the Remnants of Europe," *South Atlantic Quarterly* 112, no. 1 (2013): 79–89.
29 Ndione, *Mbëkë mi. À l'assaut des vagues de l'Atlantique*, p. 67.
30 Ndione, *Mbëkë mi. À l'assaut des vagues de l'Atlantique*, pp. 67–68.
31 Ndione, *Mbëkë mi. À l'assaut des vagues de l'Atlantique*, p. 73.
32 Suvendrini Perera, "Now, Little Ship." In *Border Thinking: Disassembling Histories of Racialized Violence.* Vol. 21 (Sternberg Press, 2018), 186. Perera aligns the treatment of African clandestine migrants in Europe and Australia

with the Chinese migrant laborers of the Morecambe Bay disaster in 2004 where twenty-one cockle pickers drowned and the 8000 Rohingya refugees who were left to die, drifting in the Bengal Bay due to the turn-back boat policies of Indonesia, Thailand, and Malaysia in 2015.

33 Meghan Beatley and Sam Edwards, "Overfished: In Senegal, Empty Nets Lead To Hunger and Violence," *Public Radio International*, May 30, 2018. https://gpinvestigations.pri.org/overfished-in-senegal-empty-nets-lead-to-hun ger-and-violence-e3b5d0c9a686 (accessed May 27, 2022).

34 Beatley and Sam Edwards, "Overfished."

35 Beatley and Sam Edwards, "Overfished."

36 See Chidinma Irene Nwoye, "The EU Subsidies Which Cause Overfishing in West Africa's Waters Also Drive Illegal Migration," *Quartz Africa*, February 27, 2020. https://qz.com/africa/1807878/eu-subsidies-boost-overfishing-in-west-africa-and-migration/ (accessed May 27, 2022).

37 The Free, "140 Migrants to Europe Die in Sinking of Boat in Senegal .. Factory Fishing Decimated Local Industry." https://thefreeonline.wordpress .com/2020/10/31/140-migrants-to-europe-die-in-sinking-of-boat-in-senegal-factory-fishing-decimated-local-industry/ (accessed May 27, 2022).

38 Lewis R. Gordon, *What Fanon Said: A Philosophical Introduction to His Life and Thought* (New York: Fordham University Press, 2015).

39 Frantz Fanon, *Peau noire masques blancs* (Paris: Seuil, 1952), 33.

40 Fanon, *Black Skin White Masks*, p. 41.

CHAPTER 15

Mediterranean Afterlives of Slavery
Refugees and the Politics of Saving

Ewa Macura-Nnamdi

"[T]o be Black is to be continually produced by the wait toward death," writes Christina Sharpe in her book devoted to the afterlives of slavery, to living *in the wake*, that is, to living the violence of anti-blackness in the aftermath of the slave trade.[1] To be in the wake is "to occupy and to be occupied by the continuous and changing present of slavery's unresolved unfolding" where "insistent Black exclusion, ontological negation . . . [and] un/survival" keep marking "blackness's ongoing and irresolvable abjection."[2] In contexts outside North America, living in the wake "means the disastrous time and effects of continued marked migrations, Mediterranean and Caribbean disasters."[3] These disasters bring to the foreground the violability of black "bodies to which anything and everything can be and is done."[4] The proximity of black life to death is what ties the Black Atlantic to the deadly crossings of the Mediterranean. Within "the semiotics of the slave ship," Sharpe says, blackness is (what is) caught in the movement towards a port. It is a discontinued journey which arrests the moving bodies as dead, dying, or about to die.[5] In this poignant meditation on what it means to be black in the aftermath of slavery, dying is the mode of being of blackness, the form it must assume to be apprehended: "They, we, inhabit knowledge that the Black body is the sign of immi/a/nent death."[6]

In her attempt to think "the inheritance of non/status"[7] through the material and symbolic meanings of the wake and to theorize the deadly scripting of back lives across global contexts, Sharpe is joined by other scholars who likewise connect the death of migrants in the Mediterranean to the gratuitous violence inherited from the Atlantic slave trade and who likewise define this connection in/as the structural, ontological, and physical proximity of black bodies to death. These scholars insist on reading what has come to be known by now as the Black Mediterranean[8] not simply in relation to the history of slavery but as its logical protraction, one that lays bare this history's structuring role in the unending production of

present-day racial violence. For P. Khalil Saucier and Tryon P. Woods, the
policing of the Mediterranean borders of Europe operates on the same
premises black bodies came to be policed under slavery, the jurisprudence
of which positioned "*all* white people [as] empowered to discipline, control
and punish – to *police* – all black people"[9] regardless of their legal status.
Bringing all black people who were "so far inferior, that they had no rights
which the white man was bound to respect," this jurisprudence subjected
all blacks to "the authority of whites," simultaneously rendering all forms
of "black self-possession" criminal and thus punishable.[10] What the Black
Mediterranean shares with the Black Atlantic is what Khalil and Woods
emphasize is gratuitous violence which does not follow any transgressive
acts but which is simply "punishment for *being*."[11] The migrants left to
drown crossing the Mediterranean are *a priori* "disempowered by the racial
economy of value" and its "matrix of violence."[12]

Likewise, Jill H. Casid suggests to read the rising migrant death toll in
the Mediterranean "in terms of an anti-black violence" and "the violence
of an anti-blackness" that have a history and are not, in other words,
"exceptional" or "contingent."[13] Casid argues that the boats with refugees
have redefined "refugees" by making them "synonymous with
criminalized . . . non-Europeanness" and with "a blackness already sentenced to death."[14] The EU policies have tied the refugees to the tactics of
death calculation, to "necrometrical tabulation of the ways in which the
biopolitics of migration have become a matter of not merely letting people
die or, rather, drown, but a necropolitical calculus whereby those seeking
asylum are forced to risk death by becoming as close to death as possible in
order to gain entry as the potentially rescued."[15] To properly comprehend
the "refugee crisis," Casid suggests reading the necropolitical calculus in
terms of "the excessive and incalculable evidence of Europe's indissoluble
implication in an unfinished present of the history of slavery."[16] Casid's
major argument is that the real and symbolic proximity of black migrants
to death, their reduction to calculated deaths which nourish the "fantasies
of rescue," debilitates any potentially radical politics because, rather than
challenging refugees' dehumanization, it "convert[s] the terror-figure of the
migrant as threat into a countable and grievable loss."[17]

15.1   The Logic of Slavery

Yogita Goyal's pithy reflection on the frequently drawn parallels between
slavery and the contemporary refugee cautions against too easy analogies
between the past and the present. On one hand, such analogies may end

up suggesting that slavery has been adequately dealt with while in fact it continues to carry an "unstable meaning . . . in political culture today."[18] On the other, they can unwittingly obscure what is politically and historically distinct about present-day refugees in the Mediterranean. These analogies call for a nuanced approach sensitive to the particularity of the present moment so that it becomes possible to "comprehend the forms of power at play today and to imagine paths of resistance."[19] Goyal alerts us to the pitfalls of an unproblematic transfer of the "conceptions of black humanity" across times and geographies.[20] Such a transfer may inadvertently turn race into a uniform, essentialized category at the same time framing contemporary contexts of the global South as posterior to an originary spatial and temporal location and thus derivative rather than coexistent. In Goyal's words: "the power and prominence of slavery as a prism through which conceptions of black humanity, agency, and futurity refract and become visible should not obscure the contradictions race acquires as it travels across the globe. Rather than seeing the past of the United States as the present of the global south, in a familiar move denying coevalness, what new relationships mapping space and time might be obtained?"[21]

Heeding Goyal's calls for more nuanced analogies, this essay proposes to seek analogies not in/on "the black bodies at sea,"[22] but in the relations brought into being between black and brown bodies and other involved actors, and in the values thus generated. Rather than suggesting that the analogy lies in their common experience of anti-black violence, I would like to seek this analogy in what Tim Armstrong calls the logic of slavery. What Armstrong suggests is a reading of slavery where it is not only "history and experience" but also a way of thinking: "there is more to be said about the figural implications of slavery's presence in Western tradition, the way it subtly infiltrates the fabric of other modes of thoughts and shapes what is thinkable, informing what could be called a culture of slavery."[23] This culture manifests itself in economic practices we perform on a regular basis when we, for example, "insure ourselves;" in our expressions of sympathy when we "emote at the pain of others;" when we ponder "the power of machines."[24] Slavery has permeated our modes of being and seeing the relations among ourselves and other entities; it has shaped economic operations and productive processes. As Armstrong argues, "the history of slavery . . . is knitted into the way in which we see ourselves as having an assignable value; the way we understand technology and making."[25] In other words, Armstrong claims that the culture of slavery is "both historical and discursive" and entails "binding slavery to the way we see a range of economic, social and legal relations."[26]

This essay takes *saving* as a practice based on one such mode of thinking. It delves into the eighteenth-century insurance practice, humanitarian discourses, and the *Zong* case to tease out the ways in which ethics, economy, and humanitarian sentiments came to be entangled in the culture of slavery. In particular, it probes the meanings of saving that emerge from the general average, a concept of marine insurance which legally enabled the *Zong* massacre. It argues that contemporary acts of saving in the Mediterranean, and the ethics and politics which have coalesced around them, derive their logic from what saving meant in eighteenth-century moral and economic sentiments underlying insurance theory and practice. Reading Helon Habila's 2019 novel *Travellers*, I examine how Habila's novel speaks to and of the inherited paradigm of saving, re-scripting the refugees' "wait toward death" into the political and economic utility of their life. Looking at the novel and the context which it addresses via eighteenth-century insurance discourses and how they informed the slave trade, allows us to discern who and what is at stake in the Mediterranean rescue scene. The main claim of this essay is that those discourses of saving re-emerge in the maritime realms of southern Europe establishing continuities between slavery and the so called "refugee crisis" that go beyond the Afropessimist paradigm. These discourses also bring to light and help to formulate a set of other significant claims: that drownings in the Mediterranean are not exceptional and should not be regarded as states of exception; that to keep some bodies as structurally beyond saving is a form of border control; and that the scenes of rescue that unfold at sea redefine refugees as those who fail to arrive.

15.2   The *Zong*, Shipwreck, and Eighteenth-Century Humanitarianism

Exploring the reasons why the *Zong* story continues to resonate so strongly, Armstrong situates the case "in a broader stream of humanitarian activity in the late eighteenth century" which, among others, involved a concern for "the drowned and drowning."[27] For instance, the Royal Humane Society, originally founded in 1774, devoted its efforts to resuscitation and subsequently to "rescue, promoting lifeboats, lifebelts, and other life-saving apparatus."[28] Armstrong argues that the Society owed its interests to "the central place of the shipwreck in accounts of the perils and individual costs of maritime enterprise in the period."[29] This centrality found ample room in the literature and art of the period where the shipwreck became "a sublime scene of sympathetic identification."[30] Indeed, it constituted a real and imaginary site of moral interpellation: "Man never beholds with indifference his fellow-creatures struggling with adverse fortune," opined Archibald Duncan in the introduction to his work *The Mariner's Chronicle* from 1810.[31] Given the status of shipwreck as an object of aesthetic and moral contemplation as well as of humanitarian practice, it is not surprising that it also made its way into abolitionist writings.[32] Here, shipwreck becomes an event through which the misery and hardships experienced by the enslaved can be registered and revealed.

Whether objects or agents of saving, in these narratives of the "shipwreck as a moral scene,"[33] enslaved lives are tied to the sentiments and rhetoric of rescue. According to Armstrong, in abolitionist writings such narratives of shipwreck, real or imagined, offered a lesson in ethics and urged audiences to become politically engaged. Importantly, Armstrong argues that it is through the prism of such narratives that the notorious *Zong* case would come to be seen: "readers of abolitionist accounts would have been primed to read the *Zong* in this way: as a melodramatic scene of shipwreck in which spectators are impelled into political action; in which the failure to see or 'count' the Africans involved as part of the ship's company is underscored."[34] The political and cultural resonance of the *Zong* case has therefore rested on a very specific distribution of affect and disposition deriving from humanitarian discourses of the time and productive of the "sympathetic identification" and thus of political activism. Within this affective framework, the enslaved are seen as shipwrecked lives in need of saving.

Thematizing saving, such eighteenth- and early nineteenth-century narratives of shipwreck and the slave trade seem to implicitly speak to another "moral scene," one also unfolding at sea, under disastrous conditions where both animate and inanimate lives are at stake, their salvage likewise dependent on finer feelings and incalculable values. This scene derives from the eighteenth-century culture of insurance, and more specifically, from one of its concepts called general average, that is, "the idea that losses undertaken voluntarily to save a boat (jettison, cutting down masts in a storm, ransom) represent a risk shared among those investing in a voyage."[35] John Weskett's 1781 *Complete Digest of the Theory, Law, and Practice of Insurance* provides a more extensive definition of the principle:

> Whatever the master of a ship in distress . . . deliberately resolves to do, for the preservation of the whole, in cutting away masts or cables, or in throwing goods overboard to lighten his vessel, which is what is meant by

jettison or jetson, is, in all places, permitted to be brought into a general, or
gross average: in which all concerned in ship, freight, and cargo, are to bear
an equal or proportionable part of what was so sacrificed for the common
good, and it must be made good by the insurers in such proportions as they
have underwrote: however, to make this action legal, the three following
points are essentially necessary; viz–1st. That what was so condemned to
destruction, was in consequence of a deliberate and voluntary consultation,
held between the master and men:–2dly. That the ship was in distress, and
the sacrificing the things they did was a necessary procedure to save the
rest:–and 3dly. That the saving of the ship and the cargo was actually owing
to the means used with that sole view.[36]

It was general average that became the pivotal point of the *Zong* case,
playing a crucial role in its court proceedings. As Armstrong tells us, the
enslaved people thrown into the sea were claimed by their owners to be
"general average sacrifice made to avert an insurrection and further
deaths."[37] In other words, in order to claim insurance money, the owners
argued that the murdered men and women were in fact a necessary
sacrifice made to save the lives of the crew and other cargo. The owners
of the ship were initially awarded damages, but the underwriters successfully challenged the decision, arguing that no immediate peril, as was
required by insurance law at the time, necessitated the jettisoning of the
enslaved people aboard the ship. The trials thus revolved around matters of
definition, their aim to determine whether the enslaved people killed by
Collingwood, the captain of the *Zong*, indeed constituted general average,
that is, "the loss of goods under duress at sea" also called "sacrifice."[38]
What is significant to note here, as Ian Baucom insists, is that the enslaved
had been assumed to be "subject to the general average," and that is,
assumed to be insurable commodities.[39]

Within "loss-value protocols of insurance" as Baucom claims, "the slaves
were . . . regarded by the law to have vanished . . . *prior* to the moment of
their murder."[40] Baucom's most crucial point is that the *Zong* case provided the typical example and an exemplary illustration of that vanishing.
If the *Zong* case functions as a paradigm of the translation of value from its
material into its abstract form, and at the heart of this translation lies the
concept of general average, it is also important to ponder the role that
saving plays in this translation. While Baucom and Armstrong do not
dwell on the idea of saving that emerges from Weskett's definition of the
general average, it is nevertheless interesting to note that what Baucom
calls "the loss theory of value" rests on saving, and that the detachment of
value from the life of things is conditioned by an act of saving.

15.3 Shipwreck in the Mediterranean

Helon Habila's most recent novel *Travellers* (2019) offers a story which exposes the paradigm of saving as it (re)emerges across the Mediterranean in the current so-called refugee crisis, generating narratives of rescue which bring together boats, bodies, and seascapes.[41] Set across countries and continents, the plot travels together with the characters we meet across the six books which comprise the text. Each book relates an individual refugee/migration story which connects with the following and preceding ones in unexpected and surprising ways. While it is set predominantly on land, Habila's narrative nevertheless repeatedly references maritime contexts and shipwreck. They are a site where the narrated travels and travails begin and end; they are what enables and propels the characters' journeys, even on land, and what facilitates or impedes their movement. The sea recurs in recollections, similes, literary citations, nested stories, and nightmares. Thus the sea is where the refugees' thoughts repeatedly return as they relive the trauma of the fatal crossing;[42] the sea is what encroaches upon land in nightmarish visions replacing the solid landscape of the city with the turbulent texture of seawater;[43] the sea is also what we hear of in a handful of references to Milton's "Lycidas" in which water is summoned as a site of burial;[44] the sea reappears in the stories the characters recount, becoming a character it its own right and a venue for another, more distant story;[45] the sea is also the terrifying subject of dreams where it serves as a medium and a locus of death.[46] As such, it no doubt recalls the "visual imagery of black bodies lost at sea,"[47] evoking the scene of the Zong massacre but also, more generally, images of "people perishing in the hold of overcrowded ships."[48] And yet the link between the Atlantic slave trade and the current plight of refugees trying to reach Europe extends here beyond such visual similitude.

The narrative uses of the sea are nearly always tied to shipwreck. One might say that shipwreck haunts Habila's novel, quietly yet insistently inhabiting the story's background, occasionally coming centre stage. Lived or recalled or imagined, shipwreck is both an experience and a figure; it is also an event distributing lives and destinations, delineating the characters' aquatic and terrestrial itineraries. Shipwreck is what organizes the lives of Matteo and his father in Book 5, two inhabitants of the anonymous island and regular witnesses to the human and non-human flotsam and jetsam beached in their vicinity. Shipwreck is reminisced in the floating wreckage and personal items seawater carries along and lands on their threshold.[49] Shipwreck is an always anticipated event, continually on the brink of unfolding, an inherent element of the maritime landscape: "In the distance the old man appears, heading for the house, the dog by his side, in the sea a rescue boat rises and dips on the water, searching for distressed migrant boats."[50] Shipwreck is imagined, far away from the seaside, as its aftermath, as drifting "shipwrecked lives" strangely alive in their testimony to the discontinued journeys of the missing yet implied ships: "Beyond it was what looked like a river, or a lake. *Watery bier.* She [Portia] imagined drowned bodies floating in the water."[51]

The novel's thematic investment in the sea and shipwreck no doubt also generates instances of saving and scenes of rescue. Habila's ingenuity lies in the challenge his novel poses to the acts of saving which derive its logic from the eighteenth-century insurance and slavery culture. More specifically, Habila interrogates saving for its distribution of safety across bodies, for its *a priori* ascription of safety to some but not others, for its production of saveable and unsaveable bodies, for its reliance on the annihilation of what is "condemned to destruction," in Weskett's words, and, finally, for its concealment of the safety/destruction dialectic that structures and mars it. Importantly, Habila exposes the underlying logic of the general average: to save is to keep hidden from view a tautology that implicitly defines "the preservation of the whole" defined by the eighteenth-century discourse of insurance. In a sense, one saves what is beforehand (considered and recognized as) safe from destruction.

15.4 Salvation

"The Sea," Book 5 of Habila's novel, opens with one of its main characters, Matteo, reimagining a scene of rescue that will constitute not only its narrative backbone but also another story, itself subject to narration, a story Matteo will recount to the narrator in the course of the Book, both thematizing saving and revealing it to be limited and regulated by the conventions derived from eighteenth-century insurance. Narrated from alternating perspectives (Matteo's and the novel's unnamed narrator's), the Book tells the story of both: the latter's sojourn at a refugee camp on the unnamed island and Matteo's rescue of a female refugee and his subsequent relationship with her. In fact, Matteo happens to also save the narrator, apparently engulfed by a resignation to the fate that befell him. Offering refuge, Matteo tells him of how he chanced upon, took home, and tended a female refugee and her son. Unable to remember who she is, the woman is finally supplied a name by Matteo, who invents a story of their past encounter. Now, desperate to have an identity, she believes Matteo's tall tales, accepting his proposal to marry him soon after. Expectedly enough, she comes to recover her memory, leaving the despairing Matteo in order to search for her husband she hopes survived the sea crossing.

"The Sea" begins with Matteo recalling her beached, lifeless Aphrodite-like body and arrival: "As he drove down the sloping road to the camp he caught a glimpse of the sea below. The southern Italian sun was gleaming on the waves and for a moment it all came back, the woman lying half-covered in the foaming waves on the beach, and he running toward her. At first he thought she was dead."[52] Alongside this romanticized recollection lies a brief but vivid description of the sea: "Today the sea was restless, roiling and snapping at the foot of the hill, spouting foam like an enraged leviathan."[53] The contrast between the mercy and the ferocity of the sea is significant for the implication it carries about the provenance of the violence that has befallen the woman, suggesting that containing it lies beyond human powers and that its infliction remains unrelated to any conditions beyond the realm of the sea. It therefore naturalizes this violence, reducing survival to a matter of miracle, something depending on the vagaries of the sea and one's ability to brave them. To be saved means to have withstood the elemental frenzy of the seawater, something that countless "images of Black subjects in conditions of radical precarity, struggling for survival" against nature rather than the border regime evidence again and again.[54] And yet this idea of survival is deliberately misleading, conveying an impression that it is the woman and others like her who are at stake in the scenes of rescue which unfold in the littoral spaces of the West. In the course of the Book, however, it becomes clear that Habila toys with the conventions of representation and the rhetoric deployed to speak of the reality of the refugees' struggle for survival at sea.

Echoing the logic of eighteenth-century maritime insurance, Habila's narrative underscores the refugees' disappearance before their journeys begin and points to the way they are, to rephrase Baucom, regarded to have vanished prior to the moment of their drowning, regarded as "bodies which disappear," as Armstrong might call them, or, as bodies "condemned to destruction" (as Weskett's framing of the general average might define them). Thus, when she finally recovers her memory, Sophia (as Matteo named her), recalls her name and the circumstances of the crossing, recounting in horrific detail the disaster that befell them:

> I was scared. I didn't want all four of us on the same boat. . . . The boat was really nothing but a death trap, an old rickety fishing trawler that should

have been retired a long time ago. . . . Some, who were down below in the
hold, stacked on top of each other, died within hours of departure – the
children and the pregnant women died first. We saw them bring up
the bodies and throw them in the water. . . . A helicopter appeared overhead, and we thought we were finally safe, but after circling for a few
minutes, it left.[55]

What is striking in this passage is the way it conveys a sense of
resignation, a calculated anticipation of the failure to make it and a quiet
acceptance of the coming catastrophe. Embarking on the trawler means
acquiescing to this catastrophe, reckoning with it and with its likelihood.
Basma's foreboding about drowning renders survival a matter of contingency, an unlikely event in the face of deliberate neglect. Indeed, the
departing helicopter only evidences this neglect, signifying the withdrawal
of help and the denial of safety. Basma's account suggests that to abandon
the refugees is already to make them disappear before they even vanish in
the depths of the sea. Abandonment as disappearance defines the conditions of radical unsafety in which to disappear is not to be saved yet
continue to exist. Interestingly the ship is also what makes them dead
before they drown: literally (some die under the deck) and symbolically
(once at sea, they lose their political life unable to claim due rights and thus
remain non-existent to international law). The ship functions, therefore, as
a technology that effects their demise while still ostensibly providing
mobility to the bodies who have already vanished. Aptly called a "death
trap" it is, paradoxically, a vehicle that both moves and stills; mediates and
withholds movement, providing an infrastructure of escape and capture.
The refugees on the boat are quite literally bodies in motion, beyond the
safety of seaworthy vessels and the protections granted by international
legal frameworks. Basma recognizes this precariousness when she describes
the ship as a "death trap" and when she recalls her well-founded fear of
perishing at sea, very clearly pointing to what she believes defines her as
unsafe from destruction before their passage begins.

15.5 Boats

If "the overcrowded vessel has become a visual type that migrates across
information and media platforms,"[56] often to speak of porous boundaries,
wicked smugglers, and heroic states, (and also undeniably to evoke the
specter of the slave trade), Habila's novel resorts to the image in order to
stake a set of different claims. Enhancing the tenor of Basma's narrative,
the recurring images of the ship in Book 5 work to expose the normative

character of the conditions of unsafety and unsaveability under which the refugees embark on their journeys. It is interesting to see how the narrative uses ships to underscore the link between refugees and un/safety, revealing thereby the political and affective values that have coalesced around it. Book 5 represents the seascape as a site of familiar and quotidian disasters contemplated from ashore with a sense of familiarity that renders them totally unexceptional:

> They sat, the three of them [Matteo, Pietro, his father, and a camp doctor], eating and watching the sea through the window, in the distance a boat circled the water. . . . Coast guards, Matteo said; no, that is the *carabinieri*, the police, the doctor argued; wrong, Pietro said, squinting his old eyes, it is a private boat, one of the rescue volunteers. . . . [the doctor] volunteered at the refugee camp, and old as he was, he went out with the rescue boats daily to search for capsized migrant boats.[57]

What is striking in these passages is not only the way the novel inscribes refugees' unsafety into the texture of the aquatic vistas but also how these rising and dipping boats address and speak of assumptions and expectations, their presence paradoxically indicative of how normalized (and also ubiquitous) the "distressed migrant boats" have become; and, more significantly yet, of how the refugees' systemic deprivation of safety is taken for granted as something unfortuitous, something reckoned with, and something matter-of-factly anticipated.

The migrant and the rescue boats that populate the maritime landscape of Book 5, simultaneously reproducing unsafety and alleviating it, tell us something about the ways border regimes enlist unsafety as means of control and regulation that require no human actors for their enactment and operation. Habila's travelers evidence how the distribution of safety across bodies redefines borders and border crossing. If vehicles, increasingly used to police and inspect migration routes, allow us to see the border as "taking new shapes and topographies,"[58] unsaveable bodies demonstrate how conditions of radical unsafety get to be mobilized in the service of migration control and the regulation of movement. The rising and dipping vessels, continually on the lookout for "distressed migrant boats," are revealing in three respects. For one, they speak of failed crossings, always looming on the horizon and indicative of how this Mediterranean border comes to be controlled by the very bodies not subject to saving whose foundering reproduces and enacts the border and keeps it uncrossed. For another, they expose how the migrants become a body of control: in their intention to cross, they are, simultaneously, producing and halting their movement, embodying it and constituting both its boundary and its terminus. In a startling sense, the body becomes the border; it is the topography borders assume, a checkpoint and a coastguard to control its own movement. Thus, to be unsaved and unsaveable is not an outcome of control but its means and precondition.

There is, therefore, something tragic, outrageous as well as banal about Pietro, Matteo, and the doctor, sitting at home, doing the guessing and impassively contemplating the maritime horizon in anticipation of drowning migrants, pondering the readiness of the rescue boats to assist vessels in distress, but thereby also laying bare the paradoxical logic underlying these aquatic vistas: the migrants are not helped to safely cross the sea; they are offered help only when they end up unable to complete unsafe crossings, having already been deprived of safety before their capsized boats secure the attention of rescue vessels. The assistance offered in conditions of emergency effectively conceals this prior state of unsafety, turning the rescue operations not only into spectacles of heroic struggle amidst the ferocity of the sea and sheer misfortune, but also into an end in itself and a sufficient remedy to singular incidents. What this saving leaves unsaved, and thus also unchallenged and intact, is precisely the refugees' condition of systemic vulnerability which both precedes and succeeds their maritime ordeals.

The narrative establishes a structural affinity between Basma and the boats by having both bring into visibility what the paradigm of saving ostensibly makes them conceal, namely, the systemic refusal on the part of border regimes to save the refugees from having to undertake the perilous journeys rather than from drowning. By rupturing the distribution of safety (the boats do so by pointing to the perils they anticipate and alleviate; Basma by temporarily living out the safety created for someone she is not) they paradoxically designate that space where unsafety remains reality and norm. Yet they also reveal how this paradigm comes to redefine the refugee from someone who must escape to seek safety into someone who is not allowed and/or expected to arrive. The title Habila chose for this collection of books loosely combined into a novel might already imply and capture the redefinition at stake. After all, travelers is a word that lends a certain amount of permanence to the movement undertaken by those who travel. Traveling is redolent of leisure and pleasure, suggesting something done out of curiosity rather than necessity. To travel is to relish the process and the activity more than the arrival at eventual destinations. The incongruity this apparent misnomer creates by naming people whose movement has nothing to do with recreation highlights, however, both the indefinite duration of the travels Habila's characters undertake as refugees and the critical project his novel engages in. Differently put, traveling may paradoxically seem the most apposite description of the movement Habila's refugees undertake: the erasure of arrival turns refugees into travelers.

15.6 Proximity to Life

Book 5 ends with an altogether different image, one that foregrounds unsaved refugees whose floating, drowning bodies speak of the withheld arrival. On a boat towards Africa rather than Europe, the narrator dreams of "Bodies floating face-up, limbs thrashing, tiny hands reaching up to me. Hundreds of tiny hands, thousands of faces, until the surface of the water is filled with silent ghostly eyes like lamps shining at me, and arms reaching up to be grasped; they float amidst the debris of personal belongings, toys, shoes, shirts, and family pictures all slowly sinking into bottomless Mediterranean."[59] The sea is here not only a hellish realm where lives are wasted but also a site where the moral economy of saving comes to the foreground. Its cadaverous materiality stands in contrast not only to Basma's story of survival but also to the rescue boats whose presence persistently promises saving rather than foundering. To end the chapter so explicitly tied to the ethics of salvation with an image so disruptive of this narrative import seems to strike a rather jarring note. And yet it also seems perfectly in line with the logic of saving that Book 5 propounds. The magnitude of this maritime catastrophe is but the other side of the same coin.

   Like the enslaved in eighteenth-century moral scenes of shipwreck, the refugees become shipwrecked lives in need of saving, the dissected bodies flailing for help a graphic visualization of this need. Whether saved or abandoned to drown, they are never, however, the real objects of saving. After all, their precarity remains tied to their bodies beyond the outcome of the rescue efforts which are limited to alleviating what is already an upshot of that precarity. To put it simply, no one saves them from having to undertake the deadly maritime crossing. As such they remain the sacrificial element of the transatlantic moral economies, the disposable unsaveable bodies that may or may not occasionally be salvaged from destruction. Though ostensibly redolent of Kevin Bales's disposable people, these refugees attempting to cross Europe's maritime borders are neither cheap nor economically exploitable in any immediate way and sense. Unlike Bales's "new slaves" whose disappearance in no way bears upon these economies they shore up because there is "an absolute glut of potential slaves,"[60] the refugees' disposability is precisely where benefits are to be reaped. It is their disappearance, or potential for disappearance, that generates value, both symbolic and material.[61] "Regarded by the law to have vanished ... *prior* to the moment of their [drowning]," to paraphrase Baucom once again, they embody the salvation value that materializes once they become subject to saving.

Travellers conveys the sense of bewilderment at the practice of saving that does not extend further than the realm of the sea. It implicitly critiques the border regimes that have elevated saving to a value detached from the bodies and material realities it purports to serve. It registers exasperation at the "resurgent European isolationism"[62] that continues to view refugees as the "empty bearers," to quote Baucom again, of the salvation value which masks that *prior* vanishing and the distribution of safety which, as in the eighteenth-century insurance culture, already marks some bodies for (potential) destruction. For this critique to work, however, Habila needs to narrate the analogy between the enslaved and the refugees in a different way to those scholars discussed at the beginning of this essay. Indeed, his narrative shifts the critical focus from the proximity to death seen as the defining aspect of blackness, towards the proximity to life. In a startling way, his novel articulates what could be called, borrowing from Alys Eve Weinbaum's different though related context, the "extraction of value from life itself."[63] While Weinbaum investigates how life has come to be commodified in biocapitalism, centering on surrogacy as a racialized process historically enabled by breeding the enslaved, Habila's novel renders "life" into "living" itself to underscore the significance of protracting and/or sustaining life so that scenes of rescue can be staged and salvation value generated. What is at stake in Habila's insistence on the refugees' proximity to life rather than death is the way border regimes subject refugees to the harrowing ordeal of maritime crossing simultaneously placing a political premium on their living and surviving that come to be shorn of value once ashore.

It is saving that redirects the Mediterranean afterlife of slavery towards life rather than death. Saving needs surviving even if some lives are lost along the way. Saving calls for living bodies whose surviving can retrospectively testify to the success of rescue efforts. Moreover, life and living implicitly speak of and confirm the efficiency of the border. In the peculiar moral and monetary economy underlying the border regimes as they currently operate in the Mediterranean, survivors are much more vital to their maintenance than the bodies sunk to the bottomless Mediterranean.

Juma, Habila's Nigerian refugee who survives the maritime crossing but fails to continue living on land, comes closest to both embodying and recognizing the moral and economic value of continuing to live in the face of unliveable circumstances. On the last pages of the novel, Juma gives an account of his ordeals at sea and on land. After he relates the gruesome details of the passage, he asks rhetorically: "Why did I survive? I often wonder."[64] The bitter remark probes into the politics, rather than ethics, of survival. Seeking to understand the sense of his survival that he sees so compromised by the unfreedom he is plunged into the moment his life is no longer imperiled at sea, Juma goes on a hunger strike in protest against the inhuman treatment he receives and the impending deportation he awaits. As the deportation is bungled, and Juma returns to Harmondsworth Removal Centre, as the place is perniciously called, no one comes to save him when he gradually withers in the cell of the detention centre. Like the salvaged slaves in the eighteenth-century literary scenes of "sympathetic identification";[65] or the survivors of the insurance logic which affected, among others, the legal and political life of the *Zong* case; Juma's stormy passage speaks of the significance of life over the necropolitical undoing which marks southern Europe's maritime realms. In the wake of the slave trade as it materializes in the waters of the Mediterranean, (saved) life makes more political and economic sense than death. As Juma pungently puts it: "I see, we are the TV, a reality show about survival."[66]

Acknowledgments

This work was supported by the National Science Centre, Poland, under research project *Fictions of Water: Refugees and the Sea*, grant number UMO-2019/33/B/HS2/02051

Notes

1 Christina Sharpe, *In the Wake: On Blackness and Being* (Durham and London: Duke University Press, 2016), 88.
2 Sharpe, *In the Wake*, p. 14.
3 Sharpe, *In the Wake*, p. 15.
4 Sharpe, *In the Wake*, p. 16.
5 Sharpe, *In the Wake*, p. 21.
6 Sharpe, *In the Wake*, p. 71.
7 Sharpe, *In the Wake*, p. 15.

8 The term "Black Mediterranean" was coined by Alessandra di Maio. See her, "The Mediterranean, Or Where Africa Does (Not) Meet Italy: Andrea Segre's *A Sud di Lampedusa* (2006)." In *The Cinemas of Italian Migration: European and Transatlantic Narratives*, ed. Sabine Schrader and Daniel Winkler (*Newcastle upon Tyne*: Cambridge Scholars Publishing, 2013).

9 P. Khalil Saucier and Tryon P. Woods, "Ex Aqua: The Mediterranean Basin, Africans on the Move and the Politics of Policing," *Theoria* 141, no. 61 (2014): 62.

10 Khalil and Woods, "Ex Aqua," p. 61.

11 Khalil and Woods, "Ex Aqua," p. 61.

12 Khalil and Woods, "Ex Aqua," p. 71.

13 Jill H. Casid, "Necropolitics at Sea." In *Migration and Contemporary Mediterranean: Shifting Cultures in Twenty-First-Century Italy and Beyond*, ed. Claudia Gualtieri (Oxford: Peter Lang, 2018), 196.

14 Casid, "Necropolitics at Sea," p. 195.

15 Casid, "Necropolitics at Sea," pp. 194–195.

16 Casid, "Necropolitics at Sea," p. 196.

17 Casid, "Necropolitics at Sea," p. 194.

18 Yogita Goyal, "The Logic of Analogy: Slavery and the Contemporary Refugee," *Humanity: An International Journal of Human Rights, Humanitarianism, and Development* 8, no. 3 (2017): 544.

19 Goyal, "The Logic of Analogy," p. 545.

20 Goyal, "The Logic of Analogy."

21 Goyal, "The Logic of Analogy."

22 Goyal, "The Logic of Analogy."

23 Tim Armstrong, *The Logic of Slavery: Debt, Technology, and Pain in American Literature* (Cambridge: Cambridge University Press, 2012), 1.

24 Armstrong, *The Logic of Slavery*, p. 2.

25 Armstrong, *The Logic of Slavery*.

26 Armstrong, *The Logic of Slavery*.

27 Armstrong, *The Logic of Slavery*, p. 21.

28 Armstrong, *The Logic of Slavery*.

29 Armstrong, *The Logic of Slavery*.

30 Armstrong, *The Logic of Slavery*.

31 Quoted in Armstrong, *The Logic of Slavery*, p. 22.

32 Armstrong, *The Logic of Slavery*, p. 22.

33 Armstrong, *The Logic of Slavery*, p. 21.

34 Armstrong, *The Logic of Slavery*, p. 24.

35 Armstrong, *The Logic of Slavery*, p. 14.

36 John Weskett quoted in *Ian Baucom, Specters of the Atlantic: Finance Capital, Slavery, and the Philosophy of History* (Durham and London: Duke University Press, 2005), 137.

37 Armstrong, *The Logic of Slavery*, p. 25.

38 Armstrong, *The Logic of Slavery*, p. 24. See also Baucom, *Specters of the Atlantic*, pp. 315–340.

39 Baucom, *Specters of the Atlantic*, p. 139.
40 Baucom, *Specters of the Atlantic*, p. 149.
41 Helon Habila, *Travellers* (London: Hamish Hamilton, 2019).
42 Habila, *Travellers*, pp. 97, 112, 200, 230, 288.
43 Habila, *Travellers*, p. 80.
44 Habila, *Travellers*, pp. 105, 111, 112, 131.
45 Habila, *Travellers*, pp. 229, 175, 148.
46 Habila, *Travellers*, p. 243.
47 Goyal, "The Logic of Analogy," p. 543.
48 Goyal, "The Logic of Analogy."
49 Habila, *Travellers*, p. 222.
50 Habila, *Travellers*, pp. 233, 220.
51 Habila, *Travellers*, p. 112.
52 Habila, *Travellers*, p. 199.
53 Habila, *Travellers*.
54 Charles Heller and Lorenzo Pezzani, "Forensic Oceanography: Tracing Violence within and against the Mediterranean Frontier's Aesthetic Regime." In *Moving Images: Mediating Migration as Crisis*, ed. Krista Lynes, Tyler Morgenstern, and Ian Alan Paul (Bielefeld: Transcript Verlag, 2020), 122.
55 Habila, *Travellers*, pp. 229–230.
56 William Walters, "Migration, Vehicles, and Politics: Three Theses on Viapolitics," *European Journal of Social Theory* 18, no. :4 (2015): 475.
57 Habila, *Travellers*, p. 220.
58 Walters, "Migration," p. 478.
59 Habila, *Travellers*, p. 234.
60 Kevin Bales, *Disposable People: New Slavery in the Global Economy* (Berkeley: University of California Press, 2012), p. 15.
61 On the economies of Frontex politics, see Kaamil Ahmed, "EU accused of abandoning migrants to the sea with shift to drone surveillance," *Guardian*, October 28, 2020 (accessed November 8, 2020); Jasper Jolly, "Airbus to operate drones searching for migrants crossing the Mediterranean," *Guardian*, October 20, 2020 (accessed November 8, 2020).
62 Stefan Helmreich, "Seagoing Nightmares," *Dialogues in Human Geography* 9, no. 3 (2019): 308.
63 Alys Eve Weinbaum, *The Afterlife of Reproductive Slavery: Biocapitalism and Black Feminism's Philosophy of History* (Durham and London: Duke University Press, 2019), 5.
64 Habila, *Travellers*, p. 289.
65 Armstrong, *The Logic of Slavery*, p. 21.
66 Habila, *Travellers*, p. 290.

Further Reading

Abderrezak, Hakim, "Burning the Sea: Clandestine Migration across the Strait of Gibraltar in Francophone Moroccan 'Illiterature.'" *Contemporary French and Francophone Studies* 13, no. 4 (2009): 461–469.

Abruzzo, Margaret, *Polemical Pain: Slavery, Cruelty, and the Rise of Humanitarianism* (Baltimore, MD: Johns Hopkins University Press, 2011).

Ajayi, Lady Adaina et al., "African Migrant Narratives, Modern Slavery, and Human Rights Violations in Libya." *Handbook of Research on the Global Impact of Media on Migration Issues* (Hershey, PA: IGI Global, 2020): 48–67.

Allain, Jean ed., *The Legal Understanding of Slavery: From the Historical to the Contemporary* (New York: Oxford University Press, 2012).

Alryyes, Ala, *The Life of Omar Ibn Said: A Muslim American Slave* (Madison, WI: University of Wisconsin Press, 2011).

Austin, Allan D., *African Muslims in Antebellum America: A Sourcebook* (New York: Garland Pub., 1984).

Baderoon, Gabeeba, "The African Oceans: Tracing the Sea as Memory of Slavery in South African Literature and Culture" *Research in African Literatures* (Bloomington, IN: Indiana University Press, 2009).

   Regarding Muslims: From Slavery to Post-apartheid (Johannesburg: Wits University Press, 2014).

Baghoolizadeh, Beeta, "Seeing Race and Erasing Slavery: Media and the Construction of Blackness in Iran, 1830–1960" (2018). *Publicly Accessible Penn Dissertations.*

Bales, Kevin, *Disposable People: New Slavery in the Global Economy* (Berkeley: University of California Press, 2012).

Barker, Hannah, *That Most Precious Merchandise: The Mediterranean Trade in Black Sea Slaves, 1260–1500, The Middle Ages Series* (Philadelphia: University of Pennsylvania Press, 2019).

Bawden, Charles R., *The Modern History of Mongolia* (New York: Frederick A. Praeger, 1968).

Bernstein, Elizabeth, *Brokered Subjects: Sex Trafficking and the Politics of Freedom* (Chicago: University of Chicago Press, 2019).

Best, Stephen M., *The Fugitive's Properties: Law and the Poetics of Possession* (Chicago: University of Chicago Press, 2004).

Biran, Michal, "Forced Migrations and Slavery in the Mongol Empire." *The Cambridge World History of Slavery: Volume 2, AD 500–AD 1420*, eds. Craig Perry, David Eltis, Stanley L. Engerman, and David Richardson (Cambridge: Cambridge University Press, 2021): 76–99.

Bragard, Véronique, *Transoceanic Dialogues: Coolitude in Caribbean and Indian Ocean Literatures* (Bern: Peter Lang, 2008).

Bunting, Annie and Joel Quirk eds., *Contemporary Slavery: Popular Rhetoric and Political Practice* (Vancouver: University of British Columbia Press, 2017).

Campbell, Gwyn, *Africa and the Indian Ocean World from Early Times to Circa 1900* (Cambridge: Cambridge University Press, 2019).

Clarence-Smith, William G., *Islam and the Abolition of Slavery* (Oxford: Oxford University Press, 2006).

Crone, Patricia, *Slaves on Horses* (Cambridge: Cambridge University Press, 1980).

Crossley, Pamela Kyle, "Slavery in Early Modern China," *The Cambridge World History of Slavery, Volume 3: AD 1420–AD 1804* (New York: Cambridge University Press, 2011).

Curtin, Philip de Armond ed., *Africa Remembered: Narratives by West Africans from the Era of the Slave Trade* (Madison, WI: University of Wisconsin Press, 1967).

Desai, Ashwin and Goolam Vahed, *Inside Indian Indenture: A South African Story 1860–1914* (Cape Town, South Africa: HSRC University Press; Second Edition, 2010).

Diouf, Sylviane A., *African Muslims Enslaved in the Americas* (New York: New York University Press, 1998).

Eden, Jeff, *Slavery and Empire in Central Asia* (Cambridge: Cambridge University Press, 2018).

Epstein, Steven A., *Speaking of Slavery: Color, Ethnicity, and Human Bondage in Italy* (Ithaca and London: Cornell University Press, 2001).

Fredrickson, G. M., *White Supremacy: A Comparative Study in American and South African History* (New York: Oxford University Press; First Edition, 1987).

Frydman, Jason, "Scheherazade in Chains: Arab-Islamic Genealogies of African Diasporic Literature." *The Global South Atlantic*, eds. Kerry Bystom and Joseph R. Slaughter (New York: Fordham University Press, 2017): 65–80.

Gikandi, Simon, *Slavery and the Culture of Taste* (Princeton and Oxford: Princeton University Press, 2011).

Gomez, Michael Angelo, *Exchanging our Country Marks the Transformation of African Identities in the Colonial and Antebellum South* (Chapel Hill, NC: University of North Carolina Press, 2001).

Goyal, Yogita, *Runaway Genres: The Global Afterlives of Slavery* (New York: New York University Press, 2019).

Gqola, Pumla Dineo, *What Is Slavery to Me: Postcolonial/Slave Memory in Post-Apartheid South Africa* (Johannesburg: Wits University Press, 2010).

Halperin, Charles J., *The Tatar Yoke: The Image of the Mongols in Medieval Russia* (Bloomington: Slavica; Corrected Edition, 2009).

Harms, Robert, Bernard K. Freamon, and David W. Blight eds., *Indian Ocean Slavery in the Age of Abolition* (New Haven, CT: Yale University Press, 2013).

Hartman, Saidiya V., *Scenes of Subjection: Terror, Slavery, and Self-Making in Nineteenth-Century America* (New York: Oxford University Press, 1997).

Heers, Jacques, *Les négriers en terres d'Islam* (Paris: Perrin, 2003).

Hesford, Wendy S., *Violent Exceptions: Children's Human Rights and Humanitarian Rhetorics* (Columbus, OH: The Ohio State University Press, 2021).

Ifekwunigwe, Jayne O., "'Voting with Their Feet': Senegalese Youth, Clandestine Boat Migration, and the Gendered Politics of Protest." *African and Black Diaspora: An International Journal* 6, no. 2 (2013): 218–235.

Laffin, John, *The Arabs as Master Slaves* (Eaglewood, NJ: Sbs Publishing, 1982).

Latham-Sprinkle, John et al., "Migrants and their vulnerability to human trafficking, modern slavery and forced labour." *International Organisation for Migration* (2019).

LeBaron, Genevieve, *Combatting Modern Slavery: Why Labour Governance Is Failing and What We Can Do about It* (Cambridge: Polity Press, 2020).

Mirzai, Behnaz, *A History and Emancipation in Iran, 1800–1929* (Austin, TX: University of Texas Press, 2017).

Moreno-Lax, Violeta, Daniel Ghezelbash, and Natalie Klein, "Between Life, Security and Rights: Framing the Interdiction of 'Boat Migrants' in the Central Mediterranean and Australia." *Leiden Journal of International Law* 32, no. 4 (December 2019): 715–740.

Martinez, Jenny S., *The Slave Trade and the Origins of International Human Rights Law* (New York: Oxford University Press, 2012).

Menefee, Samuel Pyeatt, "The Smuggling of Refugees by Sea: A Modern Day Maritime Slave Trade." *Regent Journal of International Law* 2 (2003): 1.

Murphy, Laura T., *The New Slave Narrative* (New York: Columbia University Press, 2019).

Nesiah, Vasuki, "Freedom at Sea." *London Review of International Law* 7, no. 2 (2019): 149–179.

Newby, Laura, "Bondage on Qing China's Northwestern Frontier." *Modern Asian Studies* 47, no. 3 (2013): 968–994.

Nichanian, Marc, *The Historiographical Perversion* (New York: Columbia University Press, 2009).

Northrup, David, *Indentured Labor in the Age of Imperialism: 1834–1922* (New York: Cambridge University Press, 1995).

Obokata, Tom, "Boat Migrants as the Victims of Human Trafficking: Exploring Key Obligations through a Human Rights Based Approach." *"Boat Refugees" and Migrants at Sea: A Comprehensive Approach* (Leiden, Netherlands: Brill Nijhoff, 2017): 145–168.

Patterson, Orlando, *Slavery and Social Death: A Comparative Study* (Cambridge, MA: Harvard University Press, 1982).

Perera, Suvendrini, *Australia and the Insular Imagination: Beaches, Borders, Boats, and Bodies* (New York: Palgrave Macmillan, 2009).

Popović, Alexandre, *The Revolt of African Slaves in Iraq in the 3rd/9th Century* (Princeton, NJ: Markus Wiener Publishers, 1999).

Quirk, Joel, *The Anti-Slavery Project: From the Slave Trade to Human Trafficking* (Philadelphia, PA: University of Pennsylvania Press, 2011).

Rossum, Matthias van, Alexander Geelen, Bram van den Hout, and Merve Tosun eds., *Testimonies of Enslavement: Sources on Slavery from the Indian Ocean World* (New York: Bloomsbury Academic, 2020).

Scheussel, Eric, *Land of Strangers: The Civilizing Project in Qing Central Asia* (New York: Columbia University Press, 2020).

Schrikker, Alicia and Nira Wickramasinghe eds., *Being a Slave: Histories and Legacies of European Slavery in the Indian Ocean* (Leiden, Netherlands: Leiden University Press, 2020).

Sharpe, Christina, *Monstrous Intimacies: Making Post-Slavery Subjects* (Durham, NC, and London: Duke University Press, 2010).

Shell, Robert C-H, *Children of Bondage: A Social History of the Slave Society at the Cape of Good Hope, 1652–1838* (Middletown, CT: Wesleyan University Press, 1994).

Skrynnikova, Tat'jana D., "Boghol, A Category of Submission at the Mongols." *Acta Orientalia Academiae Scientiarum Hungaricae* 58, no. 3 (2005): 313–319.

Slaughter, Joseph R., *Human Rights, Inc.: The World Novel, Narrative Form, and International Law* (New York: Fordham University Press, 2007).

Suchland, Jennifer, *Economies of Violence: Transnational Feminism, Postsocialism, and the Politics of Sex Trafficking* (Durham, NC: Duke University Press, 2015).

Toledano, Ehud R., "The Concept of Slavery in Ottoman and Other Muslim Societies," in Miura Toru and John Edward Philips eds. *Slave Elites in the Middle East and Africa: A Comparative Study* (London: Kegan Paul International, 2000): 164.

Uberti, Stefano degli, "Victims of their Fantasies or Heroes for a Day? Media Representations, Local History and Daily Narratives on Boat Migrations from Senegal." *Cahiers d'études africaines* 213–214 (2014): 81–113.

Verges, Francoise, "Writing on Water: Peripheries, Flows, Capital, and Struggles in the Indian Ocean." *Positions: East Asia Cultures Critique* 11, no. 1 (2003): 241–257.

Vreeland, III, Herbert Harold, *Mongol Community and Kinship Structure. Behavior Science Monographs* (Westport, CT: Greenwood Press, 1973).

Waley-Cohen, Joanna, *Exile in Mid-Qing China: Banishment to Xinjiang, 1758–1820* (New Haven, CT: Yale University Press, 1991).

Waltner, Ann, *Dream of the Red Chamber: Afterlives* (Minneapolis, Minnesota: University of Minnesota Libraries: Twin Cities, 2021). https://open.lib.umn.edu/redchamber/

Witzenrath, Christoph ed., *Eurasian Slavery, Ransom and Abolition in World History, 1200–1800* (London: Routledge, 2015).

Worden, Nigel and Gerald Groenewald eds., *Trials of Slavery: Selected Documents Concerning Slaves from the Criminal Records of the Council of Justice at the Cape of Good Hope, 1705–1794* (Cape Town, South Africa: Van Riebeeck Society for the Publication of South African Historical Documents, 2005).

Young, Bhana, *Illegible Will: Coercive Spectacles of Labor in South Africa and the Diaspora* (Durham, NC: Duke University Press, 2017).

Index

Bold = extended discussion or key reference; n = endnote

Cambridge Companions To . . .

AUTHORS

Ernest Hemingway edited by Scott Donaldson

Hildegard of Bingen edited by Jennifer Bain

Homer edited by Robert Fowler

Horace edited by Stephen Harrison

Ted Hughes edited by Terry Gifford

Ibsen edited by James McFarlane

Henry James edited by Jonathan Freedman

Samuel Johnson edited by Greg Clingham

Ben Jonson edited by Richard Harp and Stanley Stewart

James Joyce edited by , Derek Attridge (second edition),

Kafka edited by Julian Preece

Keats edited by Susan J. Wolfson

Rudyard Kipling edited by Howard J. Booth

Lacan edited by Jean-Michel Rabaté

D. H. Lawrence edited by Anne Fernihough

Primo Levi edited by Robert Gordon

Lucretius edited by Stuart Gillespie and Philip Hardie

Machiavelli edited by John M. Najemy

David Mamet edited by Christopher Bigsby

Thomas Mann edited by Ritchie Robertson

Christopher Marlowe edited by Patrick Cheney

Andrew Marvell edited by Derek Hirst and Steven N. Zwicker

Ian McEwan edited by Dominic Head

Herman Melville edited by Robert S. Levine

Arthur Miller edited by , Christopher Bigsby (second edition),

Milton edited by , Dennis Danielson (second edition),

Molière edited by David Bradby and Andrew Calder

Toni Morrison edited by Justine Tally

Alice Munro edited by David Staines

Nabokov edited by Julian W. Connolly

Eugene O'Neill edited by Michael Manheim

George Orwell edited by John Rodden

Ovid edited by Philip Hardie

Petrarch edited by Albert Russell Ascoli and Unn Falkeid

Harold Pinter edited by , Peter Raby (second edition),

Sylvia Plath edited by Jo Gill

Plutarch edited by Frances B. Titchener and Alexei Zadorojnyi

Edgar Allan Poe edited by Kevin J. Hayes

Alexander Pope edited by Pat Rogers

Ezra Pound edited by Ira B. Nadel

Proust edited by Richard Bales

Pushkin edited by Andrew Kahn

Thomas Pynchon edited by Inger H. Dalsgaard, Luc Herman and Brian McHale

Rabelais edited by John O'Brien

Rilke edited by Karen Leeder and Robert Vilain

Philip Roth edited by Timothy Parrish

Salman Rushdie edited by Abdulrazak Gurnah

John Ruskin edited by Francis O'Gorman

Sappho edited by P. J. Finglass and Adrian Kelly

Seneca edited by Shadi Bartsch and Alessandro Schiesaro

Shakespeare edited by Margareta de Grazia and Stanley Wells (second edition)

George Bernard Shaw edited by Christopher Innes

Shelley edited by Timothy Morton

Mary Shelley edited by Esther Schor

Sam Shepard edited by Matthew C. Roudané

Spenser edited by Andrew Hadfield

Laurence Sterne edited by Thomas Keymer

Wallace Stevens edited by John N. Serio

Tom Stoppard edited by Katherine E. Kelly

Harriet Beecher Stowe edited by Cindy Weinstein

August Strindberg edited by Michael Robinson

Jonathan Swift edited by Christopher Fox

J. M. Synge edited by P. J. Mathews

Tacitus edited by A. J. Woodman

Henry David Thoreau edited by Joel Myerson

Tolstoy edited by Donna Tussing Orwin

Anthony Trollope edited by Carolyn Dever and Lisa Niles

Mark Twain edited by Forrest G. Robinson

John Updike edited by Stacey Olster

Mario Vargas Llosa edited by Efrain Kristal and John King

Virgil edited by Fiachra Mac Góráin and Charles Martindale (second edition)

Voltaire edited by Nicholas Cronk

TOPICS

For EU product safety concerns, contact us at Calle de José Abascal, 56–1°, 28003 Madrid, Spain or eugpsr@cambridge.org.